Agamben and Indifference

Agamben and Indifference

A Critical Overview

William Watkin

ROWMAN & LITTLEFIELD
INTERNATIONAL
London • New York

Published by Rowman & Littlefield International, Ltd.
16 Carlisle Street, London, W1D 3BT
www.rowmaninternational.com

Rowman & Littlefield International, Ltd. is an affiliate of The Rowman & Littlefield
Publishing Group, Inc
4501 Forbes Boulevard, Suite 200, Lanham, Maryland 20706, USA
With additional offices in Boulder, New York, Toronto (Canada), and Plymouth (UK)
www.rowman.com

British Library Cataloguing in Publication Information Available
A catalogue record for this book is available from the British Library
ISBN: HB 978-1-78348-007-4
ISBN: PB 978-1-78348-008-1

Library of Congress Cataloging-in-Publication Data

Watkin, William, 1970-
Agamben and indifference : a critical overview / William Watkin.
p. cm.
Includes bibliographical references and index.
ISBN 978-1-78348-007-4 (cloth : alk. paper) -- ISBN 978-1-78348-008-1 (pbk. : alk. paper) -- ISBN
978-1-78348-009-8 (electronic)
1. Agamben, Giorgio, 1942- 2. Apathy. I. Title.
B3611.A44W36 2013
195--dc23

2013024919

∞™ The paper used in this publication meets the minimum requirements of American
National Standard for Information Sciences Permanence of Paper for Printed Library
Materials, ANSI/NISO Z39.48-1992.

Printed in the United States of America

Contents

Acknowledgements

I would like to sincerely thank Giorgio Agamben for his continued support for my work and exceptionally kind and generous words as regards this particular study. I would also like to thank Sarah Campbell and more widely Rowman & Littlefield International for providing a fresh and innovative approach to academic publishing, and a proper home for the book. Finally my gratitude to Gerhard Richter for permission to use 'Betty' on the front cover.

Excerpts from *The Sacrament of Language: An Archaeology of the Oath* by Giorgio Agamben, Copyright © 2011 by the Board of Trustees of the Leland Stanford Jr. University English Translation; (c) 2008 Gius laterza and Figli original; *The Kingdom and the Glory* by Giorgio Agamben, Copyright © 2011 by the Board of Trustees of the Leland Stanford Jr. University; *Potentialities, Collected Essays in Philosophy* by Giorgio Agamben, Copyright © 1999 by the Board of Trustees of the Leland Stanford Jr. University; *Homo Sacer* by Giorgio Agamben, Copyright © 1998 by the Board of Trustees of the Leland Stanford Jr. University, all rights reserved, used with permission of Stanford University Press, www.sup.org. Excerpts from *The Coming Community* by Giorgio Agamben, Copyright © 1993 by the University of Minnesota Press, used with permission of University of Minnesota Press. Originally published in Italian in *La communità che viene*, copyright 1990 Einaudi, Turin. English translation copyright 1993 by the Regents of the University of Minnesota.

Introduction

The ways in which we do not know things are just as important (and perhaps even more important) as the ways in which we know them.... It is possible, in fact, that the way in which we are able to be ignorant is precisely what defines the rank of what we are able to know and that the articulation of a zone of nonknowledge is the condition—and at the same time the touchstone—of all our knowledge ... articulating a zone of nonknowledge does not mean simply not knowing; it is not only a question of lack or defect. It means, on the contrary, maintaining oneself in the right relationship with ignorance. (Agamben, *Nudities* 113–14)[1]

Across the majority of Giorgio Agamben's work a pattern emerges. At the end of a detailed philological study of the various paradigms of a particular phenomenon spanning, usually, extended periods of time, the essay or book reveals that the multiplicity of the various paradigms can be organised beneath a single overarching conceptual structure: power, language, potentiality, poetry, life. This conceptual structure is dominated, he explains, by an economy made up of an element which seems to found the phenomenon and a series of subsequent elements which appear to actualise this founding element or simply which are allowed to occur because of a held-in-common foundation. The founding or originating element is what Agamben calls the common, while the elements founded he terms the proper, although the most familiar name for these in his work is paradigms. There is nothing intended to be new here. The common-proper dialectic is simply another way of citing the "*gigantomachia peri tes ousias*, the 'battle of giants concerning being,' that defines Western metaphysics",[2] namely, the three-millennia-long skirmish between the one and the many.

Agamben then insists that the consistency assumed for this economical system, a common foundation for a set of paradigms that operate as a named set due to their sharing this common foundation, is actually inconsistent. Again no innovations here; like his numerous forbears Agamben has no time for structures of consistent unity or what Derrida calls presence, Deleuze territorialisation. At this stage, however, Agamben habitually places the reader in what he calls a zone or threshold of indistinction, inoperativity, indiscernibility, suspension or indifference.[3] He uses various terms to name the zone and various other terms to designate its specific quality, but the structure is always the same. In this zone of indifference, the clear difference between the founding common and actual instances of this common foundation (the proper) becomes confused. First, it is difficult to ascertain which element _is_ the common and which the proper. Second, it becomes therefore impossible to say that the common _founds_ the proper as often the proper seems to construct the common as its foundation at a later date retrospectively and retroactively. Or simply, one cannot be sure which is really the common and which is the proper. Finally, the energy of the dialectical system, one and many or common and proper, dissipates as this energy or economy depends on oppositional difference. The one and the many must be different from each other, and, across our Western metaphysical tradition they must always be in a state of contest, _gigantomachia_, with each other.

For Agamben all Western concepts of any significance derive their longevity, consistency and operativity from the dialectical conflict internal to them between elements which are common and elements which are proper. The common is meaningless as a founding element if it founds nothing; thus, it needs the proper. The proper is mere random multiplicity unless the elements can find a set-consistency, so they need a held-in-common foundation for their legitimacy and identity. Yet the common must be one, so it cannot admit to being an element of the system. The one must be outside the system to guarantee its consistent delimitation. And the proper must be many if the system is to be able to take account of and, thus, basically control the wide diversity of changing human experience over large periods of time encompassing huge numbers of people held within different cultures. Therefore, every concept in the West is bifurcated. One part must always be a founding common, the other an actuating proper. One element is meaningless without the other, yet each element must retain a radical oppositional difference from the other. This machine of tensile interchange is Agamben's description of metaphysics and his overall aim the eradication of a philosophy of division without recourse to that of transcendent unity.

If something occurs within the machine, and it always does because the machine is faulty, which makes the clear difference between the two elements questionable, blurred, illogical or indistinct, then the necessary differential interrelation between common and proper becomes inoperative or simply indifferent. The clear difference between common and proper is now obscure, and as the whole system depends on the distinction between common and proper, the system is rendered inoperative due to indistinction. Rendering indifferent the metaphysics of dialectical difference between founding common and actuating proper is the aim of every work Agamben has written since, at least, 1978. It is, in other words, those zones of indistinction at the end of _Language and Death_, _The Coming Community_, _Homo Sacer_, _The Time That Remains_, _The Open_, _State of Exception_ and so on, that provide the real evidence for Agamben's lasting originality. His description of metaphysics is as old as philosophy itself.

His project to dismantle metaphysics dates back to Nietzsche and owes much to Heidegger, Derrida and Deleuze. But the manner in which he renders philosophical dialectics indifferent is entirely original to him and hence forms the basis for this critical overview of his work. Without indifference Agamben is essential and fascinating, but with indifference he is philosophically remarkable.

To recap, Giorgio Agamben's philosophical project is the making apparent and then rendering indifferent all structures of differential opposition that lie at the root of every major Western concept-signature or discursive structure. It is important here to accept that we are dealing with a philosophy of immanent discourse inspired and made possible by the work of Foucault and a philosophy of concepts that owes a good deal to the late Deleuze. Taking our lead from this stipulation we can then say that Agamben's philosophy can be termed a form of metaphysical critique that argues all abstract concepts are only quasi transcendental. By this would be meant all concepts are historically contingent, not logically necessary, yet such concepts (we should get used at this stage to calling these signatures as Agamben now does) sanction a common intelligibility over very large scales of time covering significant communities of people. His then is a philosophy of radical contingency yet one marked by very notable historical quasi necessity. If, for example, a signature is not actually true, self-evidently true for all people for all time, they are usually taken to be true for centuries, often millennia, distributed across that group of subjects we call the West, which includes, of course, due to the Western penchant for imperialism, large numbers of people outside that geopolitical designation as well. Within the process of communicable intelligibility, there are at least two necessities. The first is the context of discourse itself, which, if it knows of finitude, and I am arguing that it does, it is a rare, probably singular cut or limit. The second is that irrespective of the discursive signature in question, the metaphysical economy of common-proper is always in place. While these two necessities are contingent in that the situation could be otherwise, they are primarily extremely stable and thus quasi necessary for how we think, speak and act.

At this point it is probably obvious to the reader that Agamben willingly participates in a tradition that includes Nietzsche, Heidegger, Deleuze and Derrida, thinkers he regularly engages with and, one would add, the four cornerstones of this method of practicing a metaphysics that destabilises itself from the inside. Where he differs from all of these is that he is not a philosopher of difference. This is a particularly neat way of explaining Agamben's critical relationship to Derrida and Deleuze as we shall see. Arguably all his predecessors undermine philosophical structures of consistent identity through the valorisation of difference in some form. Is not this the basic signature of continental philosophy since Nietzsche: difference precedes identity, and thus, because identity is supposed to be foundational and so original, by definition difference negates identity?

Agamben does not participate in this tradition, making its basic presupposition indifferent or indistinct because he insists that difference is as much implicated in the system of metaphysics as that of identity, or the proper is as much a part of the metaphysical machine as the common. If, he argues, like his predecessors, that identity structures are historically contingent, not logically necessary, then so too are differentiating structures, which can then further be said to be complicit in metaphysics, not a means of overcoming it. Put more simply, if the philosophy of difference showed that identity was founded on difference, Agamben shows that difference is part of a consistent, foundational metaphysical identity. Rather than undermining identity with difference, therefore, Agamben reveals that identity and difference themselves are not necessary terms in the development of ontology, say, but historical contingencies that in fact form one single entity within our tradition, what one might call identity-difference metaphysics since the Greeks, and based on these observations one can suspend their history of opposition by rendering them indifferent to each other. I am aware that my portrait of the philosophy of difference is contestable to say the least here, but we will justify this likeness in due course. [4]

For Agamben as for many postwar thinkers identity, self-identical full presence, the one, universal truths, tautologies, self-evident statements, unity and God are all discursive entities. The common is not an actual, existent ontological or transcendent state. This is a position made available to him by the philosophy of difference, specifically, he admits, that of Jacques Derrida. Difference, the other, absence, the many, specific examples of universal truths, multiplicities, statements in context, chaos, the human, division and finitude, what Agamben calls simply the proper, are the same. Further, concepts are no longer to be taken as identity-concepts: ideational structures possessive of communal consistency around an agreed set of referents that can be held under the same conceptual heading. Instead they should be termed identity-difference-signatures. This then opens out into the second essential element of Agamben's philosophy, his philological method that he names philosophical archaeology.

In Agamben's philosophical archaeology one always starts with a very large scale concept that has been in place for a large period of time crossing various discursive and disciplinary boundaries and which can clearly be seen to sanction and organise behaviour. These concepts will, from now on, be called signatures. Signatures have a historical moment of arising when they become active in sanctioning knowledge systems. This is not the first time the word was used but the first demonstrable moment when the word becomes a signature through the means by which, due to it being sanctioned through power and our complicity, it controls how we think, speak and act. Agamben calls this moment of arising the *archē*. It would be (and has been for some already) a significant mistake to think of this as origin in any normal sense of the word.

Next, every signature has a mode of distributing itself across time, space and discourses to control large and stable discursive formations over centuries under the auspices of the signature. These areas in Agamben include language, power, poetry, the sacred, the secular, glory and life. The signature, our common, is actualised across a variety of different discourses through time, place and peoples but is kept consistent by each discourse or period sharing in common a series of terms all of which are meaningfully operative due to their commonality of signatory 'origin' and continued activity. These elements are called paradigms in Agamben's work.

At this point we now need to map the method onto the metaphysics of indifference that we commenced with. How does philosophical dialectics affect signatures? is perhaps the central question when understanding Agamben's work in its entirety. Put as transparently as we can at this stage, signatures operate as the common while paradigms are the proper of any discursive formation. This being the case, signatures are in a mode of opposition to the very paradigms they sanction and legitimate. Anyone who has read Aristotle or Russell or Badiou is aware of this philosophical problem, namely, how does a genus oversee a species without the genus being a species to a larger genus and the species becoming a genus of a smaller species and so on ad infinitum? This can be reposited via the simultaneous and interrelated problems of transcendent infinity and infinite regress. A signature presents itself as the founding commonality of an array of paradigms to solve the second problem of difference: the chaos of the too many that are too different and themselves also infinitely divisible. While the paradigms operate to facilitate a signatory consistency, that is not, however, entirely transcendental because the signature exists only as the overall name for all these instances of the signature.

This is a neat solution but an ill-fated one for, as we saw, signatures, whilst foundational, are proven to exist as such only if they can make a consistent set of paradigms over time sufficient to be named Life, for example. Until these paradigms are corralled under the signatory term Life, Life as a signature does not exist. So the signature Life occurs 'after' its paradigms. It cannot, therefore be, a *founding* common. In addition, the paradigms of Life are only paradigms because they have been sanctioned as such due to the signature in operation. If the signature is not a *founding* common, paradigms are not examples of a founded *commonality* either. There is nothing specifically that they have in common except that discursively they are collected as proper examples of the common under one signature. So the foundation of commonality is not foundational, and the commonality of the actualisations of proper elements is not due to anything intrinsic to those elements. The common first needs the proper, yet the proper exists only because of the common. There is obviously a logical problem of causal succession here. Take this model and add in the convention of history as a traceable, sequential causal chain, and you transform a logical problem into a logical impossibility.

To sum up, the economy of the common-proper is illogical. As everything is discursive for Agamben, then the relation between philosophy and history is a given. Yet as history is based on foundational, causal sequential strings of events, it is even more susceptible to the logical impossibility of the retrospectively founded foundation or future anterior. Thus, philosophy is made inoperative through philological statements rather than logical deduction or empirical intuition, for example, while history is made inoperative due to a formal philosophical impossibility: there can be no actual consistency without a common foundation, and there can be no common foundation unless there are actual differences to found as common.

This leads us to the messianic potential of Agamben's work which, for the record, has no commitment to synthesis, unity, a return to an ideal state of grace or a quasi-religious final day of retribution or historical redemption and is not even, in any lasting sense, theological. In philosophical archaeology there is inevitably an almost-fated period of indifference where the clear oppositional distinctions of the system, always based on identity versus difference, either break down or can aggressively be shown to be assailable contingencies. The method of tracing these moments for the purpose of suspending identity-difference constructs, what he calls signatures, is the overall methodology that Agamben names philosophical archaeology. Its aim is *not* to give a clearer account of history or to redeem lost fragments but to render historiography as a mode of metaphysical identity-difference indifferent. In a way it takes the discipline of the common, philosophy, and undermines it using the discipline of the proper, history. Yet at the same time it takes the presupposition of the proper, effectively all disciplines based on a quasi-scientific empirical method of some sort, and argues it is entirely dependent on a metaphysical commonality, the common-proper differential dialectic.

On this reading, philosophical archaeology, as the name suggests, is nothing other than the rendering indifferent of the two oppositional methods of Western thought: logical deduction and empirical induction. If Andrew Gibson is right in stating that Alain Badiou's work is a form of ethical ontology of intermittent disruptive events as 'good',[5] then Agamben's is an ethical epistemology using the philosophy of how we know things to allow us to stop knowing them always in the same way and thus liberate ourselves from the economic control of our held-in-common signatures.

NOTES

1. See also Giorgio Agamben, *The Open: Man and Animal*, trans. Kevin Attell (Stanford, CA: Stanford University Press, 2004), 90–91, on the zone of nonknowledge.

2. Giorgio Agamben, *State of Exception*, trans. Kevin Attell (Chicago: University of Chicago Press, 2005), 59.

3. See, for example, David Kishik, *The Power of Life* (Stanford, CA: Stanford University Press, 2012), 67.

4. Laruelle is the first thinker I am aware of who openly attacks the philosophy of difference based on a careful stipulation as regards how such diverse thinkers as Nietzsche, Heidegger, Derrida and Deleuze can be thought of constituting a consistency. See François Laruelle, *Philosophies of Difference: A Critical Introduction to Non-Philosophy*, trans. Rocco Gangle (London: Continuum, 2010), 9–14. More generally there is a great deal here that is in agreement with Laruelle. For example, the syntax of difference as he calls it is the economic articulation of difference according to Agamben, while his definition of the One as indivision is naturally directly related to our own formulation of indifference, although in our case not yet directed to any wider conception of a radically immanent real of some order. There is no time to present a comparative study of the two thinkers here, but this is a fairly pressing project for the future as at present Agamben and Laruelle constitute the two central voices presenting a critique of philosophical decision in the form of differential dyads.

5. Andrew Gibson, *Intermittency: The Concept of Historical Reason in Recent French Philosophy* (Edinburgh: Edinburgh University Press, 2012), 26.

Part I

The Archaeology of Indifference

ONE

The Signature of All Things, Paradigms and Signatures

For such a momentous work, Agamben opens *The Signature of All Things* (2008) rather modestly with a polite rejoinder to the clamour of criticism following the publication of *Homo Sacer* (1995) attacking what has been perceived as his faulty methodology. Agamben explains that while he has used historical phenomena in his work, they were treated as "paradigms whose role was to constitute and make intelligible a broader historical-problematic context".[1] He accepts this approach has generated a few "misunderstandings", based primarily on the assumption that Agamben is a bad historian, an inept philologist or naïve philosopher, and so has decided to reflect on the role of the paradigm in the human sciences. Given the number of criticisms Agamben's work has garnered and the degree of misreadings contained therein, these comments show incredible restraint.

The Signature of All Things is the vital companion for our own work. Much of what I have said so far of a general nature is bracketed and thus made operative by two key works by Agamben in relation to indifference: *The Coming Community* and *The Signature of All Things*. Moreover what calls to me from 1990 in *The Coming Community*, a fundamental text on the nature of singularity and indifference, is given articulate voicing by what is written in *The Signature of All Things* twenty years after. This remarkable later work forms part of a suite of essential treatises published in recent years that include *The Kingdom and the Glory* (2007) and *The Sacrament of Language* (2008). Taken together these three tomes answer, for me at least, all the problematic questions of the earlier works in terms of three key areas in Agamben's project: method, power and language. Of these, it is *The Signature of All Things* that has been our main reference point thus far; we will turn to sustained reading of the other texts in the final part of our work, and it is time to present a careful study of that book in preparation for the rereading of the earlier works that are to follow, notably *The Coming Community* and several important essays from the 1999 *Potentialities* collection, which in turn will make more intelligible the full importance of the other recent works.

THE METHOD AND ITS AIMS

Although Agamben suggests the role of *The Signature of All Things* is to explain the paradigm, the text is actually divided into three parts which constitute three elements of a single system called philosophical archaeology. These three elements are the paradigm, the signature and archaeology itself (specifically the moment of arising or *archē*). Summarising at this early stage we can define paradigm as the name of the particular mode and function of historical examples, the main site of controversy around Agamben's work. The paradigm has a specific nature: "it is a singular object that, standing equally for all others of the same class, defines the intelligibility of the group of which it is a part and which, at the same time, it constitutes".[2] Signature (*la segnatura*) describes the mode of the distribution of paradigms through time and across discourses and again has a specific nature in that it is suspended between signifier and signified, so that rather than being a sign as such, it is "what makes a sign intelligible" (*rende il segno intelligibile*)[3] by determining its existence through its actual usage. Finally, philosophical archaeology captures the purpose of the overall method, specifically in terms of its relation to the *archē* or moment of arising of a historically inscribed concept and how this is accessible only through the contemporary moment of its being accessed. At the very end of the study he says of the *archē* that it is "not a given or a substance, but a field of bipolar historical currents [*un campo di corrente storiche*] stretched between anthropogenesis and history, between the moment of arising [*punto d'insorgenza*] and becoming, between an archi-past and a present".[4]

The overall method of Agamben's work as philosophical archaeology is a process that is composed of three elements: paradigms, signatures and archaeology. The main purpose of this opening chapter then is to delineate the detail of this complex mode of what can only be termed revolutionary hermeneutics defined by a radical intent towards change in the present through a critical relationship to what is determined as 'past' within contemporary structures of transmissible intelligibility. A secondary intention pertains to answering Agamben's critics in that, thus far, most of the criticisms levelled against him are based on a reading of his work that one can say is substantially wrong. I will not, however, pursue systematic and patient rebuttal of all the angry voices thus far raised; I have responded to some and de la Durantaye has made a detailed defence in his recent work.[5] Instead, I want to present a clear indication as to how one cannot read Agamben, which will hopefully be a corrective for more constructive criticism in the future.

Without then going into detail, common criticisms can be identified. It is often argued that Agamben misuses his historical source material in at least three key ways. He claims to have discovered hidden origins of modern political structures, he misreads philological material and he makes drastic abbreviations and unacceptable emphases by concentrating on only a very partial set of historical facts. Then there are also the philosophically inspired criticisms. It is often said that he has a naïve dependence on a philosophy of origins, as well as a commitment to a philosophical messianism which has been proven in the last century by several thinkers to be fundamentally aporetic. Both positions are exacerbated by the myth of the 'two Agambens' for whom we have to blame Antonio Negri, who suggests that Agamben's methodological combination of historiography and philosophy is tragically bifurcated.[6] As my essay will show time and again, this is the most misleading and ill informed of all the criticisms one could level against Agamben. The image that one gets from these hasty dismissals is a thinker who is trying to use historical data to support an already discredited philosophical project of foundations and final unities, using the empirical power of historical material to gain purchase in the philosophical community, whilst applying outmoded philosophical arguments to mask what is effectively a partial and inaccurate set of historical-philological observations. Without offering further encouragement for future attacks, what I want to show is that if one wishes to undermine Agamben's increasing influence, it is the overall system and its philosophical and methodological underpinnings that need to be addressed, and this can come only from a full understanding of the method, its originality and its radical intent. Agamben is a controversial thinker not because he 'misuses' historical sources but because he is proposing a fundamental reconsideration of what constitutes the historical, our intent towards it in the contemporary moment and the means by which systems of intelligibility are not just revealed, as in Foucault, but ultimately suspended.

In what follows I will trace the precise detail of the method he uses to arrive at this destination of suspension, but at this stage let us first lay out once again the bare bones of the overall purpose of such a method. As you recall, Agamben perceives, like Derrida, that all the concepts of our culture are based on a limited set of fundamental philosophical structures presented as necessary and transcendental but which are in fact historically determined. Differing from Derrida in ways we will return to later,[7] he sees the basic model of the metaphysical tradition to be the presentation of a concept through a primary scission between two heterogeneous and asymmetric elements. One element always occupies the position of the common or unconditioned power, the other that of the proper of the supposed singularity of the conditioned fact. The common operates in this model as the foundation, while the proper is what is founded, hence the supposed heterogeneity and asymmetry between the two. We do not need reminding of the first aporia of this system, as Western philosophy has been pursuing this complex articulation almost since its inception: it is illogical, paradoxical and self-negating and does not work. This is primarily because the founding and unconditioned power of the common is what Zartaloudis defines as the self-founding fiction of "the mythologeme or fiction of (bipartite) presence".[8] As the arguments across Agamben's *The Kingdom and the Glory* (2007) show most clearly, the power that is assumed to found and legitimate the factical existence of government and law is itself a product of that law. The common thus founds the realm of the proper, which itself invents each day the need for the fiction of foundation through the modes of its operations. This constant movement between common and proper defines the economy (*oikonomia*) of every conceptual-discursive formation in the West.

While the system is machine-like and robust, it is only apparently indefatigable and unassailable. In fact we can promote three clear opportunities for its arrest and deactivation, ever Agamben's aim. First, as we saw, the logical impossibilities of the system are well known and can be used against the system. Second, the historical contingency of every conceptual system, however abstract, including logic itself, means that archaeological work can reveal the 'true' origins of the system in the development of the founding fiction of oppositional division as a basis for the intelligibility of lasting concepts. Third, each system is dependent on the comutuality of an identity (the common) and differences (the proper) and their constant communication. At certain key moments then, due to the paradox logic of the system, the ceaseless movement from common to proper and back again, the lack of clear distinction over precedence and the historical truth at the root of the system (that in fact there need not be such a division at all), the oppositions within the system blur, become indiscernible, are suspended, reach a state of indistinction, become inoperative and so on. The very basis of all our concepts on a particular structure of oppositional differences becomes indifferent; that is, their clear difference is suspended. Agamben's philosophical system is simple and single-minded in this regard:

1. Identify which concepts control the intelligibility of our culture.
2. Reveal their historical contingency through the fiction of their divisive nature.
3. Trace the economy of their oppositional, binary interchange.
4. Hone in on the moments of indifference in the economy.
5. Invite the reader to observe the inoperativity at the heart of a concept as a positive potential.

6. Finally, valorise and occupy indifference against the inbred tendency to demonise and negate it.

Radically at the root of the totality of this system is that even the very basis of thinking, the opposition between identity and difference, the very terms 'identity' and 'difference', even the idea of an economy between them, are historically contingent. This means that it is possible to exist in a world where our intelligibility as living human beings is not dependent on structures of identity or of difference or the opposition between the two. I do not know what this world can or will be like, but it will not be a messianic future return to an ideal state of predivisive unity, as some critics have suggested.[9] Rather, it will commence with the occupation of the logic of indifference to either identity or difference, which this book attempts to make more widely communicable.

WHAT IS A PARADIGM?

The Signature of All Things is a sustained reading—and critical modification—of the methodology that Foucault calls archaeology. The theory of paradigms is presented through readings of Foucault, Melandri and Melandri's reading of Foucault. Agamben then argues that his conception of signature matches that of statements in Foucault. While finally philosophical archaeology is, like Agamben's use of biopolitics, a critical development from out of Foucault's own method. Consequently the opening comments on the paradigm pertain to the lack of direct engagement between Foucault and T. S. Kuhn over what constitutes the paradigm in relation to 'normal science'. Kuhn's thesis is that, in science, paradigms are composed of two elements. First, they name the set of techniques and values a community adopts as normal science, specifically determining if a set of problems are scientific or not. Second, they focus on a single element of this set of processes, such as Einstein's special theory of relativity, that serves as an example which replaces a set of abstract rules and also locates the process within a "coherent tradition of inquiry".[10] After Kuhn, therefore, a paradigm is not a set of rules determining how science goes about its business but constitutes a field of enquiry, 'normal science': "a paradigm is simply an example, a single case that by its repeatability acquires the capacity to model tacitly the behaviour and research practices of scientists".[11]

Agamben correctly indicates that Kuhn's paradigm, less interested in rules that determine the norm than a means of determining behaviour, finds precisely the same form of expression in Foucault's concentration on the integration of power in the life of individuals rather than a "juridical theory of power".[12] We can also say the same of Agamben's own extensive work on power and his use of examples such as *homo sacer* and the *Muselmann*, to name the two most often cited.[13] These paradigms do not determine what power is but how it organises and controls, to the point that we can say that power is nothing other than this mode of organising control or, rather, that sovereign power is determined by, in a complex way, the modalities of government that it is presumed to found. This argument comes to the fore in *The Kingdom and the Glory*, where, as regards the relation between government, *oikonomia* (economy), and kingdom, Agamben concludes,

> The ambiguity that consists in conceiving government as executive power is an error with some of the most far-reaching consequences. . . . *What our investigation has shown is that the real problem, the central mystery of politics is not sovereignty, but government; it is not God, but the angel; it is not the king, but ministry; it is not the law, but the police — that is to say, the governmental machine that they form and support.*[14]

One might say in fact that they form and support that which forms them through defining them as the founding power.

Where Foucault parts company with Kuhn is over the precise nature of the comportment and distribution of paradigm sets. This episteme is not something like a worldview[15] but rather the total set of all relations that come together at specific periods to allow such things as the concept of a world-view, the concept of a discipline and the concept of a formal system to occur at all. As Agamben concludes: "Unlike Kuhn's paradigm, the episteme does not define what is knowable in a given period, but what is implicit in the fact that a given discourse or epistemological figure exists at all".[16] Citing Foucault, Agamben draws our attention away from what exists as knowledge, in favour of the simple fact that it exists or rather that it *can* exist: an ontology of epistemology. This brings together the paradigm and its distribution through the signature which, as we have already seen, constitutes the intelligibility of a sign, not its content as such. This crucial distinction links the paradigm specifically to Agamben's earlier work on language as pure communicability,[17] a concept Agamben develops from Benjamin but which can actually be found most clearly stated in the pages of Foucault's *Archaeology of Knowledge*.

Agamben goes on to consider another feature of the paradigm, in relation to the suggestion by some that Foucault's examples replace the metonymic function of relation in history with a metaphoric one. Agamben disagrees with this assessment, as, he notes, paradigms do not constitute the transfer of meaning but rather an analogic logic. Analogy, he contends, refers to a third order of relationality. Metonymy is relation due to contiguity and metaphor due to meaning transfer, but analogy presents an entirely different order of deactivated relationality that is neither contiguous nor transferable but a hybrid of the two occupying a space of suspensive, supplemental mediation. Explaining this he gives us two further rules of the paradigm:

- It is a singular case that in being isolated from its context, taken as exemplary and thus raised up, constitutes this isolation by making intelligible a new set that it constitutes by revealing its own singularity.
- This means the term taken as paradigm is "deactivated" from its normal use, not so that it can move into a new context, which would be metaphoric, but so as to present the rule of its original usage "which can not be shown in any other way".[18]

The reason the rule cannot be shown in any other way is that since Aristotle, through Kant right up to Badiou's great innovations, every theory of set composition is hampered by the law of infinite regress, and by the impossible relation between whole and part or genus and species. To confirm this Agamben spends time on Aristotle and Kant in this first chapter to raise several related problems. In Aristotle's *Prior Analytics*, for example, where the opposition between inductive and deductive thinking is consecrated through the standard law that induction proceeds from the particular to the universal and deduction from the universal to the particular, the paradigm is defined in the same text as that which goes from particular to particular.[19] While in Kant the same terms are in play in reference to aesthetic judgement and the example without the rule. As Agamben concludes, "A paradigm implies the total abandonment of the particular-general couple as the model of logical inference. The rule . . . is not a generality pre-existing singular cases and applicable to them, nor is it something resulting from the exhaustive enumeration of specific cases. Instead, it is the exhibition alone of the paradigmatic cases that constitute a rule".[20]

ANALOGIC: TO THE SIDE

Agamben now turns to Melandri's *La linea e il circolo*, which presents analogy as an alternative to the logic of contradiction and excluded middles that dominates Western thought including analytical philosophical pseudo-problems and set theory. Agamben summarises this mammoth work as follows:

> Against the drastic alternative 'A or B', which excludes the third, analogy imposes its *tertium datur*, its stubborn 'neither A nor B'. In other words, analogy intervenes in the dichotomies of logic (particular/universal; form/content; lawfulness/exemplarity; and so on) not to take them up into a higher synthesis but to transform them into a force field traversed by polar tensions, where . . . their substantial identities evaporate. . . . The analogical third is attested here above all through the disindentification and neutralization of the first two, which now become indiscernible. The third is this indiscernibility.[21]

Thus, an analogical paradigm is the process by which the standing for all cases (identity) and being one case amongst many (difference) is suspended in a state of indistinction, indiscernibility or indifference (all terms Agamben regularly uses to refer to this crucial aspect of his work). Taking this to be the case Agamben then concludes: "We can therefore say, joining Aristotle's observations with those of Kant, that a paradigm entails a movement that goes from singularity to singularity and, without ever leaving singularity, transforms every singular case into an exemplar of a general rule that can never be stated a priori".[22]

One final element of the paradigm remains to be conveyed, and that is its relation to the problem of the sensible by means of its intelligibility. In section 10 of the first chapter Agamben considers the work by Victor Goldschmidt on paradigms, a work he thinks Foucault may have been familiar with. Goldschmidt raises a central point in relation to the paradigm and relationality. He notes that while the paradigm, as singular instance, is sensible, the singular instance, in being exemplary, also carries with it the *eidos* of the set or form it is exemplary of. He concludes that this does not mean that the sensible is present in two places, but that the paradigm is the relationship between the sensible and the supersensible. Agamben develops this point in relation to Plato's work on recollection as a paradigm for knowledge where the sensible is placed in nonsensible relation with itself. He goes on to conclude after Plato that "the paradigm is not a matter of corroborating a certain sensible likeness but of producing it by means of an operation. For this reason, the paradigm is never already given, but is generated and produced . . . by 'placing alongside'".[23] From this we can deduce three things about the paradigm. The first is that it is neither sensible nor supersensible, but rather their relation. Then that it is not pre-pregiven but a produced identity of a certain order. Finally, this relationality is located alongside, to one side (para-).

This last point is important, as it ties the paradigm into a long consideration of the space to one side in Agamben's work from considerations of the *corn* in *Stanzas* through his discourse on halos in *The Coming Community*.[24] In addition, it confirms the earlier point that paradigmatic relations are not metonymic nor metaphoric, entirely sensible or the transport of meaning from the sensible into the abstract. This relationality partakes of metonymy—there is proximity after all, as it is alongside or to the side or, as in the case of heaven, entirely like only slightly different—yet it also facilitates the transport of meaning, it being intelligibility as such. Paradigm therefore can be termed displaced metonymy and arrested metaphor combined through a dynamic process of relational, suspensive interchange. As Agamben says, "The paradigmatic relation does not merely occur between sensible objects or between these objects and a general rule; it occurs instead between a singularity (which thus becomes a paradigm) and its exposition (its intelligibility)".[25]

GRAMMAR AS PERFORMATIVE EXAMPLE OF INTELLIGIBILITY

Highly significant at this point in the argument is the choice of grammar as an example because intelligibility as such is the quality of language, often called communicability, that was the central concern of Agamben in his founding statement *Language and Death* and has widely been taken to be perhaps his main concern.[26] Here he repeats a consideration of language that is developed in other texts, notably *The Coming Community*, and that he develops in greatest detail in his consideration of the oath in *The Sacrament of Language*. The grammatical example, he notes, for example, the declension of the word 'rose', must suspend the denotative function of the word. The example makes possible the intelligibility of a grammatical group which it is both member of and paradigmatic of. Interestingly he then uses a grammatical consideration of the oath, explaining that the 'I swear' of the grammatical example carries none of the power of a real oath. We must add here that Agamben is being slightly puckish in that his definition of the oath is precisely the suspension of the denotative function of the word. Anyway, he explains in relation to the grammatical paradigm: "To be capable of acting as an example, the syntagma must be suspended from its normal function, and nevertheless it is precisely by virtue of this non-functioning and suspension that it can show how the syntagma works and can allow the rule to be stated".[27] On this reading the example shares a great deal with the oath, important not least because language as oath, as we shall go on to consider in great detail, is the end point of Agamben's many statements on language.

Agamben defines the oath as confirming the lack of division in speech between word and thing by taking language 'back' to the divine consonance between word and act. For God, words are acts in that his logos is purely generative and needs no division between word and thing. God's words make things or are things. The oath operates in the same fashion in that in swearing, your words are an act, which is another way of saying oaths are speech acts. However, in agreement with Deleuze and, I suppose, at odds with Derrida, Agamben believes that the essence of language is the oath. Performatives are self-referential uses of language, (we can see here parallels with the consideration of Platonic recollection), and it is this self-referentiality that allows oaths to take on the quality of facticity rather than referentiality. "It is necessary," he adds, "to specify that the self-referentiality of the performative is constituted always by means of a suspension of the normal denotative character of language . . . the performative substitutes for the denotative relationship between speech and fact a self-referential relation that, putting the former out of play, puts itself forward as decisive fact".[28] The first thing that one can conclude from this is that the paradigm operates in accordance with one of Agamben's main philosophical contentions: the pure communicability of language as such or, here, the pure intelligibility of the example-oath.

When I swear, or when I give an example, I commit my language to fact, not to reference. Thus, what I produce is not a sign, for a sign is divided in terms of reference; instead, I produce pure language or an indifferential language as a medium for intelligibility or what Agamben calls communicability.

NOTE ON COMMUNICABILITY

Agamben is openly dependent on Foucault's *Archaeology of Knowledge* for a central concept in his overall method, which he calls variously communicability, intelligibility and operativity. We will opt for communicability here because this term has a long philosophical heritage commencing with Kant's *Third Critique* and the universal faculty for subjective taste, reappearing most notably in Heidegger's "The Origin of the Work of Art" in terms of how a work of art makes a world for and through a people.[29] Foucault's argument is that all existence is composed of knowledge organised in discursive formations composed of statements made by subjects that are not 'people' as such, with bodies and delimited consciousnesses, but enunciative positions within said discourse. These discursive formations, when named as such and organised historically into periods, do not compose world-views or meaningful constructions, but simply *sanctioned modes of intelligibility*. It does not matter what is said in statements, Foucault argues, rather, what is significant are the contexts of intelligibility that first allow such a statement to be made by such and such a subject position, and, second, that this statement is intelligible amongst other subject positions implicated in this discourse. This much is well known, fulsomely documented.

Kant's theory of the universality of subjective taste hands downs to us two basic conditions for communicability. First, on Kant's reading you must be able to feel such and such a feeling in relation to such and such an object of beauty. This is the ontological element. Second, you must communicate this feeling to others, saying, 'This is beautiful, don't you think so?' In communicating this statement the subject assumes that said others will instantly know what is meant by this statement, not in terms not of its content but of its pure intention to signify, as Agamben often calls it.[30] Thus, other subjects may not agree with—and thus be said to really understand—how the subject communicating with them could find such a thing beautiful. This is not what the statement is communicating, however. What it communicates is communicability in terms of: I am a subject, you are a subject, and I can find objects in the world beautiful because I can feel pleasure based on the manner in which such objects prove the co-comutual operativity of the faculties of understanding and reason. This pleasure proves their co-comutuality. You may not find such and such a thing beautiful, but you do understand that one can get said pleasure from the contemplation of at least one thing in the world, confirming the universality of subjective taste and thus of the critical philosophy of the faculties. And so, if the second subject says, 'No, I don't find that beautiful,' they participate implicitly in the agreement that the faculty of pleasure from contemplation of beautiful objects in the world is entirely communicable to them. If it were not, they would have to say, 'What do you mean by "finding something beautiful?"' For Kant such a question is non-noncommunicable, although for we moderns it is perhaps the most likely response in a conversation about modern art. Putting that to one side,[31] this second stage of communicability is the epistemological aspect, which is also, of course, statement dependent. You may recognise a large part of this structure from Habermas's reframing it as communicative action. Communicative action is a contesting alternative consideration of communicability, perhaps evident from Agamben's strong attacks on Habermas.[32]

Foucault's innovation is to remove communicability from Kant's world of things, and modify the ontological aspect in terms of intelligibility and power. After Foucault, communicability means you are able to make such and such a statement from such and such a subject position at such and such a time. Intelligibility is not *what* a statement means but *that* it means, that it exists as the statement that it is, which is not dependent not on its content for its actual meaning but on who says it from which position, and how it is immediately intelligible amongst a group of other subjects for a sustained period of time in relative consistency. I will repeat this law because it is essential for all that is to come and because Agamben himself is less than clear at times as to what communicability actually is: *not what a statement means but that it is taken to be meaningful.* Communicability is the foundational term for all we are going on to consider because for Agamben communicability is first and foremost language, a central signature across all of his work, it determines the exact nature of power, another important element, and finally because it is something that allows certain meanings to be communicable between us for a relatively long, but not indefinite, period of time. Thus, communicability is Agamben's conception of consistency as well as his means of undermining concept consistency.

This last assumption composes his critical project, how we come to think, speak and act in these seemingly predetermined ways, and his messianic intent, seeing that these modes of behaviour are merely contingent, he asks: how can we think, speak and thus act in a manner not dependent on them? This project is operative only if you accept three fundamental positions. First, all concepts, modes of communication and activity are controlled by historically contingent discursive formations. There is nothing necessary in thought, speech and act. Second, these modes are organised into large-scale structures of behaviour due to a basic communicability at the root of each, namely, an oppositional structure where one term acts as the founding common, and the other as the actuating proper. This structure, the metaphysics of identity-difference, is what makes all our concepts communicable due to a long historical process of stratification. By this is meant we are able to say such and such a thing only under the sanction of this system, and we are able to understand commonalities of position because we presuppose this system at the root of all our communications (in keeping with Kant's bi-bipartite definition of communicability). Thus, even communicability as a system operates amidst communicability at large with the sanction that we are such and such a people so we can say such and such a thing or do such and such a thing, operating as the founding common, and the means by which individual statements communicate amongst many different groupings of us, being the proper element.

This leads to the final assumption, which, it must be said, is emphasised in my study in a manner not immediately apparent in Agamben's work but without which the project does not seem possible. This last stage is the suspensive indifference of oppositions as a mode of discourse critique. Revealing the oppositional structure of concepts is the first bout here. After this one must stress that this opposition is contingent, not necessary. Having done so, one then patiently and repeatedly reveals how this structure of opposition, which can run for centuries with machine-like efficiency, is always operating on a set of processes that are so ill matched that they cannot help, at certain moments, but fail. These moments are when the opposition at the heart of the system is apparent, their historical agency revealed and the nature of their oppositional difference questioned, rendered unclear or suspended for a period. Such periods of inoperativity within the system—which can occur of their own accord, can be forced or can be forced as they begin to appear, which may be retrospectively—are what I am calling indifference. *Indifference in Agamben is the suspension of clear difference between a founding common and an operative proper where even the concepts of identity and difference are themselves indifferentiated (their clear oppositional separation rendered questionable).* My last conclusion, which is only hinted at in Agamben but is surely the logical end point of the system, is that if communicability is what renders concepts visible as fictions of opposition, then communicability itself will at some point be rendered noncommunicable. Communicability must be a discursive formation, otherwise, it would become necessary. This being the case and because communicability is dependent on indifferent suspension between opposing terms to pass from discursive critique to messianic project, then indifference itself must, at some future date, be indifferentiated. The indifference of indifference then is the final destination of Agamben's work, a position still rather noncommunicable primarily because, as a community, we do not yet fully understand the nature of indifference as such and so cannot find sufficiently communicable the counterintuitive idea of the indifference of said indifference.

EXAMPLE AND EXCLUSION

Returning to *The Signature of All Things*, in the same paragraph as the discourse on grammar, Agamben also develops a powerful parallel of opposition between the example and the exception (the zone of exclusion as included exception is crucial to Agamben's most widely known work, *Homo Sacer*, and the much-read follow-up *State of Exception*). In noting that the example is excluded from the rule, as he has already stated, he explains this exclusion is "not because it does not belong to the normal case but, on the contrary because it exhibits its belonging to it. The example, then, is the symmetrical opposite of the exception: whereas the exception is included through its exclusion, the example is excluded through its inclusion, the example is excluded through the exhibition of its inclusion".[33]

Obviously, Agamben is relating the example here to his most famous example, *homo sacer*. The sacred man, like sovereign power, is the inclusion in a state of norms of that which exceeds the norm and thus confirms power on a norm-making figure. The sovereign, the guarantor of norms, is the power of the kingdom, to refer to *The Kingdom and the Glory*, so that the *oikonomia*, the real distribution of power, can purport to possess a founding legitimacy in the condition which, in truth, the conditioned actually produces following the same logic as that of the paradigm here. At the same time the sacred man is the inclusion of a subject over whom the sovereign has absolute power of life and death, and yet whose death cannot be considered as murder. Thus, they are also included as the exclusion from the norm. This being the case, power requires two included exclusions, absolute condition to found the conditioned, and abject facticity, a conditioned that escapes the condition but only through its being negated. In contrast, the paradigm works in the opposite direction. It rises up to the position of the condition; the example after all possesses the identity of the set.

This ability to be excluded from the rule, however, is in effect a promotion of the fact. The fact is not included in the rule because it is the rule-defining and composing element of any set. If we compare this to our previous exclusion we can see that the sovereignty of the example is based on its exemplary yet still singular facticity. Unlike God, sovereign or Führer, however, this condition does not succumb to indifferent indetermination, the impossible to conceive of illimited, eternal and founding absolute power of the condition, but rather presents a clearly identified and determined condition. It actually constitutes the self-conditioning of the conditioned, matching the self-referentiality of the oath-speech act. So the example possesses an exclusion of facticity but unlike the exclusion of facticity that composes the sacred man, a bare life which is pure factical existence but without connection, the exemplary exclusion of facticity is fully connected, as it is excluded precisely because it is connected to all the other elements of the set. This connection is not determined, however, by things the elements have in common, or their co-comutual relationality to the condition of the set, but rather in that they all share in common the potential for set definition and composition. Agamben ends this quite astonishing section with a simple reminder in terms of the spatiality of exclusion. The paradigm is beside itself, to one side of itself. The being of the paradigm is this self-referentiality or being beside itself. Whereas the ontology of sovereignty is that of Being beyond all beings, and that of the *homo sacer* beings which are denied possession of Being.

PARADIGMATIC, POIETIC DIALECTIC

The following two sections reveal the ambition of Agamben in that they take the two major modalities of modern philosophy, the dialectic and hermeneutics, and solve their two main paradoxes by means of the paradigm. First, we find that since Plato there has been a problem as regards the founding of the dialectic mode of thought in relation to grounding or condition. Science, Plato notes, is based on hypotheses which it takes as ground because they are presuppositions based on known principles which are tautological and apodictic. In contrast the dialectic does not take the hypothesis as a ground, but as a stepping-stone or leaping-off point that leads one to the non-hypothetical first principle of all things. Agamben defines the dialectical hypothesis as that which is exposed rather than presupposed, and sees direct parallels with the paradigm whose knowability is never "presupposed, and that on the contrary its specific operation consists in suspending and deactivating empirical givenness in order to exhibit only an intelligibility".[34] Thus, the dialectical hypothesis can be renamed the paradigm, whose modality is the utilisation of the sensible as the "medium of its intelligibility" or the production of the supersensible.

He then maps this onto modern, post-Hegelian dialectics when he recounts that the double meaning of *aufheben*, to raise and to eliminate, is finally explained by the modality of the paradigm as dialectic. The paradigm, after all, raises up the sensible to the position of supersensible, set-defining exemplarity. Thus, it is taken from its sensible facticity, and elevated to supersensible exemplarity. This effectively allows Agamben to radically recuperate Hegel by proposing absolute knowledge as philosophical archaeology through the operation of paradigms, answering any criticism that assumed Agamben was simply repeating Hegel's mistakes. In a sentence almost impossibly contracted considering its implications, he concludes: "The intelligibility in which dialectics moves in its 'descent toward the end' is the paradigmatic intelligibility of the sensible".[35]

Unpacking this thicket of philosophical shorthand we can propose the following. The paradigm takes a sensible singularity and raises it to the status of example. In this manner it is dialectic in that, after Hegel, it alienates immediate sense certainty. Further, the process of exclusion in play here is one of self-referentiality, so that again the dialectic is confirmed by the inclusion of self-alienation, the second stage of the dialectic. Yet unlike the dialectic, the paradigm is not a movement. If you recall, the dialectic moves because it cannot resolve the paradoxes of the Also (conditioned) and the One (condition). The paradigm is able to resolve these logical impossibilities by not entering into them and so is static, although this does not mean it is dead. Rather, the dynamism of the paradigm is in its genetic productivity. The paradigm negates its facticity so that it can generate the condition of its facticity. This means that rather than present a narrative of the dialectic, moving towards an impossible resolution in absolute knowledge, the paradigm presents a poiesis that is constantly productive through the double motion of poetics, rising up and falling away.[36]

PHENOMENOLOGICAL HERMENEUTICS: THE PARADIGMATIC CIRCLE

Having, in two pages, presented the history of the dialectic and, I would contend, its solution, Agamben then takes up the other major modality of the modern tradition, phenomenological hermeneutics. Noting the ancient problem of the hermeneutic circle—knowledge of the whole presupposes knowledge of parts and vice versa—Agamben accepts that Heidegger's solution was, in the interim, significant. Yet he wonders, as we all have, after Heidegger, "if the activity of the interpreter is always already anticipated by a pre-understanding that is elusive, what does it mean 'to come into [the circle] in the right way'?".[37] He is not alone of course in trying to redraft Heidegger's hermeneutics, one could argue modern philosophy has been nothing other than an attempt to do that on the part of Gadamer, Habermas, Derrida, and Deleuze. Agamben's innovation is to suggest that the only real solution to the hermeneutic circle, which of course delimits not only modern epistemology but also, since Heidegger, ontology, is to present it as the "paradigmatic circle." In such a circle the assumed duality between whole and part, as we have seen, is void or better suspended in indifferentiation. The whole is the result of paradigmatic demonstrations through particular cases. More than this, there is no succession of pre-preunderstanding and interpretation, the before and after of Heideggerian hermeneutics, as in the paradigm intelligibility does not precede the phenomena but stands to one side of it, and is indeed produced by it. "The phenomenon, exposed in the medium of its knowability, shows the whole of which it is the paradigm. With regard to phenomena, this is not a presupposition (a 'hypothesis'): as a '"non-presupposed principle,' it stands neither in the past nor in the present, but in their exemplary constellation".[38] We are forced through indirection to retain the Benjaminian overtones of constellation here as a mere background motif, for now Agamben seems content to list six features of the paradigm as a means of refuting the misunderstandings around his work. Although reader beware, in composing the paradigm as solution to one set of problems, how Agamben uses historical examples, he is in truth presenting the paradigm as future source of a new set of controversies, how modern thought's investment in the dialectic method contained within the hermeneutical circle, which is perhaps the best summation of philosophy in the last hundred years or so, is resolved by something as simple as an example.

Rather than repeat these six features, all of which we have covered, perhaps it is better to simply explain the qualities of the paradigm through them. The paradigm is a mode of knowledge that moves between singularities. It refutes the general and the particular. It refutes dichotomous logic in favour of a "bipolar analogical model".[39] The paradigm is always both suspended from its group and belonging to it. Thus, the separation of exemplarity and singularity is false or at least impossible. All groups are immanent to their paradigmatic members, never presupposed. With this weapon in hand, Agamben marches on to a greater engagement, the total control of all knowledge through the sanction of communicability under the auspices of the signature.

THEORY OF SIGNATURES

Having dealt with one half of this equation, singularity as paradigm, we now must turn our attention to the other element, the exposition of intelligibility, or what Agamben calls the signature. It is typical of Agamben that he chooses to make use of the medieval theory of signatures developed by Paracelsus and Böhme to address perhaps his most central idea, intelligibility (in the earlier works communicability, in the most recent operativity), even naming perhaps his most important work to date after Böhme's major work on the healing properties of plants based on their similarities to parts of the body or symptoms. To justify this provocative gesture Agamben commences this section by describing the signature as akin to the paradigm. There are, indeed, several qualities of the signature that refer back to the logic of the paradigm. So we find that the signature is composed of at least two parts, the *signator* and the signature, wherein the *signator* operates as the condition but, through the act of signing, is affected by the signature retroactively. Then we find that there is a signatory art of which the originary structure is Adamic language as the true names of all things. These true names are what Agamben calls oaths, not acts of denotation but rather speech acts of facticity wherein each name gives the true nature or being of the animal: pigs are filthy, horses strong and so on. We can thus deduce that the signature is mappable across Agamben's ideas on language as communicability and operative facticity (oath).

Then in terms of how a signature is assigned/found we see it is not a matter of straightforward resemblance. For example, in the *Euphrasia*, which has markings in the shape of an eye, the fact that it is good for curing eyes is not because it looks like an eye. The signifier, eye resemblance, and the signified, curative of eye problems, do not determine the signature. Instead, a signature is composed of at least five elements within which the differentiation between signifier and signified via material resemblance is problematized, and the clear divisions between *signator* and signature "seem to enter a zone of undecidability" so that the precedence of the *signator*, man's eye, over the signature, marking on the *Euphrasia*, is suspended. Already this logic of suspensive indifference is familiar to us, as is the logic of Böhme that a sign is created mute and must, to bring about knowledge, "be animated and qualified in a signature . . . the signature here clearly does not coincide with the sign, but is what makes the sign intelligible".[40] This is the basic formula of communicability. Having established several strong links between the paradigm, the signature and indeed wider themes in his work, Agamben then goes on to present us with a paradigmatic history of signatures and the resemblance, after Böhme, of signature to the idea of character, before arriving at Foucault's crucial appropriation of the term.

FOUCAULT'S STATEMENTS AS SIGNATURES

Foucault notes that in the sixteenth century knowledge operated by superimposing semiology, that which allows us to recognise what a sign is or is not, and hermeneutics, the set of knowledges that make a sign speak. Being able to recognise a signature in a sign produces knowledge out of resemblance: that which looks like an eye cures the eye. That said, there is not a perfect consonance between sign and meaning, which is why we have the signature or mark of secret knowledge that Adam imbued in every sign when he first created them. Every sign is made up of two degrees of signifier, its neutral signifier and its secret meaningful signature, and two degrees of signified, the object it refers to as sign and the knowledge it releases as signature. Melandri's interpretation makes this most clear when in writing on *The Order of Things* he calls the signature a "sign within a sign; it is the index that in the context of a given semiology univocally makes reference to a given interpretation . . . that it indicates, by means of the sign's making, the code with which it has to be deciphered".[41] It is clear then that the signature in the earlier text becomes the statement in *The Archaeology of Knowledge*, but Agamben further facilitates this shift through a reading of Benveniste's development of the problem of the lack of communication between sign and sentence because the semiotic sign must be recognised while semantic discourse must be understood. This is, of course, a restatement of the famous problem that motivates modern philosophy through Kant: how can sense immediacy and supersensible mediation come together and/or communicate? Agamben says of Benveniste's observations: "Signs do not speak unless signatures make them speak [they] render thinkable the passage between the semiotic and the semantic".[42]

A brief note on method is applicable here. The overall concept of the signature is developed in a paradigmatic manner. No one thinker is responsible for the intelligibility of the signature, and Agamben's role is certainly not the innovator of the term but something more akin to its curator. I think this term is preferable to, say, an archivist in that Agamben is making telling, paradigmatic selections from the archive to present a developmental argument. As Zartaloudis says of this method, Agamben "is not in search of problem-solving recommendations, but rather attempts to expose the empirical remainders of such problem-solving recommendations that defy any attempt at a transhistorically preordained essence or substance".[43]

Having presented his paradigmatic archaeology of the signature up to and including Foucault, Agamben is able to place the statement within the signature by observing that the statement is not a mode of traditional reference, such as we find in the sign, but operates in semiological structures "at the level of their simple existence, as a bearer of efficacy, which each time allows us to decide whether the act of language is efficacious".[44] As Foucault's work makes clear, a statement does not determine what is said or its meaning but the facts, circumstances, relations and networks that mean such a thing can be said at that moment in history. This becomes, in Foucault, the enunciative function, which is the cocreation of a subjective position from a statement which both validates the operativity of the statement, (this can be said by such and such a subject), but whose operation also facilitates the creation of such and such a subject-position. The enunciative function of the statement then is the modern equivalent of the signature. Definable neither as sign nor as meaning, it is a signing that allows for the existence of a meaning. Agamben concludes:

> Statements, then, are situated on the threshold between semiology and hermeneutics where signatures take place. Neither semiotic nor semantic, not yet discourse and no longer mere sign, statements, like signatures, do not institute semiotic relations or create new meanings; instead they mark and "characterize" signs at the level of their existence, thus actualizing and displacing their efficacy. These are the signatures that signs receive from the sheer fact of existing and being used — namely, the indelible character that, in marking them as signifying

something, orients and determines their interpretation and efficacy in a certain context.[45]

ONTOLOGICAL EPISTEMOLOGY

To clarify the central point in all of this, Agamben says that "the sign signifies because it carries a signature that necessarily predetermines its interpretation and distributes its use and efficacy according to rules, practices, and precepts that it is our task to recognize. In this sense, archaeology is the science of signatures".[46] This helps us better understand the following assertion that a statement/signature/paradigm has no real properties, rather, "it is a pure existence, the sheer fact that a certain being—language—takes place".[47] In other words, a statement is what allows for a certain fact of language to happen. This must not be taken as a pure and abstract state, as we must have signatures to have language; rather, it cannot be separated from its facticity: in order for such and such an act of language to occur, a signature must be presented through a statement that confirms such and such an act of language can be recognised as occurring, the semiotic, and be seen to take on consistent meaning, the semantic. This is where the signature of all things becomes its most radical potential by presenting an ontology of knowledge or of epistemology, revealed as Agamben clarifies the distinction between signatures and statements. Signatures stand in relation to being in the same manner that statements stand in relation to language. They mark being in its state of pure existence so that *On haplos* or pure being stands as the "archi-*signator* that imprints its transcendental marks on existential entities".[48]

Having said this Agamben refuses to fall into the usual problems attendant on this statement, for example, precedence, part-whole, or origin, by having recourse to the Kantian, and, for that matter, Wittgensteinian, mainstay that existence is not a real predicate. Thus, we cannot predicate existence on a founding subject of being, the concept of something added on to the concept of a thing, precisely because being is not a concept but a signature, not a specific, universal meaning confirmed by an empirical object, but the means by which a specific being can be said to come into existence at a precise moment in time, in history. "Hence ontology is not a determinate knowledge but the archaeology of every knowledge, which explores the signatures that pertain to beings by virtue of the very fact of existing, thus predisposing them to the interpretation of specific knowledges".[49] It is, in other words, the ontology of knowledge as an archaeology of knowledge as basis for the operativity of every being that is the main purpose of this text and Agamben's work as a whole.

SIGNATORY DISPLACEMENT

We cannot leave the second chapter of the work without attention paid to the final section, section 25. The first reason is that it explains a confusion raised in *The Kingdom and the Glory* over the definition of signature as displacement. In the earlier text the image of the signature given there strikes me as of a different order of emphasis than that which we find in the full consideration given here. This cannot be due to Agamben changing his mind or developing the concept, as there is only a year between the publication of the two books. In *The Kingdom and the Glory* at the very beginning, excavating the same authors, Foucault and Melandri, Agamben is considering the signature of secularization defining it thus because a signature *"is something that in a sign or concept marks and exceeds such a sign or concept referring it back to a determinate interpretation or field, without for this reason leaving the semiotic to constitute a new meaning or a new concept. Signatures move and displace concepts and signs from one field to another . . . without redefining them semantically"*.[50] Due to this, signatures connect different times and fields and so can be called "pure historical elements.". Thus, he further states, Foucault's archaeology, Nietzsche's genealogy, Derridean deconstruction and Benjamin's theory of dialectical images are all "sciences of signatures". From this basic law of signatory displacement the rest of this vast work then considers the "transposition" of *oikonomia* from the domestic into the theological field and from the theological into the political, defining *oikonomia* as a signature whose meaning remains the same but whose location alters. Order, the essence of *oikonomia*, is also defined in this manner, and the model of movement of a sign from one context to another, (and back again in some instances), without modifying the semiotic or semantic element is repeated throughout the book as the definition of the signature.

Significant though this is as an observation, I think it does not quite capture the signature, and indeed such a clear statement of the case is not presented in *The Signature of All Things*, which seems rather to speak of signature as a kind of fate for concepts, determining how they will be distributed rather than simply that they will and can be displaced. Further, displacement is presented more in terms of the paradigmatic logic of suspension between semiotic and semantic, rather than simply the manner in which one signature-statement can move from one discursive strategy to another without having to change its name or meaning. Of course the analysis of paradigm and signature explain how this can be so, in that the 'meaning' of a signature is not found in the sign or the semantic content but in the manner in which the signature allows things to be said or understood. For example, the displacement of *oikonomia* from home economics, for the Greeks, into theological economy and then political economy describes merely how certain things could be said in terms of theology and politics, rather than how one proceeds from the other. It is certainly not an argument for a theological basis for all politics, for example, with Christianity being as devastated by a signatory indifference in *The Kingdom and the Glory* as modern politics is in the earlier parts of the *homo sacer* project.[51]

INDIFFERENT MARKING, POTENTIAL AND PRIVATION

Now if we return to section 25 the same material is presented more briefly in some ways, and yet also more expansively in others. Here secularization, debated as a concept in the last century in key debates on theology and modernity, is presented not as a concept but as a "strategic operator" that functioned in modernity as a signature that presented the possibility of considering modernity in relation to theology by opening up a way back from modernity to theology. Secularisation, like a badge of office, the yellow mark on a Jew's coat or the sign worn by secularised priests referring to their previous order, is a mark worn that refers back to a past location, it "marks or exceeds a sign or concept in order to refer it to a specific interpretation or a specific sphere without, however, leaving it in order to constitute a new concept or new meaning".[52] This modality of marking is then considered in terms of the zero-degree of marking which we may call indifferent marking: the mark that indicates the presence of an absence. Indifferent marking allows Agamben to further establish a relation to perhaps his most enduring philosophical consideration, potentiality, when he likens the mark of a signature to Aristotelian privation. Privation is not absence but in fact is an actual referral back to the form it is the privation of, which is another word for actualisation defined by Agamben as the negation not of a potential but of the impotential. Impotentiality then operates as a strategic interim mode of privation linking, essentially, potentiality to the signature. Agamben summarises the situation as the presence of the signature: "The zero degree is not a sign but a signature that, in the absence of a signified, continues to operate as the exigency of an infinite signification that cannot be exhausted by any signified".[53] The signature is the impotentiality that allows a potentiality to come to actualisation without negating potentiality as such or presenting actualisation as plenitude. The impotentiality of the privative capacity not to do something means that actualisation only ever negates the impotentiality of a potential, the capacity not to do something removed by actually doing it. This provides, for me at least, a much more satisfying model for displacement and explains the direct relation between the two lasting legacies of Agamben's work, the logic of potential or the ontology of potential, as he calls it, and the epistemological project of the method which, in the signature, come together to form a crystalline and challenging consistency.

SIGNATURE AS CRITICAL PHILOSOPHY:
DERRIDA VERSUS DELEUZE

In this section the hint as to the signatory nature of different philosophi-cal systems is also addressed, specifically by opposing Derrida to Fou-cault. It is no surprise that Derrida appears to come out of this compari-son the worse off, but that is not to say that Agamben's theory of signa-tures is simply mappable onto Foucault's archaeology and his use of statements. In fact, it is more accurate to say that signatures compose the different philosophical sets of our age around differing instances of how the signature works and that, thus far, the true power of the signature has not been fully realised. That aside, deconstruction is presented here as the "interpretative practice that suspends signatures and makes them idle, in such a way that there is never any access to the realized event of mean-ing".[54] As such, deconstruction, he says, thinks about signatures "as pure writing beyond every concept, which thus guarantees the inexhaustibil-ity—the infinite deferral—of signification".[55]

The issue for Agamben is actually quite simple. The signature has a specific origin, a historical moment of arising, and a large number of historical presentations, all of them paradigmatic. It is also tied to specific signs in a manner that is not free. In addition a signature is held to specific meaning possibilities. In this way it is not supplemental or in excess, and contrary to Derrida's insistence, the trace is not produced as its own erasure, but is in fact productive of a suspension between specific instances of meaning. Thus, unlike *différance* with which in all other as-pects it concurs, the signature is not endless deferral, does not indicate a permanently other-to-come, can be traced by to a specific origin, can take on a defined significance, and can also be inoperative. Or, as Agamben says, negatively presenting the trace here as signature: "A signature's auto-signification never grasps itself, nor does it let its own insignificance be; rather, it is displaced and deferred in its own gesture. The trace is then a signature suspended and referred toward itself, a *kenōsis* that never knows its own *plērōma*".[56]

One could perhaps best summarise this by saying that the trace re-leases a series of undecidables around concepts that open up a freedom of potential, supplemental meanings that disallow any concept coming to full presence. While a signature marks a series of decidables but at the level of material particularities, that do not operate around concepts but around modes of efficacious discourse, that do not open up a freedom but rather help us to see the massive weight of determination around everything we say or do, and that, rather than denying the full presence of concepts by introducing a supplemental other, instead reveal the pow-erful presence of ideas across time and disciplines where there are no supplemental others, in that nothing can come to discourse unless it is allowed to by conforming to the signature of its communicability. This being the case, the radical power of signatures to undermine states of meaning is to do with their own suspensive operations, rather than end-less deferrals via tiny supplemental alterities that hint at a larger, never-to- be-recuperated alterity.

Foucault's strategy is presented positively here as the opposite to Der-rida's. Like Derrida, Foucault begins with a signature and its excess over signification, and he accepts there is no pure sign without signature (trace), but he also says that "neither is it possible ever to separate and move the signature to an originary position (even as supplement)".[57] Foucault never seeks for an origin or an absence of origin, such a designa-tion makes no sense to how statements operate. That would indicate a traditional historiography applied to a radical project of disjunction. In-stead, for Foucault the statement-signature means "keeping events in their own proper dispersal, lingering on the smallest deviations and the aberrations that accompany them and determine their meaning. In a word, it means seeking in every event the signature that characterizes and specifies it and in every signature the event and the sign that carry and condition it". Or, as Foucault has it, "'to show that to speak is to do something other than express what one thinks'".[58]

While Agamben is still very much in the camp of Foucault in this regard, he does not see this as the final destination for the signatory method. Here I think we have the real purpose of the text, which is in fact to use paradigms and signatures as interim strategies only. This being the case, his critique of Derrida and Foucault is the same: they are both bril-liant strategists of the signature, but they present a limit to thought not an exit from it. In contrast, Agamben imagines a practice that does not dwell on pure signatures (deconstruction) or investigate their relationality to signs and events of discourse (Foucault's archaeology) but "reaches back beyond the split between signature and sign and between the semiotic and the semantic in order to lead signatures to their historical fulfil-ment".[59] In other words, signatory philosophy's role is not to reveal the paradigmatic strategies of, say, power, or life, these are a mere by-prod-uct. Instead, it is to suspend itself as the final strategy of the dialectic method (deconstruction) within the hermeneutic circle (archaeology) re-sulting in a position of the nonmarked "that, according to Paracelsus, coincides with the paradisiacal state and final perfection".[60] But, as Agamben accepts here, that is a story "for others to write"; he seems satisfied to merely lay out the method here in preparation for its sus-pended fulfilment by those of us who follow after.

NOTES

1. Giorgio Agamben, *The Signature of All Things: On Method*, trans. Luca D'Isanto and Kevin Attell (New York: Zone Books, 2009), 9.

2. Agamben, *Signature*, 17. Although there has been much confusion over this issue of historical paradigms, the basis of this method can be found in Agamben's early work. He first mentions the idea of a philosophical philology in *Infancy and History* (1978) (Giorgio Agamben, *Infancy and History: On the Destruction of Experience*, trans. Liz Heron [London: Verso, 1993],159–67), where the importance of the paradigm is also addressed (Agamben, *Infancy*, 119–137), and speaks at length about the example in *The Coming Community* (1990) (Giorgio Agamben, *The Coming Community*, trans. Michael Hardt [Minneapolis: University of Minnesota Press, 1993], 9–12). It is worth noting here the centrality of two Italian terms. The first is *valere*, translated here as "stands for," which would rather be *rappresentare*, suggesting a mode of secondary signification, or *sopportare*, which instead has the sense of being a founding support. If we neglect these two options we may have a cleaner sense of this all-important relationship. In this context *valere* means to be of equal worth, equal use or equal validity. That a paradigm is not a representation of something else or a founding support is essential for understanding the specificity of this term in Agamben. As for *intelligibilità*, the issue is quite different. There is no ambiguity of translation here but rather a philosophical and historical debate as to what constitutes intelligibility. Agamben is using Foucault's term here, of course, so he specifically calls to mind the means by which discursive statements can be said to be intelligible based on their communicability. In this context, then, intelligibility, or how concepts can be known to the intellect, and communicability, how they can be known in common amongst a group of subject positions, are synonymous, taking us much closer to the communal and discursive presentation of all concepts in Agamben.

3. Agamben, *Signature*, 42. In the future *segnatura* will rank as perhaps the most important single term in Agamben's work. The first thing to ask is why the translators of *Signatura Rerum* chose not to keep the Latin term, a term in common currency with its own peculiar and important discursive history, when, for example, *Homo Sacer* was retained for the 1995 text? The obvious reason why *Homo Sacer* was not translated is that it is a paradigm, and its manner of rendering a sign intelligible is not reproducible in any of the translated options. The same is surely true of *Signatura Rerum*. This is made apparent if we try to translate *segnatura* from the Italian as simply "signature", as the English edition does. In fact signature is more commonly *firma* in Italian, while the term *segnatura*, if not obscure, is not really in common usage. Agamben clearly has in mind the specific meaning in Italian of marking, especially in publishing, and indeed this is how he begins his consideration of the term in the second part of the study. As we shall go on to see, the signature must be a mark which is stable but which bears no defined meaning and so can be used in a myriad of ways. The English term "signature" derives directly from the Latin but almost always takes the meaning of a *distinguishing* mark. While I cannot easily think of an alternative, this is rather misleading in relation to how Agamben uses the term, for in fact *segnatura* is a general, meaningless and thus, in a sense, indistinct mark. This indistinct generality is central to my own reading of the term. Obviously, the translators are following orthodoxy in translating *Signatura* as "signature", but if they had retained the Latin term, it would have been truer to Agamben's methodological intentions.

4. Agamben, *Signature*, 110. The choice of translating *punto d'insorgenza* as "moment of arising" in the text neglects two inferences here. The first is the long philosophical consideration of the temporality of the point in relation to extension and space. The choice of 'moment' blunts this somewhat, as does the word 'arising', which neglects the obvious indication here of uprising and insurgency. One can see why point of insurgency was not chosen, but it contains much more that is true philosophically and politically than our tamer "moment of arising".

5. I respond to the large majority of major criticisms throughout the pages of *The Literary Agamben: Adventures in Logopoiesis* (London: Continuum,mm, 2010), as does de la Durantaye in *Giorgio Agamben: A Critical Introduction* (Stanford, CA: Cal.: Stanford University Press, 2009), 219—223 & 345—351.

6. See specifically my comments in relation to this in William Watkin, *The Literary Agamben: Adventures in Logopoiesis* (London: Continumm, 2010), 1–3, and Alex Murray's, *Giorgio Agamben* (London: Routledge, 2010), 3–4.

7. Agamben's repeated criticism of Derrida's work is another rich source of aggressive misreadings of Agamben's work, to some degree solicited by the frequency and increasingly incendiary tone of Agamben's remarks. We will return to this in the second part of the study.

8. Thanos Zartaloudis, *Giorgio Agamben: Power, Law and the Uses of Criticism* (London: Routledge, 2010), 13.

9. Agamben states in a recent essay, "And yet, following the rule that history never returns to a lost state, we must be prepared, with neither regret nor hope, to search . . . for a new figure of the human" (Giorgio Agamben, *Nudities*, trans. David Kishik and Stefan Pedatella [Stanford, CA: Stanford University Press, 2011], 54). See also Zartaloudis's excellent differentiation of bare life from any Hobbesian originary state of nature in Zartaloudis, *Giorgio Agamben*, 146–47.

10. Agamben, *Signature*, 11.

11. Agamben, *Signature*, 12.

12. Agamben, *Signature*, 12.

13. See Giorgio Agamben, *Homo Sacer: Sovereign Power and Bare Life*, trans. Daniel Heller-Roazen. (Stanford, CA: Stanford University Press, 1998), 71–74, and Giorgio Agamben, *Remnants of Auschwitz: The Witness and the Archive*, trans. Daniel Heller-Roazen (New York: Zone Books, 2002), 41–86. Agamben's use of the *Muselman* as a paradigm has perhaps raised the most amount of controversy. So far Žižek is probably the most fair and perceptive critic in this area; see Slavoj Žižek, "Neighbours and Other Monsters: A Plea for Ethical Violence," in Slavoj Žižek, Eric L. Santner, and Kenneth Reinhard, *The Neighbour: Three Enquiries in Political Theology* (Chicago: Chicago University Press, 2005), 160–62.

14. Giorgio Agamben, *The Kingdom and the Glory: For a Theological Genealogy of Economy and Government*, trans. Lorenzo Chiesa with Matteo Mandarini (Stanford, CA: Stanford University Press, 2011), 276.

15. See Michel Foucault, *The Archaeology of Knowledge*, trans. A. M. Sheridan Smith (London: Routledge, 1972), 3–17.

16. Agamben, *Signature*, 15.

17. See Giorgio Agamben, *Potentialities*, trans. Daniel Heller-Roazen (Stanford, CA: Stanford University Press, 1999), 27–38, and Watkin, *Literary Agamben*, 48–51 and 54–57.

18. Agamben, *Signature*, 18.

19. See Giorgio Agamben, *The Man Without Content*, trans. Georgia Albert (Stanford, CA: Stanford University Press, 1999), 94–103.

20. Agamben, *Signature*, 21.

21. Agamben, *Signature*, 20.

22. Agamben, *Signature*, 22.

23. Agamben, *Signature*, 23.

24. See also Giorgio Agamben, *The Time That Remains*, trans. Patricia Dailey (Stanford, CA: Stanford University Press, 2005), 69.

25. Agamben, *Signature*, 23.

26. Murray takes this tack, for example, not without justification. See Murray, *Agamben*, 5–6 & 52–53.

27. Agamben, *Signature*, 24.

28. Giorgio Agamben, *The Sacrament of Language: An Archaeology of the Oath*, trans. Adam Kotsko (Stanford, CA: Stanford University Press, 2010), 55.

29. Agamben's first engagement with communicability is as Heideggerian cultural transmissibility; see, for example, Agamben, *Man Without Content*, 107, and then *Potentialities*, 104. He then returns to it in the form of Heidegger's language as saying in Giorgio Agamben, *Language and Death: The Place of Negativity*, trans. Karen E. Pinkus with Michael Hardt (Minneapolis: University of Minnesota Press, 1991), 13, and as

pure taking place Agamben, *Language and Death*, 56—57. He has settled on communicability by the time of *Means Without Ends*; see Giorgio Agamben, *Means Without Ends*, trans. Vincenzo Binetti and Cesare Casarino (Minneapolis: University of Minnesota Press, 2000), 98—99. That said, he is still using the idea of transmissibility in the recent work, for example, Agamben, *Time That Remains*, 40.

30.   One of the earliest references to the signifying function as such is Agamben, *Infancy*, 94. He then returns to this in Giorgio Agamben, *The End of the Poem*, trans. Daniel Heller-Roazen. (Stanford, CA: Stanford University Press, 1999), 67.

31.   See Watkin, *Literary Agamben*, 87—116, for a consideration of this issue.

32.   Agamben, *Kingdom*, 253—259.

33.   Agamben, *Signature*, 24.

34.   Agamben, *Signature*, 25—26.

35.   Agamben, *Signature*, 26.

36.   This double nature of the poetic was the basis of my first study of Agamben. For more, see Watkin, *Literary Agamben*, 135—165.

37.   Agamben, *Signature*, 27.

38.   Agamben, *Signature*, 28.

39.   Agamben, *Signature*, 31.

40.   Agamben, *Signature*, 42.

41.   Cited in Agamben, *Signature*, 59.

42.   Agamben, *Signature*, 61.

43.   Zartaloudis, *Giorgio Agamben*, 4–5.

44.   Agamben, *Signature*, 63. The more accurate translation of *funtore* would be "functor", that is, not something that simply bears or carries efficacy but that in doing so allows it to function. This comes closer to Agamben's sense, after Foucault, that the material presence of the signature is the key here, irrespective of any sense of the sign as meaning.

45.   Agamben, *Signature*, 64.

46.   Agamben, *Signature*, 64.

47.   Agamben, *Signature*, 65.

48.   Agamben, *Signature*, 66.

49.   Agamben, *Signature*, 66.

50.   Agamben, *Kingdom*, 4.

51.   *Homo Sacer* is but the first and most well-known of the series of texts that compose what I term the Homo Sacer project, a project, Agamben tells us, that is drawing to a close with the publication of the *Homo Sacer, II, 5 Opus Dei. Archeologia dell'ufficio*, (Torino: Bollati Boringhieri, 2012) but is, as I write, being extended into a volume entitled *L''uso dei corpi*, which Agamben cannot confirm for certain will be the last volume. That this series of texts extends increasingly into theology is not testament to a particularly theological bent in Agamben's work, but merely evidence of the fact that when excavating the origins of our current signatures, naturally a large part of all statements made originate in religious texts. Agamben is no more a theological thinker than he is a political or philosophical. All these determinations are essentially signatory and so, over time, would be rendered indifferent and thus inoperative. Agamben then does not sign up to the death of God but to his deactivation, and this is the basis of his often misunderstood messianism.

52.   Agamben, *Signature*, 77.

53.   Agamben, *Signature*, 78.

54.   Agamben, *Signature*, 78.

55.   Agamben, *Signature*, 78.

56.   Agamben, *Signature*, 79.

57.   Agamben, *Signature*, 79.

58.   Agamben, *Signature*, 79—80.

59.   Agamben, *Signature*, 80.

60.   Agamben, *Signature*, 80.

TWO

Philosophical Archaeology

The project by which an ontology of epistemology is developed wherein all being is defined as the intelligible, communicable operativity of knowledges is complex enough. That this project is merely preparatory for the suspension of the assumed division between ontology and epistemology or Being as such and beings as facts adds an additional level of complexity which is, however, essential both for a full understanding of Agamben's method and a proper appreciation of his importance. This combination of signatures operating through time due to a signatory logic in such a manner as existence and knowledge become coimplicated to the degree that their clearly sanctioned difference in our culture is suspended is named, by Agamben, in the last chapter of the book, philosophical archaeology.

The final section of the book is concerned with the problem of the *arché* and as such is a clear departure from both Derrida and Foucault. While Foucault makes it clear that the question of origins does not pertain to signatures, for Agamben, Derrida replaces the legitimacy of the question, How did this begin? with the archi-trace. This is problematic for at least two reasons. The first is that for Agamben difference does not in any fashion undermine structures of metaphysics but founds them through an imposed division between issues of identity (the common) and difference (the proper). The second is that, after Foucault, Agamben believes in the legitimacy of tracing historical materialities. This being the case, why does Agamben then retain the issue of the *arché*? The answer is that for Agamben the tracing of the *arché* of particular discursive formations, as Foucault calls them, reveals the deep-seated structures of Western thought as problematic, profoundly contingent and so surmountable. Against the best wishes of Derrida and Foucault, Agamben recuperates the idea of origins for contemporary philosophy so as to end the great narrative of origins and destinations that is the vast, fallacious epic of this tradition.

ARCHĒ: PHILOSOPHICAL ARCHAEOLOGY[1]

Considering the controversy that has raged around Agamben's philosophy and/or historiography of origins, it is not insignificant for these reasons also that the final chapter of the book begins with the *archē* of the idea of philosophical archaeology in Kant. Kant, Agamben notes, struggles with the empirical and temporal nature of a historical enquiry versus the reasoned ahistorical nature of philosophic thought. Philosophical history, he realises, cannot be simply the written opinions of philosophers, for that would never capture the truth or essence of thought, so that in the end one would have a history of everything that happened except the thing itself. This is our first lesson. In philosophical archaeology, "the *archē* it seeks can never be identified with a chronological datum".[2] As the philosopher always commences with the fact that philosophical truth has not yet been established and also because, as such, of all disciplines it lacks a specific object of enquiry, all philosophy is built on the ruins of those that came before, and the origins of any such project can only ever act as *Urbilder* or archetypes, a place that can never be reached, Kant says, and must serve instead as a guideline. This reading from Kant forms a refutation for the larger majority of Agamben's critics: the question of origin is of the order of the *archē* outside of a traditional concept of a chronological datum.

Next Agamben develops his relationship with Foucault by drawing out a difference in Foucault's work on Nietzsche between Nietzschean genealogy or *Ursprung*, which Foucault associates with the now-discredited idea of origin and his own version of genealogy. In Foucault's system, any quest for the origin of something commits two cardinal errors. It first presupposes an ideal identity at the base of any set of discursive formations, and, second, it commits to the hermeneutics of silence or the unnamed true motivator behind the statement which is traceable to its root. If you recall, the most radical element of Foucault's statement is that it is what it is, and it says what it says. It is not a secret index or cipher of a deeper meaning. This is a position that surely influences Agamben's first major philosophical attack on the tradition of linguistic ineffability in Hegel and Heidegger, *Language and Death*. Agamben pays close attention to Foucault's choice of verb here in his phrase "The genealogist needs history to dispel the chimeras of the origin".[3] The verb *conjurer*, he notes, has an apotropaic structure in that it means to evoke and to expel. Agamben rightly points out that the two meanings of the word are not in opposition: "for dispelling something—a spectre, a demon, a danger—first requires conjuring it. The fact is that the alliance between the genealogist and the historian finds its meaning precisely in this 'evocation-expulsion'".[4]

REPRESSION

Several things need to be noted here. The first is that, contrary to what critics have regularly contended, the Agamben search for 'origins' is in fact an alliance between historical data and genealogical method. Second, the role of history is to reveal origins that allow one to dispel the myth of origins. In this manner one can see clear agreement between Agamben, Foucault and Derrida as regards the spirit of this project but profound methodological disagreement as regards the efficacy of historical document. Third, it is quite clear that the apotropaic structure of attraction-expulsion mirrors that of perhaps the discipline that might seem most at odds with Foucauldian genealogy, namely, Freudian repression. In repression it is the expelled that exerts a hidden attraction at the root and origin of a symptom, and the role of the analyst is to go back to this origin and dispel it. That said, both methods share a commonality of disdain for the veracity of factual *archē*; after all, Freud famously says in a footnote at the end of the "Wolfman" case study that the fact of the actual existence of a primal scene is irrelevant as long as the patient believes this factuality in such a way as a cure is produced. The same is true to a degree for the genealogist who works in the opposite direction to the symptom producing an antisymptomology. They also care nothing for the 'veracity' of *archē*—there is no such veracity except as an assumed element of the discursive formation that allows statements that require *archē* to come into existence[5] —but instead of seeing a repressed repulsion at the root of a symptom, they concentrate on a regularly expressed attraction at the basis of the antisymptomatic nature of the statement, meaning, if Žižek is correct in his contention that Marx invented the symptom, that not only is there no place for Freud in philosophical archaeology, neither is there any room for Marx.

Leaving Marx to one side, much of the final section of the book is an acceptance of the similarity between repression and archaeology and also a careful oppositional difference between the two. For example, reading Melandri on Foucault, Agamben considers the precise relation of archaeology and repression where the historian goes back to the point when a phenomenon splits into a conscious and unconscious element. But what is of concern, Melandri argues, is not regression to the hidden and repressed element, bringing it back to life so to speak, but simply a questioning as to why it was made unconscious in the first place. Here again there is an implied criticism of Derrida, who does clearly state that one part of the role of deconstruction is the restitution of the other in discourse although not, of course, its hypostatisation. Agamben, Melandri and Foucault are in this sense much more reactionary in that they do not want to write the history of the repressed; they simply want to show how repression is capable as a discursive process relating to a set of materials at a particular time.

The parallel between Freudian repression and Agambenian archaeology is so marked that, rarely for Agamben, he spends quite some time on psychoanalysis, coming to the conclusion that both methods gain access to the past through something that has not been lived through and so cannot actually be called past: it remains with us. Yet for genealogical inquiry, the not-yet-past is revealed through the moment of arising, not of origin. For genealogy, unlike psychoanalysis, it is not a case of endlessly replaying the infantile scene or of making conscious all unconscious material:

> On the contrary, it is a matter of conjuring up its phantasm, through meticulous genealogical inquiry, in order to work on it, deconstruct it, and detail it to the point where it gradually erodes, losing its originary status. In other words, archaeological regression is elusive: it does not seek, as in Freud, to restore a pervious stage, but to decompose, displace, and ultimately bypass it in order to go back not to its content but to the modalities, circumstances, and moments in which the split, by means of repression, constituted it as origin.[6]

At this point the unlived past is revealed as contemporary with the present and thus accessible for the first time in the form of a source. When this occurs the contemporary attains copresence with one's own present, seeing it as an "experience of an unlived and the memory of a forgetting". Thus, it renders inoperative an operativity, experience is unlived, and operative an inoperativity, forgetting is remembered. Agamben further develops this by saying that the moment of arising is then an example of the future anterior, as it occurs only after the inquiry into its historical status is complete. It is produced, in other words, by the inquiry that it structurally produces. Archaeology is neither memory nor forgetting but "at the threshold of their indifference".[7] One could say in this register that archaeology unearths a past that will have been when contemporary work unblocks those unconscious elements that disallowed access to this past.

THE MOMENT OF ARISING

We now turn to perhaps the key element of the method. In that Agamben's philosophy is a call for the movement beyond a metaphysics of both presence and difference which, be believes, does not disrupt presence but actually forms and distributes it, his interest in the origins of discursive formations such as sovereignty, sacredness, law, economy, secularisation, democracy and so on is campaigning. His patient archaeology of paradigms wishes to render all these inoperative over time. This is not a project he shares with Foucault, and perhaps at this moment we must say that in addition, while the signature resembles the statement, the statement is limited to linguistic phenomena while the signature goes beyond this limit.[8] The messianic intention of Agamben to render inoperative the conditioning, binary logic of Western thought through careful exposition of paradigmatic order and its signatory distribution through a dialectic of common and proper is what Agamben means by *archē* or, as he also calls it, the moment of arising, of the phenomenon. Here *archē* is very far away from any sense of constituting origin, as it is, in Agamben, necessary only as a tool to render major discursive formations inoperative. In this way it is not founding and generative but suspending and inoperative. Thus, when Agamben considers his own project of philosophical philology, for after all he is much more a philologist than a historian,[9] he questions the value of the philological datum in a manner his critics are not able to do. For him what is in question is "the epistemological paradigm of inquiry itself". In a rather Derridean moment, then, the tools of philology are turned against philological, historical and genealogical presuppositions.

What follows is a definition of archaeology that really must silence any critic questioning the historical or philological prowess of Agamben's work:

> Provisionally, we may call 'archaeology' that practice which in any historical investigation has to do not with the origins but with the moment of a phenomenon's arising and must therefore engage anew the sources and tradition. It cannot confront tradition without deconstructing the paradigms, techniques, and practices through which tradition regulates the forms of transmission, conditions access to sources, and in the final analysis determines the very status of the knowing subject. The moment of arising is objective and subjective at the same time and is indeed situated on a threshold of undecidability between object and subject. It is never the emergence of the fact without at the same time being the emergence of the knowing subject itself.[10]

Another reflection of this logic, after Foucault, would be that the moment of arising is the identifiable point when it became possible for a set of discursive formations to be operative. This concerns the regulation and transmission of concepts and ideas but also practices and methods via the construction of a subjective enunciative position or set of positions, which constitute through their perspective, being and behaviour the objective world around them. In a radical revision of the Kantian revolution, yes the objective realm exists for the subject who has a set of concepts which it uses to make sense of this realm, only this does not happen once and for all but more than once over periods of time where the world of things is composed by subjective positions which can be taken up only by virtue of the very realm of things that they have composed. The *archē* in Agamben, nearly always represented by subjective positions, *homo sacer*, sovereign, God, judge and so on, constitutes the first moment of the intelligibility of a new discursive formation. Thus, Agamben is concerned with the coming into existence of a historical and discursive exigency, usually one we have enshrined as founding, external and beyond the norm: founding and governing power.

BENJAMINIAN NOW-TIME AND DIALECTICS AT A STANDSTILL

In the final pages of the text Agamben once again repays his debt to the work of Walter Benjamin. It is Benjamin's conceptions of the Angel of History, weak messianism, dialectic images at a standstill, profane redemption and the constellation of now-time that form the real inspiration of the Agamben revolutionary method.[11] This method consists of three parts, as we saw. First, identify paradigms and the logic of the paradigm. This logic is suspensive and considers the regulation between issues of the common and the proper. Thus, it tells us how examples can be formed in such a way that lay bare the machinery of the condition and the conditioned but also through these examples how this machinery came about, allowing us to see how we could, if not dismantle it, at least render it inoperative. Next, trace the signatory element of these paradigms, that destinal distributive process that allows for the transmission of concepts across time and discourses in a kind of meta- or transparadigmatic fashion. Finally, the *archē* gives us the moment of arising of this regulatory practice, the point when it was first possible to say such and such a thing from such and such a subject position, seen from our own current enunciative position within our own current structures of intelligibility—not the first time such and such a thing was said or the first time such and such a subject position was allowed but the first co-originary and approved consonance of the two as an approved intelligibility of a discursive practice traceable within actual textual materials at the current time.

Where Benjamin's work is essential here is in terms of the temporality of now-time (*Jetztziet*). Now-time allows one to say of the moment of arising that one has *not* discovered something hidden about the past that has influenced us ever since and which, now that we know this, we can do something resistant about it. This is not Agamben's message at all, especially not in the much-misread *Homo Sacer*. Rather, now-time is the moment when we can redeem a historical fragment, another name for the paradigm, in the modality of composing our own contemporary enunciative and discursive position.[12] Thus, archaeology is primarily about how we are constructing our own discursive formations from our sanctioned enunciative positions through the contemporary organisation of statements. For Agamben, Freudian regression and Benjamin's Angel are two sides of a single process. The Angel travels into the future gazing at the past, and regression moves to the past while looking to the future. Both have an element they cannot see and know. Powerfully opposed to the metaphysics of occlusion implicit in these two figures,[13] Agamben then calls for the two gazes to be merged, which allows him to say, of the moment of arising when a discursive formation is split into its conscious and unconscious element, "it should by now be obvious that our way of representing the moment before the split is governed by the split itself".[14] The split is not based on a 'before', therefore, an ideal state of unity or happiness, but on a 'now' composed as the 'after': "before or beyond the split, in the disappearance of the categories governing its representation, there is nothing but the sudden, dazzling disclosure of the moment of arising, the revelation of the present as something that we were not able to live or think".[15] So, it is not even the case that, as in Foucault, before the split there was another set of split-dependent operations relating to a different split. And it is certainly not the case, as he says here, of a Freudian infantile scene. Rather, the temporal category, before the split, is what arrives to us now in the realisation that our present situation does not belong to us as something we can either live or think. What we see in the *archē*, the moment of arising, the predivisive moment, is our dispossession of selves right now.

Agamben summarises the *archē* in the closing section as being in possession of the following qualities:

- It is not placed in a chronology of past origination.
- Rather, it is an operative force within history emanating from the moment of its arising.
- The example chosen is the 'big bang', whose effects we still feel as contemporary moments, but, unlike the big bang, the *archē* has no date.
- The *archē* has no substance per se but is "a field of bipolar historical currents stretched between anthropogenesis and history",[16] or between moment of arising and of becoming, archi-past and present.
- This is a moment that is supposed to have taken place but cannot be reproduced as an actual chronological event.
- The whole role of the *archē* is merely to give historical phenomena their intelligibility/communicability or their possibility of existence.
- All of which is directed to one end, as regards historical phenomena, namely, "'saving' them archaeologically in a future anterior in the understanding not of an unverifiable origin but of its finite and untotalizable history".[17]

From these maxims we can now easily assert that Agamben's work was never about unearthing hidden origins but rather about rendering the conditions of the intelligibility of our own current discursive formations through the complex archaeological process to, ultimately, reveal and then make inoperative the underlying signature of all things in our culture. This signature is the act of presenting as necessary what is in fact a deep historical contingency: the imposed division of common and proper at the heart of every form of knowledge and the peculiarity of the co-originary yet asymmetrical relation (the common founds the proper as the precondition of its own authority or power).

This is not the place to trace the complex relation between Agamben and Benjamin, a project that has in any case been exhaustively covered by de la Durantaye's comprehensive introduction. That said, Agamben pays as much of a debt to Benjamin as to Foucault when it comes to the construction of the method, and, for our own study, this was in fact the first gate that opened onto the dependency of the method on indifference. And as we are lingering on now-time it seems apt that we add a clarification as regards the source of Agambenian indifference in Benjamin's work. For it is true that Foucault has little to say by way of indifference, whereas the Benjaminian method is defined by indifference in the vast, incomplete arcades project. There, speaking of ambiguity in Baudelaire, he says this is "the manifest imaging of dialectic, the law of dialectics at a standstill. This standstill is utopia".[18] Although this does not explain what dialectics at a standstill can mean, the relation of this proposed state and a conceptual utopia is found across all of Agamben's major works.

A good deal more detail of this discomposing formulation is then found hundreds of pages later in the famous entry on the dialectical image:

> It is not what is past casts its light on what is present, or what is present its light on what is past; rather, image is that wherein what has been comes together in a flash with the now to form a constellation. In other words, image is dialectics at a standstill. For while the relation of the present to the past is a purely temporal, continuous one, the relation of what-has-been to the now is dialectical: is not progression but image, suddenly emergent.[19]

Within this passage there is much that is recast in Agamben's method. If we understand image here as not merely an actual visual image or a simple schema of thought, following Havercamp's logic, but instead a schema of reading whose effect is more decisive than its cause,[20] then we can see that an image is an alternative description of the visibility of signatures and paradigms in Agamben's work. Indeed, the whole logic of the method is then available to us in Benjamin's wonderful vocabulary.

The image here, which is a realisation of a suspension as the only true images we are told are dialectical ones and their purpose moreover is to present the dialectic (past and present) at a standstill, appears in the suspension of normal temporality. The past is seen in now-time as if for the first time, and now-time is composed out of images and fragments from the past. Instead of a sequential and naïvely causal movement between past and present, typifying the historiographer's art, the movement is suspended in the image and disseminated horizontally in the form of an immobile and extensive constellation. Of course, there is much here that is in turn Mallarmé, with the throw of the dice being the punctual moment of the event of the image and the dissemination of multiplicity that is not negated by the throw the constellation (constellation of course being one of Mallarmé's most important symbolic reservoirs).

The clear relation between Agamben's method and Benjamin's is confirmed later on in the text when Benjamin says,

> To thinking belongs the movement as well as the arrest of thoughts. Where thinking comes to a standstill in a constellation saturated with tensions—there the dialectical image appears. It is the caesura in the movement of thought. Its position is naturally not an arbitrary one. It is to be found, in a word, where the tension between the dialectical opposites is greatest. [21]

The combination of movement and arrest as a modality of thought, the emphasis on the tensile standoff as the mode of the appearance of the dialectical image, [22] the definition of the caesura as the movement of thought [23] and the nonarbitrary nature of the standstill, occurring as it does in moments where the tension is greatest, are all concepts that have found a place in Agamben's development of his own system. [24] Thus, the dialectical image, which in a flash facilitates the dialectic at a standstill, giving access to a constellation of material elements redeemed from history as continuum, that suspends the opposition between past and present through the new occasional temporality of now-time whose final aim is "historical apocastasis", [25] all as a form of weak messianism, is a pretty good first summation of Agamben's work.

However, and this was indeed the question that in effect created the 'image' of my own study, what does a dialectic at a standstill look like when dialectics is defined by movement? A dialectic at rest cannot be, in truth, a dialectic as such. Therefore, to build a philosophical system out of what at best in Benjamin is a logopoietic invention rather than a logically worked out term seems akin to saddling up Pegasus in a horse race — superlative if you can locate a Pegasus but disastrous when the magical horse is proven to be chimerical. To overcome the Pegasus objection one must therefore return to Hegel and, especially, the much-overlooked reliance of the dialectic on a mode of negating indifference, not so much to give the concept wings or to ground it but, as ever, to suspend it. This will be the main task of the subsequent chapter.

NOTE ON NYMPHS AND PLATES

In the final pages of the first section of *The Signature of All Things*, Agamben chooses Aby Warburg's theory of the *Pathosformeln* as an example of the paradigm in action.[26] This refers to a project Warburg worked on, an atlas of images which he named *Mnemosyne*. The atlas consists of pages or plates made up of various images often treating the same theme. Plate 46, for example, is handed over to the theme of the nymph. We are engaged with the same material source that informs much of the debate in the small book *Ninfe* (2007) with Warburg operating as a modern end point to the much-neglected yet apparently essential theory of these in-between and interim, in that they will not attain salvation or redemption, creatures.[27] While there are hints in *Ninfe* as to the significance methodo-logically of the *Pathosformeln*, not least references by Warburg to the Ben-jaminian 'dialectic at a standstill' to refer to the status of the nymph, it is in the later weightier tome that we begin to see how so slight a creature as a nymph could hold in its mortal hands that will never see prayer, accept the host or bear stigmata, the potential future direction of that most ex-hausted and threatened beast, Western metaphysics.

Agamben explains that plate 46 contains 27 images of 'nymphs' but that it would be a mistake to see it as merely an iconographic repertoire of images in reference to a woman in movement, which one would ar-range chronologically to trace back this theme to the original archetypal image or 'formula of pathos' from which all subsequent images emerge. Rather, Agamben argues it was not Warburg's intention to present any image as the original or to say that the rest of the images are copies. Instead, Warburg's *Pathosformeln* are

> hybrids of archetype and phenomenon, first-timeness (*primavoltità*) and repetition . . . the nymph herself is neither archaic nor contemporary; she is undecidable in regards to diachrony and synchrony, unicity and multiplicity. This means that the nymph is the paradigm of which the individual nymphs are the exemplars. Or to be more precise, in accor-dance with the constitutive ambiguity of Plato's dialectic, the nymph is the paradigm of the single images, and the single images are the para-digms of the nymph.[28]

To explain the nymph's status as both general and particular in a perpet-ual, promiscuous exchange representing a certain categorical-hierarchical nymphomania, Agamben likens this to Goethe's much more sober term *Urphänomen* referring to a modality of the organisation of experience that renounces Aristotelian genus-species organisation patterns in favour of a system of Nancyean reticulation, where a point stands in equal relation to all other points in every direction. Goethe terms this analogy, or the placement of one existent alongside another and, indeed, every other. Analogy, Agamben explains, can be taken as another name for the paradigm or "the place where analogy lives in perfect equilibrium beyond the opposition between generality and particularity".[29]

The nymph, therefore, is a paradigm of the paradigm or the analogy of the analogous per se. Plate 46 is an example of the paradigm, but further than that its choice of paradigm is paradigmatic. The nymph is neither human, nor animal nor something else. Rather, it is a creature held between *zōe* and *bios* in a state of revelatory suspension. Thus, the nymphs in plate 46 are all examples of paradigm, neither general nor particular, neither *archē* nor recurrence, but each a part that brings to presentation and definition a whole of which they, however, also remain a part. At the same time the nymph as such is itself paradigmatic as a being that exists alongside the human and the animal constituting the set, existing beings yet also being but a part of the set.

STATEMENTS—PARADIGMS—SIGNATURES

Through a consideration of first Benjamin and then Warburg, what we have presented here is one of the more complex elements of Agamben's method that, to my mind, he does not adequately explain. This is the specific relationship between statements, paradigms and signatures. We know from his own comments on Foucault that any statement, in being communicable, is potentially paradigmatic. Being exemplary is not to do with any content in the statement but is entirely due to conditions of inclusion-dictated placement (para-), reticulation (inter-) and movement (how para- comes to be temporarily meta-). It is also apparent that nothing stops a paradigm becoming a signature, although it does so by a modification of placement, reticulation and movement. Thus, a paradigm is placed to one side of other statements on a delimited level formed by the inter-reticulation of each paradigm to each other, and the possibility of a meta-movement where one element can stand for all others. I will call these levels plates, using a term Agamben adopts in his readings of Aby Warburg's Atlas both in this text and the related study *Ninfe*. A statement becomes a paradigm through this movement or this second order of existence where it moves from pure communicability as such to a named field of communicability. It is worth noting that the movement from statement to paradigm is not a change in the ontology of the statement or facticity of its being as *dasein*; rather, it is an unnecessary supplemental being, so that while not every statement is a paradigm, every paradigm remains a statement whilst also being a paradigm. This is also true of signatures, which stand in the same paradigmatic relationship to paradigms as paradigms stand in relation to statements.

At this juncture we need to clarify the nature of statements which Foucault calls the "the atom of discourse",[30] a description in keeping with Agamben's designation as no longer sign and not yet discourse.

Foucault is at pains to indicate that on the level of signification, the state-ment is not language dependent, and on the level of materiality, the statement is not an object in the world. Therefore, it is an enunciative element that has material presence in the world that is neither language nor object. This leads him to the revelatory conclusion for our own study as regards the statement:

> It is not so much one element among others, a division that can be located at a certain level of analysis, as a function that operates vertical-ly in relation to these various units, and which enables one to say of a series of signs whether or not they are present in it. The statement is not therefore a structure . . . ; it is a function of existence that properly belongs to signs and on the basis of which one may then decide, through analysis or intuition, whether or not they 'make sense' . . . it is not in itself a unit, but a function that cuts across a domain of structures and possible unities, and which reveals them, with concrete contents, in time and space.[31]

To this explanation we can also add a few more qualities of the statement. The same verbal utterance can be more than one statement. Every state-ment is singular and nonrepeatable. Even if the same statement is issued in the same context, if it succeeds in becoming a statement again, it is a different statement. It must have a material presence, but this presence is ontologically indifferent, in a Badiouan sense of simply dictating a neu-tral situation of presentation: there is.

As there are innumerable, singular statements and as each statement is singular and nonrepeatable, while paradigms are statement based, they must differ from statements. Paradigms are the recurrence of statement regimes in effect, each one a material element which reneges upon singu-larity to be part of a closed sense-making environment. So it must be the case that statements dictate the movement of signs, all material marks, to composed sets, paradigmatic plates. The same is in part true of signatures except that signatures are of course statement-limiting entities. It is signa-tures that determine how signs become paradigms through the demands of the signatory location and logic. After all, signatures contain no con-tent, being simply the economy of placement. So while it is true at a basic level that signatures are statements, I think Agamben is perhaps too loose in easily equating the two and not clarifying the difference in relationship between paradigms and statements and signatures and statements.

It may be that I am oversystematising Agamben here for my own purposes, but it must be the case that a signature is made up of state-ments only inasmuch as a signature is a sense-making engine of consis-tency. Paradigms must be made of statements because, like statements, they are transsignificant, being the movement from sign to discourse. This being the case, then, we must say that the modality of a sign becom-ing a statement within a material discourse determines whether the statement is paradigmatic, part of a mobile yet relatively fixed set of sense-making corelating units, or signatory, brought from sign to sense by the dictates of the signature. If this is so, then statements are much freer in the signatory element in that they are simply included in the sense-making realm, becoming paradigmatic over time through processes of habituation and sedimentation that only Agamben's most recent work takes time to fully detail. That said, such statements are *not* signatures any more than a statement can be said to *be* a paradigm. Instead, from my perspective at least, statements negotiate the structure of signs—paradigms—signatures determining if a sign becomes paradigmatic and/or signatory based on a differing movement across the vertical.

From this consideration we can say that the plate of signatures, the Atlas as such (and yes my own study operates here as an Atlas of Agambenian signatures), stands in the same relationship to its plates (paradigms) as its plates stand in relation to all the possible signs that could have been included (here all the images of nymphs that exist). What we cannot say is that the reticulation (inter-) and movement (meta-) are the same in the case of the signature. More clearly than even in the case of the paradigm the signature has no content. In fact, it helps us to accept that there is a form of particular content in terms of the paradigm; it is just that their inclusion together as a set is not actually determined by a special quality of their content. Thus, they share content in common, but they are not paradigmatic because of a particularly exemplary element of their content. Rather, one has to say that their content is indifferently proper or particular, by which I mean they each share in common their own particularity, but each particular quality is indifferent in status of quality: one image is as exemplary as another, as exemplarity is determined by inclusion due to placement, not due to intrinsic essence or property possession.

None of this is true of the signature whose radical lack of content means it cannot be said to stand in a state of reticulation in relation to other signatures. This is one of the counterintuitive laws of the indifferential method: the greater the reduction of qualities, the more a term stands out as singular. Thus, there is no given reticulation between the signature of Kingdom and that of Potential or Poetry in terms of content. By the same gesture, signatures do not move in the same direction as paradigms. The signature is not a term that has risen up above the plate to form a paradigmatic plate of signatures, and the signatures on that plate do not vie for dominance. If this were the case, then there could be a further meta- plate of plates, or the signatory plate of all signatures and so on into infinite progress. This would make the method perilously Hegelian, requiring a transcendental capping device. Rather, signatures mark the maximal end point in the same way as statements mark the minimal, or, as Agamben says, not yet discourse and no longer signs. We now see the brilliance of this demarcation, for the level below the paradigm-statement, signs, is of course infinitely multiple, whilst the level above signature-statement is transcendentally unitary. Thus, in collusion with Foucault, the statement allows us to retain a field of multiple singularities that do not consort with infinite regress or formlessness and a field of consistency that is not transcendental and unconditioned. What is fascinating and what marks the difference between Agamben and Badiou—after all, both are looking to solutions to the same problems with the same structures—is that while Badiou sees set theory as a means of retaining the ancient dialectic of the multiple and the one, Agamben effectively solves this paradox simply as a means of dispensing with it. Badiou's set theory allows him to keep metaphysics; Agamben's discourse analysis permits him to suspend it.

The stability of the signature in relation to the paradigm does not mean that signatures do not move, for indeed, as we have seen, they are defined precisely because they move. Signatures are therefore paradigms entirely divested of content that move laterally without regression or involution and are defined entirely by the history of what they have made operative through the agency of their communicability. Therefore, they are determined in terms of placement as meta-, in terms of reticulation as void or a- and in terms of movement as trans-. One might even add in here that inasmuch as all statements are signature dependent but not all statements are paradigms, although they can be and all paradigms are statement made, then the vertical-lateral movement of the paradigm must occur after the simple vertical movement of the statement. A statement passes over the paradigmatic plate directly to the signatory plate before dropping down, or not, onto the paradigmatic plate.

In addition, if a signature moves to a new discourse, it does not take those paradigms with it. They remain within their specific discursive realm. That said, the new paradigm plates that are formed are equivalent to parallel worlds not in terms of the content they compose, this must be different, and especially not in terms of their semiotic make up, but rather due to their structural dependency on the same signature. This is another reason why a signature movement does not affect the content or semiotic makeup of a sign, for if it did, it would be unable to move and cease to function as a signature. Thus, a signature can be said to be the means by which heterogeneous paradigms cobelong, copying a formulation from Deleuze also found in Badiou, through parallels in composition, dynamism and genealogy.

Agamben never says this, but to my mind signatures must remain radically heterogeneous from each other for precisely the reasons just given. Yet if this is so, what signatures have in common, what makes them a consistent multiplicity that can be named, is first of all their context, Western metaphysical-discursivity, and, as we shall increasingly see, its conceptual economy, primarily the complex cofounding relation between common and proper, the machinic nature of the constant change of placement of terms along this axis and finally the inevitability of a moment or period of inoperativity due to the logic of indifference. This then is the essence of the a-reticulation of the limited set of terms called signatures; there are very few signatures in Agamben's work in the end, while there are numerous paradigms and innumerable statements. At this stage perhaps, we can usefully use the term "void" from the work of Badiou, as both thinkers are contending with sets.

BADIOU AND SET THEORY

For Badiou the being of any set is void, present as subtracted, an operational negation which therefore cannot be said to be inexistent but which cannot also be said to have a negative being either. Being then, as the void subtracted from any situation in order that it be presented in the count, has a great deal in common with Agambenian indifference, and indeed Badiou states more than once that the quality that most defines being as void is indifference (although his sense of indifference does not match that of Agamben's insistence on indifference as suspension of the dialectic). Thus, indifference as the presented situation of suspension between two opposed elements, made operative here by a signature, is itself determined by a name which is void or at least devoid of content. This then is the indifference of signification which defines each signature. Second, indifference is what is never presented in a situation so that the situation can be presented, in the first instance, by the indifferential logic of the paradigm. Finally, the mode in which indifference suspends the operation of the signature, which also by necessity must negate the paradigms it makes communicable and operative, is the means by which the nonpresented element of a situation which makes a situation operative must also, due to the inherent conflict between presentation and the void, render it inoperative or, in Badiou's terms, inconsistent. This is further facilitated by the fact that the two sides of the indifferential equation, the multiplicity of paradigms and the one of the signature, are obviously composed along the same lines of presentation, the common-proper economy, as any signatory construct.

Thus, indifference as such is what is subtracted from the indifference copula so that it can be first rendered operative for large periods of time, then its operativity rendered transparent, and finally so that this operativity can be rendered inoperative. To put it in terms Badiou would recognise but using the same logic presented in Agamben, indifference must be presented as the void term so that a situation, here a signature, can be presented. However, when that situation comes to be represented, in terms of signatory distribution and also Agamben's archaeology (the identification of paradigms) the logic of the void in terms of belonging, in collusion with the excess of inclusion attendant on any signature, which is after all what the paradigm is supposed to control, means that the same agency that makes a situation possible to present is also what makes a situation, eventually, impossible to sustain. In this way Agamben and Badiou are entirely mappable onto each other except for two elements, the value of the event as it is proposed by Badiou and his confidence in a dialectic between common (one) and proper (multiple) which he contends can be retained if its paradoxes are solved by set theory. Agamben has no theory of the event as successive development, indifference is a theory of suspension not supersession, and he cannot accept that set theory makes identity-difference an operative ontology, when for him it always remains an operative historical contingency.[32]

To conclude, the slight form of the nymph surprisingly contains the solution to this most complex problem. What we have are two plates, the paradigm plate which operates via the logic of belonging-indifference and the signatory plate which operates via the logic of inclusion-indifference. The signatory plate is made up of signatures from different disciplines, Poetry, Potential, Secularization, Kingdom, Power, Glory, Economy, Time, Life, the Animal and so on. There are a number of these but not a significant number, perhaps so far in Agamben fewer than twenty. The paradigm plate is made up of the elements which are said to belong to the signatory situation, underneath which of course are all signs which at any point can belong to a situation but only after they have been included. All statements are included in every signature, but those which belong, paradigms, are controlled by the signature. That is indeed all the signature does: control which of its included elements, statements, can be said to belong at any one time or discursive place, paradigms. The signature then determines which included elements are counted twice to form a representation or state. Indifference then is what is subtracted from each element here or, more accurately, what is doubly subtracted at the level of belonging (paradigms) and inclusion (signatory exclusion in fact) so that the system is made operative.

Agamben is brilliant enough to be able to compose his system along these lines and also more straightforwardly in terms of the material nature of Warburg's Atlas. The plates are the paradigm level, the closed covers of the book the signatory level, and all the mobile elements that are included or excluded as the project developed over time, all statements to hand. What is crucial to indicate here is that indifference is an articulation of the two plates facilitated by the differing elements of indifference. That indifference as not-presented matches perfectly Badiou's theory of the void of Being. And the system is thus carefully composed so that the two plates are restricted in terms of proliferation. There is a point of expansion at the paradigm level, but because they are paradigms this is only actually infinite, in terms of the infinity of countable multiplicities. And there is clearly a hierarchical augmentation between paradigm and signature plates. But this is kept to two plates due to the indifferent logic of paradigms; in other words, however many plates there are, they are all indifferently placed side by side in every direction in only two dimensions, and of the signature, as signatures are contentless, there can be no signatory signature. Finally, the level below the paradigms is not subject to infinite regress because it is a composed propriety by virtue of the dictates of a signatory commonality. Statements can be said to be statements only if they have agreed to be included in a sense-making situation (a signatory situation). Nor can any one signature become the signature of all signatures because of the a-reticulated void of their noninterrelation which disallows *Aufhebung* due to the inevitability of its opposite, indifference.

PHILOSOPHICAL ARCHAEOLOGY

We can now compose in clear conscience a final summary of the Agamben method. Philosophical archaeology has two elements. The *archē* represents a moment of arising of specific discursive formation—not the origin of the formation but the moment when a certain set of paradigms operate in signatory fashion to make it possible to compose a set or named discourse based on what it allows to be said. However, the point of tracing such a moment of arising is to answer a contemporary moment of discursiveness and render it inoperative. Here Agamben diverges from Foucault in that Agamben believes that in revealing the moment of arising, identifying its paradigms and tracing its signatory transmissions, one is able to close the book on an element of Western thought. This is because each of the three elements depends on a logic of conditioning conditions which create their own condition as origin, as part of the modality of their distributive mode of 'being conditioned'. The paradigm renders inoperative common and proper (whole and part). The signature renders inoperative signifier and signified (fact and norm). And archaeology renders inoperative foundation and effect (origin and influence).

Any critical reading of Agamben that does not take into consideration this system and try to undermine it by philosophically tackling the presuppositions and consistencies of the system is, I believe, a misreading. Any reading that assumes Agamben is a historian or philologist, good, bad or indifferent, has entirely missed the point. Any critique of Agamben in terms of his reliance on the now discredited logic of origins or teleology has ignored innumerable statements and demonstrations to the contrary. Finally, as a careful reading of *The Signature of All Things* shows, any approach to Agamben that does not understand that the entirety of his project is to use paradigms to trace signatures as part of a radical archaeological means of suspending metaphysics by rendering inoperative its basic logical presupposition, a division between common (identity) and proper (difference) wherein the common operates as founding condition of the various instances of the conditioned, is simply not ready to mount even a basic objection. If Agamben is one of the most controversial thinkers alive today, the controversy must, from now on, focus on the true ambitions of his work which, when understood in full, present a powerful attack on the totality of all our systems of knowledge and indeed, more than that, the indifferent suspension of everything we take to be foundational, intelligible and productive. With the method fully laid out, we are now in a position to revisit the key works of Agamben in specific relation to the methodology of philosophical archaeology to trace the moment of arising of indifference whose *archē* has only recently become available with the publication of *The Signature of All Things*. While it is my hope that all future readings will take into account the dependency of his thought on indifference, it is my assumption that they will certainly have to take into account the methodology mapped out and signed for by this remarkable text.

NOTES

1. See also Giorgio Agamben, *Potentialities*, trans. Daniel Heller-Roazen (Stanford, CA: Stanford University Press, 1999), 155–59.
2. Giorgio Agamben, *The Signature of All Things: On Method*, trans. Luca D'Isanto and Kevin Attell (New York: Zone Books, 2009), 82.
3. Cited in Agamben, *Signature*, 83.
4. Agamben, *Signature*, 84.
5. This answers the criticisms of Agamben's philology in relation to the *zōe-bios* bifurcation such as is to be found in Laurent Dubreuil, "Leaving Politics: Bios Zoe, Life", *Diacritics* 36, no. 2 (2006): 83–98, which may be described as a category error, judging Agamben within the discourse of classical philology when his work was never designed to be judged as such.
6. Agamben, *Signature*, 102–3.
7. Agamben, *Signature*, 106.
8. There are several key differences to be drawn between Agamben and Foucault. Foucault's epistemes occupy epochs of much more limited scope than Agamben can accept. Foucault's system concerns primarily statements, whereas Agamben's signatures concern acts as well as utterances (indeed all utterances are for him acts). As mentioned here Foucault is strongly opposed to origins and destinations, while Agamben wishes to expose false origins for a messianic project of metaphysical suspension. Finally, while Agamben himself says that statements are the equivalent to signatures, Foucault supports a vast field of singular statements, while Agamben focuses on a strictly limited set of signatures. A more accurate breakdown would be that each discursive formation is made up of a constant stream of statements, that these statements become formalised in repeated paradigms, and that these paradigms are composed in accordance with large-scale signatures of intelligibility.
9. Originally, his method was to be a form of philosophical philology; see Giorgio Agamben, *Infancy and History: On the Destruction of Experience*, trans. Liz Heron (London: Verso, 1993), 159–67.
10. Agamben, *Signature*, 89. The choice of "engage" as a translation of *confrontarsi* is perhaps lacking in the more proactive sense of philosophical archaeology in play here, in part redeemed by the choice of "confront" as the translation of *misurarsi*, yet this then raises another problem related to the clear intention of the author to explain how his method has the "measure" of tradition, meaning it also passes judgement on said

tradition. The method is both aggressive confrontation with the presuppositions of historiography and a mode of deciding or judging.

11. I think Mills was the first to truly articulate the nature this essential relationship when she says that "Benjamin provides Agamben with the tools for the *euphoric* overcoming of the *aporias* that he diagnoses as underpinning the violence of modern democracy" (Catherine Mills, *The Philosophy of Agamben* [Stocksfield: Acumen Press, 2008], 6). De la Durantaye's work (*Giorgio Agamben: A Critical Introduction* [Stanford, CA: Stanford University Press, 2009]) is also an exemplary study of the relation between Benjamin's concepts and Agamben's development from them of his weak messianic system. Indeed, all the major works in the field acknowledge the debt Agamben owes to and has paid Benjamin.

12. See Slavoj Žižek, *Did Someone Say Totalitarianism? Four Interventions in the (Mis)Use of a Notion* (London: Verso, 2011), 146.

13. Agamben's first major work of philosophy, *Language and Death: The Place of Negativity*, trans. Karen E. Pinkus with Michael Hardt (Minneapolis: University of Minnesota Press, 1991), is based on a radical critique of the metaphysics of the unsaid and the ineffable. A very strong and radical element of both Agamben's and Foucault's system is their resistance to the logic of depth and otherness. Agamben is seeking to unearth not the hidden but the widespread distribution of the signatures of all that has been said.

14. Agamben, *Signature*, 99. "Split" is the best translation of *scissione*, but it is useful to keep in mind that *scission*, a key philosophical term, is felt in the Italian and not in the English term. It is after all the metaphysics of scission that Agamben's first major philosophical interventions were concerned with suspending.

15. Agamben, *Signature*, 99.

16. Agamben, *Signature*, 110.

17. Agamben, *Signature*, 110.

18. Walter Benjamin, *The Arcades Project*, trans. Howard Eiland and Kevin McLaughlin (Cambridge, MA: Harvard University Press, 1999), 10.

19. Benjamin, *Arcades*, 462.

20. Anselm Havercamp, "Notes on the 'Dialectical Image' (How Deconstructive Is It?)", *Diacritics* 22, no. 3–4 (1992): 72.

21. Benjamin, *Arcades*, 475.

22. The issue of tension in Agamben is not widely commented on, but there is extensive consideration of it in my own work where it is repeatedly mentioned in *The Literary Agamben: Adventures in Logopoiesis* (London: Continuum, 2010). A good place to commence is in that work(pp. 135–39).

23. Consideration of Agamben and caesura is now fairly widespread. For a full consideration of the issue again, see Watkin, *Literary Agamben*, 166–93.

24. For example, see Giorgio Agamben, *The Open: Man and Animal*, trans. Kevin Attell (Stanford, CA: Stanford University Press, 2004), 81–84, and Giorgio Agamben, *What Is an Apparatus?*, trans. David Kishik and Stefan Pedatella (Stanford, CA: Stanford University Press, 2009), 50–53.

25. Benjamin, *Arcades*, 459.

26. Agamben undertook extensive research at the Warburg Institute. For more on this intimate relationship, see de la Durantaye, 65–72, and Agamben, *Potentialities*, 89–103.

27. See also Agamben's essay "Aby Warburg and the Nameless Science" in *Potentialities*, 89–103.

28. Agamben, *Signature*, 29.

29. Agamben, *Signature*, 30.

30. Michel Foucault, *The Archaeology of Knowledge*, trans. A. M. Sheridan Smith (London: Routledge, 1972), 80.

31. Foucault, *Archaeology*, 86–87.

32. To my mind, the best comparative reading of Agamben and Badiou is to be found in Gibson's comparison of bare life to inexistence through a reading of Badiou's increasing use of the term *exception*. I cannot subscribe to Gibson's presentation of Agamben's philosophy as reducible to bare life, where for me the key term is *indifference*, of which bare life is one instance, but the reading is important and the first time, I believe, that anyone has presented this relation, so crucial for the future direction of philosophy in our age. See Andrew Gibson, *Intermittency: The Concept of Historical Reason in Recent French Philosophy* (Edinburgh: Edinburgh University Press, 2012), 51–54, 261.

THREE

Language and Death: Indifferent Difference as Such in Hegel and Heidegger

Careful readers might note an archaeological structure to the rest of our study. Having commenced with one of Agamben's most recent texts, we now need to travel back around twenty-five years to identity the moment of arising of Agamben's philosophy of indifference before we can then move forward identifying the paradigmatic moments within the vast Agamben oeuvre. Again in keeping with Agamben's philological tendencies, we also cannot content ourselves with concentrating on just one voice, Agamben's. Rather, we have to listen to the signatory distribution of the communicability of the term *indifference* across the modern era of philosophy. Specifically, we have to come to terms with the fact that Agamben's mature career begins with *Language and Death* (1982) through a sustained critique of the philosophy of difference represented by Hegel and Heidegger, yet this book itself is not a paradigmatic work of indifference. *Language and Death* is a critique of nihilism in the philosophy of difference based on two contentions Agamben identifies in the work of both Hegel and Heidegger. The first is that Being is unthinkable outside of language. The second is that language as such always remains ineffable or unsayable or, as Heidegger famously says, never has the floor. This is actually just another way of restating probably the most significant axiom of twentieth-century thought, Gödel's first, famous incompleteness theorem: a self-consistent system cannot prove from within the system the truth of the elements that make it self-consistent. If language is the self-consistent system of Being, the one element of language that cannot be said is the system itself (in mathematics this pertains rather to natural numbers). This is why, according to Hegel and Heidegger accord-

49

ing to Agamben, Being is always in withdrawal. The Being of Being is language, but language as such can never be said because it is the ground of all saying. This is another early version of Agamben's contention that language is communicability as such. Agamben concludes that the metaphysics of negation, or difference as we prefer to term it here, is founded on an element he calls Voice, echoing the capitalisation of Being in Heidegger, which is only ever found under negation. The book closes by saying first that the philosophy of difference is defined by this idea of Being opening onto an ineffable and unsayable language, Voice.[1] And second, by arguing that to escape this nihilism, Being is always based on the 'death' or negation of language, one simply has to conceive of the voice as "never having been".[2]

This argument seems a very long way away from our own contention that the philosophy of difference is in default due to indifference, and it is not perhaps until the final chapter that we can clarify that language as communicability is effectively indifference. Having said that, one can see here, indirectly, that Voice pertains to the problem of the Being of beings, or the common of the proper, by making common that which is always taken by philosophy as archetypally proper, language. However, to more fully understand how Agamben's philosophy of indifference finds its moment of arising in 1982, we have to move to one side, away from the considerable shadow cast by *Language and Death*, another rather Agambenian gesture, and look at a shorter essay published on Hegel and Heidegger in the same year, "**Se*: Hegel's Absolute and Heidegger's *Ereignis*," before we can move forward to Agamben's first and perhaps only real treatise on indifference, *The Coming Community*. This is a somewhat awkward procedure, so I crave the reader's indulgence if we take a detour through the history of philosophical indifference, specifically the contributions made by Hegel and Heidegger in developing a philosophy of difference based on what Hegel calls indifferent difference and Heidegger heeding the difference as difference. Hopefully, there will come to be seen ample justification for this diversion when it is shown how interlinked Agamben's work is with Hegelian and Heideggerian dialectical pure difference and how studiously he works to developmentally distance his philosophy from the two most significant modern representatives of the philosophy of difference, Derrida and Deleuze. For now we must, in an Agambenian mode, travel back through time and discourse to the moment of arising of the signature Indifference.

THE THREE AGES OF INDIFFERENCE

Indifference has a complicated entry in the *Oxford English Dictionary*. It means or has meant being neutral (neither good nor bad), absence of bias in favour of one side or the other, absence of active feeling for or against, lack of difference between things, of something making no difference (i.e., not mattering), and freedom of choice of thought or the equal power to take either of two courses. It also means being moderate, something of no more advantage to either party and not definitely possessing either of two opposing qualities. Finally, it has also meant unimportant things. It is primarily a state of disinclination to either party or position, leading to neutrality and impassivity. It has a strong connection to dualistic thought patterns, as most of its definitions pertain to logical structures of neither one nor the other rather than, for example, neutrality in the face of multiple options.

As a term it recurs again and again in Agamben's work at the same key concluding moments of his argument, often in the form of various synonyms, such as *suspension, indistinction, indiscernibility, inoperativity* and *neutrality*.[3] Out of all these terms, I have chosen *indifference* because it has a long philosophical history comprised of three key stages commencing with stoicism and scepticism. In these philosophical approaches indifference refers to the disinclination to choose, as whichever choice is effectively equal due to the wider power of God, nature or, later, doubt, in relation to which your local choices are as if indifferent in that they make no difference to the overall totality. This indifferentism in philosophy, Kant explains in the preface to the *First Critique*,[4] is one of the prime motivations for his critical system, and the extensive "Antinomies" section of that study is entirely directed at dispelling philosophical indifferentism in four key areas due to the logical impossibilities of the two contesting modes of his day, idealism (thinking due to the common) and empiricism (thinking due to the proper).[5]

The second stage of philosophical indifference, which is fully developed by Hegel, has a more technical definition meaning pure difference as such. In the first section of the *Phenomenology* the choice of A or B is defined as indifferent when the identities of A and B are not fixed but mere abstractions. Second-order indifference then defines difference without identity or, as Deleuze will reconceptualise it in *Difference and Repetition*, difference before identity. Not always called indifference, pure difference as such can be sourced in Nietzsche and later Heidegger, Benjamin, Levinas and Blanchot, finding its real advocate in Deleuze. Deleuze's system of difference and repetition is founded on three differing aspects of the primacy of difference over identity, all of which are described in terms of indifference.[6]

The final use of indifference is to be found in Agamben, who takes indifference, in all its synonyms, as the suspension of difference between identity and difference. This last use combines first- and second-order indifference to some degree by using the disinclination to choose or act of the first, to negate the presupposition of the second, namely, that difference precedes and is in some sense preferable to and undermining of identity, an option made communicable, however, only after the development and distribution of second-order indifference as difference as such.

It is this sense of indifference, the suspension of opposition between identity (common) and difference (proper), that Agamben's philosophy repeatedly turns to and is what marks him out as a truly original thinker for our century. His is not a philosophy of identity or of difference but of the indifference between the two, and our century, if it can be said to be anything after a lamentably banal first chapter, will be taking its lead from Moravia's first precocious work, the age of indifference.[7] This then is both our local thesis and our wider intent expressible in the following syllogism: Agamben unthinkable without indifference, thinking now unthinkable without Agamben, future thinking unthinkable without indifference.

SECOND-ORDER INDIFFERENCE: PURE DIFFERENCE AS SUCH

As already stated, after Hegel second-order indifference names the active process of differentiation itself, best described as the difference between A and B before A and B take on any determinate identity.[8] It also describes a medium of differentiation or a place that allows for and supports the differentiation of two entities or units, usually traversed by a tireless dynamic or economy of interchange. This location is, in reality, little more than movement between two positions and is as much composed in temporality as it is in space. The issue of Agamben and time will be a central one as we progress. Indifference of this sort is how difference occurs, what it is in itself, what allows for it to come about, 'when' this happens and 'how long' it takes. To paraphrase Deleuze, indifference is nonidentical differentiation as such, or the fact that there is difference before one stipulates precisely which two elements are being differentiated[9] or which multiple of terms establish a set of differentiations or even how one term, say the subject, is differentiated from or within itself. Indifference is the combination of all these elements into what philosophers term difference as such.

Although second-order indifference can be found in the work of many philosophers, it is attributable to Hegel, who defines it across the three moments of the dialectic in great detail in the first section of the *Phenomenology*. These three moments pertain first to indifference at the heart of sense certainty in terms of neutral deictic indication (the not-this); then to indifference as the neutral medium of perception of singular elements placed alongside each other, the famous problem of the Also and the One; and finally as regards the indifferent realm of pure understanding typified by what he calls the abstract realm of inert laws. Thus, we have indifference of sense, of perception and of understanding, for Hegel necessarily in that order, as these three indifferences are not three different instances of indifference but a three-part construction of the first stage of the dialectic, that of understanding. Consciousness therefore passes through indifference three times, according to Hegel, because in each instance it finds a contradiction it cannot accept. Yet while Hegel presents this as a sequential compound of the dialectical first stage of self-conscious negation (understanding), what one actually sees is that indifference is negated by the passage between sense-indifference (stage 1) and law-indifference (stage 3) of property-indifference (stage 2). This is because the problem of the pure abstract medium of indifference, as Hegel terms it, contains within it both particularity (Also) and generality (One).

To sum up the Hegelian position, the first moment of supersession which he calls understanding depends on the negation of three kinds of indifference. Each of these is a form of second-order indifference, namely, not disinclination to choose but differentiation in the abstract. Each stage of indifference must be negated to access the next. That said, the actual negation of indifference is not a simple sequence of overcoming, this is only one element of the *Aufhebung* after all. Rather, to overcome Indifference 1 one passes through Indifference 2 to Indifference 3. Then to overcome Indifference 3 one passes through Indifference 2 to Indifference 1. Only once one has achieved this reiteration of Indifference 2 is the method in place to negate indifference once and for all. That method is the dialectic. Thus, the dialectic is a system designed to negate indifference that comes into existence only after or rather through the process of indifference-negation. Indifference then is not a sequential ascending narrative but a reiterative double-order dynamic across the pure abstract medium of the endless interchange between Also and One (proper and common) that defines the essence of a thing, without the application of self-conscious negation. As we shall see, this economy or *oikonomia* both leaves its indelible mark on Agambenian third-order indifference and marks the very system, the dialectic, that indifference is primarily involved in suspending in such works as *Language and Death* and the essays found in *Potentialities*. Specifically in relation to *Language and Death*, if the dialectic negates indifference, then a case must be made that language is indifference, as Agamben argues it is actually language as negation that facilitates dialectics, a case we have already deposed through our comments on communicability.

HEIDEGGER: HEEDING THE DIFFERENCE AS DIFFERENCE

In second-order indifference, if we were to take the formula A is not B — indifference is the 'is not' of the equation, that which differentiates without conferring identity on either term — one can also write this A ≠ B. The "is not" denies identity in particularity: A is not B because A contains these properties that B does not. And it denies identity in general: A is not B because A has this essence and B has this other essence. It separates two terms, the is *not*, by relating them, the *is* not. We have Heidegger's *Identity and Difference* to thank for preparing the ground for this observation without which Agambenian indifference is noncommunicable. Specifically, indifference is differentiation as such previous to the relation of difference to the specific identities of two or more elements. It is, in this sense, disidentified difference, as Agamben also terms it in relation to analogy.[10] Perhaps at this stage it is more apt to say that indifference is a form of relational nonrelation. As we shall see, a key distribution in this text will be the distinction between Agamben's nonrelational relationality, Derrida's oscillation between two oscillations and Deleuze's quasi-causal cobelonging separation systems (to which we must also add-in Badiou's nonrelation theory of relationality in *Logics of Worlds*).[11]

Disindentification is a strong contender as a substitute for indifference, as it reminds us that indifference is as much neutral identity as it is neutral difference. However, when we speak of disindentification in Agamben we do not mean the attack on presence by means of difference but the disidentifying of identity and difference together in the fundamental copula of Western thought patterns. Indifference is between identity and difference, and this is the identity and the differentiation that it attacks: the presence of the differential oppositional structure at large.[12] Indifference taken in this way confirms that there is difference or that difference is potential and inevitable in some form within our common history thus far, but it is indifferent to the nature of the two identities differentiated. Taking this on board, if indifference is the differentiation of nonparticularised units, it presents the precondition for all particularization yet resists the metaphysics of identity. This observation, dependent as it is on the coupled concepts of disidentification and nonrelation, is communicable only because of the work of Heidegger in critically developing the Hegelian dialectic in relation to pure difference.

As we have said, Agamben's first major philosophical work is *Language and Death*, and the first interlocutor of this book is Hegel, specifically his contention that language is necessary to access knowledge of the world but falls short in its indicative brevity. Thus, the means by which one can refer to objects' sense-immediacy using *Deise*, 'this', renders the world out there in terms of mediation only at the expense of retaining an unspeakable element within all language, the shortfall between the actual thing and the means of deictic indication. Hegel's problem with deixis in the 'this–not this' formulation of the first section of the *Phenomenology* is universally known. While deixis allows us to speak of sense-immediacy, it both falls short of the actual thing as such and, as we saw, also negates it. This then leads Agamben to conclude that for Hegel language is negativity, or language is death. This is not as clear a statement of the problem of Hegelian difference as one might wish, but as we shall see time and again and as I have already indicated, the issue of the linguistic and the specific importance of deixis are foundational elements to both Agamben's own rejection of Hegelian pure difference and his pursuit of his own indifferential system.

The second interlocutor in the book is, inevitably, Heidegger, inevitable not only because Heidegger has bequeathed two key concepts to modern thought debated in the work, the pure medium of thinking and the finitude of being, but also because of course Heidegger is the great thinker of difference. Perhaps the philosophy of difference began with Hegel, certainly it was in full force by the time of Nietzsche, but *the* thinker of difference for us is surely Heidegger. As should now be apparent the modern theory of indifference is not primarily one of disinclination to choose but of abstraction from difference. Indifference is a specific kind of difference, or rather a specific element of the compound of difference that is so often presented as an *a priori* analytical element; there can be nothing smaller than difference, and so difference is a fundamental of thought, when in fact it may be an *a posteriori* positing of an *a priori* synthesis: one element within a development of difference over time that has then been reinscribed in the history of philosophy as foundational. Actually, the situation is more complex than this in that the temporality of indifference, by which I mean both its presence in the history of thought and its internal sequential structure of operation and development, does not succumb to the linear before-and-after model so central to the designations *a priori* and *a posteriori*. This is a point we have already addressed in relation to the archaeological method, so here it suffices to say that difference as indifference functions precisely to present a different model of cognitive temporality entirely, by demonstrating a moment of temporal suspension between before and after that is not, however, reducible to a now (instead Benjamin calls it now-time and Agamben *kairatic* time).

In 1957, Heidegger published *Identity and Difference*, a work he saw as his most important since *Being and Time*, although as Agamben shows it is not stand-alone but part of a flurry of texts dealing with *Ereignis*. [13] A significant feature of this slim volume is that it deals not with the opposing terms of the ontico-ontological difference but rather the very precondition of their opposition. He explains this with direct reference to the Hegelian dialectical methodology concluding on the fundamental difference between the Hegelian and Heideggerian dialectic:

> For Hegel, the matter of thinking is: Being with respect to beings having been thought in absolute thinking, and as absolute thinking. For us, the matter of thinking is the Same, and thus is Being—but Being with respect to its difference from beings. Put more precisely: for Hegel, the matter of thinking is the idea as the absolute concept. For us, formulated in a preliminary fashion, the matter of thinking is the difference *as* difference. [14]

If we add into this two other conditions of difference posited by Heidegger in this text, then we will begin to understand how, essentially, Heideggerian difference is the first real valorisation of indifference, Friedlaender and Schelling's work notwithstanding.

Previous to this statement Heidegger explains that in the formula of identity, A is A, one ought to concentrate not on the self-identity of the term in play, A, but in the manner in which one can posit this self-belonging: *is*. In saying that a thing is the thing it is, one is essentially saying that the being of the thing is its belonging to its Being. "With this 'is', the principle tells us how every being is, namely, it itself is the same with itself. The principle of identity speaks of the Being of beings. . . . To every being as such there belongs identity, the unity with itself".[15] The formula A is A therefore means A is the same as A but not equal, for sameness is the total compound statement A belongs with itself which presupposes a degree of difference of A from itself to facilitate such a state of belonging. To belong with means to presuppose separation from. If identity were instead reduced to the formalism A = A, then it would be so tautological as to be meaningless. That we can make a formal representation of identity means that identity contains a speck of disindentification within itself. Thus, within identity there is always the difference between beings and their Being, and man, he goes on to explain, "*is* essentially this relationship of responding to Being, and he is only this".[16] Or human being is the process of living self-reflexivity in self-conscious fashion. This being the case, identity is a question of difference, but not only is difference a part of identity—one cannot think identity without thinking the essential difference of an Also to a One, a part to its self-same identified whole—but more fundamentally difference precedes identity; as he says, "Whenever we come to the place to which we were supposedly first bringing difference along as an alleged contribution, we always find that Being and beings in their difference are already there".[17] Heidegger concludes by explaining that metaphysics has always progressed by the manner in which it "represents beings in respect of what differs in the difference, and without heeding the difference as difference".[18] Heeding the difference as difference is, as far as I can tell, effectively the first positive formulation of indifference proper in the history of Western thought, effectively because Heidegger never uses the term *indifference* in this respect.

We can now see that Heideggerian difference is defined as the presupposition of difference as regards Being. Identity as such is difference of equality within the same. A being can differ from its Being, indeed must differ, but this difference is determined not by the difference between the terms but by the differential relationality of their differentiation. What constitutes 'A is A' is not the A but how the relational 'is' operates. It is a similar point to Agamben's own observation that it is the 'and' that is central to *Being and Time*, or how Being and beings can be said to sit together, and is part of a wider commitment on his part to what he calls syncategorematic thinking. The same logic is also to be found in Derridean *différance*, which insists that in every identity there is a speck of alterity without which identity as identity could not be posited (indeed Derrida is indebted primarily to Heidegger for this observation without which deconstruction is impossible). Finally, such a difference, difference qua differentiation or difference as such, must be said to be foundational. Difference precedes identity operating as its precondition, a maxim that also forms the basis of Deleuzian difference so that in one short phrase Heidegger effectively predisposes an entire generation of thinking around the philosophy of difference.[19]

All we need to add here is that in terms of how we have been formulating indifference, it is clear that although he never says it, when Heidegger uses *difference*, what he means is differentiation as such, and thus he refers to second-order, Hegelian indifference. Thus, Heideggerian difference is the isolation of the centrality of indifference to the thought of Being and the negation of the Hegelian dialectic which posits difference (indifference) only so as to overcome it with the identity of the absolute concept as the perfect unity of beings and thought. And inasmuch as all modern continental philosophy is a response to the Hegelian-Heideggerian dialectic, that is, a dialectic of dialectics, indifference is a foundational element of modern thought. Having said all of that, again these are not the issues in Heidegger's work that concern *Language and Death*, whose main concerns are Heidegger's statements on language, death and the ineffable nature of being in withdrawal. Indeed, *Identity and Difference* is not even cited in that work.

SE: WHAT IS PROPER

At this point it would appear that, given the opportunity to write a clear critique of the philosophy of difference based around Hegel's and Heidegger's reliance on a pure and indifferent difference as such, Agamben chooses to do otherwise. Not that *Language and Death* is not already marked by the philosophy of suspensive indifference, as my own earlier study confirms,[20] but it is just that pure difference as such is not its main concern; rather, the metaphysics of negativity resultant from a view of language as ontologically necessary yet ineffable is what exercises Agamben's mind at this stage.[21] Yet in the same year Agamben also publishes what must be considered the simultaneous sequel to *Language and Death*, the essay "*Se*: Hegel's Absolute and Heidegger's *Ereignis*". As the essay title suggests, it is, essentially, a developed consideration of Heidegger's own self-differentiation from Hegel and in this sense is, subtly but indubitably, an essay on indifference. This is flagged up early in the essay by an explanation that *Se* is, in Indo-European languages, the reflexive that indicates "what is proper".[22] Tracing its etymology Agamben discovers that *Se is at the root of words pertaining to what is proper to a group via habit, character and custom and also to solitude, represented in its presence both in the Greek for 'proper' and 'appropriation' and in the Greek for 'itself'. Agamben thus concludes, "Insofar as it contains both a relation that unites and a relation that separates, the proper—that which characterises every thing as a *se—is therefore not something simple".[23]

Nor is it simply something composite, for the qualities in play here that define the proper, habit and solitude are then disseminated across Western habits of thinking as essentially oppositional. What is proper therefore is both what defines a being as being, what is proper to them or what qualities they possess, and what defines said being in relation to other beings. This therefore recasts the proper in terms of the paradox of immediate being that is mediated by properties and by relationality. Every thing is proper to itself, owns itself, appropriates itself. Thus, it is immediate and infinite. Yet the very act of self-reflexivity enshrined in the grammaticality of the term *se suggests an act of one being on another, of being acting on itself, appropriating itself. For this to logically be possible, until Hegel at least, such a being needs must be mediate and finite. This results in a double paradox. Internally a being is the immediate collocation of all its mediated qualities (its character), and externally a being sees itself as an immediate self and also sees that self in terms of a communally held set of qualities as if from the outside (mediated).

Agamben traces this double paradox back to one of the most ancient texts of Western thought by Heraclitus which is traditionally translated as "for man, character is the demon" but which he retranslates in characteristic fashion as "For man, *ethos*, the dwelling in the 'self' that is what is most proper and habitual for him, is what lacerates and divides, the principle and the place of a fracture," or as Agamben puts it in his own words, "Man is such that, to be *himself*, he must necessarily divide himself",[24] which is little more than a rephrasing of Heideggerian difference of course. By now we should recognise this as a formulation of such irresolvability; Heidegger finds no solutions, for example, that there are two options presented, either negation or the indifferential suspension of the terms. Agamben's choice of indifference over the philosophy of negation accuses Hegel and Heidegger of indulging in the reification of difference in relation to the aporia of the identity-difference construction is what sets him apart within the modern philosophy of difference and is essentially the journey taken across the early works, specifically *Infancy and History* and *Language and Death*.

HEGELIAN ABSOLUTE AND THE APOTROPAIC
ECONOMY OF THE DIALECTIC

Before we get to that, we need to pay attention to how the indiscernibility in *se between being and division, the one and the many, is transmitted through the history of Western philosophy, coming to rest in the debate in question here between Hegel and Heidegger. Agamben commences this essay, for example, by explaining that *se is at the heart of the most important question for thinking, the Absolute, and that its transmission through the Latin verb *solvo* facilitates the subdivision of the verb into the self-reflexive *se-luo* that "indicates the work of loosening, freeing (*luo*) that leads (or leads back) something to its own *se*".[25] Here Agamben raises a structural thematics that is not merely at the heart of Western thought as it currently stands, that is, post Hegel, Heidegger and the philosophy of difference, but also central to any sustainable theory of indifference.

The Absolute is that which sets out from what is proper, via a property or set of properties, to an act of self-appropriation. This is a classic example in fact of the Agambenian methodology of archaeology. Here what is not at stake is the total veracity and unquestionable status of Agamben's layers of philology and etymology. It would be tempting yet wrong to ask why all previous scholars of Heraclitus, Indo-European, Greek and Latin missed this essential conglomeration of themes until now. The reason they did not is that they are not contemporary philosophers, and it is only within the contemporary moment of thought, after Hegelian, Heideggerian, Derridean and Deleuzian dialectics, that the moment of arising of the problem is made historically available via a confrontation with the current state of philosophical thought.

The structure in question here is what I have previously called the apotropaic *periplus*.[26] It marks a movement forward and back, an oscillation familiar to us from Derridean and Deleuzian presentations of difference and repetition, but also up and down. These positions may be recast as space, extension of a point into a line and contraction of a line to point, and time, extension of a line into a field or plane in which trace and history are retained and created within an extended field of temporal positions which I term tabularity.[27] Agamben reveals that this apotropaic theme, which is not a theme but a habitual method or thought modality, is central to both Hegel's theory of the Absolute and Heidegger's modification in the impossible to translate *Ereignis*, the central term of his later work including of course *Identity and Difference*.

It is first of all obvious why the Hegelian dialectic fulfils the terms of the apotropaic *periplus*. The coming to self-consciousness requires that the subject become self-alienated so that it may return to itself first locally and seemingly endlessly and then finally in the conclusion of all thinking, absolutely and singularly. The dialectic consists of a double layer of abso-

lution, of coming to self by letting go, a progressive conglomerate of
particular journeys which finally lead spirit to one last journey. The
movement of the dialectic comes to a rest within itself, but only after an
epic narrative of apotropaic loosenings via self-negation/self-conscious-
ness (*loosenings* being here another term for the successive series of super-
seding *Aufhebungen*). Agamben cites the final chapter of *The Science of
Logic*, which I will also cite although for a different emphasis. The context
of this citation, which is not entirely clear in Agamben's essay, is the
differentiation or moment of division between the logical Idea and the
Absolute Idea and the final argument of the *Science of Logic* wherein, it
would seem, the dialectic as a method for arriving at the Absolute seems
to actually become the Absolute itself. The passage goes as follows:

> Logic exhibits the self-movement of the absolute Idea only as the origi-
> nal *word*, which is an *outwardizing* or *utterance* [*Äusserung*], but an utter-
> ance that in being has immediately vanished again as something outer
> [*Äusseres*]; the Idea is, therefore, only in this self-determination of *appre-
> hending itself*; it is in *pure thought*, in which difference is not yet *other-
> ness*, but is and remains perfectly transparent to itself.[28]

Agamben naturally, considering the themes of *Language and Death*, focuses on this idea of an originary word that is totally externalized and
likens it to the animal voice, "like the singing of birds and the braying of
donkeys", or perhaps glossolalia, "a word whose meaning has been forgotten".[29] (Agamben's critique of Hegel in *Language and Death* centres
around Hegel's contention that it is only in death that an animal is possessed of voice.) Naturally, my emphasis would be rather less on the
choice of the term 'word', accepting that at this point it was essential for
Agamben's argument that Being be encountered through language as
negated, than the reference here to a difference that is not yet otherness,
namely, an indifference.

Whether it be an immediately vanishing pure exteriority of language
or language as an instance of the vanishing pure exteriority of indifference is perhaps a moot point. Agamben's definition of method shares
much in common with Hegel's own in the closing pages of his logic,
wherein method or form is not merely a means of accessing content but
in fact takes "the *infinite form* for its content" that at the moment of Abso-
lution "has for its content merely this, that the form determination is its
own comprehended totality" so that "what remains to be considered here
is not content as such, but the universal aspect of its form — that is, the
method".[30] Said method is, as Hegel goes on to argue, the dialectic.

Just as for Hegel the dialectic is not an indeterminate formalism providing access to determinate content, the traditional and modern presentation of logic, but rather a formalism that becomes its own content, so
too as we saw in Agamben the relation between a paradigmatic instance
of indifference, say infancy, a signatory distribution of indifference, lan-

guage, and indifference as such as medium of inoperative suspension, which is the particularity of indifference I am arguing for here, is both the meaning of indifference as a potential, postphilosophical thinking and the method of bringing this about. Or to put it more succinctly, indifference as such can come only out of the archaeological indifferentiation of paradigmatic indifferents through the systematic suspension of signatures.

EREIGNIS AND THE UNSAYABLE IN HEIDEGGER

All of this prepares us for Heidegger's own admission across several works, which Agamben traces with great facility, that his view of *Ereignis* as the experience of Being as such as appropriation and being appropriated comes very close to that of the Hegelian Absolute. *Ereignis*, habitually translated as event, as "the ultimate and the highest," differs from the Absolute in that Hegelian dialectics seeks to overcome human finitude, whereas for Heidegger "it is precisely finitude that comes to view—not only man's finitude, but the finitude of *Ereignis* itself".[31] One can see here a profound structural similarity of method nestled in this clear differentiation, or at least a similarity of negation in the way profound opposition often results in the most fearful filiations, as in an eclipse that reveals a hidden pathway that full sunlight could never make manifest or a ghost that can show the truth on this earth that stands directly in front of the prince but which he cannot see. For just as the dialectical method, in sublating finitude, becomes not merely method but also the content of Absolute thought, the thing of thought itself as self-evident being which is after all Hegel's conclusion to his whole project, so for Heidegger the finitude of Being reveals the finitude of the method, namely, that in appropriating Being one is simultaneously appropriated by the truth of Being as such; namely, its being always in withdrawal.

As Agamben shows, *Ereignis* is "the reciprocal appropriation, the co-belonging of time and being" or the relationality of difference as such which we discovered in the pages of *Identity and Difference*.[32] What *Ereignis* reveals then is the finitude of the relationality of finitude to itself — not, as he stipulates in "Time and Being", finitude in relation to infinity but the finitude of finitude, or what we have called the difference of difference as such. *Ereignis* is thus differentiating as the corelational differentiation between beings which are all around us but devoid of essence and Being which runs through all beings but only as permanently in withdrawal. *Ereignis* is, therefore, another name for a second-order indifference or rather the second stage of the second-order indifference. Like Hegel, Heideggerian indifference is still the negation of indifference in favour of a positing of Being via language as under negation, (at least this is Agamben's argument), but unlike Hegel, Heideggerian indifference posits difference qua difference as the final resting point of thought, not merely a stage to pass through towards the Absolute. That said, indifferentiation in Hegel and Heidegger, as we now expect, finds a commonality of negation of Voice, and it is now that we return to the passage from *Identity and Difference* that began this excursus.

Following Heidegger's criticism of Hegel, Agamben agrees that Hegel "strives to think the becoming equal of itself of speech . . . he attempts to consider the word as wholly comprehended".[33] This is somewhat of a compound projection, for the passage in question on Heidegger has little or nothing to do with language in actual fact. Heidegger, Agamben argues, again extrapolating, rather

> wants to think the difference between saying (*Sage*) and speech (*Sprache*) in itself; he thus searches for an experience of language that experiences the *Es* ('it') that destines itself to speech while itself remaining without destiny, the transmitting that, in every event of speech and every transmission, remains untransmissible. Thus is the Proper, **se* . . . not the absolute concept, Being that has become equal to itself in being-other, but rather difference *itself*, led back to itself.[34]

Agamben summarises by saying that for Hegel the unsayable has already been said, the 'this' is always already the not-this as a stage in the ongoing circle of circles of negation that is the dialectical juggernaut. In contrast, for Heidegger "the unsayable is precisely what remains unsaid in human speech but can be experienced in *human speech* as such".[35] In other words, there are three stages of language as indifference. The first is indifference as destined to *Aufhebung*. The second is indifference as trace or mode of access to being through its being what facilitates transmission between Being and beings but, in being itself nontransmissible in that it is transmission as such, it reveals the true access of *Ereignis* as content to *Ereignis* as method. In that indifference, as *Ereignis*, or as language, fails to provide access to Being as such as a method, this methodological failure becomes the content of Being: Being accessed through the failure of access or Being in withdrawal. The third stage is Agambenian indifference, which merely requires that the negative, the unsaid in Language, be said without being sublated, the essential argument of *Language and Death*. How this comes about in language and its wider implications are questions we cannot answer until the final chapter of this study.

NOTES

1. Although I am not entirely in agreement with the presentation of the signature Language here, still Dickinson's comments on the implication of Voice for theology around the question of Anselm's ontological proof are very informative. See Colby Dickinson, *Agamben and Theology* (London: Continuum, 2011), 23–24.

2. Giorgio Agamben, *Language and Death: The Place of Negativity*, trans. Karen E. Pinkus with Michael Hardt (Minneapolis: University of Minnesota Press, 1991),104.

3. See particularly Giorgio Agamben, *Potentialities*, trans. Daniel Heller-Roazen (Stanford, CA: Stanford University Press, 1999), 233, 235, 256–57.

4. Immanuel Kant, *Critique of Pure Reason*, trans. Marcus Wiegelt (London: Penguin, 2007), x.

5. Kant, *Critique*, 378–484.

6. See Gilles Deleuze, *Difference and Repetition*, trans. Paul Patton (London: Athlone Press, 1994), 1–27.

7. Moravia's title *Gli Indifferenti* is more accurately translated as "The Indifferent Ones", but the translator's choice of "The Age of Indifference" is much more provocative and truer to the wider intentions of this vibrantly jaded debut.

8. Another name for second-order indifference is of course formal abstraction. Since at least Aristotle, the neutrality of formalism was destined to eventually fetch up on the shores of an indifferent, because formal, pure difference as such. We do not have the space to pursue this here, but the predominance of indifference in Badiou at the level of the void and the generic is entirely facilitated by the indifferent abstraction of the mathematic formalism he employs throughout *Being and Event*. That formal notation contains no reference to quality facilitates the possibility of talking about such a concept as pure difference (event) and indeed pure identity (being) without succumbing to any of the aporias of a qualitative ontological quantification also inaugurated by Aristotle. It has taken, in other words, more than two millennia to simply get Aristotle to listen to his own reason.

9. Deleuze, *Difference and Repetition*, 13–14.

10. See Giorgio Agamben, *The Signature of All Things: On Method*, trans. Luca D'Isanto and Kevin Attell (New York: Zone Books, 2009), 18–19.

11. Nonrelational relationality in terms of a consistent conceptualisation of multiplicity that has no use for a transcendental whole and which has built into it a sense of affirmative and radical change, forms perhaps the greatest challenge to twenty-first-century thought. It encompasses the work of both Agamben and Badiou, both of whom apply a nonrelational methodology to the idea of relation based around three key elements: multiplicity, localised immanence and change.

12. In this sense Agambenian indifference operates in the opposite direction to that found in Badiou. Whereas in Badiou indifference as void and generic forms the outer limits of thinking, presenting a halting point for regression and an actualisation of the infinite so that a being can count as one, in Agamben indifference negates infinite regress and bad infinity by disidentifying them from a central position. Put simply Badiou constructs multiple counts as one by bracketing it in indifference, while Agamben creates indifference through the suspension of the one and the many.

13. See Agamben, *Potentialities*, 128–31.

14. Martin Heidegger, *Identity and Difference*, trans. Joan Stambaugh (Chicago: University of Chicago Press, 1969), 47.

15. Heidegger, *Identity and Difference*, 26.

16. Heidegger, *Identity and Difference*, 31.

17. Heidegger, *Identity and Difference*, 62.

18. Heidegger, *Identity and Difference*, 70.

19. Although lamentably I came to Laruelle's work after the completion of this study, I was naturally gratified by the parallels between his work and my own. His analysis of Heideggerian indifference along these lines is profound and important, going far beyond what I have been able to present here. It is essential reading for any future postdifferential philosophy. See especially François Laruelle, *Philosophies of Difference: A Critical Introduction to Non-Philosophy*, trans. Rocco Gangle (London: Continuum, 2010), 24, and the third chapter.

20. See William Watkin, *The Literary Agamben: Adventures in Logopoiesis* (London: Continuum, 2010), 126–34.

21. See Catherine Mills, *The Philosophy of Agamben* (Stocksfield: Acumen, 2008), 9–34.

22. Agamben, *Potentialities*, 116.

23. Agamben, *Potentialities*, 116–17.

24. Agamben, *Potentialities*, 117–18.

25. Agamben, *Potentialities*, 116.

26. Watkin, *Literary Agamben*, 132–33, 198–99.

27. Watkin, *Literary Agamben*, 155–56, 199–201.

28. G. W. F. Hegel, *Science of Logic*, trans. A. V. Miller (New York: Humanity Books, 1969), 825.

29. Agamben, *Potentialities*, 126.

30. Hegel, *Logic*, 825.

31. Heidegger, *Identity and Difference*, 128.

32. Agamben, *Potentialities*, 29.

33. Agamben, *Potentialities*, 132.

34. Agamben, *Potentialities*, 132.

35. Agamben, *Potentialities*, 132.

FOUR

The Coming Community: An Essay on Indifferent Singularities

The Coming Community (1990) is widely recognised as significant, although most commentary focuses on the fact that the book is ostensibly about ethics contributing to debates on communal singularity to be found in Blanchot and Nancy. It is certainly not subtitled "An Essay on Indifferent Singularities", but my position is that it is the one work of Agamben's that comes closest to being 'about' indifference. The more it is read in this vein, and also with the retrospection of Agamben's later work on politics rather than ethics per se, the more the ethical component of community in the work seems to fade into the background. (We have already stated, for example, that the primary ethical impulse in Agamben is the ethical epistemology of his method.) This is not to say that the indifferent elements then shine through. The book is complex, at times excessively dense or impossibly lapidary, and requires a sustained commentary, I believe, to open up the work so as to locate it at the heart of Agamben's philosophy. This is what I will attempt so as to provide a systematic consideration of the primary concern here, namely, the relation of indifference to singularity, a stipulation of no small importance as we clarify that the proper in Agamben is always to be taken as the particular, leaving a space for the singular which is not critical but constructive.

WHATEVER

In keeping with the gnomic tonality of this work, the book commences with an initially obscure maxim of messianic, third-order indifference: "The coming being is whatever being".[1] For the English, a translator's footnote immediately interposes to explain that the Italian *qualunque* is

65

poorly rendered by the term "whatever", and for that matter the French *quelconque*, which easily renders the Italian, has however been poorly rendered in English translations of Deleuze and Badiou as sometimes particular, at other times general. In fact, the estimable Hardt explains that 'whatever' "refers precisely to that which is neither particular nor general, neither individual nor generic".[2] The point is well made.[3] In this poverty of translation resides the whole issue of 'whatever-ness' which could have been more freely translated here as indifferent being: the coming being is indifferent being, any being, whatever being.[4] The formulation becomes central by relating being, for indifference as much pertains to ontology as it appears to be central to a certain Foucauldian epistemology, indeed presents an ontology of epistemology, to the futural moment of indifferent being. This is the theme of ethics for Agamben: the arrival of ontological indifference or suspension of the opposite terms that have defined the project of human existence since the Greeks, an arrival, however, that is as dangerous to the human being as it is potentially liberating.

That Agamben projects forward to coming indifference and then the next sentence looks back to Scholastic philosophy's use of the Latin term for "whatever", *quodlibet*, presents a miniaturisation of his method that reaches an almost unbearable level of intensity. The oppositional categories of being, or of Being and beings, is presupposed here, the futural moment of their indifferentiation predicted. And a possible paradigmatic moment of arising is then immediately laid before the reader when Agamben then gives a brief history of the term *quodlibet*:

> In the Scholastic enumeration of transcendentals . . . the term that, remaining unthought in each, conditions the meaning of all the others is the adjective *quodlibet*. The common translation of this term as "whatever" in the sense of "it does not matter which, indifferently" is certainly correct, but in its form in the Latin says exactly the opposite: *Quodlibet ens* is not "being, it does no matter which," but rather "being such that it always matters".[5]

Again we come up against those troublesome problems of translation. It is not just that *quodlibet* cannot be rendered from Latin to Italian, *qualunque* from Italian to French to English, that something is "lost" in translation or another meaning gained. Rather, in translating the term across time-languages, indifference seems to suffer in each case as being doubly translated into opposing terms: that which does not matter/that which always matters, the particular *and* the general. This is an early indication in fact of the final argument we will arrive at, that indifference is a signature itself that must be suspended, it being the indifference of the particular and the general. As we will repeatedly realise, contradiction is one of the first indicators of the operativity of a signature, primarily because its operativity is based on a dynamic interchange of inoperative logical positionings in relation to common and proper that will inevitably suspend themselves.

This is perhaps confusing at first glance but need not be, especially if we keep in mind Heideggerian difference as outlined in *Identity and Difference*. Whatever-being here is indifference not because difference is suspended but because being as-such is foregrounded and put in play by indifference. The being as-such here is the equivalent of the difference qua difference of Being and beings to be found in later Heidegger. To clarify these issues, Agamben adds, "The Whatever in question here relates to singularity not in its indifference with respect to a common property (to a concept, for example: being red, being French, being Muslim), but only in its being *such as it is*. Singularity is thus freed from the false dilemma that obliges knowledge to choose between the ineffability of the individual and the intelligibility of the universal".[6] The essence of indifference for Agamben is a resolution of the Aristotelian heritage of part and whole which Hegel seems to in fact invent the totality of the dialectical system to overcome in those few pages in the *Phenomenology* concerning the troublesome properties of salt which are central to his redefinition of indifference.[7] Like Hegel, Agamben does not seek to solve the problem of part and whole, what Stern terms in relation to analytical philosophical debates bundle and substratum,[8] but instead seeks to use the problem to step out of the debate altogether through the formulation of his conceptualisation of whatever singularities or the being as-such of beings. Being-such or whatever (indifferent) being suspends the basis of the whole history of the debate relating to part and whole in that singularity is the very point of indifference between the unknowability of multiple particulars and the supersensuous reductive abstraction of general laws. This is naturally straight out of Hegel, who constructs the need for understanding, the first key stage of dialectic self-conscious negation, to solve this age-old contradiction as we saw. For now, however, Agamben is not thinking of Hegel but has in mind the medieval Jewish philosopher Gesonides's formulation in relation to intelligible universality consisting of "singularity insofar as it is whatever singularity".[9]

If we place these different elements together, we have in miniature the whole system of indifference that, however, will not be systematised in Agamben's work for another twenty years. Indifference is the difference as-such between singularities, not merely the difference as-such but more profoundly the difference of as-such that is the essence of Heideggerian difference qua difference ("heeding the difference as difference" being Heidegger's fundamental ontological statement). Such an in-difference, by which I mean both indifferent and also internal to difference as difference, suspends the opposition between general and particular traceable back to Aristotle and so central to the whole drama of Western thought, most notably the source of modern continental thought patterns: Hegel's dialectic. What will come in being therefore is the suspension of this dialectic, particular-general (part-whole [beings-Being]) resulting in a state of singularity in which "such-and-such being is reclaimed from its having this or that property, which identifies it as belonging to this or that set . . . and it is reclaimed not for another class nor for the simple generic absence of any belonging, but for its being-*such*, for belonging itself".[10] (One cannot ignore the appropriation of the key Badiou term belonging in this passage.[11])

This statement clearly needs some unpacking. Indifference puts into play indifferentiation between neutralised elements belonging to opposing sets. In so doing it makes elements of the sets singularities rather than particularities. Singularity here can be taken to mean lacking particularity and yet not being subsumed under another one-identity. Singularity then not merely neutralises the differentiation in identity of two terms but renders neutral the very modality of categorisation in this manner. When this occurs we are not left with a neutral set of two singularities, pure abstraction as that would be (A is not B), but singularity as Heideggerian belonging-difference as-such. Read under this stipulation, singularity does not refer to neutralised particulars or even the simple suspension of particular and general by giving one a generalised, neutral particularity. Rather, singularity is the Heideggerian (self) relational state of belonging or the as-such of the as-such. There is nothing neutral, particular or general about it. In this short essay therefore is the whole basis of Agambenian indifference, not merely indifferentiation of two opposing terms creating two abstract singularities, Hegelian indifference, but the mediation of indifferentiation as a singular self-relating but not self-identical medium: singularised-singularizing immediate mediation. This then forms the basis of what Agamben takes the ontological term 'is' to actually mean. A is A or A belongs with itself as a nonidentical consistency. That he is appropriating the same fundamental law of what we might call the difference-minimum that we find in Derrida *and* Deleuze will be the topic of the following chapters, but for now we need to concern ourselves as to how Agamben can retain the Heideggerian ontology of difference as difference without succumbing to negativity. As I have already stated, the only means I believe he can do so is through an innovation and application of a new order of philosophical indifference.

EXAMPLE

The rest of the book provides examples of the fundamental ontological logic of indifference, or, better, paradigms, and thus provides us with a clear model of how the archaeological method will develop in *Homo Sacer* and the works which follow. It also, in commencing quite early on with the example *of* the example, maps out the logic of the paradigm which will return relatively unchanged in *The Signature of All Things*, making many of us rather shamefaced that we did not pick up on this much earlier on. Finally, although other works previous to this are essential to Agamben's ideas on language, the comments on language in *The Coming Community* are the first moments where the clarity of communicability comes to the fore as the defining characteristic of what Agamben takes to be language. Thus, in the chapter "Example" he states,

> The antimony of the individual and the universal has its origins in language. The word "tree" designates all trees indifferently, insofar as it posits the proper universal significance in place of singular ineffable trees . . . it transforms singularities into members of a class, whose meaning is defined by a common property (the condition of belonging ε).[12]

Here we have delineated the basic, faulty logic of the West's idea of language, or what is consistently communicable under the signature 'Language'. In the dialectic of common and proper, language operates as the common element which founds the possibility of the singularity of the natural-ineffable by summarising singularities into named particularities. Yet, as we know, the history of metaphysics argues the opposite, namely, that the world as such is the universal, founding common, for which instances of language are supplemental, conventional contingencies which communicate only because there is a commonality of natural experience at the base of being (Wittgenstein's influential form of life). Thus, the communicability of language is the manner in which its operativity is based on a logical inoperativity. Language summarises the proper through its common modality of naming as summary, singularities made into members of a class, yet it can do so only if founded on the opposite logic that nature is the founding common of the contingent instances of linguistic propriety. The name and the world then change places here, both operating as the founding common of a proper position they also come to occupy. This interchange is what makes communication possible and what reveals its inevitable collapse. Language of this order is the operativity of communicability as destined to become inoperativity wherein the communicability of language will become communicable for the first time only when it is rendered inoperative and indifferent.

The entire history of the signature of language in the West is marked out by the ancient paradoxes of singularity, class and belonging then handed down to modern set theory and its implications for analytical philosophy and of course the work of Badiou, who exists as one of the spectres at the frugal feast of this book.[13] What was also bequeathed to set theory were certain paradoxes, not least that of the set of sets. "Linguistic being (being-called) is a set (the tree) that is at the same time a singularity (*the* tree, *a* tree, *this* tree)".[14] To solve this paradox, Badiou explains, set theory invented a series of counterintuitive axioms.[15] Agamben notes a simpler solution in the example. "The example," he says, "is characterized by the fact that it holds for all cases of the same type, and, at the same time, it is included among these. It is one singularity among others, which, however, stands for each of them and serves for all. . . . Neither particular nor universal, the example is a singular object that presents itself as such, that *shows* its singularity".[16]

We need not analyse this logic too much as change 'example' to 'paradigm', and we can see that the example is an early formulation of the logic of analogy, here termed singularity. What is significant rather is that the example *of* the example, nouns, is linguistic, for this allows Agamben to conclude, "Exemplary being is pure linguistic being". As we are speaking here of the medium or process of singularization, not simply singularities, we can then add to our definition of indifference that it is the medium-process of singularization that shows its singularity and in doing so shows us the being of singularity as such: language (although this is a particular sense of language as communicability).

Keeping with the theme of particular and general, which is after all the paradigmatic differential of indifferent singularity, Agamben concerns himself with medieval considerations of this problem, not least Duns Scotus. The essay on the scholastic *principium individuationis* (individuation) begins in conclusion to previous points and in clear consort with Badiou: "Whatever is the matheme of singularity, without which it is impossible to conceive either being or the individuation of singularity".[17] Having clarified therefore that what binds his work to Badiou is indifference as matheme and further that indifference is not simply a state of being or a state of singularity but the process of differentiation as such I have called singularization, Agamben then considers how the history of individuation, or how an indifferent mass becomes individualised, stems from Duns Scotus's debate with Saint Thomas, which in turn originates as ever with Aristotle. What makes a thing the thing it is, something inherent to the thing or something added to the thing? is the question here. Duns Scotus famously goes for the latter but solves the problem of how the defining essence of an immediate unity can be found in a mediated extra property brought in from outside by explaining that "individuation as an addition to nature or common form (for example, humanity) [is] an addition not of another form or essence or property, but of an *ultima realitas*, of an "utmostness" of the form itself. Singularity adds nothing to the common form, if not a 'haecceity'".[18]

The solution is neat enough. Singularity comes in from the outside to define the thing as the thing it is, by speaking generally and in the abstract of individuation or the process of becoming differentiated from other things into its identity. At this point we should note that haecceity is carefully differentiated in Duns Scotus from mere quiddity. Quiddity defines the whatness of a thing in relation to qualities it shares with other things, making it a species of a genus. Haecceity rather names the particularity of the thing or what it shares with nothing else. That said, haecceity is not singular enough to Agamben's mind. He criticises Duns Scotus on four counts: (1) he sees common nature as prior to the thing in question, and (2) this means it is "indifferent to whatever singularity, and to which singularity adds on haecceity";[19] (3) as such, he ignores that fact that the whatever or quodlibet is inseparable from singularity, (4) so that finally he makes indifference the root of individuation. In a sentence initially disastrous for our study, Agamben concludes, "But 'quodlibetality' is not indifference" before asking, "What then is the relationship between quodlibetality and indifference? How can we understand the indifference of the common human form with respect to singular humans?"[20]

The answer to this problem resides in two rather incompatible areas, love and Spinoza. Commencing with Spinoza, Agamben explains that according to the *Ethics*, while all bodies have it in common to express extension, "yet what is common cannot in any case constitute the essence of the single case". He explains this further with reference to the idea of inessential commonality or "a solidarity that in no way concerns an essence": "*Taking place, the communication of singularities in the attribute of extension, does not unite them in essence, but scatters them in existence*".[21] If we pause for a moment, we can try to differentiate haecceity-singularity from inessential commonality. All that haecceity adds is a held-in-common nature which stipulates the thing as what it is. Yes, it removes the thing from held-in-common species-genus qualitative hierarchical comparative groupings, but still it poses individuality as indifferent to the singular. Here we now see that Agamben is using indifference in the historically current, medieval sense of simply without inclination. In Duns Scotus, therefore, singularity is simply singularity as-such, or a pure abstraction, and Agamben is warning us against indifference as-such, or a general indifferentiation that is not tied to actual, singular qualities. Such a theory of abstract indifference denies the very element that the theory is supposed to protect: what makes something singular, precisely the problem of indifference of sense-certainty for Hegel. Here is where love comes in. Speaking of quodlibet as the being-such, Agamben says, "The singularity exposed as such is whatever you *want*, that is, lovable".[22] This statement stresses not just the indifferentiation of the whatever but also the inclination. *Whatever* means whatever you *want*. To clarify he gives the example of love never being love of only one attribute of the loved one, yet neither is it neglect of properties in favour of "insipid generality": "The lover wants the loved one *with all of its predicates*, its being such as it is".[23]

In place now we have an essential element of indifference which almost seems to conform to the law of nontranslation we found in relation to quodlibet and *qualunque* in that indifference means, within the history of Western thought, both noninclination and the specificities of inclination as such.[24] What is key is that indifference is not itself emotionally indifferent (first-order indifference predicated on prephilosophical indifference). The suspension of differentiation of identity does not result in a general, featureless indifference as difference as such. Rather, it frees properties from being the particular of a general, or from being simply "the concept of the property", allowing them, as Spinoza has it, not to unite in essence but to scatter in existence: actually to come to being as if for the first time. Agamben clarifies, "Whatever is constituted not by the indifference of common nature with respect to singularities, but by the indifference of the common and the proper, of the genus and the species, of the essential and the accidental. Whatever is the thing *with all its properties*, none of which, however, constitutes difference. In-difference with respect to properties individuates and disseminates singularities, makes them lovable (quodliterable)".[25]

To capture what is one of the most challenging formulations in Agamben, he presents us with a cluster of examples. We have of course love. He also mentions the "right word", which is neither language as such; each word does not equal the held-in-common language, but nor is it heard as if for the first time, which would make it glossolalia. He gives the Levinasian example of the face of which there is an implied criticism. Each face is noted for its individuation of the human being, yet there is such a thing as "whatever face, in which what belongs to common nature and what is proper is absolutely indifferent".[26] The final example is perhaps the most charming and powerful, combining, as it does, language, human form, lovable idiosyncrasy and act: handwriting. Agamben first gives the medieval view that "the passage from potentiality to act, from common form to singularity, is not an event accomplished once and for all, but an infinite series of modal oscillations. The individuation of a singular existence is not a punctual fact, but a *linea generationis sunstantiae* that varies in every direction according to a continual gradation of growth and remission, of appropriation and impropriation".[27] Noting that the image of the line is not accidental, Agamben suggests that in writing a letter the hand moves continually from the common form of the twenty-six letters, twenty-one in Italian, to the "particular marks that identify its presence". Thus, he says, "It is from the hundred idiosyncrasies that characterize my way of writing the letter *p* . . . that its common form is engendered. *Common and proper, genus and individual are only two slopes dropping down from either side of the watershed of whatever*".[28]

This magisterial image of verticality, however, an indirect citation of Blanchot surely,[29] is then immediately undercut by a concluding image that instead defines the constant oscillation between potentiality and act, common and proper as something that "comes about every time as a shuttling in both directions along a line of sparkling alternation on which common nature and singularity . . . change roles and interpenetrate".[30] I believe this double structure is essential to the understanding of how the two different elements of indifference, local examples and indifferentiation of common and proper as such, work together to produce a totality of indifferent indifferentiation which avoids the danger of purely abstract, noninclined indifference yet which does produce a general law of indifference as presented here: namely, the suspension of differentiation between common and proper that constitutes the very law of differentiation as such.

The motion of indifference is both a rising up and a shuttling across. It is a point of ecstasy and an ongoing oscillation. It combines, in other words, meta- and para- spatial positioning such as we already identified in relation to the paradigm and the signature. As far as I am aware there is no term for the meta-para-, but in my earlier work in relation to this interactive spatial dynamism in poetic rhythm, I have called it the tabular-planar.[31] This is an interaction of localised indifferentiations, back-and-forth linearity (paradigms) and historical hierarchies of a vertical nature (signatures) or indifferentiation as general suspension between common and proper. Take a point and extend it horizontally and vertically, and you have the two-dimensional space-arena that captures the double-modality of indifferent singularization as it is presented in *The Coming Community*. This is what I mean by the medium of indifference, a space-movement across the heterogeneity of the horizontal and vertical temporal-spatial coordinates.

BEING-NAMED

In Agamben's work the many critical considerations of the signature language can be reduced to two formulations. The first is that language as naming results in the paradox, which Agamben traces across several sources, ancient and modern, continental and analytical, that there is no name for the name. In other words, in the set of names which is language, the name as such cannot be named, as that is the meta-name or genus-name of which all other names are species. We might here term this the indifferent name or empty act of naming something but nothing in particular, a gesture which of course negates the assumed purpose of naming. The second is that language as such is not simply naming but a medium of communication. What is not named in language therefore by the set language is not simply an empty name but the ability of language to act as the medium of communication wherein language as such, as medium of truth, remains unsaid, by which we could say is not presented. Here language is what he calls, after Benjamin, in *Potentialities*, pure communicability of immediate mediation.[32] It would be tempting to say that language's lack of name becomes its communicability as such, as names combine into discourse, but I believe this is too simple a solution. Indifference as language, like indifference in all areas, is the complex combina-

tion of the proper, the name and the common, naming as such or language as a whole, and in Agamben's early work this plays out across a
dynamic between the name and the medium of language.

To trace the moment of arising of these issues Agamben begins with
the famous and divisive establishment of analytical philosophy in the
debate between Frege and Russell at the beginning of the last century
over "the class of all the classes that are not members of themselves",[33]
what has come to be called Russell's paradox, the same paradox, of
course, as Badiou explains, that eventually leads to the set-theory event
of the last century.[34] Russell explains that when we say an object has a
property, we assume the property is definite and distinctive from the
object in question. A London bus is red, inasmuch as it also has wheels,
but a London bus does not equal red, or, to put it more clearly, the bus is
red, but red is not the bus. In addition, Russell argues all objects that
share this property form a class, red things, and just as the property is not
the same as the object, so the class of objects is not the same as the object.
A bus belongs to the class red things, as does a strawberry, but a bus is
other things besides red, while the class red is not determined, say, by
properties such as must carry passengers, makes excellent ice cream and
so on. Thus, each name denotes an object by presenting a presupposed
and paradoxical three-part differentiation: object as such, property and
class. These paradoxes appear in their most intense form if the object in
question is the name of the class, for the name is a property, being-
named, which it coincides with absolutely. This is entirely what naming
is, forming a class, the being-named, of which it is the only member but
of which it cannot be a member; the name cannot belong to the class
Name because it is the external law of that class. Yet nothing else can
belong to that class. Thus, the class is 'empty'.

This debate will eventually be solved by certain axioms of set theory
central to Badiou's application of this paradox to ontology.[35] In the mean-
time Russell comes to the rescue by suggesting that the presupposition
"every concept forms a class that constitutes an extension" by deciding
that certain concepts do not form a class. These "nonpredicative" concepts have, as the term suggests, no extensions as regards properties and
class, relating them to another set of words relating to nonpredicative
multiplicity: all, every, any, some and so on. As Agamben explains, "The
classes that arise from these expressions are 'illegitimate totalities,' which
pretend to be part of the totality they define (something like a concept
that demands to be part of its own extension)".[36] Analytical philosophy
then makes as one of its central tenets that such nonpredicative terms
must be bracketed from logic, as they represent false totalities, properties
and classes, leading to Russell's lasting contribution to the discipline, his
theory of types. Agamben is willing to concede this prohibition only on
the grounds that analytic philosophy accepts that nonpredicative expressions are in fact very common; in fact, they are an element of every

moment of expression: "since every term refers by definition to every and to any member of its extension, and can, furthermore, refer to itself, one can say that all (or almost all) words can be presented as classes that . . . both are and are not members of themselves".[37] Inasmuch as words are multiplicities within a consistent count, Badiou would concur.

This possibility relates not to the confusion, say, of the word shoe and the thing shoe. This would be a presupposition of language as bifurcated into *phone* and *logos* which Agamben's work has tirelessly presented as the false moment of definition by division of language as negative being. Rather, it relates to the "word 'shoe' precisely in its signifying the shoe . . . the shoe in its being signified by the term 'shoe'".[38] So that while one can separate, with effort, the word shoe from the thing,

> it is still much more difficult to distinguish a shoe from its being-called-(shoe), from its *being-in-language*. Being-called or being-in-language is the non-predicative property par excellence that belongs to each member of a class and at the same time makes its belonging an aporia. . . . In other words, if we try to grasp a concept as such, it is fatally transformed into an object, and the price we pay is no longer being able to distinguish it from the conceived thing.[39]

Here we find combined several lasting themes pertaining to Agamben's valorisation of language as the thing of thought as such as he presents it in *Potentialities*.[40] First, language does not consist of a sign made up of signified and signifier, logos and phone. In such a formulation language remains silent, negated or unnamed. Language is not the representation of the classic metaphysical division between word and thing, proper and common, but is in fact the very medium of the staging of the problem. Language does not represent this problem but facilitates and presents it. This can be found in various functions of language but here specifically in the process of naming. Naming something is not representation, a sound image representing a concept, because naming does not consist of the division property and set. Rather, naming is the process of being-named or being-in-language. This is an indifferent naming or naming as such: how does one come to be named, how can naming as such occur? If one tries to name the name, one comes up against a nonpredicative paradox, yet the name is not a property, object or class but the very potential and activity of the act of naming. Inasmuch then that each moment of naming exists within the action of being named as such, each name contains the problem that its being as name is its status of that which is being-named. Naming therefore does not denote a thing in terms of a concept, class and properties but places naming as-such before us as a modality of communicability. That most differential of processes, giving something a specific name, actual properties, locating it within a class, is the very essence of indifference, the suspension of actual differences in the moment of pure difference as such: how some thing becomes presented in some situation. At this point it is hard to fit an iPad between Agamben and certain key elements of Badiou.

In the earlier works on this problem, such as *Infancy and History*, *Language and Death*, *The Coming Community* and the essays which open *Potentialities*, these formulations remain, for this reader at least, rather indistinct. However, within the framework of the recent texts the whole problem is rather easily explained by saying language is not a mode of expressed, referential communication but rather is communicability. What is not said in our signature Language is that language is not a bifurcation at the level of the word (sign) but a process at the level of discourse. And if language never has the floor, because there is no word for the word itself, it is more precisely because language is the floor and is not composed of word-referrals. Language operates in a complex manner in Agamben's work because there is the signature Language, which he is merciless in undermining in text after text, and the process of linguistic communicability by virtue of discursive statements, upon which the method depends. In fact it is neater to speak of language as communication, which suffers from the metaphysics of bifurcation, and language as communicability, which hosts this metaphysics, distributes it, organises its meanings and has the potential to render it inoperative.

Returning to the text at hand, Agamben traces the history of the problem of the relation of name to concept, especially the name of the concept of naming as such, to Aristotle. This is inevitable in that indifference is directly related to the paradox of genus and species which is traceable to Aristotle's various presentations of his theory of categories that we have alluded to more than once. Agamben specifically highlights what he sees as a mistranslation of the *Metaphysics* that pertains to the distinction and interrelation of synonyms and homonyms. For Aristotle, synonyms are objects that have the same name and the same definition, not as we have it different names but the same definition. Homonyms in contrast are objects with the same name but different definitions: "Thus the single horses are synonyms with respect to the concept horse, but homonyms with respect to the idea of the horse—just as in Russell's paradox the same object both belongs and does not belong to a class".[41] To clarify, horses are synonymous with the concept of horse in that they share "participation in a common concept". They all share horse-ness, as they constitute the concept inductively. Yet at the same time the idea of horse as such, horse-ness per se, is not a horse and does not belong to the class horses. At some point the inductive aggregation of the set making up the concept horse, that is a horse, that is a horse, that is a horse, until one feels confident enough to say therefore horse is thus, must become deductive: horse as such is not in any one of those horses but in the properties they all share in common. Every synonym at a certain point must find its homonym, but "that with respect to which the synonym is homonymous is neither an object nor a concept, but is instead its own having-name, its own belonging, or rather its being-in-language. This can neither be named in turn nor shown, but only grasped through an anaphoric movement".[42]

We will come back to anaphora. Here we need to note only that Russell's paradox stretches all the way back to the beginning of Western thought not only coming to the fore in 1902 when he wrote that fateful letter to Frege and in 1985 with the publication of *Being and Event* but again in 1990 when Agamben identified this as our current moment of arising of the problem. The problem is of course as ancient as it is current: how can a thing be said to be the thing it is? If it is defined by properties, here represented by the concept, how do said properties, which do not belong to the thing as such but only the thing as concept (in other words, red does not belong to the bus it only borrows it to be defined as "bus"), purport to combine to form the essence of the thing when they do not belong to said essence? If it is defined by a pure substance or idea, the horse as-such, then what defines the horse is the precise thing that is not part of the horse but something brought in from outside. Either a thing is all set and no class, or it is pure class without a set.

Agamben does not go back to Aristotle to embarrass Russell for not spotting this, or at least I do not believe so, any more than he ignores Badiou's solution to the problem five years earlier; rather, he finds in Aristotle's formulation of the homonym a potential moment of instability which may in fact have a positive outcome. His emphasis then is of a different order. For him an idea can be rendered in language, you will recall, only by anaphora or a neutral mode of indication that refers one back to the first moment of naming. In that the idea has no proper name, it cannot be named as it is naming as such; it is in effect a nongenerative anaphora or a reference back to a nonpresent name. This is rendered in Aristotle by the Greek *autò*: "the idea of the thing is the thing itself. This anonymous homonymity is the idea".[43] The idea as such is therefore the process of anonymous homonymity of a nonnamed or not specifically named difference between all names and the very definition of naming as the being-named. It is for this reason, Agamben argues, that the principle in question, of anaphoric self-reference as nonreference to any specific name, allows one to note that Aristotelian homonym constitutes the whatever: "*Whatever is singularity insofar as it relates not (only) to the concept, but (also) to the idea.* This relation does not found a new class, but is, in each class, that which draws singularity from its synonym, from its belonging to a class, not toward any absence of name or belonging, but toward the name *itself*, toward a pure and anonymous homonymy".[44]

The effects of this process are, first, that while the concept is always forming networks of synonymous relations, at each juncture the name reveals that these networks are nonabsolute, something is always missing from the set. That said, contra Badiou, the whatever does not simply name the indiscernible in any set, albeit said indiscernible is the indifferent subtracted void in Badiou, but rather activates "pure being-called", which is unnameable only because the whatever designates "the being-in-language of the non-linguistic".[45] Naming, therefore, in there being no name for the name, does not confirm the history of metaphysic's negation of language but reveals it as if for the first time via a confrontation with contemporary ideas about language and their historical foundation that occurs in our current age. Naming's not being named does not move from specific, naming an actual thing, to generality, the concept of naming as such, but suspends the difference between the nonlinguistic, ineffable proper and the antilinguistic, intelligible common. That language has no name does not define language as without name but forces us to rethink entirely what it means to be-named, to be in the process of naming. Simply put, it is the paradigmatic example of the greatest problem in philosophy, how to get from the specific nonlinguistic to the general postlinguistic, paradigmatic not because indifference is reducible to language but simply because the history of the problem has always been presented as a problem of denotation. The paradox of the name then makes language as communicability appear in a logic that is used in Agamben's early work, specifically *The Man without Content* in relation to modernism and *Infancy and History* in relation to the sign, wherein the negation of a signature is an essential moment in making the signature appear to us such as it is under the sign of its inoperativity. Thus, the interrelation between operativity and inoperativity within signatures, which I am consistently trying to elucidate, is present from the very beginning of Agamben's work in what may originally have been seen as a kind of negative onto-theology.

Agamben's first important statement on language as signature is to describe how the communicability of language as such or the manner in which language allows for communication or naming in general remains itself noncommunicated, in such a way that the noncommunicable does not become reduced to ineffability, the failure of language to render things, but becomes the presentation of communicability itself. This is the agenda he sets for himself in *Language and Death*. That language does not communicate itself in communicating reveals the singular whatever in every act of naming, denoting and communicating. Communicability therefore is language as a potential medium which is always available for communication but which is never exhausted by communication. Language is always communicating, but no one communication renders communication as such. Rather, communicability comes about only in the act of communication as the suddenly encountered precondition of all communication. In a sense communicability is what is left unsaid by a specific communication and is thus *a posteriori* (whatever was said, saying as such was never said), yet it is also the foundation of all communication (in never being said I see that it is the basis of all saying). This is what Agamben means by the apparent paradox of communicability as immediate mediation:[46] one is always within the midst of a mediation, and language is therefore the medium of pure mediation.

It is useful here to consider communication as the movement across the assumed abyss between common and proper represented both by naming as signification and also by single (self-present and thus common) subjects communicating with other (hence proper) subjects, while communicability is the wider discursive context that sanctions this fiction so as to allow certain statements and behaviours to consistently occur over large periods of time. If we believe in language as communication, a large number of other predicates are sanctioned pertaining to subjectivity, agency, intention, intersubjectivity, truth as agreement, reference, common sense and so on, going all the way back to the foundational need of our system to present language, fictively, as the bifurcation between word and thing. Communication does not facilitate the free exchange of ideas amongst subjects pertaining to objects in the world, thoughts are also objects of course, but sanctions the controlled and closed system of a set of central concepts through the idea of free exchange. The relation of this to the idea of freedom in democracy will become increasingly clear in the final chapters of the work.

SPACE AND TIME

One of the peculiarities of *The Coming Community* is that, as the title suggests, it is a messianic text which, however, has no overall theory of time. Not that time does not dominate certain sections, for example, in terms of potentiality, but essentially *The Coming Community* is, perhaps confusingly at first, a treatise on different forms of space. Now that we have in our possession, so to speak, Agamben's treatise on temporal indifference, *The Time That Remains* (whose obviously messianic title suggests some order of cobelonging between the two texts), this is not so strongly felt. That said, as we shall see in relation to similar thoughts regarding *Homo Sacer*, there is an argument to be made that *The Coming Community* suffers from incompletion of method in terms of a general conceptualisation of indifferent temporality and, in the sections that conclude our argument on the irreparable, the specific nature of temporal redemption. Then again there is a counterargument that the later work is possible by virtue of these earlier excursions into time to be found in *The Coming Community*. The question remains, however, if this is a work of messianic ethics, how does it stand in relation to time? The response is in two parts. First, the sustained consideration of space, by definition, implies time. Second, the conclusion of the work pertains to the irredeemable or irreparable portion of singular ontology, so that while not ostensibly about time, from the announcement of the title to the challenge of the appendix, this is an impossible to ignore element of the work.

What could link space and time in Agamben's work of this period is the indifference of their assumed difference. This is one of the major observations of Derrida's early work in *"Ousia* and *Grammē"*, for example. To bring this about in Agamben, at least one element would have to occupy the position of the common, the other the proper, then these placements would continually alternate resulting in the same order of time-space suspension you find in Derrida's work. One could argue in this manner then that time is the extension of a point in space with the point being the proper and the extension of the point into the generality of past and future resulting in time as the common. This could suggest then that space is the proper, the point, and time the common. Yet this does not wash of course. Since Kant, Space and Time have been parallel signatures, and if Derrida is able to render them indifferent in *"Ousia* and *Grammē"*, it is only by virtue of the implied realisation that they share in common an indifferential structure. Derrida does not say this, but what makes space and time indistinguishable is the means by which the propriety of the point-moment in relation to the commonality of extension-time repeatedly changes places so that the point-moment both founds its extension and is founded by extensivity-movement, explaining the peculiarity of *"Ousia* and *Grammē"*, which attempts to collapse the opposition of space and time rather than find the supplemental element of each.

That Agamben does not attempt a suspension of the pairing space and time reveals an important element of his theory of signatures, which does not allow for transsignatory indifference, a law that inadvertently Derrida subscribes to whilst at the same time flouting said rule in his own essay. If transsignatory indifference were possible, then Agamben's system would resemble a pyramidal, Hegelian *Aufhebung* leading up to the final, ultimate indifference. What is highly significant is that the distribution of signatures is restricted to two plates: the set of paradigms and the signature which sanctions their communicability. The signature Glory is of the same status, in this way, as Time, even if in relative terms Glory would appear as dramatically epiphenomenal in relation to Time in philosophical discourse. Thus, Space and Time exist not in a corelational state of indifference but in a paradigmatic state of analogy even if, within metaphysics, the time-space dichotomy is highly pronounced. Otherwise, Agamben would be forced to make a special case of time-space, as Kant did, for example. Instead, in Agamben, the signature Time is related to the signature Space in terms of a certain to-the-side location, traditionally communicable under the signature Space, but which also makes concepts of Time communicable as well, while both the signatures of Space and Time are temporally inscribed within the messianic temporality of the method.

For example, at the end of *The Time That Remains* referring to the dialectics at a standstill method, Agamben says apropos of Benjamin's hermeneutic principle, "Benjamin's principle . . . proposes that every work, every text, contains a historical index which indicates its belonging to a determinate epoch, as well as its coming forth to full legibility at a determinate historical moment".[47] This includes the signature Time of course. Thus, we can see here that Time as signature has the same temporality as Space as signature, as Power as signature, as Language and so on. Similarly, the para-logic of the paradigm or analogy operates through a to-the-side spatiality which is undermining of the signature Time as well as Space. To call the first a temporal category is to conform to the communicability sanction of our age, when in fact there is nothing temporal about it, even if Agamben calls it archaeology. By the same gesture the para-logic is communicable through conceptions of space but is not spatial in any empirically observable or ontologically consistent sense. It is in this way that Agamben could never indifferentiate space and time as such, as Derrida does in his work, as, for Agamben, Space and Time would be either signatures of communicability in a para-logical relation whose only commonality is their dependence on the common-proper fictive division or paradigms of a larger signature, say, metaphysics as a whole. If they are paradigms, then again their interrelation is structured in an analogical fashion that is nonoppositional inasmuch as the set would, in any case, include other paradigms. It is this second situation that *The Coming Community* addresses in fact, presenting an indifferentiation of metaphysics as signature, through the work of various signatures such as Language, Space, Time, Potentiality and so on.

TEMPORAL INDIFFERENCE: *THE TIME THAT REMAINS*

To understand how the method relates space and time in this paradigmatic and analogical fashion, let's consider again the argument of temporal indifference in *The Time That Remains*. Here, Agamben traces the signature of Time back to St. Paul and the very temporality of the messianic that occurs at key concluding moments of the argument in so many Agamben texts. Explaining that traditionally time has been represented as *chronos*, linear sequential time, moving towards the *eschaton*, the conclusion of time, Agamben reveals that true messianic time is to be found not in the eschatological completion of linear temporal sequentiality, as might be assumed, but in the *kairos* or the occasion of one's being called to the messiah (messianic *klesis*). *Kairatic* or true messianic time is not the end of the time but, as he says, the time it takes for time to come to an end. It is in fact not a temporal category as such at all; it is not a valorisation of the now, as some have said,[48] but the occasion, which is a process. *Kairatic* time folds back the *eschaton* into the *chronos*, recalling in the end every instant before and leading up to the end while at the same time it projects forward the *chronos*, whose every moment or now is a presaging of the final moment of temporal completion. In this way *kairatic* time is a mode of temporal suspension or indifference, where proper time of moments and common time of fulfilment are overlaid, so that their positions become blurred and their differentiation suspended.

In *The Time That Remains*, Agamben stresses that *kairatic* time, or temporal indifference, is involuted time. It finds a space within time that is in effect out of time according to three measures. It refutes sequence, it negates destiny and it is the very end of time as the nontemporal period of its ending. Yet although *kairatic* time is a space tucked into time, this space is a location of exteriority. In the key section "*Kairos* and *Chronos*", Agamben explains that although *kairos* and *chronos* are usually opposed, what is central is not their opposition but their possible relation. Citing the *Corpus Hippocraticum* he finds the following formulation of relational difference: "*chronos* is that in which there is *kairos*, and *kairos* is that in which there is little *chronos*".[49] Agamben notes that *kairos* and *chronos* are not opposed here but overlaid, "literally placed within each other," so that *kairos*, the messianic moment of one's being called from one's day-to-day life to serve the messiah, "is not another time, but a contracted and abridged *chronos* . . . *kairos* is nothing more than seized *chronos*".[50]

At this precise moment Agamben almost seems to present a transtextual example of this process when he cites here, in brackets, the rabbinic apologue which states that the messianic world will be not another world but our world with just a slight difference "which results from my having grasped my disjointedness with regard to chronological time".[51] What we can conclude from this is that temporal indifference, defined in terms of the messianic, is possible only through another messianism which is a kind of messianic space, not in order to differentiate space and time, as I have said, but to show how, in this instance, the "spatial" logic of the analogy can be found distributed across a wide diversity of texts: abstract considerations of category and class, Christian texts of redemption, Judaic works of redemption and so on. All of this confirms the second point that all these ideas are to be excavated using the archaeological method in tandem with the paradigmatic logic with the messianic aim of suspending such and such a signature. These terms are not in play in *The Coming Community* but are being excavated archaeologically in my work for various, I hope, legitimate exegetical reasons, not least the possibility of the indifferentiation of Agamben's philosophy of indifference.

PARADIGMS OF SPACE: EASE AND HALOS

The same example of involuted, exterior space to-the-side pertaining to indifferent temporality is given midway through *The Coming Community* under the chapter heading "Halos", which itself relates back directly to the section entitled "Ease". Both are paradigmatic concepts taken from rabbinic Talmudic tradition. The second, ease, refers to a law in the Talmud that two places are reserved for each of us, one in Eden and the other in Gehenna. If you are saved, therefore, you get your own place, plus that of a neighbour who was damned and vice versa. Agamben realises this is an early formulation of the very modern philosophical issue of alterity and is basically quasi Hegelian. If you are saved, you find yourself not in the space proper to yourself but the common space of the neighbour. "What is most proper to every creature is thus its substitutability, its being in any case in the place of the other".[52] Agamben, via the theology of the community called Badaliya, a theology of self-substitution, interprets this legend as the allowance of the taking-place of alterity or the other: "This substitution no longer knows a place of its own, but the taking-place of every single being is always already in common—an empty space offered to the one".[53]

One can see here that the space in question, which is called ease, brings together problems of space and time in a unique fashion. In that the tradition speaks of the end of time, it is messianic. Yet it relates to one's place after redemption, so it is spatial. In that the subject takes its rightful place only by taking the place of an anonymous neighbour, this spatiality is confirmed, but in so doing it allows alterity as common anonymity to take place, to occur, and so is in fact temporal. Agamben concludes thus: "In this way, the multiple common place . . . is nothing but the coming to itself of each singularity, its being whatever—in other words, such as it is. Ease is the proper name of this unrepresentable space . . . the space adjacent . . . the empty place where each can move freely, in a semantic constellation where spatial proximity borders on opportune time (*ad-agio*, moving at ease)".[54]

It is Agamben himself who ties the space of ease to another rabbinic tradition, that of the messianic world of the tiny displacement. Agamben equates this displacement-as-salvation theory with the problematic theology of the halo, which runs the risk of adding something to indicate perfection, which debases said perfection by adding a questionable supplement. This will become a much more complex debate in *The Kingdom and the Glory* for precisely the reason that glorification of God is the addition of something to a being, God, who is self-present and complete in its own ontological state of glory. The same problem also attends the issue of displacement, which he explains "does not refer to the state of things, but to their sense and their limits. It does not take place in things, but at their periphery, in the space of ease between every thing and itself".[55]

The halo and the displacement add something to perfection which Agamben immediately relates to the issue of Duns Scotus's problem of individuation which we have already explained. In that the halo is the "individuation of a beatitude, the becoming singular of what is perfect," it resembles Duns Scotus's theory yet differs in one essential element. The halo does not add something to a class or change its nature, the problem we addressed in relation to the categorical, because it is added to an already perfectly completed and thus infinite and determinate being. The halo represents something other than determination, "an unravelling or an indetermination of [being's] limits: a paradoxical *individuation by indetermination*. One can think of the halo, in this sense, as a zone in which possibility and reality, potentiality and actuality, become indistinguishable".[56]

The halo passes, he concludes, from absolute finitude, accessible of course only after death and salvation, to a moment "that makes its limits indeterminate and allows it to blend, to make itself whatever",[57] the procedure of becoming whatever is, he argues, accomplished by an act which both displaces the world and raises matter up so that it "does not remain beneath the form, but surrounds it with a halo".[58] Here Agamben may as well be speaking of the matter of commonality without concept in relation to that of propriety without ideality, or indeed of X in relation to Y. In both instances of singular indifference the process of indifference cannot be captured by the act of horizontal or vertical figuration but only, and this is exceptionally significant, in the metrical combination of the two into planar space-time.

The space of ease equates directly with the involuted pocket of the temporality of *kairos* because, as the taking-place, it is the transitional zone between space and its extension into time. Taking-place therefore designates the peculiar space-time of the messianic, which is both punctual and extensive through an open-to-exteriority intensity. Taking-place is the process of being-in, being-such, the suspensive moment between the specificity of the proper and the generality of the common. As such, yes, it is a point of suspension between the two, the name as anonymous homonym, but it is also the zone of passage, an extension of space into time that constitutes the pure medium of language as a zone of immediate mediation. The taking-place therefore is both the transition from proper X to common Y, a place between, and the place to one side or permanent pure exteriority of the medium of transition, the Z below the X and Y—below, to the side and around but never above. Thus, singular indifference is not merely space and time but also in relation to time, completion and sequence and in relation to space, inside and outside.

TAKING PLACE OUTSIDE

In the essay "Taking-place," a profound and troubling discourse on the necessity of evil, Agamben again turns to the theological tradition of indifference by rereading the heretic doctrine of the followers of Amalric of Bena who were all burnt alive for their indifferent interpretation of the dictum "God is all in all". They took this to be a radical development of Platonic *chora* or place of space from which one must conclude, "God is in every thing as the place in which every thing is, or rather as the determination and the 'topia' of every thing. The transcendent, therefore, is not a supreme entity above all things; rather, *the pure transcendent is the taking-place of every thing*. God . . . does not take place, but is the taking-place of the entities, their innermost exteriority".[59]

Six hundred years later, and Kant is grappling with the selfsame concept when he comes to define the essence of singularity. Here under the heading "Outside," Agamben relates taking-place to the issues of singularity which most concern any theory of the indifferent time-space formulation:

> Whatever is the figure of pure singularity. Whatever singularity has no identity, it is not determinate with respect to a concept, but neither is it simply indeterminate; rather it is determined only through its relation to an *idea*, that is, to the totality of its possibilities. Through this relation, as Kant said, singularity borders all possibility and thus receives its *omnimoda determinatio* not from its participation in a determinate concept of some actual property (being Red, Italian, Communist) but *only by means of this bordering* . . . the relation to an empty and indeterminate totality.[60]

We could speak of this logic in relation to naming and category, as Kant does, or within a different context of communicability, the space of ease/halo as the messianic indeterminacy of the perfect completion of messianic redemption (a communicability one would suspect would be noncommunicable to Kant and his contemporaries). So as to develop this paradigmatic, analogical link, Agamben says, "In Kantian terms this means that what is in question in this bordering is not a limit (*Schranke*) that knows no exteriority, but a threshold (*Grenze*), that is, a point of contact with an external space that must remain empty. Whatever adds to singularity only an emptiness. . . . Whatever is singularity plus an empty space, a singularity that is *finite*".[61] Here the legend of the two spaces in heaven for the devout is reconfigured in rational terms as the problem of belonging without being determinate (again surely Badiou is on his mind here). Agamben accepts from this set of deductions that a singularity plus an empty space, which is a singularity become singular due to the empty space, can only be pure exteriority, in that the space to the side of the singular is an empty yet indeterminate totality bordered by a finite indeterminate singularity. "*Whatever*," he says, "*is the event of an outside*. What is thought in the architranscendental *quodlibet* is, therefore, what is most difficult to think, the absolutely non-thing experience of a pure exteriority".[62]

Yet before one comes to view a contradiction here between the space of pure exteriority and the outside/inside of the taking-place of singularity, one must take into consideration, Agamben contends, what outside actually means, in that historically across many European languages it has meant at the door or threshold. Thus he concludes on space, presenting the final piece of the puzzle so to speak as to what constitutes this strange time-space, point-extension, linear-tabular, inside-outside phenomenon (whatever [indifferent] singularity),

> The *outside* is not another space that resides beyond a determinate space, but rather it is the passage, the exteriority that gives it access. . . . The threshold is not, in this sense, another thing with respect to the limit; it is, so to speak, the experience of the limit itself, the experience of being-*within* an *outside*.[63]

Thus, if *kairos* is a time becoming space of the outside-inside, so the space of whatever singularity is the space becoming time, place becoming taking-place, of the inside of the outside. We are, in other words, centrally located within yet another indifferent suspension, not merely between two opposing terms in one unit but also in the constructive combination across two levels of indifference, the specific and the general. If indifference suspends the differentiation between proper and common, it does so not by negating proper and common but by applying proper and common across its own logic. Indifference of indifferents, the suspension of difference as such across two proper terms, is accessed via the abstract logic of indifference as difference as such. Yet difference as such alone, remember, is not "whatever", singular indifference, as then it becomes merely indifference as universal abstract law (a mistake, after Hegel, we all know not to make). Thus, while the proper example of suspension between cases of proper and common is suspended, it is reactivated in the proximate space of its own dissolution from proper into common.

Certainly there is no name without medium, no example without the general condition of indifference as such, yet there is also no medium unless activated by the example, no absolute outside, outside of the example in question. There is no general law of indifference, nor is any one of the several instances of indifference, including most pertinently language which does seem almost to operate as archetypal indifference (Agamben says, after all, "Exemplary being is purely linguistic being"),[64] the example of indifference, which is tantamount to saying there is no indifference as-thus, as precisely this thing, nor indifference as-such, general law, without a radical appraisal of the thus and as-such as modalities of thinking in the key of identity and/or indifference. This is the theme and contention of the final essay in the collection, "The Irreparable", which, Agamben explains, is a set of loose reflections on Heidegger's *Being and Time* and Wittgenstein's *Tractatus*.

NOTES

1. Giorgio Agamben, *The Coming Community*, trans. Michael Hardt (Minneapolis: University of Minnesota Press, 1993), 1. As should be clear, I have designated three 'stages' of indifference: critical indifference between two categories, their point of

arising, and the messianic moment of their suspensive indifference. These three make up only one element of indifference, which we should term proper indifference. They are instances of indifference within the history of our thinking. The other element of indifference is common indifference or the general law of indifference as difference as such. Indifference as a whole, echoing the Hegelian dialectic, is not a concept at all but a dynamic process of movement across and between specific indifference and general indifference. This movement is the overall suspension of proper and common in favour of singularity which is a nonparticular differentiation which, however, keeps in play all the particulars of a being so as to refrain from becoming and abstract general law.

2. Agamben, *Coming Community*, 107.

3. Although indifference falls from the agenda of the sustained criticisms of Agamben's work, he was well served in his early commentators, Hardt, Wall and Düttman, all of whom see early on the significance of indifferent suspension to Agamben's work, although none of them use this precise terminology. See Hardt's notes in Agamben, *Coming Community*, 107–8; Düttman's introduction in Giorgio Agamben, *Idea of Prose*, trans. Michael Sullivan and Sam Whitsitt (Albany: State University of New York Press, 1995), 3–28; and the entirety of Thomas Wall's groundbreaking study.

4. See also Giorgio Agamben, *Profanations*, trans. Jeff Fort (New York: Zone Books, 2007), 58. See also David Kishik, *The Power of Life* (Stanford, CA: Stanford University Press, 2012), 82.

5. Agamben, *Coming Community*, 1.

6. Agamben, *Coming Community*, 1.

7. I refer here to the section "Perception: Or the Thing and Deception", in G. W. F. Hegel, *The Phenomenology of Spirit*, trans. A. V. Miller (Oxford: Oxford University Press, 1977), 67–79.

8. See Robert Stern, *Hegel and the Phenomenology of Spirit* (London: Routledge, 2002), 51–56.

9. Agamben, *Coming Community*, 1.

10. Agamben, *Coming Community*, 1–2.

11. Indeed, Badiou himself notices the proximity of terminology in his detailed response to the piece Alain Badiou, "Intervention dans le cadre du Collège international de philosophie sur le livre de Giorgio Agamben: *La Communauté qui vient, théorie de la singularité quelconque*", http://www.entretemps.asso.fr/Badiou/Agamben.htm.

12. Agamben, *Coming Community*, 9. He is pointedly using the same notation as Badiou here.

13. I have no time to trace this here, but *The Coming Community* is in critical dialogue with three thinkers with whom at this time Agamben still seems to be in sympathy but not in agreement, namely, Badiou and his theory of the event, Deleuze and his theory of immanent vitalism, and Nancy's theory of singular community. Agamben is clearly influenced by Nancy, with whom it is reported he has been very close. For example, he debates one of Nancy's central concepts, communicability, through Nancy's conceptions of the common in Giorgio Agamben, *Means without Ends*, trans. Vincenzo Binetti and Cesare Casarino (Minneapolis: University of Minnesota Press, 2000), 115–17.

14. Agamben, *Coming Community*, 9.

15. This is the significance of forcing in set theory. See Alain Badiou, *Being and Event*, trans. Oliver Feltham (London: Continuum, 2005), secs. 35 and 36, and Christopher Norris, *Badiou's Being and Event* (London: Continuum, 2009), 68–69.

16. Agamben, *Coming Community*, 9–10.

17. Agamben, *Coming Community*, 17.

18. Agamben, *Coming Community*, 17.

19. Agamben, *Coming Community*, 17.

20. Agamben, *Coming Community*, 17–18. This is a good example of the overlay of the different themes of Agamben's critique of metaphysics. Ostensibly talking about

singularity, the example of the human, immediately implicates this abstract debate in essential and current debates as regards the biopolitical sphere of modern democracy.

21. Agamben, *Coming Community*, 18–19.
22. Agamben, *Coming Community*, 2.
23. Agamben, *Coming Community*, 2.
24. Although a common synonym for indifference is disinclination, within our systems this smacks too much, at times, of not wanting out of dislike. As our prephilosophical conception traces how simply not being inclined one way or another habitually takes on the apotropaic dialectic of wanting X out of active not wanting Y, I will use the term "noninclination" here to make it clear we are speaking of not being inclined towards and nothing more.
25. Agamben, *Coming Community*, 19.
26. Agamben, *Coming Community*, 19.
27. Agamben, *Coming Community*, 19.
28. Agamben, *Coming Community*, 20.
29. See Maurice Blanchot, *The Work of Fire*, trans. Charlotte Mandell (Stanford, CA: Stanford University Press, 1995), 332–33.
30. Agamben, *Coming Community*, 20.
31. See William Watkin, *The Literary Agamben: Adventures in Logopoiesis* (London: Continuum, 2010), 142–44.
32. See Giorgio Agamben, *Potentialities*, trans. Daniel Heller-Roazen (Stanford, CA: Stanford University Press, 1999), 48–61.
33. Cited in Agamben, *Coming Community*, 71.
34. For an overview of Heidegger's version that there is no word for the word, see Giorgio Agamben, *Language and Death: The Place of Negativity*, trans. Karen E. Pinkus with Michael Hardt (Minneapolis: University of Minnesota Press, 1991), 61–62.
35. By which we mean the axiom of the void set; see Badiou, *Being and Event*, 66–69.
36. Agamben, *Coming Community* , 72.
37. Agamben, *Coming Community*, 73.
38. Agamben, *Coming Community*, 73.
39. Agamben, *Coming Community*, 73–74.
40. See Agamben, *Potentialities*, 27–38.
41. Agamben, *Coming Community*, 75.
42. Agamben, *Coming Community*, 75–76. While I concentrate on the relation of Aristotelian homonym to the self-predication paradox, another key source for this work is of course that of Jean-Claude Milner. Agamben is indebted to Milner and Benveniste throughout his early work, although his relationship to them is both respectful and critical.
43. Agamben, *Coming Community*, 76.
44. Agamben, *Coming Community*, 76.
45. Agamben, *Coming Community*, 76.
46. Agamben, *Coming Community*, 47.
47. Giorgio Agamben, *The Time That Remains*, trans. Patricia Dailey (Stanford, CA: Stanford University Press, 2005), 145.
48. See Agamben's clarification on this error in Giorgio Agamben, *Ninfe* (Torino: Bollati Boringhieri, 2008), 41.
49. Agamben, *The Time That Remains*, 68–69.
50. Agamben, *The Time That Remains*, 69.
51. Agamben, *The Time That Remains*, 69.
52. Agamben, *Coming Community*, 23.
53. Agamben, *Coming Community*, 24.
54. Agamben, *Coming Community*, 25.
55. Agamben, *Coming Community*, 54.
56. Agamben, *Coming Community*, 56.
57. Agamben, *Coming Community*, 56.
58. Agamben, *Coming Community*, 56.

59. Agamben, *Coming Community*, 14–15.
60. Agamben, *Coming Community*, 67.
61. Agamben, *Coming Community*, 67.
62. Agamben, *Coming Community*, 67.
63. Agamben, *Coming Community*, 68.
64. Agamben, *Coming Community*, 10.

FIVE

Towards a Deictic Ontology or Being-Thus As-Such

The Coming Community is a profound consideration of ethics, a fact we have bracketed so as to access its second use as the foundational text of singular indifference or being-whatever. It is also a sustained consideration of the golden age of German prose, both Kafka and one of Agamben's favourite authors, Robert Walser.[1] Many of the essays turn to Walser's oddly indifferent prose. In particular Agamben is interested in how Walser's characters exist in limbo. They are, he says, "irreparably astray . . . in a region beyond perdition and salvation". They are self-consciously null, he contends, because there is nothing in them that can be saved. It is because of this nullity that Agamben says, "The irreparable is the monogram that Walser's writing engraves into things",[2] by which he means the elements of Walser's fictional world as consigned to pure being-thus, precisely what they are, no more and no less. The fictional elements in Walser are not aggregations towards some totalizing realism or symbols of something exterior to the world presented. Walser himself showed remarkable prescience in this regard when he spoke of his own "fascination of not uttering something absolutely",[3] laying down a law for indifferent prose which has yet to come to its fruition in the kitsch, late realism of the contemporary moment of the novel. Yet what is the language of the nonabsolute? Agamben calls it, in an essay of the same name, "Pseudonym."

PSEUDONYM[4]

"Pseudonym" precedes the essay "Homonym" in *The Coming Community*, yet its full significance in relation to the total schema of indifference is apparent only after coming to terms with naming and anonymous homonym. The essay begins with an excellent summary of Agamben's position on linguistic indifference and its direct relation to the discipline and history of Western thought at least since Plato:

> Every lament is always a lament for language, just as all praise is principally praise of the name. These are the extremes that define the domain and scope of human language, its way of referring to things. Lament arises when nature feels betrayed by meaning; when the name perfectly says the thing, language culminates in the song of praise, in the sanctification of the name. Robert Walser's language seems to ignore them both.[5]

There is a direct reference here to the later work of Heidegger on poetry of course, especially his work in *The Ister*, where he considers Hölderlin's contribution, via the hymn, to the history of the songs of praise in contrast to those of lament (Agamben will pick up the topic of the hymn in *The Kingdom and the Glory* many years later). Thus, the very history of literature echoes that of language (here we mean Language as signature) and thinking. Each demonstrates a clear dialectical process with lament being the process of commonalisation which we might term archetypal philosophical reduction coming to its end point with Husserl and Heidegger and praise being absolute propriety, the perfect coincidence between name and world. The significance of Walser's prose, in being archetypally indifferent, is its renunciation of the terms of the dialectic. While in the West, according to Agamben, "language has constantly been used as a machine to bring into being the name of God and to found in the name its own power of reference", for Walser, "language has outlived its theological task".[6] Walser's is a prose neither of absolute meanings nor of realistic specificity; his work names neither God (the common) nor the world (the proper). It is, in this sense, a zone of perfect indistinction: the prose of indifference.

Would that Agamben termed it thus, perhaps life would be easier. However, instead of naming it indifferent prose as I have done, he calls it the language of the pseudonym or nickname: "It is as if every word were preceded by an invisible 'so-called,' 'pseudo-,' and 'would-be'",[7] almost as if every term raised an objection against its own denominative power. Such a pseudonymity results in a literature of exhaustion: "If any grammatical form corresponds to this exhausted state of language it is the supine, that is, a word that has completely achieved its 'declension' in cases and moods and is now 'stretched out on its back,' exposed and neutral".[8] The pseudonym exists, of course, in relation to the synonym and the homonym but operates at a different level of modality, I would contend. In one sense it is synonymity in that it finds a new name, a nickname for something. On the other hand it is homonymy, at least in Aristotelian terms, in that it draws attention to the very being-named of nomination: the so-called in all acts of being-named. Pseudonymity combines, therefore, the failure of individuation and universality within the process of naming in a clear, self-conscious and everyday manner.[9]

The nickname is ubiquitous and is the human means of indicating the fundamental being in indifference of the human in that the nickname is a synonymity of concept that introduces a homonymity of idea. The name both refers to the person as such and flags up that this is not their actual name but something they are being-called. Yet in a sense it operates in opposition to the anonymous homonymity of the anaphora of 'itself' in that while anaphora uses a neutral term to refer back to a specific name, 'he' instead of 'Walser', for example, the pseudonym operates in a very different fashion. It is not a process of generalised and retroactive nomination, the trace of synonymous 'Walser' in the anonymous 'he', but of specific, redemptive renomination. In adding an extra name to Walser, a pseudonym, one does not name naming as-such, but one ties the thing down to an extra nominal specificity: you name the same thing twice, making it more than specific but less than abstract. That this is a redemptive gesture is perhaps here less than clear in that it relates to the final, most central category of this extraordinary text: the irreparable.

THE IRREPARABLE

Of the two essays with this name in the book, the first considers yet another theological problem of scholastic thought, Saint Thomas's consideration of the nature of the world after its final judgement. If, the saint wonders, the world was set up to fit imperfect humanity, what is the role of nature after the final act of human perfection? Walser's answer, Agamben believes, which we have already perused, is that "all will be just as it is, irreparably, but precisely this will be its novelty". Irreparable means both that things "are consigned without remedy to their being-thus, that they are precisely and only their *thus*", but also that "in their being-thus they are absolutely exposed, absolutely abandoned".[10] The state of being-thus of irreparable redemption, the absolute thus-ness of naming the same thing twice, one with its actual name and one with its not-actual name, means that necessity and contingency disappear in the world of redemption. "The world is now and forever necessarily contingent or contingently necessary. Between the *not being able to not-be* that sanctions the decree of necessity and the *being able to not-be* that defines fluctuating contingency, the finite world suggests a contingency to the second power that does not found any freedom: It *is capable of not not-being*, it is capable of the irreparable".[11]

I would imagine this needs some gloss. One can see here that necessity names thus-ness: this is thus. Naming therefore nominates thus-ness; this horse in being named horse is thus a horse or, rather, is thus a being-

named horse. Yet it is also contingent, as the previous formulation suggests. Naming is a convention in the world of signification and representation that we have lived in for several thousand years. The name is
added to the thing over time and is therefore contingent. Naming the
horse is simply the horse as thing rendered as the horse as being-named
horse. Yet within contingency there is necessity: the horse, to be rendered
as thing for thought, must be named, so being-named is necessary. (One
might say necessary for presentation leaving aside here the determinants
for the necessity of a presentation except to say that in the system of
communicability at least one presentation must occur, the communicable
state as such.) Similarly within necessity, this thing is named thus as the
thing it cannot otherwise be, there is contingency; absolute thus-ness is in
fact not horse-ness but the actual, singular thus-ness of everything.

Everything has a potential pseudonym in that to truly render any
thing in language as the thing it is, it must be both what it is named as
being, a horse, a man, red, and an additional name which presents it as
more than that: he is my classmate John Smith, but he is also Smithy.
There is an empty space beside every name, which is filled both with its
generality, every name is also abstractly being-named, and with a more-
than-specific specificity, it will always need an extra name to specify its
actual specificity. In this fashion every pseudonym, which is 'onymous',
is also an-onymous. In a very odd turn of logic, in finding extra names for
things, one renders them singularly and indifferently anonymous.

This is the logic of the irreparable thus-ness: extra-specific nomination
reveals at the same juncture generalised anonymity; being named an extra name reveals also the general, indifferent linguistic mode of the being-
named. And it is here that the irreparable transgresses in the space of
indifference as adjacent and all around. In a sense this is a representation
of certain tendencies across Foucault, Deleuze and Agamben to differentiate language from the simple act of nomination. Put simply, every act of
language is a statement, not a word (even if it is just one word), operating
in terms of an enunciative position (not being simply a subject) whose
'meaning' is determined by its happening within a context that also
makes said context occur. It is then the communicable operativity of every utterance, not what it means but that it means or not what it means but
that it matters (to paraphrase first Foucault and then Deleuze), that determines its irreparable statement of necessary, contingent thus-ness. One
might abstract even further, provided that the reader is now conversant
with the centrality of indicative deixis in all these debates, and say not
this but thus or, better, every this is as-thus.

In a recent essay on "Parody," Agamben traces the origin of the term
to the breaking of the harmony between speech and song in Greek poetry
so that the singing produces discordant melodies which are said to be
singing *"para tēn ōidēn,* against (or beside) the song".[12] Parody then was
the moment of arising of prose in that it was the first moment of loosen-

ing (differentiating through oppositional schism) the coincidence of speech and song, *logos* and *melos*: "It is precisely this parodic loosening of the traditional link between music and *logos* that made possible the art of prose with Georgias. Breaking this link liberates a *para*, a space beside, in which prose takes place".[13] If prose is easeful, operating in the space of ease to one side, it is also haloic, as the closing lines of the first irreparable essay show. In speaking of the world of irreparable redemption, Agamben answers Saint Thomas's question via the parodic prose of Walser: in the redeemed world all of nature will appear in a state of incorruptible "fallenness—above them floats something like a profane halo".[14]

As the second essay in question here, "Appendix: The Irreparable," is presented as fragments, I will take the liberty of merely enumerating the various properties of the term as they are presented almost aphoristically by way of an interim conclusion:

- The irreparable is "things just as they are."
- According to Spinoza what is essential to the irreparable is "that every cause of doubt has been removed."
- It is "pure *being-thus* without any attributes."
- What changes in the redemption into irreparability is not things but their limits, "as if there hovered over them something like a halo."
- It is neither "an essence nor an existence . . . neither a possibility nor a necessity" and so on.
- "It is not properly a modality of being, but it is the being that is always already given in modality, that *is* its modalities. It is not *thus*, but rather it *its* thus".[15]

Thus is being-thus.

DEICTIC ONTOLOGY: THE THUS AND THE AS-SUCH[16]

I think the arguments surrounding the irreparable state are familiar enough to us now, as each refers to a state pertaining to the metaphysics of indifference as it is present in Agamben. Further, we will have to return to these issues one more time in relation to the relevancy of redemption in *The Kingdom and the Glory*. Therefore, we will linger no longer in the neutral and impassive defiles of irreparable prose, with the proviso that a true theory of para-prose or of prose as such is yet to be written, and without it our current understanding of this world of prose is severely lacking.[17] Instead, I want to ease to closure by concentrating on two anaphoric ontological devices in relation to the irreparable state of singular indifference: the thus and the as-such.

For Agamben, thus or, rather, being-thus means "not otherwise", the very thus-ness of being standing not as a predicate for a presupposed being, all being must be thus, that is, what it singularly is and not otherwise, but instead "*is* its *thus*". This quality of the presence of singular being is a modification of one of the fundamental qualities of ontology: quiddity or that it is. As we saw in our earlier considerations of singularity and haecceity, being-thus is not simply that it is but also that it is something in its singularity (it is thus to a singular situation). Thus-ness therefore is not an abstract quality that links all species of being, that is, every being, to a general genus Being, namely, what possesses quiddity, but is always a specific what-ness, that which saves particularity and generality from their traditional paradoxical relationship by the insistence of a disseminating singularity rather than an appropriating *Ereignis*, as one appears to find in Heidegger. Thus-ness indeed questions the necessity for an ontico-ontological difference. If this is the case, Agamben, who is well schooled in the ways of ontology and its strict logic, wonders if within this tradition, which also means in relation to ontology in general, as for him there is no thought outside of archaeology, as we have seen, "can one conceive of a being-thus that negates all possibilities, every predicate—that is, only the *thus*, such as it is, and no other way?"[18]

He rapidly admits that such a being is a kind of negative theology but does not shy away from this traditional riposte, instead concluding, "*Not otherwise* negates each predicate as a property (on the plane of essence), but takes them up again as im-properties or improprieties (on the plane of existence). (Such a being would be a pure, singular and yet perfectly whatever existence)".[19] This then is the final throw of the dice of Agamben's high-risk gamble that will not come to fruition for two decades with the publication of *Altissima povertá* and its consideration of nonproprietary use. The greatest of all suspensions, the most powerful of all indifference, ontological indifference (not least because it allows indifference to supplant Heideggerian difference and of course sets Agamben apart from his great contemporary Badiou), is to be located in this small, anaphoric act of deixis: thus.

Agamben's quarry here is not the valorisation of negativity, absence or weakness. For Agamben impotentiality is not weakness but the origin of real strength, so here the being-thus as the not-otherwise is not simply that being must be defined by being not-otherwise, the classic gambit that a sign is defined as the not-being of all other signs in the system. This is because being-thus and, as we shall also see, the as-such are modes of deixis which suspend the very basis of all indication at the heart of abstract thought. It seems odd that it all comes down to this. Deixis and anaphora are, after all, only technical terms within linguistics that do not say anything about language as such, as, say, the theory of signs or generative grammar do, but merely show one of the local operations in language: how language indicates.

Indication is sparse. It is not even denoting. It is merely pointing. More than that, such devices are almost invisible within discourse: he, she, it, that, this, now, then, thus, as and so on. They are bald conveniences either referring to a much richer experience exterior to language, the world out there, or anterior to language, the original meaning or being of which he, she and it are shorthand. That a total reappraisal of ontology through indifference should depend on deixis seems almost a crime to the rich language of all our philosophers with their marvellous networks of categories, neologisms and reinventions. Can the suspension of ontology depend solely on the operations of such a technical footnote to the history of linguistics?

If it can, then the clue here comes from Agamben's earlier work on deixis and anaphora in *Infancy and History* and *Language and Death*. In the first of these two texts, for example, deixis provides a crucial moment in Agamben's discovery of the moment of arising of scission within our history of language as signification and the potential for its suspension. Deictics, or, as Jacobson and Benveniste term them, deictic shifters, have a special role in structural linguistics, the crowning moment of the long history of signification in the West. In that Saussure stipulates that the signified and the signifier, although bound together, are radically hetero-geneous, he is merely rehearsing the history of metaphysics and its divi-sion of common meaning from proper matter. Yet with deixis the pos-sibility of suspending this radical difference right at the heart of the very essence of its perpetration, language as signification, makes itself present.

The deictic 'it', for example, in 'there it is', refers to a thing in the world; thus, it is pure signified. As indication, therefore, deixis and anaphora are entirely exhausted materially by their pure referentiality. That said, deixis itself carries no meaning of its own. It is not a name but an indication of a thing which can be named in the world, deixis proper, or which has already been named, anaphoric deixis. In this sense it is a sign without referent or, by definition, pure semiotics. In addition, the possibility, in literature, of references to things in the world which are not in the world but merely discursive and references back to events that never occurred means that deixis can be both meaning without matter and matter without meaning. That deixis shifts from common to proper is its linguistic interest, that, as is shown in *Language and Death*, modern thought is based on the use of deixis to render being as ineffable lan-guage, is philosophically explosive, as here deixis is not merely a shifter; it is a suspender: deixis suspends difference through its application of indifference.

It is more complex than this. As the analysis of Leopardi's *"L'Infinito"* in "The Seventh Day" chapter of *Language and Death* shows, deixis must always be cut across by anaphora. Anaphora, reference back to a preced-ing originary term, and its sister concept cataphora, reference forward to the arrival of the originary term, take deixis from the simple, shuttling back-and-forth of local indifference to the verticality of indifference in general. As I have already written extensively on this section of Agam-ben's work, forgive me if I refer the reader to that passage for the detail and rush, instead, to its relevancy for ontology. In *"L'infinito"*, Agamben notes, the insistent deixis of the poem which begins specifically with *questo*, *"This* lonely knoll", and then becomes general and externalised by a distribution of "that" and "there" already emulates the structure of indifference: both proper, this, and common, that there. Indeed, the first line, *"This* lonely knoll *was* ever dear to me", by implication, sets up this dynamic in that we effectively read it as *"This* lonely knoll *that* was ever dear to me". More than this, the spatial referentiality of the poem is always already temporal. The poem begins, citing the Italian version now, *"Sempre caro mi fu quest'ermo colle / e questa siepe, che da tante parte / dell'ultimo orrizonte il guardo esclude"* (This lonely knoll was ever dear to me, / and this hedgerow that hides from view / so large a part of the remote horizon), thus instigating the law of poetry for Agamben which is "a place of memory and repetition". The place of the poem, its "this", will not only therefore shift to the place that is not the poem, "that", via deixis, but also always shift from the place of the poem to its temporality. Thus, here the famous "knoll", of greater actual significance than any other knoll in history after the one made famous by the violence of Dallas, is already recollected, while the metaphysical hedgerow, *siepe*, which actually means hedge or hurdle, provides a point of separation between the now of recollection and the to-be of the poet's reflections on infinity. Here deixis refers to the time of indication and as such is operating already, functionally, as anaphora. This is confirmed by Agamben's analysis of the manner in which the poem's last line, *"e il naufragar m'e dolce in questo mare"* (and in this sea is foundering sweet to me) recalls that of the first line, making the whole poem a complex circle of interreferentiality.[20]

Having presented the main elements of Agamben's interest in deixis and its relation to anaphora, we can return to *The Coming Community*, where, in trying to define the pure being-thus as, you recall, that which negates all predicates, Agamben likens it to "an anaphora that no longer refers back to any meaning or any referent".[21] Such an anaphora without presupposition, there are innumerable examples in poetry of course, would, he contends, require that we rethink entirely deixis and anaphora, the examples of ostension and relation, and in so doing rethink philosophy, which, he believes, has relied on these modes to determine being since its inception. Pure being, for example, has always been rendered by ostension, "what is presupposed is the immediate being-there of a non-linguistic element, which language cannot say but only show",[22] while in anaphora reference is to a term already mentioned so that the presupposition is an already existent meaning providing the model for essence and meaning. Here Agamben then binds together the two modalities into a matrix that, for me, captures the structural essence of indifference in all its levels of operation. I will cite the section in full for this reason:

The pronoun, through *deixis*, presupposes relationless being and, through anaphora, makes that being "the subject" of discourse. Thus anaphora presupposes ostension, and ostension refers back to anaphora (insofar as *deixis* presupposes an instance of discourse): They imply each other (This is the origin of the double meaning of the term *ousia*: the single ineffable individual and the substance underlying its predicates). The originary fracture of being in essence and existence, meaning and denotation is thus expressed in the double meaning of the pronoun, without the relationship between these terms ever coming to light as such. What needs to be conceived here is precisely this relation that is neither denotation nor meaning, neither ostension nor anaphora, but rather their reciprocal implication . . . it is the being-in-language-of-the-non-linguistic . . . not the presupposition of a being, but its exposure.[23]

Behold the modality of the thus, facilitated by the metrical interchange or what he calls implication or the model of indifference that I have repeatedly emphasised. Deixis is the indifference of singular nonlinguistic difference as manifested in the being-named. Anaphora is then a planar, multidimensional interindication within language that makes language exterior to itself in that discourse takes discourse as its externality. Indifference at the local level of the name or deixis, pure ostension, is always already implicated in the medium of discursivity. Yet discourse cannot refer to itself without the presupposition of ostension, just as ostension cannot occur without anaphoric interdiscursive indication. As we have seen, the two levels of indifference are also the two levels of poetry, typified in Leopardi as the metrical musical element of interchange between poetic memory and repetition. Memory is ostensive deixis, the presupposition of the nonlinguistic thing as the basis of naming. Every name is a memory of a thing in that the thing always precedes it. Repetition is anaphora, the intermediate repetition of the already existent name, which, however, makes the name into a thing of reference.

This leaves us with the following, perplexing and counterintuitive position. Proper indifference and common indifference are two levels of a third indifference. Proper indifference indifferentiates proper and common in terms of qualities. Common indifference indifferentiates proper and common as such in all signatory situations. But then finally, proper indifference and common indifference indifferentiate each other, disallowing either position one of the following metaphysical options:

- Neither is originary.
- Neither is a teleological totalization.
- Neither is a dialectic.
- The two together are not a unity.
- The system cannot be subdivided *ad infinitum* into an infinite, abstract analytical multiplicity of ones.

- The system cannot proliferate infinitely outwards in Hegelian bad infinity.
- The system of indifference, therefore, referring back to the original problem of first-order indifference, does not need a stop to be placed on it, a judgement, a transcendent metaphysics. It stops itself.

AS SUCH

In terms of as-such, the next level of the debate, the logic is the same but this time applied to naming as such rather than reference as such, in other words, anaphora as deixis rather than, in thus-ness, deixis that becomes anaphora. Therefore, when Agamben explains the logic of as-such, one can recognise its structural similarity to that of being-thus:

> As such. Here the anaphora "as" does not refer to the preceding refe-
> rential tem (to a prelinguistic substance), and "such" does not serve to
> indicate a referent that gives "as" its meaning. "Such" has no other
> existence than "as," and "as" has no other essence than "such". . . . (The
> anaphoric relation is being played out here between the named thing
> and its being named . . .).[24]

I think we have the measure of this argument from previous considerations of being-named, and all we need add here is the following: "The
such does not presupposed the *as*; it exposes it, it is its taking-place. . . .
The *as* does not suppose the *such*; it is its exposure, its being pure exteriority".[25]

Here all the strands of the metaphysics of indifference come together
in the conclusion to this section of the essay on the maxim: "The being-
such of each thing is the idea",[26] which forms a complex bookend with
our opening maxim: the coming being is whatever being. We can now
synthesise the two statements to read as follows: the coming being is
whatever being as the being-such of the idea. This leads Agamben to a
number of conclusions on the singularity of indifferent being which project forward to the methodology that does not come to full expression for
another two decades. First, he says that the knowability of each entity, for
which we now read communicability or intelligibility, is as if detached
from it but not to such a degree that it becomes a separate entity. At the
heart of being there is no ontico-ontological split, as it has been crudely
represented out of early Heidegger, nor of course is there a split between
word and world in the form of signification. Communicability of being is
not dominated by an ontological or signifying division of common and
proper, yet, as we see, there is a division here. Agamben goes on to state
that the form of communicability, he calls it *intentio*, angel, image, is
neither simply existential nor transcendent, beings or Being, but operates
according to a "para-existence" or "para-transcendence" that is located

alongside the thing in the same status as the place of ease or the halo. As such it does not constitute the self-present identity of the thing, its repeatability as the common of a singularity; it cannot be because it is outside of the thing, an unnecessary supplement, yet because the proximity is so close that the para-existent almost merges with the thing, it is nothing other than the thing. He calls it the *"none-other"*.[27] Therefore, he concludes, the existence of the idea is paradigmatic, but, and here is perhaps the first really significant example of the logic of indifference in its full manifestation in Agamben's work, "this showing beside itself is a limit — or rather, it is the unravelling, the indetermination of a limit: a halo".[28]

This final statement is a warning shot and a lesson in how to read Agamben. Having spent a hundred pages seemingly constructing an ontology of indifferent singularity, he then undercuts this with his final comments. Up to this point perhaps, we might have been justified in finding a credible alternative to the ontologies of self-presence or self-difference on offer within the tradition, especially as the engagement with Russell, Frege and Wittgenstein in these pages seems to recuperate the question of being from the landfill of pseudoproblems over which the gulls of analytical philosophy wheel in mockery. And to some degree, as we find in Badiou, Agamben is attempting to relegitimate the question of ontology from within the continental tradition in its totality, suggesting that the question of being can be asked of being through the simple question: what is being or what is the being of all beings?

If this were so, then an ontology based on the dual modifications of existential, ontico, factical beings in the form of being-such and of transcendental, ontological, abstract Being in the form of as-such would be the proposition of offer. On its own that would be remarkable enough, taking the ontico-ontological split, revising it through the scholastic tradition, to provide a more subtle reading of the two positions should be sufficient to guarantee a place in the crumbling pantheon of ontological thinkers. Yet, as Agamben concludes, such a reading makes being in terms of its communicability haloic, that is, unnecessary, evanescent and inexistent. Instead, what the impossible para-existence of the halo shows is the indetermination of a limit, not a reinvigoration of a division such as would be possible if ontic-beings became being-thus and Being as such became the as-such. Instead, being as a problem of indifferent singularity, whatever being as the book began by foretelling, is not the future solution to the problem of being such as Badiou promises but the final indifferentiation of being through the indeterminacy of the problem of singularity. If the coming being is whatever being, then such a being must be the being-such of its communicability, and all ontology from this point on must be an ontology of epistemology, a position Badiou clearly refutes. As such it must be subject to the same laws of discourse, in this instance the logic of the paradigm.

Inasmuch as each being operates as a paradigm to itself, the problem of being is not a pseudoproblem but a problem. Each being operates, through singularity and whatever singularity, as a paradigm of itself so that that ontico-ontological difference becomes the ontico-ontological in-difference. First, because each being is a parody of being, a paradigm of the set of one, a halo, and so each being is subject to the indifferent law of the paradigm as I have outlined it. Second, because each being is also a signature of itself, a contentless physical presence that sanctions existential significance but has none of its own. This ontological signature allows being to subsist, to move through time, to operate in innumerable discursive contexts, all discursive contexts in fact; it sanctions every enunciative position, and finally it allows for the operativity of all existence inasmuch as all existence is defined here as knowability or, as we prefer, communicability. What each being carries with it then is not so much the split between immanence and transcendence, existential versus consistent being, but the indifferentiation of said split. In operating as both the paradigm of itself and the signatory sanction of its consistent existence, the coming being is truly indifferent being or the suspension of being through the indifferent logic of its double singularity: its self-present thus-ness and its consistent as-suchness. Between the thus and the such, therefore, we find being's full communicability as the indifference between the ontico and the ontological, which one could read as a radical critique of Heidegger.

Alternatively, after a consideration of the real nature of difference in terms of being as the self-belonging of the difference within each being of the equal with the same such as I presented in the our reading of Heidegger, is not *The Coming Community* simply the full realisation of Heideggerian ontology as second-order indifference, suspended by the indifference of the indetermination of a limit? In crowning Heidegger with a halo, Agamben both celebrates and renders inoperative the ontology of difference and opens the way for a sustained critique of the entirety of the philosophy of difference through his radical engagements with its two most prominent executors: Jacques Derrida and Gilles Deleuze.

NOTES

1. See also Giorgio Agamben, *Profanations*, trans. Jeff Fort (New York: Zone Books, 2007), 31.

2. Giorgio Agamben, *The Coming Community*, trans. Michael Hardt (Minneapolis: University of Minnesota Press, 1993), 39.

3. Cited in Agamben, *Coming Community*, 60.

4. See also Giorgio Agamben, *Remnants of Auschwitz: The Witness and the Archive*, trans. Daniel Heller-Roazen (New York: Zone Books, 2002), 131–32.

5. Agamben, *Coming Community*, 59.

6. Agamben, *Coming Community*, 59.

7. Agamben, *Coming Community*, 59.

8. Agamben, *Coming Community,* 60.

9. Consider the related issue of the proper name in Giorgio Agamben, *The End of the Poem,* trans. Daniel Heller-Roazen (Stanford, CA: Stanford University Press, 1999), 70.

10. Agamben, *Coming Community,* 39. See also Giorgio Agamben, *Means without Ends,* trans. Vincenzo Binetti and Cesare Casarino (Minneapolis: University of Minnesota Press, 2000), 11–12.

11. Agamben, *Coming Community,* 40.

12. Agamben, *Profanations,* 39. See Colby Dickinson, *Agamben and Theology* (London: Continuum, 2011), 32.

13. Agamben, *Profanations,* 40. A similar argument is made by Godzich and Kittay when they trace the rise of prose in relation to the use of deixis as a means of referring to someone or something over there, in the real world. For more on this, see William Watkin, "The Materialization of Prose: Poiesis versus Dianoia in the Work of Godzich & Kittay, Schklovsky, Silliman and Agamben," *Paragraph* 31, no. 3 (2008): 344–64.

14. Agamben, *Profanations,* 40.

15. Agamben, *Coming Community,* 90–92.

16. The operativity of the as-x construction is yet to be fully considered in Agamben, although I commence the study here. A more complete consideration would also include structures such as as-if and as-not within the wider philosophical context, Kant certainly, such as is presented in Giorgio Agamben, *The Time That Remains,* trans. Patricia Dailey (Stanford, CA: Stanford University Press, 2005), 37–38, 42–43. Specifically here Agamben relates impotentiality to living as-if, and, as we make a case here that impotentiality is really a paradigm of the function of indifference, naturally indifference and as-if is a topic for future scholarship to take up. See Agamben, *Time That Remains,* 38.

17. See Watkin, "Materialization of Prose".

18. Agamben, *Coming Community,* 93.

19. Agamben, *Coming Community,* 94.

20. See William Watkin, *The Literary Agamben: Adventures in Logopoiesis* (London: Continuum, 2010), 126–34.

21. Agamben, *Coming Community,* 94.

22. Agamben, *Coming Community,* 95.

23. Agamben, *Coming Community,* 95–96.

24. Agamben, *Coming Community,* 96.

25. Agamben, *Coming Community,* 98.

26. Agamben, *Coming Community,* 101.

27. Agamben, *Coming Community,* 101.

28. Agamben, *Coming Community,* 101.

Part II

Difference and Indifference

SIX

Derrida and Agamben: *Différance* Makes Indifference Communicable

A mark of Derrida's power is also evidence of the limits to his thinking; namely, of all the major philosophers of our age, he is the only one to demonstrate no clear relation to a conceptualisation of indifference. This is a peculiar observation in that Derrida's work owes such a great deal to Hegel's dialectic and Heidegger's concept of difference, both of which I have shown are unthinkable without indifference. Further, two thinkers who clearly hold powerful sway over the development of Derrida's work on alterity and literature, Levinas and Blanchot, respectively, are widely lauded for their theories of indifferent neutrality: Levinas's *il y a* and Blanchot's neuter. Yet the observation is correct; not only does Derrida rarely use the term "indifference" or any of its synonyms, but, more significantly, he does not have a structural dependence on indifferent states of any form unlike, say, Deleuze. That said, the conversation between Attridge and Derrida, "That Strange Institution Called Literature," is organised in significant portion around the idea of a suspended relation which we must now concede is a standard formulisation of any philosophy of indifference. This then seems to present an ideal opportunity to clarify Derrida's relation to indifference in preparation for the more tricky task of then teasing apart Derrida and Agamben.

Speaking of the so-called two literatures,[1] Literature as institutional convention and literature as disruptive inventive singularity, Derrida gives us this final definition of the oscillating logic of the literary: no self-present convention without the irruption of alterity in the form of invention, no pure singularity of invention as difference without the purity of singularity being immediately rendered impure by the famous logic of iteration.[2] Specifically Derrida says, "There is no literature without a *suspended* relation to meaning and reference. *Suspended* means *suspense*, but also *dependence*, condition, conditionality. In its suspended condition, literature can only exceed itself".[3] This exhortation must give one such as I have become whilst riding the juggernaut of indifference in these pages pause for thought. Specifically the question arises, Is not this tantamount to Agamben's theories on indifference? A question that is umbilically linked to another demand: in fact, is not Agamben's system of metaphysical critique of opposition, nothing other than another way of presenting Derridean *différance*?

If one may in a spirit of collegial leniency be given permission to abstract out from this a little and summarise the position, first in terms of convention, we are speaking here more widely as regards a metaphysics of presence, what Deleuze calls repetition and what Agamben takes as the common. Convention, Derrida argues, can never be fully self-present due to what is clearly an example of the logic of Heideggerian self-belonging. Even in Being as such, as we saw, there is the difference of a thing to itself as itself. From the opposite perspective, invention, or *différance* as singularity or the event, can also never become totalising or transcendental as a principle. There can be no self-presence of *différance* because of the logic of iteration. *Différance* must be repeatable, and it must also be communicable by being defined as different against the conventions of the same. Thus, singularity is never pure difference but always difference becoming presence and difference within the context of presence.[4] This then becomes the famous oscillation in Derrida: the much-spoken-of deconstruction of presence by *différance* and the less transparent but just as crucial impossibility of a transcendental difference due to the inevitability and ubiquity of presence.[5]

The basis of my differentiating Derrida and Agamben is that this oscillation is precisely what Agamben tries to halt, not by proposing a dialectic without *Aufhebung*, which is what Derrida promotes, but a Benjaminian-inflected dialectic at a standstill, as we saw. Yet here Derrida is clear that literature's oscillation between conventional commonality and differentiating singularity is a suspended relation. Now, specifically, Derrida is debating the relation of literary inventiveness to the conventional, thetic or referential element. The suspense is not precisely between convention and invention but is the means by which convention is 'deconstructed' by invention. Literature, he argues, although it opens on to everything (allows everything to be said and also allows one to say anything, the two senses of literature as the *tout dire*), is never reducible to any of the thetic discourses it opens on to.[6] Therefore, literature as a signature retains its own specificity, by which I mean is communicable as the signature that it is through what it allows to occur in its name. Yet at the same time this specificity, which is in fact defined by being the communicability of its presumed singularity, is, as we saw, possible only through what I would term the laws of conventional inevitability and ubiquity: convention will always infect invention because convention is the medium against which invention is communicable. And so literature's relation to meaning and reference, the transcendental thetic as Derrida calls it, represented by discourses that do not take singular invention as part of their essence, is one of nonrelational relationality, Agamben's term for indifferent relations. The conventional is conditioned by its nonrelation to the inventive, and the inventive is conditioned by its nonrelation to the conventional. For those interested in such a consonance, the logic of nonrelationality is what binds Agamben, Derrida, Deleuze and Badiou together and what negotiates their inevitable scattering.

On the basis of cobelonging then, we are able to prise apart the two thinkers in play here. For Derrida, suspended relations facilitate the oscillation between presence and difference. Thus, one can imagine that the collapse of convention into invention is facilitated by meaning's suspended relation to difference. The first suspense allows "big L" Literature to exceed itself into invention, while the second allows "small l" literature to exceed itself back into convention. In this system a double suspension produces an active oscillation due to the classical logic that the suspension of a suspension results in its negation.[7] At each end of the movement between common and proper in Derrida, what stops either convention or invention becoming totalised is this suspension, which is static, that is then suspended, producing movement. We can represent this as ((Invention suspends Convention) oscillation (Convention suspends Invention)) or more generally using repetition and singularity ((R oscillation S) oscillation (S oscillation R)) where oscillation is difference-minimum in repetition or presence-maximum in singularity brought about by a continuous interchange of suspensions resulting in constant movement. Agamben's view is of another order. For him suspension comes between identity and difference, by which we mean between difference suspended by identity, philosophies of identity and presence, and identity suspended by difference, philosophies of difference. This is because he believes that identity and difference are historically contingent conceptions intrinsic to metaphysics, while Derrida sees our persistent metaphysics as primarily that of presence, with his comments on difference more a warning not to valorise difference in place of presence (in my opinion).

A clue here is Derrida's reading of Heidegger. Only Derrida, I suspect, could read Heideggerian *difference as self-belonging* as indicative of a metaphysics of presence, marking both Derrida's genius and his perversity as a critical commentator. In doing so he negates the possibility of a philosophy of difference by suggesting this is still a philosophy of presence. In contrast, Agamben argues that Heidegger's *is* a philosophy of difference and that its relation to metaphysics is not a hidden-presence agenda but the fact that metaphysics is the philosophy of identity-difference in 'equal' measure. This is not to say that Derrida hypostatises metaphysics; he does not support metaphysics as *the* metaphysics or that metaphysics is anything other than historically contingent. Yet he does make clear in

Speech and Phenomena, in a passage we will turn to shortly, that deconstruction can come only from within metaphysics, creating the logic of
the inevitability and ubiquity of convention that, for example, later
frames his ideas on literary and poetic singularity.

Agamben instead argues that the oscillation factor (*oikonomia*) is intrinsic to metaphysics, not undermining of it. And if this is the case, it is
possible to think a consistency that is not presence repetition and a singularity that is not difference hypostatisation. In a sense then, the sustained
squabble of decades that will, I believe, compose one of two future ave-
nues for the philosophy of our age depends in this basic dispute. Derrida
uses suspension to make operative his critical oscillation that has been
called deconstruction. Agamben enforces suspension to halt this oscillation. Being generous to Derrida, Agamben's indifference is entirely dependent on the progress made in terms of Derridean *différance*. Being
philosophical, that is, caustic rather than kind, Agamben's indifference
attempts to radically reduce Derrida's doubly suspensive oscillation
model to the last gasp of the metaphysics of identity-difference.

Having described the overview of this difference, we can now see that
each attack Agamben makes on Derrida's work is based on this same
distinction. This means that while I will begin by detailing one such
attack, afterwards we can content ourselves with simply summarising the
later attacks on law, messianism and so on which are of the same order
because Derrida's consistency of approach means that Agamben's is a
consistency of critique spanning various different areas.

STANZAS AND SIGNIFICATION

Agamben launches his buoyant invective by attacking Derrida's early
work on the sign and the voice. He presents a summary of grammatology
which is that the metaphysics of presence represented in theories of signification as the signified is based on the supplemental use-suppression
of the signifier, which Agamben has Derrida calling an external trace.[8]
Installing the signifier and the trace as always already in place both allows for the possibility of metaphysics and disallows its central tenet,
namely, that of full and self-present presence. This then provides Agamben with his primary concern as regards his version of what he calls
deconstruction: "The origin is an *architrace*".[9] Agamben agrees with the
need for a crumbling of metaphysics along these lines, that is, pertaining
to signification, but he does not agree that this abrasion, such as he
presents it in Derrida's work, achieves the step-backward-beyond metaphysics that deconstruction attempts. For Agamben metaphysics never
presented a fracture of presence as a duality between signified and signifier, sensible and intelligible, but insists "rather, that the original experience be always already caught in a fold, be already simple in the etymo-

logical sense (*sim-plex,* 'once pleated'), that presence be always already caught in signification: this is precisely the origin of Western metaphysics".[10] This basic position will find full expression in the more recent work with the idea of metaphysics as the articulation of a common and proper whose initial scission is enforced precisely to facilitate said articulation. This being the case, writing and the trace are not means of deconstructing metaphysics through the deconstruction of presence in signification because they are instead the "reverse face" of metaphysics.

Putting aside the rather rapid reduction of *Of Grammatology* to a couple of sentences, Agamben's argument consists of the observation that the origin of the metaphysics of presence in signification already made extensive use of both *gramma* and *phonē*, with *gramma* being defined as reflection on language and *phonē* as writing in the soul.[11] Therefore, he argues, the letter cannot be used as a means of stepping backwards away from metaphysics because it is itself essential to the metaphysics of presence, which always included a representation in writing of the pure presence of the soul. In presenting this argument I am not agreeing with Agamben per se but simply trying to explain the justification for what he proposes in relation to Derridean concepts of trace and writing. For Agamben, the metaphysics of presence (*phonē*) is not undermined in any significant way by the philosophy of trace and writing (*gramma*), and it makes no sense to argue for the precedence of difference, whatever the term "precedence" or "origin" might mean.[12] The archi-trace, that there was always already difference, represented by Derrida as writing, writing as spacing between presentation and representation not writing as material marks, meaning that all structures of self-presence must founder on their dependence on and denial of the trace or the signifier, makes no sense to Agamben, at least not in the way Derrida presents it. For Agamben, the trace was always an acknowledged part of metaphysics, never occluded. The letter therefore is a key element of metaphysics, not a modality of its deconstruction.

In contrast to this view of the philosophy of difference, Agamben offers an alternate aspect. For Agamben the original nucleus of signification is not the assumed heterogeneity between voice and writing signified by the bar '/' between Sd/Sr "but in the fold of the presence on which they are established: the *logos,* which characterizes the human as *zoon logon echon* (living thing using language), is this fold that gathers and divides all things in the 'putting together' of presence. And the human is precisely this fracture of presence, which opens a world and over which language holds itself".[13] The totality of signification is entirely reducible to the barrier between signified and signifier. It is to be found not in either one or the other of the terms in play but in the barrier in which "we should not see merely the trace of difference, but the topological game of putting things together and articulating . . . ".[14] This amounts to saying that difference alone is not enough; it must always already be participating in another modality, that of putting together, or articulation.

Agamben then goes on to trace the history of the articulation of presence in the term *harmonia*. *Harmonia* was used by the ancients to present a just order governing the world, presence in other words, yet the term itself always referred less to a single unified entity than an articulation, the term originating from the idea of a join, say, in carpentry. Thus, harmony, metaphysical presence, always implied "the idea of a laceration that is also a suture, the idea of a tension that is both the articulation of a difference and unitary",[15] what Heraclitus calls the "invisible articulation," which is another way of saying that there is a difference which is always a one and a one which is always already differentiation. This is the articulation of harmony that is both a total unity and a fundamental difference. If this is the case then, as Agamben says in conclusion, "Only when we have arrived in the proximity of this 'invisible articulation' will we be able to say we have entered into an area from which the step-backward-beyond metaphysics, which governs the interpretation of the sign in Western thought, becomes really possible".[16] Or, Derridean deconstruction is incomplete because all it has revealed is the second aspect of the metaphysics of presence, namely, difference. Agamben does not advocate a unity before difference; rather, he promotes the deconstruction of metaphysics at its actual root, which for him is the suspension of the opposition between difference and presence that can occur only face-to-face with this originary unity, here called harmony, but which we are terming indifference.

LANGUAGE AND DEATH AND VOICE

In *Language and Death*, Agamben intensifies his assault on Derridean grammatology as a component of the metaphysics of representation as opposed to its presumed cessation. The basic argument of *Language and Death*, you may recall, is that the location of Being in our capacity for language and our finitude has resulted in an ontological nihilism typified by Heidegger's contention that Being is that which is in withdrawal. More than this, a fundamental association has been drawn up so that language and finitude are not merely the two qualities of the human, but they interact and infect each other. Thus, for Hegel and Heidegger alike, there can be no access to Being without language, yet both great men find the limitations of language as a mode of reference, especially in the rather bald deictic indicators of 'this' and 'there' (*Deise* and *Da*), become modes of limiting access to Being. The shortfall between signifier and signified and the barred access between the two, typical of Western signification, means the access to Being via language, the only access now left as credible, is always an access to it as ineffable, by which is meant simply that it cannot be rendered in full by language yet cannot be rendered by any other mode.

If language affects the access to Being, finitude also infects language so that, according to Agamben, the technical presentative nature of language in the form of the voice, simply that language has phonetically taken place, becomes something other, the failure to achieve full meaning. This second mode of the voice is capitalised in Agamben to show the parallel between beings and Being in Heidegger. Clearly what has happened here is that the immediate presentative capacity of the voice as *phonē*, writing on the soul, has, as Derrida tirelessly shows, made the voice an attractive possible means of unmediated access to Being: voice speaks Being immediately as pure presentation. However, due to the bifurcated nature of signification, no pure *phonē* exists without *gramma*; every access to Being in Voice instead becomes the inability to access Being, as its only mode of access, language, is not presentative but representative, and so Being in full is always deferred. So far Agamben is merely agreeing with Derrida:

> But inasmuch as this Voice (which we now capitalize to distinguish it from the voice as mere sound) enjoys the status of a *no-longer* (voice) and of a *not-yet* (meaning), it necessarily constitutes a negative dimension . . . the Voice discloses the place of language, but in such a way that this place is always already captured in negativity, and above all, always already consigned to temporality. *Inasmuch as it takes place in the Voice (that is, in the nonplace of the voice, in its having-been), language takes place in time. In demonstrating the instance of discourse, the Voice discloses both Being and time.*[17]

Obviously, Agamben is describing in this passage the differential trace as it is to be found in the early works of Derrida. Derrida argues consistently that Being as such can be accessed in Western metaphysics only by virtue of modes of language. Let us not say language pure and simple at this juncture, whatever that could mean, but rather those modes of language that have been called voice and writing, immediacy and mediation, presentation and representation. Derrida is well aware that any argumentation of presence, which he sees as primarily metaphysics from Plato to Husserl and Heidegger, needs a mode of mediating representation or, better, cannot operate without such a mode that is presented as nonnecessary. This presentation of the nonnecessary nature of mediating modes of language, we shall call all of these writing, is necessary to attain presence. Writing is not necessary itself to metaphysics, but the presentation of writing as nonnecessary supplement is itself necessary for presence to be formulated.

On the whole Agamben is accepting the terms of Derridean *différance* in this text yet, at the same time, is subtly moving away from Derrida here. As regards the critique of metaphysics, for example, as we saw

Agamben does not believe this is the uncovering of the impossibility of presence due to what Derrida calls writing. Agamben argues that metaphysics is not marked by the attempt to negate writing in favour of the voice and in doing so making voice as pure presence impossible but not possible as the impossible as such. Rather, ours it not a metaphysics of presence but a metaphysics of absence. Here then we can juxtapose Voice with writing. Voice is the already present realisation that Being can be accessed only through language and that language is marked by an essential, ineffable finitude. As Agamben stipulates, Voice occupies the space between the emergence of full presence in the voice, represented in our tradition by the animal voice, especially the animal voice at the instant of death in Hegel, before the arrival at meaning. Agamben takes as read that of course writing, *gramma*, is an essential component of the collapse of presence, but he feels that this revelation has forced the key thinkers of the modern age to then seek refuge in an ineffable Voice of Being as there only in withdrawal or under negation. The real work then is not the undermining of immediacy through mediation, *phonē* through *gramma*, but how one moves forward from this tradition of the metaphysics of negation.

All of this sets up the following three-page "excursus" which specifically attacks Derrida rather than the implicit critique we found in the preceding chapter. Agamben begins by adding meat to the bones of his earlier contention that *gramma* was as essential to the construction of Western metaphysics as *phonē* and thus that any grammatology is as subject to the problems of metaphysics as any other system seemingly based on the *phonē* as presence. If this is not hard enough a morsel for many to swallow, however, he goes further by suggesting, through a reading of Aristotle, that *gramma* was presented as one of the four interpreters that make up the interior of the voice. Thus, it is argued, signification, what is in the voice, is reference between all our voices and our mental experiences and all our mental experiences and things in general—and *gramma*, or writing. Agamben argues that rather than this supplement of writing being presented as of a lesser order, an afterthought, it is the very "ground that sustains the entire circle of signification".[18]

Ancient grammarians, he goes on, come to define *gramma* as the *"quantum of the signifying voice*. As a sign, and, at the same time, a constitutive element of the voice . . . the paradoxical status of an index of itself".[19] It is *gramma* and not *phonē* that is at the heart of Western reflections on language, meaning the ancient problem of metaphysics is not the necessity of *gramma* to attain *phonē* and the impossibility of this due to the logic of writing as *différance* but instead that "as a sign the *gramma* presupposes both the voice and its removal, but as an element, it has the structure of a purely negative self-affection, of a trace of itself. Philosophy responds to the question, "What is in the voice?" as follows: nothing is in the voice, the voice is the place of the negative, it is Voice—that is, pure temporality. But this negativity is *gramma*, that is, the *arthon* that articulates voice and language and thus discloses being and meaning".[20] The Voice on this reading is the pure taking-place of language, the support for every instance of language through the other three elements of significance, voice—mental experience—thing, but whose presence is always under negation. Certainly *gramma* allows for the voice, language, to occur, but only by occupying a temporality of always already having being, which is a spatiality of the taking-place of a nonspace or pure medium for language.

It is at this juncture that Agamben repeats his charge against Derrida. Derrida's critique of metaphysics is acute but incomplete. He then adds that Derrida's development of grammatology as a means of "surpassing" (this is Agamben's word) metaphysics is misguided because all it does is bring "the fundamental problem of metaphysics to light"[21] (for many this is more than sufficient!). If then, and we hold judgement on this 'if' for the present, Derrida's intention is to 'overcome' metaphysics through the *gramma*, it is destined to failure because valorisation of grammatology over phonetic-metaphysics is to "conceive of metaphysics without its co-existent negativity". Agamben then says that metaphysics, in being founded on the Voice as negated or always already absent, is a "fundamentology" in that "the *gramma* (or the Voice) functions as the negative ontological foundation".[22]

The case is now relatively clear even if, it would be fair to say, the philological evidence is limited. At least here, unlike in *Stanzas*, Agamben provides a sustained critique of the metaphysics of the Voice as negation through detailed readings of Hegel and Heidegger, and his point that *gramma* was always already a part of metaphysics is at least as plausible, essentially, as Derrida's that our metaphysics is definable by the impossibility of presence due to the supplement of writing. We are presented then with a clear antinomy or Kantian case of indifferentism. Even Agamben's argument that deconstruction takes one only so far is acceptable as it is clear that Derrida did not intend to step back beyond metaphysics to replace it with something else. His is certainly a critical rather than projective or positive philosophy. It is an impressive coup also to appropriate grammatology on behalf of metaphysics and to wrong-foot Derrida by suggesting that grammatology itself is the foundation of metaphysics. That said, we must raise the question here as to the regular contention that Agamben makes that Derrida wants to overcome metaphysics, as what is certainly clear is that any such gesture is presented by Derrida as itself metaphysical and doomed to failure. So the argument in play here is not so much the correctness of Derridean *différance*, Agamben clearly agrees with it as a structure, but whether *différance* is nihilistic, whether grammatology is a science set to overcome metaphysics and whether Derrida's philosophy is a mode favouring writing over speech. There is, I believe, considerable evidence to suggest this is not the case, yet this evidence does not then necessarily suggest the opposite either, as Agamben's critics have suggested, that Agamben misreads Derrida because he does not understand him. This, as I hope to have shown, is certainly not the case. Agamben understands grammatology as well as anyone, better than most. What is under contention is what he believes Derrida intends to make happen with grammatology. In other words, the problem is that of the process of deconstruction itself.

Before we move on, let us consider one last time the main charge of Agamben's early work against Derrida, that he uses negativity to overcome a metaphysics of presence while neglecting to consider that this negation, *gramma*, is not only a central and explicit part of metaphysics but actually its foundation. In *Speech and Phenomena*, Derrida is grappling with Husserl's attempt to escape another metaphysical bind, that between empiricism and idealism. Dismissing Husserl's brilliant solution to the problem of form versus being through the development of a "transcendental *experience* of pure consciousness," Derrida goes on to propose that in fact there is no choice to be made, adding that

> our task is rather to reflect on the circularity which makes one pass into the other indefinitely. And, by strictly repeating this *circle* in its own historical possibility, we allow the production of some elliptical change of site, within the difference involved in repetition; this displacement is no doubt deficient, but with a deficiency that is not yet, or no longer, absence, negativity, nonbeing. . . . Neither matter nor form, it is nothing that any philosopheme, that is, any dialectic . . . can capture. It is an ellipsis of both meaning and form; it is neither plenary speech nor perfectly circular.[23]

I am afraid this puts to bed any claims that Derrida is expounding a philosophy of negation, nor does the term overcoming metaphysics operate either. In fact, this displacement into a deficiency that is not yet a negativity is echoed very closely by Agamben's own use of the space to the side, the para-. Yet, at the same time, it is clearly a fact that in the great early texts Derrida is using singularity, here the difference involved in repetition, to undermine structures of presence, here a transcendental experience of pure consciousness. So that while the term 'overcoming' is unfortunate and the accusation of participating in a metaphysics of negation is clearly denied in this famous passage, the spirit of Agamben's early attacks is not entirely wrong. Derrida's work *does* favour difference over repetition, even if it does not expound a pure philosophy of difference. Like Deleuze, Derrida *does* claim that difference precedes repetition. In *"Ousia* and *Grammē"*, for example, he accepts that *différance* is perhaps older than Being, more unthought than the difference between Being and beings, and in fact "would be the first or last trace if one still could speak, here, of origin and end",[24] a point he reiterates in *Of Grammatology* and "Difference", hence Agamben's attack on the Derridean archi-trace.

NAMING NAMING AS SUCH AND DERRIDA'S UNDECIDABLES

Agamben makes four attempts on the Derridean peak over four decades. The first, which we have delineated, concerns a profound scepticism that the trace of difference is able to overturn a metaphysics of *phonē* through the imposition of *gramma*. This is rejected by Agamben because it misrepresents the centrality of *gramma* in the foundation of metaphysics and as such sees Derrida join the ranks of metaphysicians of absence who use an ineffable language as the means by which to overcome a metaphysics of presence, putting in its place a metaphysics of absence or negation. The second is over the issue of names and terms in relation to the metaphysics of negation, the third law, and the fourth temporality. In each case the basic argument is repeated: Derrida's insistence on difference being capable of a manner of precedence in relation to Being scuppers Being as presence but leaves us adrift in a sea of ineffable language writing. Yet, as the work proceeds, the attacks become more sophisticated and harder to dismiss. In this vein we now turn to the single most significant piece Agamben has penned on Derrida, "*Pardes*: The Writing of Potentiality" published in 1990. In the interim Agamben has dedicated a short essay to Derrida dealing with citation in *Idea of Prose*, which is largely admiring in tone, as is, on the surface at least, "*Pardes*" which, as it has been extensively glossed by Adam Thurschwell in a relatively evenhanded manner that in the end sides with Derrida all the same, we can rather rapidly move through, before coming to rest on the central heart of the argument.[25]

The text recounts a Talmudic Mishnah that deals with the limits of knowledge. Four Rabbis enter *pardes*, or paradise, looking for mystical knowledge. Each approaches the tree of knowledge differently. The first dies; the second goes mad; the third, Aher or other, cuts the branches off the trees; and the last, Akiba, escapes unharmed primarily, according to Agamben and Thurschwell's interpretation, because of the actions of Aher. Agamben presents the traditional interpretation, a counterinterpretation, then his own based on the counterinterpretation. In the counterinterpretation each Rabbi represents a different mode of interpretation as such: literal, Talmudic, allegorical and mystical. The allegorical, or Aher's interpretative deforestation, while ingenuous and of course precursive to the successful exit of Akiba unharmed (you may realise that if Derrida is Aher, then Agamben is Akiba), has serious limitations. Agamben sees the branch cutting as a means of separating the tree of knowledge from the tree of life. Taking the branches away, knowledge can be transported and possessed. Yet, "In the cutting of the branches . . . we can see a moral risk implicit in every act of interpretation. . . . The risk is that speech, which is nothing other than the manifestation and the unconcealment of something, may be separated from what it reveals and acquire an autonomous consistency".[26] This act he terms an *exprimentum linguae*, a phrase he associates in his early work with his own activities:[27] "an experience of

language that consists in separating speech both from the voice and pro-
nunciation and from its reference. A pure word isolated in itself, with
neither voice nor referent, with its semantic value indefinitely suspended".[28] The first sentence here echoes precisely the definition of the
Voice as no longer voice but not yet meaning, while the second suggests
that this pure word is a form of indifference in that it experiences suspension, yet problematically it is an isolated indifference, or what Deleuze
calls the indifference of pure determination. As Thurschwell details, the
pure dwelling in language results in a proximity to one element of God at
the expense of isolation from the other elements.

What seems to have happened in Agamben's maturity is a realisation
that Derrida has, effectively, successfully conducted the *experimentum linguae* of a pure experience of language that his own early work appeared
to attempt and, further, that the Derridean trace is entirely mappable
onto his own fundamental metaphysical concern at this time: potentiality. In this way also, as we shall see, the undecidability of Derridean
terms, an element of *différance* we have not yet considered, is equal to the
method of indifference as the later work terms it. For Agamben at least,
undecidability is a function of indifference. However, where the two
thinkers differ is that for Derrida undecidability is the institution of a
fundamental otherness at the origin of all thought, resulting in a philosophy as *oikonomia* or an oscillation between two suspending oscillations,
whereas for Agamben otherness is not prior to but produced by the imposed division of language into voice and Voice. Let's trace this complex
argument through the text itself.

The dispute is conducted through a debate we are already familiar
with: there is no name for the name so that a) one cannot name the pure
taking place of language and b) this deficiency at least gives us access to
language as such as a form of immediate mediation. Agamben gives us a
history of terms, from how they stood for something else to the point in
modern thought where the confidence that a term could stand for a being
in the form of an idea, say, is problematized. Philosophy therefore can no
longer give names to the objects of thought. This has not resulted in, as
some contend, the becoming literature of philosophy, and Derrida's attack on terms does not result in the end of naming as univocal reference.
Rather, "Deconstruction suspends the terminological character of philosophical vocabulary: rendered inde-terminate, terms seem to float inter-
minably in the ocean of sense".[29] To prove this Agamben then hands over
a whole section of the essay to three magnificent moments in Derrida's
work where he deals with the name and terminology.

Central of these is a quote taken from an interview where Derrida
defines terms as undecidables.[30] As undecidability appears very close to
Agambenian indifference, let us enumerate Derrida's argument here:

1. Derrida's terms are to be called undecidables, although even this term has more than one name; for example, they can all be called the nonname.
2. These terms are "unities of simulacrum", false propositions which cannot be included in philosophical opposition but which inhabit this opposition.
3. This occupation of the ground between philosophical oppositions does not result in a third term; thus, binary oppositions do not become, say, tertiary constructions.
4. Rather the aim is, via the fold, to take a place of strong determination and introduce a term or set of terms that disallow closure or clever reassemblage.
5. Yet this does not result in "inexhaustible wealth of meaning" or "transcendence of semantic excess" not least because a) the simulacra have a degree of unity and b) they occupy a philosophical consistency and have importance only within that consistency from which, by the way, they originate.
6. In this way any term operates in two modes which combine to form its total modality. A term marks both the mark *and* the marked becoming the remarked site of the mark.[31]

Derrida could be clearer here if he said an undecidable stands in a relationship of necessary contingency in relation to any philosophical term. It designates what the term is and to that which it would purport to refer, in such a fashion that it makes the process of reference self-referential. It comments on the site of the mark, or how a term comes into being as attempted reference to an object, and in so doing enters into the assumed agreement between term and object and makes an object of reference as such. Yet all of this it does from within the confines of the marks in play.

Agamben summarises this text along with comments on the trace as erasure and the unnameable in play in any act of naming as: "What is unnameable is *that there are names* ('the play which makes possible nominal effects'); what is nameless yet in some way signified is the name itself".[32] From this we can deduce that names or terms now name the process of naming or the taking place of the name itself. As names as such cannot name this directly for two reasons, first there is no name for the name, and, second, no name can any longer unproblematically name its object, undecidables are always caught in a process of self-referentiality. They name the 'truth' of naming, which is that each name names primarily that which is unnameable.

This logic is perhaps more clearly expressed in Derrida's later texts on the name and also on the date.[33] The date, for example, marks both a temporal singularity, now, and a reiterative generality, the now. Every date has both a fundamental singularity and a general iterability. The name is the same.[34] It is supposed to render in its specificity its referent, but to do this it uses general iterability. This problem is most adequately established by trying to name the name or the mark in time, time as-such. In a profoundly Kantian manner we discover that place and time, while the basis of all understanding of intuitions, can never be accessed themselves as pure intuitions and so in this sense can never be an object of understanding. Derrida agrees, or at least Agamben has Derrida agree: naming is the condition of all reference of intellectual objects, but what cannot be named is the name as such. Yet, in a profoundly non-Kantian fashion, Agamben argues, traditionally in terms of reference there were two orders, the word as such, which was considered acoustically consistent, and the reference to the word. In a condition of self-referentiality the word as acoustic material would form the object of the reference. If this is so, then an intuition *is* the basis of an understanding. Agamben rightly states, along Kantian lines, that this is not actually self-reference since the term signifies an element of the world, the word as sound, and not intentionality itself.

In the modern world of reference typified by the Derridean use of and deconstructive texts on names, the self-referentiality of the sign or the signification of the intention to signify, "it is necessary that a term signify itself, but *signify itself only insofar as it signifies*".[35] In a structure that echoes Heidegger's in relation to identity where the 'is' between A is A becomes the very basis of Being, so here in the structure A stands for B, true self-referentiality concerns only the 'stands for' and in a sense becomes a structure of in-significance to echo that of indifference. Indeed, here we could argue for a tripartite schema, in-identity, in-significance and in-difference, and any future study of indifference would do well to take into consideration this compound identity which we have little time to develop here to anyone's great satisfaction. Heidegger's model of identity as self-belonging concentrates on the 'is' as pure identity as such in which, however, the two terms of the A, its Being as the same and its being as not-equal, are suspended. Identity is thus self-suspending so that the very identification of A with itself remains neutral. What is most important to identity, that which is identical to itself, is neutralised by the differential-combinatorial 'is'. We have seen the same structure time and again with indifference so that A is not B suspends differential actual identities to be located in A and B in favour of their pure, presupposed difference. Here, with representation, true self-referentiality is in-significant in that the A stands for B, suspends the identity and the difference of A and B, foregrounding instead the neutral and preceding abstract possibility of the 'stands for' which, according to Agamben, stands for nothing other than another standing for. In both instances 'is' and 'stands for' are examples of the expanding roster of syncategorematic terms from which Agamben is constructing a paradigmatic plate of a neutralised or indifferent ontology.

However, there are here moments of dissatisfaction with this process revealed by Derridean, undecidable terminologies. Thus, Agamben says, "The aporia of Derrida's terminology is that in it, one *standing for* stands for another *standing for*, without anything like an objective referent constituting itself in its presence".[36] Here Agamben is almost praising this ability of the undecidable term to upend objective reference, but time and again in his later criticisms he will return to this simple point of infinite regress. In Derrida, one 'stands for' stands for another 'stands for', allowing the power of pure language to be revealed as such as the neutral basis, 'is', 'is not', 'stands for', of all constructions of metaphysics: identity, difference and representation, respectively. This in effect forms an indifferent ontology through three syncategorematic terms if you agree, with Badiou, that ontology depends on identity, difference and representation. Yet in each case nothing in language stands for language as such; rather, each time something stands for something else which stands for something else, we might call this regressive referentiality, which in Derrida's work is a constant and sustained event to be found in all of his myriad texts where language is revealed only as absent, negative and permanently divided at its root by *écriture*.

Agamben makes the point that for language to really refer to itself, it must not subscribe to structures of pure presence or absence, but, he argues, the logic of the trace in Derrida does not allow for this. So that, using here the Latin terms that have been in play in this section, whereas the aim is to suspend the division between first and second sign intention (the reference to an object and the intention of the sign), so that one isolates the 'stands for', in Derrida's system one is caught in a permanent oscillation between *secunda-primo* and *primo-secunda*. This much is quite correct and leads Derrida to a paradoxical statement or indeed many such statements: the concept trace is not a concept, the name difference is not a name and so on. "Grammatology was forced to become deconstruction in order to avoid this paradox".[37]

KHŌRA OR MATTER AS THE TAKING-PLACE

Agamben now goes on to make a case for the Derridean trace as being the same experiment in language as his own through his early comments on language and his sustained consideration of potentiality. It is this section that Thurschwell uses to attempt to collapse the case of Agamben against Derrida and side with a Derrida-Levinas nexus of an ethics of otherness rather than what he mistakenly terms Agamben's ontology of language. He argues that to make the Derridean trace into potentiality, Agamben has to define the trace as pure matter, something, it is true, Derrida agitates against more than once. This argument is then developed over the contesting readings of Platonic *khōra* in *Timmeaus*, with Agamben seeing this as a kind of pure matter and Derrida refusing to side with any of the names that have been given to the term over time, thus revealing the *khōra* as the no-place of all elements of naming: namely, the trace.

Let's first explain how trace is potentiality and then unpack what Agamben means by matter, something which Thurschwell, in his rush of blood to the head in finding what he sees as Agamben's fatal flaw, misinterprets, but in a useful manner. Agamben's question is, What is the trace's pure potential to write? He uses the Aristotelian model of thought as a blank tablet in *De Anima*, an image he returns to repeatedly during this period to try to capture potential. Specifically we are speaking here not of the tablet but the wax laid on top of the tablet, producing a useful parallel with one of Derrida's key works on the trace, "Freud and the Scene of Writing". For Aristotle thought is marked by two internal contradictions. If thought is merely pure potentiality to think a problem, then once the problem is solved, thought is negated entirely, and yet philosophy's essence is to perpetuate thought. On the other hand, if thought remains pure potential to think, then it would never come to actuality and so would think nothing. Thus, actuality negates the thing of thought while potentiality does not allow thought to think any thing. We can reconstitute this now through the sign as a mode of representing thought as a process. If a sign exists purely to signify an object in the world, then the sign itself is self-negating. Yet if it does not refer to anything, then it is useless.[38] This is a problem of course only when the sign tries to signify itself, when naming names itself and when thought thinks itself in philosophy. As we know, for Agamben, Aristotle's solution is to define potentiality as the potential not to do something. In this way actuality does not negate the potential, for in each actuality there is always a potentiality of not doing. A poet is as much a poet when writing poetry as when not. At the same time it negates pure potentiality because potentiality that is not coming to actuality is simply potentiality as not to do.

The tablet works as a metaphor for this in the following manner. Potentiality is as a wax tablet on which nothing is written. The tablet will support writing, but this does not mean to say when it is blank that it is radically dis-actualised. Nor does it mean that once written upon it is radically and permanent actualised because of course the writing can be erased. Let's now follow Agamben and map this onto the trace. The trace is an actualisation because there is no pure trace as such, only trace of something in something else. Although the trace comes before presence, there is no archi-trace as, say, pure floating negative presence. The trace occurs always historically through textual actualisations. Yet one can never actualise a trace and exhaust it in full. The total history of the trace is never to be written, not least because the trace is never present as such but always to come, even in the past.

Yet Derrida's own version of the tablet, Freud's *Wunderblock* or mystic writing pad, presents a modified version. One can also rewrite on this pad with a stylus and then erase it, but each mark leaves a trace of indentation on the cellophane cover, resulting in a palimpsest of almost invisible but, if necessary, traceable traces. Here the trace then is rather an actual historical record of writing that can never be fully erased and can be called up into actuality when needed. Obviously, Derrida is considering Freud's appropriation of the idea of repression here. We now have before us two very different writing tablets. The first remains always blank yet not negated, the second always marked, and those marks are always potentially present to disallow any final naming of presence. Yet they are also potential in the way Agamben says, for the tablet is not only traced but always to come. The trace is not simply the burden of history but the inevitability of the future as singular and yet always already repeated. That said, Agamben is speaking of a very specific function of the tablet here, that of using the tablet to write the tablet, or using thought to think itself: self-referentiality. "The thinking of thinking," he says, "is first of all a potential to think (and *not to think*) that is turned back on itself. . . . Potentiality, which turns back on itself, is an absolute writing that no one writes: a potential to be written . . . a *tabula rasa* that suffers its own receptivity and can therefore *not not-write itself*".[39]

We now enter into the most complex and challenging section of the essay and of Agamben's engagement with Derrida at which point our aim has altered. Content no longer with explaining Agamben's critique of Derrida or presenting a critique of this critique, we rather come up against the true intention of Agamben's work, which pertains to an explanation of indifference through the attempted appropriation of Derrida's work to the cause. All of this centres around a difficult consideration of matter, which seems to leave Agamben open to accusations of establishing an arche-matter. Agamben first makes the strong claim that the trace and potentiality are effectively the same entity. Arguing that the trace cannot be a form or an actualisation, naturally he is lining up the trace to be a type of matter, specifically "a writing tablet that suffers not the impression of a form but the imprint of its own passivity, its own formlessness".[40] If this is matter, it is a peculiar form of matter in that it is a matter that is not form in potential, nor is it a pure formlessness either, but a matter that bears the mark of its own formlessness or, one might say, its own potential to form in such a manner that form never cancels its formlessness impotentiality.

Significantly for us, the means by which the tablet is described opens it up to a reconsideration of our thesis here that is indifference. Specifically, what we are grappling with is this question: to what degree is Derrida a thinker of indifference, specifically through the trace of his undecidables which make naming self-referential but which open up deconstruction to self-referential self-referentiality ad infinitum, so as never to truly to be able to put on stage, so to speak, the pure stands-for of language which is its true nature? Agamben then raises the legitimate question that if thinking is the pure potentiality of thought as experienced passivity, not form in the state of matter or matter in the moment before form, how can we actually experience such a state? Can one go through indifferent passivity in the state of the stands-for of potential writing, or does one not get caught in the same endless regress as Agamben locates in deconstruction but which we might better describe as the oscillation between two oscillations? Can one have an experience of an oscillation as such, which would surely necessitate its being stilled or suspended?

Agamben turns to Plotinus, who, in "On the Two Matters", attended on a similar problem: how can one conceive of a nonform and an indetermination, something without form but which is not simply pure, chaotic matter? The section cited could have come straight from Deleuze, and it is at this stage that it becomes increasingly impossible to stay with the consideration of trace as potential without adopting the Deleuzian schema, in particular in its relation to indifference.[41] Yet as that is the topic of the following chapter, I will simply allude to key elements here with the proviso that Agamben's relationship to the work of Derrida can be resolved only through an understanding of his relationship to Deleuze.

Plotinus gives the example of how in the dark the eye cannot see anything but is aware of itself as the capacity to see colours when light permits. We are not blind in the dark, and indeed in some sense we truly see, for we see our capacity to see at the point when we are not seeing anything at all. Plotinus argues the mind is the same, relying on a residuum it cannot bring under determination but which is not the void. Thus, the eye/mind is "affected by its own incapacity to see . . . between the experience of something and the experience of nothing there lies the experience of one's own passivity. The trace (*typos*, *ikhnos*) is from the beginning the name of this self-affection, and what is experienced in this self-affection is the event of matter".[42] We will leave to one side the implicit attack here on Derrida, who is trenchant in his work that the trace undermines the logic of auto-affection, and say instead that Agamben believes that at this moment the regressive aporia of self-referentiality is halted and that aporia, in a Benjaminian moment of redemption, becomes euphoria. This represents indeed the very crux of his argument with Derrida, namely, that the aporia of the trace is negative and a means must be found of making it positive. All aporias will become euphorias if the Agamben messianic system were finally to be realised. This occurs because self-reference is displaced into potentiality, and the question is no longer that of word or thing in reference but "a pure potentiality to signify (and not to signify), the writing tablet on which nothing is written".[43]

We now become entangled in the knotty problem of matter and Thurschwell's accusation that Agamben is effectively a materialist. What we discover here is that Agamben is in actual fact an indifferent materialist favouring a matter that is not formless and then suffers an impression but rather the effective suspension of the age-old division between the sensible and the intelligible, or matter and form. Potential matter, and in some senses it is confusing to retain the term matter, is thought that "makes itself into the trace of its own formlessness, a trace that no one has traced—pure matter". This trace-matter, "far from being the inert substratum of a form, it is on the contrary, the result of a process of materialization".[44] Anyone who has read the major works of Deleuze cannot help but see his influence here. In his work he speaks of two elements of indifference within the process of determination or of virtual becoming actual, a process mappable onto Agamben's theory of potentiality as we shall see. In the predetermined realm we have indifference of indetermination or pure formlessness, while in the postactual we have the realm of pure determination or pure form. In each we have a disjunction similar to that which Derrida-Aher is accused of in separating the branches from the trunk. Pure formlessness is a potentiality or a virtuality that never becomes actualised, while pure form is a series of determinations that have no link to their material base. In the first we have the indifference of dark chaos separate from the becoming-actualised, in the second we have the lit, amnesiac, isolationist fascism of total determination where each actualisation is as if it is its own state with no link to the potential to become otherwise. We can recognise here in Deleuze the two aporias of the potentiality to think in Aristotle.

We will return to this argument, but for now suffice it to say that for Agamben, as for Deleuze, there is a stage of the material which is its virtuality or its potential for actuality. Each trace, each singularity, is and must be becoming-actualised or available to actualisation even if it never becomes actualised. This is another way of stating the law of the trace in that each actualisation, as a result of its being a determination from a virtuality, is marked by its history of predetermination, remains in touch with the virtual which at any moment can deterritorialize its determination and is reticulated at every moment with every other singularity. Here this reticulation means all those singularities a trace could have actualised but didn't, all those it could still actualise, all those it did actualise and all those which were actualised elsewhere which remain in clear or obscure reticulation at any given moment.

Agamben chooses the term *khōra* here to name this state which he has Plato to mean the nonplace, a designation also to be found in Derrida's essay. Where the controversy arises, however, is that Agamben retains the term matter for this nonstate, although now we can see this is not matter as such but the becoming-actual and remaining potential of what he calls pure matter: that which subsists between two incorrect presentations of materialism, namely, potential without actuality and actuality as the negation of potentiality. Glossing on Plato he says,

Khōra, place (or rather nonplace), which is the name he gives to matter,
is situated between what cannot be perceived (the sensible, perceptible
as *aesthēsis*). Neither perceptible nor imperceptible, matter is perceptible *met'anaisthēsias* (a paradoxical formulation that must be translated
as "*with* the absence of perception"). *Khōra* is thus the perception of an
imperceptions, the sensation of an *anaisthēsis*, a pure taking-place[45].

This definition of pure matter is not in the spirit of Thurschwell's critique;
instead, it is the perception of imperception or a pure *anaisthesis*. And as
such the tablet which supports such an *anaisthesis* is not bound by the
weightiness of pure materiality as semiotic support but rather the more
insubstantial materiality of immediate mediation as such. As pure taking
place the Agamben tablet is of course another model of communicability
which does, after all, rely on material presence as one of its preconditions
in Foucault. That said, this presence is not solid and foundational in the
manner of a stone tablet per se but the very indifference of immediate
mediation whose purpose is to suspend the difference between matter
and form and in doing so to literally suspend the physicality of the tablet
itself and make it hang, as if weightless, in the space to the side of ease, or
hover just above the head like one's halo tends to do.[46]

DIFFÉRANCE MAKES AGAMBENIAN INDIFFERENCE COMMUNICABLE

Returning to our wider schema of indifference then, we can see the case is
not dissimilar to Derrida's own use of terminology. Critics regularly seize
on these essays to suggest that first Agamben locates the origins of Being
in language and second that he hypostatises a kind of arche-matter of
total unity that precedes difference. This is not the case. Rather, this is one
of his key signatory plates of indifference, the indifference of language in
Western metaphysics. What is suspended here then is one of the most
persistent formulations of the common and the proper: the intelligible
and the sensible. By concentrating on signification and especially Derrida's work, Agamben shows that through the intelligibility of the intelligible due to the sensible use of marks, words, names and signs, what
results is not the collapse of the common on the back of the proper, a
process he attributes to Derrida, but the state of *anaisthesis* or the taking
place of the pure indifference of matter in relation to form and form in
relation to matter. To clarify before we leave this point, he then suggests
that the trace is "something like the experience of an intelligible matter"
although not enough like it for Agamben to be satisfied, hence his equation of his own thought to that of Akiba and his gratitude to his great
forebear Derrida-Aher. He does not claim that the trace is materiality;
rather, the trace comes close to the materialization of pure matter through
its similarity to potentiality as regards its indifference.

What I have detailed here is that up to and including the work of the 1990s, Agamben's constant attrition of the Derridean edifice is based on a profound respect for deconstruction coupled with an increasing fund of disappointment. Specifically, Agamben constructs a four-part attack to support a simple thesis that Derrida will give us access to paradise, in this context the final knowledge of what constitutes our metaphysics, but he will not let us leave again to reenter experience armed with this knowledge. One can phrase this, as I have done, as deconstruction does not go far enough, or perhaps deconstruction does not let us pass through and/or return home. In a sense no Derridean scholar can contest this point. Rather, they would contest Agamben's desire to exit paradise as anything other than metaphysical. I hope that I will be able to show this is not the case by the end of the book, but for now content yourself with the detail of Agamben's critique.

Derrida's history of the sign is incorrect, Agamben argues, by suggesting that writing is occluded and made supplemental when in fact it is presented and defined as central. This means Derrida succumbs to the metaphysics of negation attributable to the two thinkers Derridean deconstruction attempts most fervently to undermine: Hegel and Heidegger. This is because the trace as a mode of self-referentiality collapses into the logic of endless regress and progress, the historial contingency of the impossible to-come. That said, it also reveals, negatively, the very location from which we might be able to exit *pardes*, what Agamben here calls the very taking-place of matter or, more generally, the indifferent suspension of language as bifurcation so that we can see the pure taking place of language as such in the form of its pure communicability.

This then is the issue between Derrida and Agamben. Derrida presents the true problem of the history of metaphysics negatively, through the limitations or failings of deconstruction. Without this presentation, Agamben's philosophy of indifference is unthinkable and non-communicable, and his constant worrying at the hem of Derrida's robes of office is best described as a troubled farewell, a reluctance to leave, a need to establish distance. It is a relationship of separation full of filiation and human feeling more complex and perplexing than but infinitely more preferable to say, a simple statement of dismissal such as one finds for example in the work of Badiou.

LAW AND MESSIANISM

Having dealt with our first two topics in relation to Agamben's attack on Derrida, *gramma* and *phonē* or archi-trace and voice as negation, we are now in a position to rapidly outline the two other major areas of disagreement between the two men: law and time. As the finest work on Agamben so far is Zartaloudis's study of Agamben and law and as de la Durantaye's panoptical gaze more than captures Agamben's messianism, backed up by Dickinson's recent study I will restrict myself here to drastic, perhaps exhilarating summary. In *Homo Sacer*, Agamben infamously rereads Kafka's "Before the Law" criticising Derrida's celebrated reading of the same text.[47] For Agamben the story is a parable of his own conceptualisation of a state of exception which is, using Scholem's phrase, that law is in force without significance.[48] By this Agamben means, as he says, "law that becomes indistinguishable from life".[49] This situation that marks our contemporary moment is, as I will detail later, the indifferent suspension of law between norm and fact based on another indifference at the heart of life between *zoē* and *bios* and again, as we shall see, the indiscernibility between kingdom and governance as regards the economy of power. As we know, a suspensive point such as this, while negative, can, through the logic of indifference, have positive outcomes. Agamben's complaint against deconstruction is that it negates this option by extending indifferent suspension across every moment of history: "The prestige of deconstruction in our time lies precisely in its having perceived the entire text of tradition as being in force without significance, a being in force whose strength lies essentially in its undecidability and in having shown that such a being in force is, like the door of the Law in Kafka's parable, absolutely impassable".[50] Agamben then adds unequivocally that recognising a state of 'in force without significance' is only an interim step: "Every thought that limits itself to this does nothing other than repeat the ontological structure that we have defined as the paradox of sovereignty".[51] Clearly, the problem with deconstruction is that nothing can happen therein. In that Derrida defines the totality of the tradition as indifference, at least according to Agamben, then naturally nothing can occur to interrupt that state of indifference. This is in stark contrast to indifference in Agamben which we constantly see is something which comes about, has origins, develops over time, reaches a point of crisis and so, at certain moments such as our own the very suspension of law, its being in force without significance, can itself be suspended.

A second comment here is worth noting pertaining to the event of possible closure. Agamben openly says he thinks the door of law can finally be closed so that being can be thought beyond every idea of law. On his reading, Kafka's parable hints at the possibility of a messianic fulfilment of history in the form of first recognising our state of legal exception, as does Derrida, and second suspending its suspension. This second eventuality he believes Derrida would not allow. Reading a famous fragment of Benjamin's which states, "The Messiah will only come when he is no longer necessary", Agamben presents Derrida's version of this as the event that succeeds in not happening. It is an orthodox reading. Derrida's point is that law and democracy are like deconstruction precisely because they establish an impossibility in the form of a to-come of fulfilment, that mirrors perfectly the impossibility of foundation as full self-presence in the trace. Whereas Derrida presents the open door as the happening of a nonhappening or the endless deferral of the hypostatisation of a singular and full arrival of, say, justice, democracy or otherness as such, Agamben says the opposite: "The story tells of how something has really happened in seeming not to happen".[52] Indifference, in this instance in the form of law, which is precisely the stasis of an economy, not its endless renewal as is the case in Derrida, is an event, a singularity, a rare opportunity. Put more bluntly, contra Derrida, in Agamben origins can be traced, singular events can occur and situations can be resolved without any of these three succumbing to a metaphysics of presence. How can this be possible? The only solution I have is the logic of indifference.

Messianism is then the source of another infamous attack on Derrida in *The Time That Remains*. After a dense, detailed and accurate reading of Derrida's reading of the Hegelian *Aufhebung* in *Speech and Phenomena* and *Of Grammatology*, Agamben correctly shows how the archi-trace negates any possibility of origins and thus also negates any moment of fulfilment as regards the dialectic. Citing a famous passage from "*Ousia* and *Grammē*", he lets Derrida reveal his oscillation-between-oscillations model in relation to the trace of signification. In that the dialectic operates between presence and absence, or convention and invention (repetition and difference), the trace must be inscribed and erased constantly without pure inscription (presence) or pure erasure (absence) being allowed to have the floor for reasons we have already detailed. This is why the trace is produced as its own erasure. It must signify something, as without signification presence is of course incommunicable, but it cannot signify something absolutely different or other, totally singular, an event as such. Rather, what the trace signifies is the system of the trace: the oscillation between two oscillations. Agamben is correct in identifying this as a Hegelian dialectic without *Aufhebung* because it denies origins, and this negates completion. He then adds,

> In this instance, the arche-trace simultaneously shows its link to—and difference from—the Hegelian *Aufhebung* with its messianic theme. In this context, the movement of the *Aufhebung*, which neutralizes signifieds while maintaining and achieving signification, thus becomes the principle of infinite deferment. A signification that only signifies itself can never seize hold of itself, it can never catch up with a void in representation, nor does it allow anything to be an in-significance. . . . Deconstruction is a thwarted messianism, a suspension of the messianic.[53]

By virtue of this complex but accurate analysis, we can lay out three different solutions to the dialectic. Hegel's *Aufhebung* depends on a nostalgia for origins that fuels a messianic completion in the form of absolute knowledge. Derrida's use of the archi-trace and the other to-come means that there is no origin of presence which signification re-presents, nor is there any final other which deconstruction will reveal as some future gesture of completion. The dialectic here is Nietzschean or perpetually in motion: the oscillation between two oscillations. Finally, we have Agamben's messianism or that which will arrive after the suspension of Derrida's dialectic that does not succumb to the only other option, as Derrida tirelessly presents it, of a metaphysics of origins and fulfilment. How does Agamben propose to avoid this most obvious accusation?

In the passage just cited he presents three solutions to how we can close the door of being in force without significance. A signification needs a space to form a mode of self-referentiality that depends on neither immediate self-presence nor mediated representation. Agamben calls this the space of ease. It must be able to present the void of signification, surely a reference to Badiou, by which we mean the void of the Being of a situation must be presented as not being present and yet not given a negative ontology. Finally, and this is directly related to the previous point, the insignificant, the nonsignifying, must be allowed to become insignificant: in, on, into, towards and against significance. The void of a situation, in our model its indifference, must be allowed to signify and be seen as significant, singular and eventful without succumbing to a metaphysics of negation, negative theology or other as Other. If this is sanctioned, then a messianism of origins is possible but only by virtue of a logic of self-referential presentative void as being such that the void of a situation, here the suspension of difference between common and proper, is allowed to be seen as such, so that it can finally be rendered insignificant. It would seem then that after deconstruction it is possible to speak of origins so as to propose messianic conclusions, if instead of a permanent philosophy of difference one submits to an interim philosophy of indifference.

SYNCATEGOREMATIC THINKING: AND

This is all very well, but the suggestion that in the end Derrida's is a system of permanent indifference, a totalised 'in force without significance' of every metaphysical category that always was and ever will be, of course suggests, counter to our own previous position, that Derrida's is a philosophy of indifference. Initially, this position seems on the verge of being borne out in a text by Derrida published in 2000 and written for Royle's *Deconstructions: A User's Guide*. "Et Cetera . . . " is a consideration of the copula 'and' and is a strong example of Agamben's observations as to how syncategorematic terms have, in modern thought, ceased to be invisible supports for thinking and instead have become zones of indistinction within which thought finds its most promising operations. Derrida himself addresses this as the text progresses in relation to Husserl.[54]

Derrida explains straightaway that "deconstruction introduces an 'and' of association and dissociation at the very heart of each thing, rather it recognizes the self-division within each concept".[55] This 'and' results in the double obligation of deconstructive thought, and . . . and, which is another way of explaining our ((R oscillation S) oscillation (S oscillation R)) model of *différance*.

The very end of the essay summarises this relation by explaining the problem of X and X, for example, deconstruction and metaphysics, in terms of the X itself always being bifurcated so that if we speak of deconstruction and law, law itself is composed of X and X where the term law is repeated within the phrase: law and law, with the first law being the possibility of law and the second its deconstructive impossibility, or the radically unconditioned element to be found at the heart of any categorisation of law. That these two terms share the same name is merely the effect of a homonym "and therefore a semantic or synonymic non-relation, a relation without relation".[56] While the double use of the term "law" as both law (the conditioned) and law (the unconditional) is a mere occurrence of homonym, this is not an accidental relation, and thus the reconstruction of this relation comes into play. Derrida's interlocutor here, who is also Derrida (fulfilling the Derrida and Derrida structure necessary for deconstruction, a structure deconstruction also fulfils), clarifies this by speaking of "something like a rule, a privileged procedure in deconstruction which is, however, neither a method nor an appropriable technique, but an event or a style," which is then defined as "a sort of disjunctive conjunction at the threatened heart of each conceptual atom: this and this, this without this, this save this . . . the one getting itself deconstructed in the name of itself, or rather in the name of what, quite other, becomes its simple homonym. And the 'and' would then mark both difference and indifference. There is deconstruction and deconstruction".[57]

This is one of the rare moments when Derrida uses the term "indifference", whose frequency in his work is rare enough, in a manner that seems to go beyond simple adjectival or Kantian usage. What he seems to be suggesting here is that the 'and' of the conjunctive disjunction signifies first difference of a concept from itself, so that, to use our previous example, justice is different from justice. Following the order presented here the disjunction in the term "justice" is that there is a homonymic element to every name that produces identity through or via difference. This then is homonymic disjunction, or Justice A and Justice B, two radically dissimilar concepts, in that one is conditioned and possible and the other unconditioned and thus impossible, that, however, through 'writing' can be presented in the same moment.

Then there is the second element here, that of conjunction. What is fascinating for us is the need Derrida has to call this indifference rather than identity. If disjunction is difference, than traditionally identity is conjunction, but the manner in which Derrida has set this up, via homonym, allows a second alternative. As he is speaking of naming, not of essence, and not just naming but syncategorematic elements concatenating with naming, here the copula 'and', he is not required to oppose identity to difference. When one says "justice", he argues, one starts from a position of assumed identity; the word refers to the unified and closed concept. Then one discovers the internal disjunction of identity within this process so that each time one says "justice", one says it twice in a single composite moment. This is of course the presentation of difference as temporal spacing in the form of the action of naming. The sign, like the now, assumes full self-presence only by establishing the most infinitesimal distance between it and its auto-affective self-consciousness. The name operates in the same fashion. Yet something then happens in the naming process, which is auto-affectively auto-homonymic, that, and I am extravagantly extrapolating here because the essay rapidly comes to a close, does not mean one simply returns to identity conjunction or stays trapped in difference conjunction. Rather, one is placed in a state of indifference: deconstruction and deconstruction becomes X and X. The two terms are the same in every way, phonetically, and different in every way, referentially, resulting in what I would call a new sign: the sign of indifference.

Sadly, this is a late work by Derrida, and as I said the essay ends rapidly but not before offering one additional piece of information. Having established, after his comment on indifference, that deconstruction is never in the singular, there are always at least two deconstructions, although it is always to be found in a singular case; like a departing Colombo he, "adds one more thing": "deconstruction is not only plural, but possible *and* impossible. . . . It also tries to think . . . the 'and' of the ambiguous excess, the 'and' which places all collective order on the way to dissemination. The disseminal 'and' is the *'plus d'un'*, and the 'more than one voice,' the 'more than one language' and the 'more than two' and the 'more than three,' etc".[58] It is this formulation, presented in the final section as "Yes, yes. And yes . . . " that disallows our co-opting Derrida, belatedly, for an Agambenian project of indifference. While Derrida concedes a third form of identity construction, as do we, meaning identity is always identity different from itself through the double mediation of indifference, Derrida's formalisation of this model is one of regress that in a sense combines the two elements of condition and cause in Kant. If, for Kant, there is the conditionality of the empirical, which regresses indefinitely because we can never empirically attain a primary condition which would be the unconditioned, there is of course conditionality of reason, which regresses to the infinite, because in reason one is not only able to present an idea of a totality, as the unconditioned, this presentation, via apperception, is actually its primary role. Derrida then takes these two faculties, the sensible and the intelligible, and through the trace reveals their codependence rather than their copresence, as in Kant. Just as the singularity of deconstruction must be undermined by its reliance on repetition, so the plurality of the 'and' cannot result in a unified aggregation theory or the set of all conjunctions. One cannot close on difference.

As two disputants seem to arrive at a mutual compromise only to then recall their irreconcilable distrust of each other, suddenly the schism between our two thinkers which seemed on the verge of being bridged could not be more pronounced. For Derrida indifference leads back to identity, as there can be no cessation of conceptual *oikonomia* that does not result in some form of presence, presence of the common or presence of the proper. In addition, for Derrida, it will be one or the other, or the other so to speak; in other words, the three positions available are presence becoming deconstructed by singularity, singularity becoming deconstructed by presence and the procedural role of the dual otherness which is deconstruction as the other, not in the form of an identity but indifferent mobility. Yet the formula ((R oscillation S) oscillation (S oscillation R)) or identity-indifference-difference, with indifference here operating briefly as another name for difference, not another avenue for difference, is always caught between the two impossibilities of infinite regress in terms of the conditioned (sensible) or the unconditioned (intelligible). This then is the basis of Derridean affirmation: always another yes. In contrast, as we have seen, Agamben favours the possibility of a mode of occupying indifference, a mode we must proceed to justify against the strongest of oppositions.

Put simply, in closing, Derrida always says yes to yes, while Agamben believes before one can say yes, one has to say no. Derrida remains in a paradise of affirmation, while Agamben has to leave nirvana and wend his weary way down the grey defiles of a purgatorial indifference. I must now ask that the reader follow on, give up their place in heaven and proceed to the next stage of the suspension of the philosophy of difference, the work of Gilles Deleuze.

NOTES

1. On his version of a bifurcated signatory literature, see Giorgio Agamben, *Profanations*, trans. Jeff Fort (New York: Zone Books, 2007), 49.
2. See especially "Signature Event Context" in this regard in Jacques Derrida, *Margins of Philosophy*, trans. Alan Bass (London: Harvester, 1982), 307–30.
3. Jacques Derrida, *Acts of Literature*, ed. Derek Attridge ed. (London: Routledge, 1992), 48.
4. Due to limitations of space I cannot justify these claims across comprehensive readings, but for a fuller portrait of these issues see William Watkin, "The/Turn and the " " Pause: Agamben, Derrida and the Stratification of Poetry" (in press), and "Counterchange: Derrida's Poetry", in *Encountering Derrida: Legacies and Futures of Deconstruction*, ed. Allison Wiener and Simon Morgan Wortham (London: Continuum, 2007), 68–81.

5. Mostly I will use Derrida's term *différance* here, but in instances where I speak more generally of difference as such, for example, in these early comments, I will then use the more general and orthodox difference.

6. I have no space to consider this here, but the role of literature as the unconditional element of every thetic discourse it opens on to certainly needs to be considered more widely in relation to Badiou's alternate vision of philosophy as that which is conditioned by the generic procedures it is sutured to.

7. One issue we do not have time for here is the presupposition that indifferent states are somehow inactive. I am indebted to my colleague James Knowles for pointing out that the Renaissance state of acedia was anything but passive and reminded of Agamben's own admonition: "inoperativity is not inert" (Giorgio Agamben, *Nudities*, trans. David Kishik and Stefan Pedatella (Stanford, CA: Stanford University Press, 2011), 102). See also Slavoj Žižek, *Did Someone Say Totalitarianism? Four Interventions in the (Mis)Use of a Notion* (London: Verso, 2011), 188.

8. Giorgio Agamben, *Stanzas: Word and Phantasm in Western Culture*, trans. Ronald L. Martinez (Minneapolis University of Minnesota Press, 1993), 155.

9. Giorgio Agamben, *Stanzas : Word and Phantasm in Western Culture*, trans. Ronald L. Martinez (Minneapolis: University of Minnesota Press, 1993), 156. See also Giorgio Agamben, *End of Poem*, trans. Daniel Heller-Roazen (Stanford, CA: Stanford University Press, 1999), 77, for a critique of the trace, and Giorgio Agamben, *Remnants of Auschwitz: The Witness and the Archive*, trans. Daniel Heller-Roazen (New York: Zone Books, 2002), 129–30.

10. Agamben, *Stanzas*, 156. There is also an implied criticism of Derrida's use of the fold in "The Double Session" I would imagine.

11. See Giorgio Agamben, *Language and Death : The Place of Negativity*, trans. Karen E. Pinkus with Michael Hardt (Minneapolis: University of Minnesota Press, 1991), 32–37, 3839.

12. See also Agamben, *Language and Death*, XIII.

13. Agamben, *Stanzas*, 156.

14. Agamben, *Stanzas*, 156

15. Agamben, *Stanzas*, 157.

16. Agamben, *Stanzas*, 157.

17. Agamben, *Language and Death*, 35.

18. Agamben, *Language and Death*, 39.

19. Agamben, *Language and Death*, 39.

20. Agamben, *Language and Death*, 39.

21. Agamben, *Language and Death*, 39.

22. Agamben, *Language and Death*, 39.

23. Jacques Derrida, *Speech and Phenomena*, trans. David B. Allison (Evanston, IL: Northwestern University Press, 1973), 128.

24. Jacques Derrida, *Margins of Philosophy*, trans. Alan Bass (London: Harvester Wheatsheaf, 1982), 67.

25. Adam Thurschwell, "Cutting the Branches for Akiba, Agamben's Critique of Derrida", in *Politics, Metaphysics and Death: Essays on Giorgio Agamben's Homo Sacer*, ed. Andrew Norris (Durham, NC: Duke University Press, 2005), 173–97.

26. Giorgio Agamben, *Potentialities*, trans. Daniel Heller-Roazen (Stanford, CA: Stanford University Press, 1999), 207.

27. See Giorgio Agamben, *Infancy and History: On the Destruction of Experience*, trans. Liz Heron (London: Verso, 1993), 1–12; Leland de la Durantaye, *Giorgio Agamben: A Critical Introduction* (Stanford CA: Stanford University Press, 2009), 129–32; and Alex Murray, *Giorgio Agamben* (London: Routledge, 2010), 13.

28. Agamben, *Potentialities*, 207.

29. Agamben, *Potentialities*, 209.

30. My apologies to Derrida scholars for depending so much on interview sources; this is partly for pragmatic reasons, partly just following Agamben's lead and only

where the argument presented in the interview is clearly an accurate and profound consideration of significant portions of other work elsewhere.

31. The actual quote is taken from Jacques Derrida, *Positions*, trans. Alan Bass (Chicago: University of Chicago Press, 1981), 42–43. My comments pertain, however, to the entire interview entitled "Positions".

32. Agamben, *Potentialities*, 211. See also Giorgio Agamben, *Idea of Prose*, trans. Michael Sullivan and Sam Whitsitt (Albany: State University of New York Press, 1995), 105–6, and Agamben, *Potentialities*, 62–74.

33. See my own comments on these issues in Watkin, "Counterchange", 68–81.

34. See Agamben, *Profanations*, 22, 25.

35. Agamben, *Potentialities*, 212.

36. Agamben, *Potentialities*, 212.

37. Agamben, *Potentialities*, 213.

38. We will see the same argument in play in relation to glory and glorification in *The Kingdom and the Glory*.

39. Agamben, *Potentialities*, 216.

40. Agamben, *Potentialities*, 216.

41. In fact, we will return to the same text by Plotinus when we consider Agamben's relation to Deleuze.

42. Agamben, *Potentialities*, 217.

43. Agamben, *Potentialities*, 218.

44. Agamben, *Potentialities*, 218.

45. Agamben, *Potentialities*, 218.

46. See also Agamben, *Idea of Prose*, 31–34, and Agamben, *Potentialities*, 73, 110–12.

47. See Giorgio Agamben, *Homo Sacer: Sovereign Power and Bare Life*, trans. Daniel Heller-Roazen (Stanford, CA: Stanford University Press, 1998), 49–62.

48. He also calls it finality without end relating Kant to Derrida in Agamben, *Infancy*, 155–56. The key text in this regard is Giorgio Agamben, *State of Exception*, which is dominated by the oikonomia between fact and law/norm.

49. Agamben, *Homo Sacer*, 55.

50. Agamben, *Homo Sacer*, 54. Impassability is another synonym for indifference that features regularly in the work of Deleuze, notably *Logic of Sense*. See also Agamben's comments in *Nudities*, 94.

51. Agamben, *Homo Sacer*, 59.

52. Agamben, *Homo Sacer*, 57.

53. Giorgio Agamben, *Time That Remains*, trans. Patricia Dailey (Stanford, CA: Stanford University Press, 2005), 103.

54. Nicholas Royle, *Deconstruction: A User's Guide* (Basingstoke: Palgrave Macmillan, 2000), 292–95.

55. Royle, *Deconstruction*, 282–83.

56. Royle, *Deconstruction*, 300.

57. Royle, *Deconstruction*, 300.

58. Royle, *Deconstruction*, 301.

SEVEN

Potentiality, Virtuality and Impotentiality, Agamben and Deleuze

POTENTIALITY—IMPOTENTIALITY

While enough has been written on the fraught relationship between Agamben and Derrida,[1] and it is certainly apparent that as regards the philosophy of difference in its contemporary manifestation Agamben is antagonistic, little consideration has been paid to Agamben's relationship with the other major representative of the philosophy of difference, namely, Gilles Deleuze. Two issues hold our attention here: Agamben's allying his own work with the philosophical tradition of immanence which includes Foucault and Deleuze and opposes the transcendental model of Levinas and Derrida[2] and the clear debt or at least fundamental relation between Agamben's potentiality and Deleuzian virtuality.[3] We will return to the issue of immanence and specifically Agamben's two explicit interactions with Deleuze's work in due time, but before that we must clarify if potentiality is another name for virtuality and, if not, how do these two similar concepts relate to each other.

Before we proceed it is certainly advisable to clarify once more where Agamben stands in relation to potentiality. Contrary to what many seem to assume, his is not a philosophy of potentiality or even impotentiality.[4] Indeed, of all signatures it is perhaps potentiality which has been the most damaging in his eyes. Rather, for Agamben the potential and the actual occupy positions of common and proper, handing down limiting discursive communicabilities in such diverse fields as faculty, change, evil, matter, being and foundation. If impotentiality in Aristotle fascinates him, it is because it operates as the indifferentiating zone of suspen-

137

sion between actuality and potentiality that results in a tardy transparen-
cy, a delay of nearly two and a half millennia, as regards their logical
impossibility. Agamben illustrates this as regards the potential of a poet.
A poet has the general potential to write poems, and so they are in poten-
tial-common. When they write a poem they have actualised this potential, producing an actual poem or actual-proper. But the particular actualisation does not negate the potential, and this Agamben argues is because
of impotentiality, which suspends the clear opposition between potentiality and actualisation. For example, a poet not writing a poem is still
capable of actualisation, so that it can be said that all common contains
the proper. And when actualising, poets remain capable of this actualisation so that all proper contains the common. Add into this Aristotle's
contention that the actual precedes and thus founds the potential, meaning as ever that the actual is in fact not proper but common, and the
process of an operative inoperativity defining of indifference starts to
display itself with little or no prompting from the interested parties. Impotentiality marks a double logic of impotential incapacity. The actual is
incapable of full actualisation, and the potential is incapable of never
being actualised. These two positions exist in the *Metaphysics* in the Megaran section and then the refutation of the opposite position that there is
something possible that will never be actualised in the following section.
There can be no actualization that totally negates potential, Megaran logic, and there can be no potential that can never be actualized, by which
we mean it is impossible for it to be so, not that one necessarily will
actualise it. Impotentiality then suspends the signatory power of actual-
potential, but at no point does Agamben advocate a philosophy of impotentiality and certainly not of potentiality.

   Having made that clarification, it seems apposite to add into this portrait some additional features from the essay "On Potentiality". I won't
belabour my analysis of this piece, as I have written about it already and
it has been considered several times by others.[5] The essay opens with the
stated aim of investigating what is meant by the verb 'can', to be able, to
have the capacity to and so on. Agamben then develops this issue as
regards what it means to have a faculty for something. This possession of
a faculty, in *De Anima*, is then considered in relation to the faculty of
vision. There are two ancient problems here, not pseudoproblems per se
but certainly the result of a fault in a certain Greek logic. The first is why
there is no sensation of the senses themselves. The second, what happens
to the faculty of vision, say, in the dark when you can still see and have
the faculty to see if the lights were turned on but at that present the
faculty is inactive? Agamben concludes that faculty always means not
just a double privation, no sense of sense and no vision in the dark, but a
continuously present absence in every faculty.[6] "How can an absence be
present", he asks. "How can a sensation *exist* as anaesthesia?" This is an
important question on the back of our time spent with Derrida as it

would be all too easy for Derrideans to label Agamben, by virtue of his valorisation of impotentiality, as a philosopher of the metaphysics of absence. Perhaps with this on his mind he then concludes by claiming the problem of metaphysics is not, contra Derrida, essence, but rather "Philosophers are above all concerned with *existence*, with the *mode* [or rather the *modes*] of existence. If they consider essence, it is to exhaust it in existence, to make it exist".[7] Not that Derrida has any time for the totalisation of existential-immanent modes of thought either of course. This distinction will come into full force at the end of the essay "Absolute Immanence" where we can see Agamben strategically allying himself with the tradition of immanence or of existence rather than that of essence—not because existence is to be preferred over essence but that the problem of metaphysics is existence, not, as Derrida often has it, primarily presence.

Agamben then moves onto the famous division of potential in Aristotle between the possible (irrational potential), a child can become this, and an actual skill (rational potential); a poet can write poems, whereas a nonpoet cannot. Specifically in this essay the emphasis is on incapacity, or the presence of impotential in every moment of potentiality-actuality. In the most important section of the essay he then speaks of impotentiality, such as it is displayed in Aristotle contra the Megarans, in the following terms. After Aristotle he finds that the essence of potential is a relation: "To be potential means: to be one's own lack, *to be in relation to one's own incapacity*. Beings that exist in the mode of potentiality *are capable of their own impotentiality*; and only in this way do they become potential".[8] He then attempts a differentiation of the human from the animal along these lines: "*Human beings are the animals who are capable of their own impotentiality. The greatness of human potentiality is measured by the abyss of human impotentiality*".[9] Finally, Agamben concludes on the relation of freedom to impotentiality: "To be free is not simply to have the power to do this or that thing, nor is it simply the power to refuse to do this or that thing. To be free is . . . *to be capable of one's own impotentiality*, to be in relation to one's own privation. This is why freedom is freedom for both good and evil".[10] This last comment seems a swipe at the Kantian categorical imperative but also raises issues as regards actuality and ethics. To be good at something means you will do it and do it well; actuality. If you don't do that thing you are committing an act of evil. In between there is not the *beyond* of good and evil but the *suspension* of evil and good. Impotentiality is not the refusal to use one's capacity, which is evil, but the freedom to use or not use it.

IMPOTENTIALITY AS PARADIGM OF INDIFFERENCE

The penultimate section "The Act of Impotentiality" tries to ally these issues around the most confusing element of Book Theta, the good and evil of different degrees of potentiality pairings. Specifically, Agamben wonders how one can consider the actuality of impotentiality or of the actuality of the *"potentiality to not-be"*. Can impotentiality be actualised in such a sense as it can be said to have an existence, happening now: look I am a piano player not-playing rather than say look I am a bricklayer who cannot play piano (the banjo is more my thing). Retranslating a section from metaphysics he concludes the following:

> What Aristotle then says is: *if a potentiality to not-be originally belongs to all potentiality, then there is truly potentiality only where the potentiality to not-be does not lag behind actuality but passes fully into it as such.* This does not mean that it disappears in actuality; on the contrary, it *preserves itself* as such in actuality. What is truly potential is thus what has exhausted all its impotentiality in bringing it wholly into the act as such.[11]

What is exhausted in actualization is not potential, the Megaran paradox, but impotentiality.[12] Actuality always contains potentiality by coinciding in totality with the impotential, not the potential. This is a crucial distinction, especially in relation to Deleuzian virtuality, but also in the manner in which potentiality maps onto language.

The consideration of potentiality as the differentiator of man and animal in this essay is a clue to the relation of potentiality to Agamben's early work on language and the consideration of exclusion in *Homo Sacer*. All three can be traced to Aristotelian attempts to define the human as the being that has language, that has political existence and here, through Agamben's interpretation, that has impotentiality. The only possible solution to this is that language, exclusion and impotentiality are all names for the 'same' phenomena or, as I suggest, the same signature for the Western metaphysical project of difference such as Agamben presents it in direct attack on the Derridean version of metaphysics as presence. In each case what matters is the nature of this middle dynamic, here called impotentiality.

What impotentiality allows is, through its own negation, the suspension of the dialectic of actuality-potentiality. In becoming actualised a potentiality is not negated and preserved in a Hegelian *Aufhebung*, as some might assume, but rather impotentiality is that which is exhausted and preserved in actualisation so that, in a messianic fashion, potentiality does not have to be sacrificed. As in the case of language, impotentiality itself never has the floor, there is no capacity for impotentiality just as there is no word for the word, because impotentiality is capacity as such, the vision of vision, which ever comes to vision only in its privation or negation. It is this element of impotentiality, the indifference it shares with language in *Language and Death*, that allows Agamben to present his real project in this essay in the final section called "Salvation and Gift". Quoting a section from *De Anima* on suffering, salvation and the gift, Agamben describes how in trying to present what happens to potentiality in actuality, Aristotle presents two alternatives, the preservation of the potential in the actual that he calls here "the gift of the self to itself and to actuality" or "an alteration," from potentiality to actuality, "of a different kind". These two alternatives in fact come together in Agamben's consideration of the meaning of this text where "we are confronted with a potentiality that conserves itself and saves itself in actuality. Here, potentiality, so to speak, survives actuality and, in this way, *gives itself to itself*".[13]

If we were to line up the final positions of all the essays that make up the final two sections of *Potentialities*, we would note a striking consonance. In "On Potentiality" we find potentiality as salvation by giving itself to itself or not merely of remaining after actuality but coming to existence only then. "The Passion for Facticity" rephrases this in terms of love and the improper. Here human beings are defined as *"those who fall properly in love with the improper, who—unique among living beings—are capable of their own incapacity"*.[14] "Pardes" ends with gratitude to Derrida for allowing us a vision of an ethics of dwelling "in the paradoxes of self-reference, being capable of not-writing".[15] "Absolute Immanence" locates us in the terrain of the blessed life or of "contemplation without knowledge", the *Theoria* of a plane of immanence which "lies on the same terrain as the biological body of the West".[16] Finally, the last words of "Bartleby" and the collection tell of an arresting vision of contingency as the shadow of an angel's wing under which a "new creature" will be born in the "indemonstrable center of its 'occurrence-or-nonoccurrence.' And it is here that the creature is finally at home, saved in being irredeemable".[17] In each instance the impotential marks a suspensive and self-sacrificing moment which performs two philosophical miracles. First, it gives potentiality to itself, actualising, if you will, potentiality as such. And, second, it presents an alteration of a different kind to potentiality so that, through the equality of impotential and actuality, potentiality can be allowed to cobelong with its actuality. In this manner one could argue that impotentiality is the gift of existence or a pure immanence as such. It allows potentiality to come to being without being negated, for it is impotentiality that is negated, and it allows potentiality to exist as potential without being non-being, as it is potential in the actual by virtue of the state of impotential.

In the roster of terms/paradigms on display in these five essays, the indifference of impotential is called impotential, love, not-writing, theory and the irredeemable, but in each instance what is at play is indifference as signatory communicability. Recombining the elements of the theory one last time we find therefore that we have the common (potential) and the proper (actual) that as soon as presented in Aristotle immediately change places. Agamben sees metaphysics as defined by an imposed, not necessary, division between the quality of common and proper or repetition (presence) and difference (existence). This, remember, is his only bone of contention with Derrida, although one substantial enough for any big beast to choke on, namely, that what philosophy needs to be is not the deconstruction of presence but of difference. Potentiality is central because it concerns existence rather than presence or being. It is a theory not of what you are but what you can do (not being but act). Yet potentiality is, like language and bare life, a highly contentious element in Agamben's work. First, it enshrines oppositional difference. Then, in the apparent negation of the common in the proper, it favours the proper over the common or, better, impropriety: that which has not yet come to propriety and so cannot yet be appropriated. Finally, it is a metaphysics of negation. One can access potentiality only as under negation in actuality.

Just as in language there is no name for the name, in potentiality there is no capacity for the capacity. This is primarily because no capacity exists except as actualised, so that the capacity of the capacity, potential, which one might also call the capacity to exist, is only ever a preserved negation. Impotentiality then, or what I am calling indifference, sacrifices itself so that potentiality can finally become the capacity for capacity. It performs this miracle by, as we saw, being privation in actualisation in place of potentiality and also, in potentiality, operating as the actualisation of the capacity for the capacity which is the capacity for the incapacity. When Agamben speaks of potentiality then, he is always speaking of the double dynamic of indifference such as I have identified it in his work. What is remarkable, if only for remaining thus far unremarked, is that every time Agamben uses potentiality he is also inferring the virtual in Deleuze, and every time Deleuze uses the virtual he is speaking of the same double dynamic of indifference.[18]

DARKNESS VISIBLE

Perhaps the best place to start which such a mammoth undertaking as plotting potentiality onto virtuality in both cases through their interreliance on indifference is through the image of darkness with which we are already more than familiar from our considerations of Plotinus's influential comments on this subject. As we saw, for Aristotle, the problem of the sensation of sensation, recast in Agamben as the capacity of the capacity, which is itself a version of Russell's paradox of self-predication, pertains to how we see darkness. Defining sight as being able to see colours, Aristotle deduces that when we see darkness, we see darkness as a colour, the other colour being light. Agamben concludes from this, "When we do not see (that is, when our vision is potential), we nevertheless distinguish darkness from light; *we see darkness*. The principle of sight 'in some way possesses color,' and its colors are light and darkness, actuality and potentiality, presence and privation".[19] If, Agamben says, potentiality were only the potential for vision, we would be unable to 'see' darkness or hear silence and so on. Agamben then turns to a commentary on *De Anima* by Greek philosopher Themistius, which likens the ability not to see darkness as not being able to think absence of thought, meaning the mind would "never be able to know the formless [*amorphon*], evil, the without-figure [*aneidon*]".[20] To this Agamben adds, "The greatness—and also the abyss—of human potentiality is that it is first of all potential not to act, *potential for darkness*".[21] Returning to our ethics of impotentiality, radical evil is not this or that bad deed, doing evil, "but the potentiality for darkness," which is also, troublingly, the potentiality for light.

Darkness and light and their concomitant values of obscurity and clarity define in its essence Deleuzian virtuality and his early complex engagements with indifference in *Difference and Repetition*.[22] For example, if we take the virtual in Deleuze, the first thing we can say about it is that it is in a state of maximum obscurity in which all its potential reticulations are attenuated, and thus its essence is one of almost pure intensity. In contrast, if we take a term like "existence" or indeed "immanence", this is a term in a state of almost total clarity, which means it is profoundly reticulated, massively extended and thus at its lowest level of intensity. The virtual and the obscure then are all but synonymous in Deleuze's system.

DELEUZIAN VIRTUALITY AND POTENTIALITY

If we revise Deleuze's system for a moment, then we can say, after James Williams, that it is dominated by two principles, the transcendental deduction of infinite comprehension,[23] which he takes with radical modifications from Leibniz, and the dialectic of body and surface and their relation of quasi-causal cobelonging.[24] Starting with the deduction, at any one time any 'thing' is capable of being understood in any of its capacities. On the plane of immanence, therefore, self-reflexively in relation to the operativity of the very term "immanence", immanence stands in the form of an infinitive, to immanence, and any sense in which immanence can be taken exists in virtuality or in potentiality on that plane, but, more than this, at the next level of abstraction every term as such is subject to the command: to immanence.[25] Using the example 'green', which Deleuze applies in *Logic of Sense* to undermine Husserl, the colour green as such is not the issue here but all the means by which green can be used as an act in a sentence: or greening as a specific form of immanencing in general. Greening can be abstract colour, painting, something to do with grass, envy, a politics of ecology and many other instances aside. All of these make up the plane of consistent immanence that is the totality of the available operations of green or all its immanencies. This being the case, the plane of immanence for green is green in its totality of virtualities, whereas use of green on the plane of modern politics would be the extension of one aspect, green politics, through reticulations with other terms from the same plane of politics, and other planes as well.[26]

How does virtuality match potentiality? As for Agamben, the main issue for Deleuze is how virtuality comes to actuality and how actuality can still be a driver for change. Like Aristotle, both Deleuze and Agamben are philosophers of change who try to think a paradox of a sustained consistency of change. Thus, actualisation as both becoming actual and a completed act concern both thinkers as the very root of everything they are capable and willing to think. Agamben's concern is that actualisation negates potentiality so that, in being capable of doing something, you actually negate capability as such, and so being perpetually negates existence, which of course makes little intuitive sense. Aside from how there can be an existence for potentiality in actualisation, Agamben also worries how there can be potentiality at all in that it can be defined only when coming to actuality. Can one be a poet even when one is not writing a poem? To solve this counterintuitive paradox, he looks to find a way of retaining potentiality in actuality; otherwise, actualisation is in fact the death of change and of allowing potentiality an existence independent of its actualisation, an existence deemed essential because actuality kills potentiality. Hence, impotentiality has this double function of facilitating the movement between potential and actual and retaining their difference from each other, even if, paradoxically, it will also suspend said difference by rendering them indifferent.

For Deleuze, virtuality of course operates in the same zone of suspensive indistinction. The virtual is that which has not been actualised.[27] Yet if it is not actualised, how can one know anything of it without actualising it? More than this, if the actualisation of the virtual is its only existence, then every virtuality has effectively already been actualised; thus, the world moves towards a state of total stasis. A second problem is actualisation itself. If the actual is the actualisation of the virtual and no virtuality can be presented except in actuality, then we live in world of total structure where change is impossible, but we also live in a world of blinding clarity where every reticulation or every instance of an infinitive has to be seen all at the same time. In contrast to this world of blinding, static vision, eye-of-God position, Deleuze's pragmatic empiricism informs him that things are not this way, and indeed no phenomenologist (for what else is Deleuze?) has ever subscribed to the possibility of seeing all of the structure all of the time. The reason for this is the faith in, intuition for, empirical observation of, logical deduction from and indeed doxa-logical commitment to change in the philosophy of difference. Since Hegel it has been ever thus so that the philosophy of difference can also be termed the philosophy of change.

However, the issue is rather more complex than usual for Deleuze. Agamben seems content to work on the traditional metaphysical register of subject and predicate, being and existence, as is, for that matter, Badiou, meaning the future of philosophy is effectively predicative, bringing together, we hope, so-called analytical and continental twentieth-century traditions. Deleuze, however, is interested not in noun phrases but verb phrases, so his area of concern is not subject and predicate but infinitive and mode.[28] He not only has to contend with how a virtual becomes an actual without the negation of the virtual *and* the madness of the total actual or revelatory stasis but also needs to come to terms with how actualities interact with other actualities. In other words, separating his work from Agamben and Badiou for different but equally radical reasons in relation to indifference, Deleuze has to contend with value.[29] Thus, Deleuze sets himself the following task:

- Explain how an instance of an infinitive moves from virtual to actual status.
- Plot how this actualisation does not negate the virtual.
- Consider how one actualisation sits in relation to other potential actualisations of the virtual not yet or not at present actualised.
- Place one instance of actualisation on a plane of reticulations which open it up to other actualisations, themselves actualisations of other virtualities, in an open-ended never-ending series of reticulations.
- Finally, make this consistent in a manner that is not total chaos or blinding stasis.

The central problematics of any philosophy of change are these: If something suffers a change, how do you know it if it is now different? In other words, how does the trace of the causality of change remain if A becomes B? Then how does change occur in a manner that is plural, or how can there be many changes without one succumbing to total flux? Finally, if change is determined by this causality, then change is perceptible only once something has changed and potential to change has become actualised. Yet if this is so, how can the principle of change itself exist, as it is only a retrospective assumption of actualisation? The final, radical conclusion could be that this means that actualisation does not exist because all potential extends from an actualisation; thus, the principle of potential is reducible to the principle of the actual, and you will know that an actual is a stable actual only if it doesn't ever change. As this is an interminable wait, in the end actuality is definable only in negation and in contingency as that which has not yet changed and so for now is actual, which is another way of saying that every actual is potential, the founding tenet of speculative realism.[30] The only way traditionally to stop these issues slipping away like so many minnows from a net with too loose a weave is to insist on a ground that cannot change, for Aristotle substance or pure matter. As we know, for the modern philosophy of difference, this would mean placing an identity before difference, a situation that cannot be countenanced.

DIFFERENTIATING DELEUZE AND AGAMBEN THROUGH INDIFFERENCE

As Deleuze begins *Difference and Repetition* with an insistence that difference always precedes identity,[31] he needs the deduction of a system of infinite comprehension that states that any object can be comprehended at any point in any of its potential actualisations through the process of reticulation.[32] This replaces the grounding of identity with a consistent plane of immanence to avoid the logical paradoxes and theories of infinity and regress that plague the Aristotelian tradition century after century. The plane of consistency for greening then is the total number of potential reticulations of verb with noun in phrase existence. This is a radical solution quite different from Agamben's theory of potentiality. It does not concern simply the capacity to do something but the concatenation of capacity with specific instance in terms of value and mode.

However, Deleuze is more than aware that this innovation leaves him open to two traditional fears of Western thought: chaos and isolation. If every actualisation is traceable back to a plane of total available virtualities, hard enough, and if each virtuality is the actualisation of one verb in the phrase of other verbs which themselves must become virtualities of the first plane *and* take our first actualisation as a new virtuality in their own plane, a system of reticulations becomes that of pure, chaotic connectiveness in every direction, slipping away not so much like minnows from a net but like a net woven in every direction at every nodal point. Such a plane of consistency has no consistency or any right to be called a plane. In contrast, if an actualisation is always so specific as to be this moment of reticulation of these actualities in relation to these virtualities, then every existence would be isolated to itself. Pure actualisation of connection without a plane of virtualities results in a splendid isolationism where each atom floats in a state of perfect, unique self-singularity. These two positions could be called the nightmare of absolute darkness, the terror of total light or, more simply, the problem of the Hegelian Also and One. This is why Deleuze has recourse to a dialectic to supplement the problems of his transcendental deduction of total comprehension.

How does Deleuze's use of dark and light in relation to the virtual map onto Agamben's use of the same terminology? As we saw, Agamben concentrates on the fact of incapacity in relation to seeing darkness. If one has the capacity to see, then one can see when one is seeing due to the coloration of light; one can see when one has one's eyes closed, as, due to the refutation of the Megaran paradox, one does not lose the capacity to do something just because one is not currently doing it; and finally, Agamben insists, one can still see even in darkness where what one sees is the colour of incapacity. This colouration is the colour of the dark, which, in showing that you can still see even if there is no light, allows one to see one's capacity as such, to see sight, which we are told is impossible, not directly but through the presentation of one's incapacity.[33] This may sound very much a confirmation of the very tradition of the philosophy of difference (Hegel, Heidegger, Derrida) that Agamben is rejecting. Rather, it is a necessary sojourn in incapacity to reveal not that the being of sight here is permanently in withdrawal, accessible only as unconcealed or located in a moment of permanent difference as deferral and self-spacing, but rather that incapacity allows one to see the problem of capacity and demands that one find a solution of sorts. This solution, for Agamben, is indifferential suspension between potential and actual through an incapacity that is sacrificed twice so that the assumed division between potential and actual can be suspended, meaning that both elements coexist in direct contravention of the rule of potential, namely, that of *dynamis*, or the movement of change.

Deleuzian obscurity is, like Agamben's incapacious darkness, a darkness that allows one to see. Again, like Deleuze, it is not a darkness that belongs only to one side or the other. If we take the virtual here to stand for potential, then the virtual is both clarity of differential complete structure and obscurity of differenciated actual wholeness. At the same time, in the actual clarity is the ability to see a global wholeness which individuated moments of differentiation merely add to and restabilise. However, such apperception negates perception of the singularities themselves. It would be tempting to say you can see either the parts or the whole, but this is not the case, as we saw. Both realms are made up of parts which combine into unified structures. That said, we can put this to one side, as the issue we are concerned with is otherwise. Is it the case, as in Agamben, that incapacity (obscurity) allows one to see one's capacity albeit in negation, and what does that mean in Deleuzian terms? Certain features of Deleuze make this consonance unlikely. The first problem is that for Agamben the faculty seems to be, if not a singular thing, an entity of strict limitations. If we speak of the capacity to write poetry, for example, the issue is whether one can retain the faculty under a single name even when one is not actualising this capacity. If we speak of writing poetry, in Deleuze we see a constant process of plane actualisation becoming habituated, and then we encounter the third stage of virtual possibility which Deleuze calls counteractualisation (virtual determinability-actualisation-counteractualisation).[34]

In other words, Agamben wants to take the basic operation of difference, the common (the virtual) and the proper (actualisation), and suspend it in favour of indifference. His is a theory of change as difference-negation opening to a field of static suspension which will then lead to real, revolutionary, evental change. Deleuze aims for the opposite. His system is to take a suspension of difference, the moment when actualisations forget entirely their virtuality and origins in difference, and reintroduce a difference, that of differen*t*iation, which results in counteractualisation.[35] Put simply, for Agamben radical change comes from impotential suspension of difference and for Deleuze counteractual destruction of the same. Agamben's is the revolution of the weak, while Deleuze's is the counterinsurgency of the strong, suggesting of course a very different political makeup to their two complementary yet ultimately contesting systems.

The central issue here is the double relations on offer. We already saw that incapacity is a double system allowing potential and actuality to see their own capacities through their very different incapacities. For Deleuze, as we saw, this is also the case. The virtual has an obscurity as much as the real. We also have a nontranslatability in both systems. Potentiality cannot pass over into actuality without being negated, so incapacity does this job for it by making actuality admit to the permanent present of a 'nonactualised' part and allowing potentiality to exist as not-yet-actualised. This is very similar to the relation of virtual to actual. The virtual does not precede the actual operating as the nonreal possible that is then realised. The virtual is always virtual. Yet in being thus, it is always available for actualisation for reasons pertaining to indifference that we will clarify in the next chapter.[36] Virtuality always has a capacity, which is that it is determinable. At the same time actuality is not the realisation of a virtuality but is a negotiation with its virtualities which can be in one of three stages: preactualised, being hidden by an imposed clarity or counteractualising. Thus, just as we saw with potential, the virtual can never be actualised and remain virtual, yet the actual never actualises all virtualities even through it always proposes a whole global system that seems to represent this. I would argue that Agamben is as reliant on Deleuze as he is Aristotle for his conceptualisation of impotentiality in this regard.

Thus, it can be said that there is much to say in favour of mapping Agambenian potential onto the Deleuzian virtual; in fact, the future of philosophy depends in part on this project in my opinion, especially in relation to the centrality of Badiou for that future. Yet there are also central features of the two systems that make this impossible. The question then, as was the case with Derrida, is how to choose? What are the conditions that determine a commitment to a philosophy of indifference over the remarkable texts of the philosophy of difference at least since Hegel? This choice, and one must choose, I contend, as the two modes of thought are ultimately incompatible, is made easier in this instance (as opposed to the tense contestation between Agamben and Derrida) due to my second line of argument, namely, that Agamben's indifference is a positive development from Deleuzian indifference rather than, as we saw previously, Agamben presenting his indifferential method as a negative break from the limits of Derridean undecidability. To prove this we now have to turn to Agamben's specific comments on Deleuze and his complex relationship with immanence.

NOTES

1. The most recent being David Kishik, *The Power of Life* (Stanford, CA: Stanford University Press, 2012), 75–77.
2. Giorgio Agamben, *Potentialities*, trans. Daniel Heller-Roazen (Stanford, CA: Stanford University Press, 1999), 239.
3. We must make it clear that Agamben is not siding with immanence per se and supports a clear suspension between immanence and transcendence as is logically consistent with the method of indifference. See Giorgio Agamben, *The Time That Remains*, trans. Patricia Dailey (Stanford, CA: Stanford University Press, 2005), 25.
4. An excellent clarification of the issue of impotentiality can be found in Giorgio Agamben, *Nudities*, trans. David Kishik and Stefan Pedatella (Stanford, CA: Stanford University Press, 2011), 102.
5. All the major single-authored works on Agamben, de la Durantaye, Dickinson, Kishik, Mills, Murray, Watkin and Zartaloudis spend ample time on potentiality, and it is from this stable platform that my own, perhaps more speculative comments are freed to leap from.
6. See also Giorgio Agamben, *What Is an Apparatus? And Other Essays*, trans. David Kishik and Stefan Pedatella (Stanford, CA: Stanford University Press, 2009), 46–47.
7. Agamben, *Potentialities*, 179.
8. Agamben, *Potentialities*, 182.
9. Agamben, *Potentialities*, 182.
10. Agamben, *Potentialities*, 183.
11. Agamben, *Potentialities*, 183.
12. See the relation of this idea to the messianic as-not of *klesis* in Agamben, *Time That Remains*, 26–27.
13. Agamben, *Potentialities*, 184.
14. Agamben, *Potentialities*, 204.
15. Agamben, *Potentialities*, 219.
16. Agamben, *Potentialities*, 239.
17. Agamben, *Potentialities*, 27.
18. Agamben makes clear the relation to Deleuze's ideas and potentiality in the short essay "On What We Can Not Do" (Agamben, *Nudities*, 43–45). See also *Nudities*, 7–8.
19. Agamben, *Potentialities*, 181.
20. Cited in Agamben, *Potentialities*, 181.
21. Agamben, *Potentialities*, 181.
22. Gilles Deleuze, *Difference and Repetition*, trans. Paul Patton (London: Athlone Press, 1994), 28–29.
23. James Williams, *Gilles Deleuze's* Difference and Repetition (Edinburgh: Edinburgh University Press, 2003), 17–18.
24. For an excellent consideration of quasi-causal belonging in Deleuze, see James Williams, *Gilles Deleuze's* Logic of Sense (Edinburgh: Edinburgh University Press, 2008), 129–32, and Sean Bowden, *The Priority of Events: Deleuze's Logic of Sense* (Edinburgh: Edinburgh University Press, 2011), 42–47.

25. Deleuze, *Difference and Repetition*, 302–4; Gilles Deleuze and Félix Guattari, *A Thousand Plateaus: Capitalism and Schizophrenia*, trans. Brian Massumi (London: Athlone Press, 1992), 506–8; Gilles Deleuze and Félix Guattari, *What Is Philosophy?*, trans. Graham Burchell and Hugh Tomlinson (London: Verso, 1994), 35–60.

26. Gilles Deleuze, *The Logic of Sense*, trans. Mark Lester (London: Continuum, 2004), 24–25.

27. Deleuze, *Difference and Repetition*, 207–11.

28. Deleuze, *Logic of Sense*, 8, 211–12.

29. In Badiou the quality of the multiple is in fact as indifferent to the formulation of sets and their interruption by event, while for Agamben all values are actually indifferent propers in relation to signatory commons which themselves, as we saw, carry no content and so can be said to have indifferent value.

30. See Quentin Meillassoux, *After Finitude: An Essay on the Necessity of Contingency*, trans. Ray Brassier (London: Continuum, 2008), esp. 50–81, where the critique of correlation is based on a valorisation, of sorts, of the absolute necessity of contingency in 'nature'.

31. What he terms "difference without negation"; Deleuze, *Difference and Repetition*, xix–xx and, later, "difference without concept", 13–14.

32. Deleuze, *Difference and Repetition*, 11.

33. Deleuze, *Difference and Repetition*, 28–29, 119–24, 275. Although I do not agree with his overall critique of Agamben, Gaston's consideration of these issues from the perspective of colour and sensation is elegant and provocative (Sean Gaston, *Derrida, Literature and War* [London: Continuum, 2009], 40–53).

34. Deleuze, *Logic of Sense*, 169–75, 203–7.

35. Deleuze, *Difference and Repetition*, 209–10.

36. Deleuze, *Difference and Repetition*, 206–7, 209–21.

EIGHT

The Two Bartlebies: Deleuze, Agamben and Immanence

A LIFE AS IMPERSONAL INDIFFERENCE

Deleuze's late essay "Immanence: A Life" seeks to explain the specific nature of the transcendental field of his work, the plane of immanence, in relation to what he calls, after Kant, transcendentals, which we will take to mean actualisations. The transcendental field is defined as "a pure stream of a-subjective consciousness, a pre-reflexive impersonal consciousness, a qualitative duration of consciousness without a self".[1] It is, therefore clearly possessed of qualities that allow us to say that it is both virtual and indifferent in essence. In relation to this field, consciousness occurs only when out of this a subject is produced at the same time as an object. Contra Kant therefore, consciousness is a production of the transcendental field, meaning that not only is the object produced by and for the subject but the subject as such as consciousness is produced at precisely the same time. This, in a nutshell, is perhaps Deleuze's main contribution to Western metaphysical systematic thought: consciousness is produced from the plane of immanence. That the transcendental field be composed of immanence is of course no surprise, but Deleuze is careful to restate here one of his most important maxims, namely, that immanence is "not related to Some Thing as a unity superior to all things or to a Subject as an act that brings about a synthesis of things: it is only when immanence is no longer immanence to anything other than itself that we can speak of the plane of immanence".[2] For our purposes this is a timely reminder that the virtual is not the possible or even the potential. It is not the latent realisation or actualisation of a subject or world of objects but is as real as the actual. We might just as well say that the actual is the realisation of the virtual in that both are produced in a circularity which

151

makes it impossible, once the process is underway, and it is always underway due to Deleuze's orthodox commitment to hermeneutics,[3] to state which term precedes the other and which produces the other. One could easily contend that the actual world is produced from the transcendental field of virtualities in that all the world is there, yet this field itself does not exist except in the act or process of production.

Deleuze then determines the field of pure immanence, or the virtual, as "A LIFE, and nothing else". This is not immanence to life but life as the immanence of immanence: "it is complete power, complete bliss". He illustrates this with an example from Dickens's *Our Mutual Friend*, where Riderhood, a much-despised character, is assumed to be dying. The closer the villain comes to death, the more the onlookers work to take care of him. As soon as Riderhood revives, the same onlookers become colder towards him. Deleuze explains this by saying,

> Between his life and his death, there is a moment that is only that of *a* life playing with death. The life of the individual gives way to an impersonal and yet singular life that releases a pure event freed from the accidents of internal and external life . . . a "Homo tantum" with whom everyone empathizes and who attains a sort of beatitude. It is a haecceity no longer of individuation but of singularization: a life of pure immanence, neutral, beyond good and evil.[4]

It is not remarkable that Agamben chooses this text of all of Deleuze's to comment on specifically. Here we have laid out before us a level of indifference pertaining to capacity which is also directly related to life. Inasmuch as there is a single project for Agamben, it is the indifferentiation of the category of life that his work on potentiality, politics and even aesthetics facilitates. The terms of the presentation of *a* life are familiar to us. The haecceity of singularization is, in effect, the project of Agamben's first great tract on indifference, *The Coming Community*. The neutral and impersonal being describes well the complex presence of the homo sacer or bare life in Agamben's work. And finally Agamben's utilisation of Aristotelian potentiality opened him up to the problem of the ethics of capacity. In fact, the difference between generic, irrational potential and skilful, rational potential is very instructive here. Inasmuch as we all live, one might say that life is generic potential. We all have the potential to live. Yet of course, life, like substance in relation to Aristotelian irrational potentiality, resembles pure matter. We must have life to have a generic capacity; thus, to speak of life as generic capacity is incorrect, for we do not have a capacity for life. That would be like arguing that there is a substance which precedes pure matter or a grounding of the ground.

However, the means by which Deleuze describes *a* life make this matter more complicated. The evil man, as he plays with death, enters a zone of indistinction between life and death which is also the suspension of morality. Although he may not have the capacity for life, he just lives it;

life is not a skill he acquires, he has the capacity for *a* life, a specific way or form of life as Agamben calls it, and he also has the incapacity for *a* life seen as a purely impersonal life. *A* life here then is the suspension of the division between life and death, which is the ultimate relation of potentiality and actuality. It has two effects. First, it makes life specific, not generic, which, for Deleuze, means it reveals that life is the balance of value and power through which a subject is produced through its relations with, production of and forgetting about objects. This life, the actualised life, is not given but made and remade constantly. Second, below this is a life as impersonal life. This is the absolute immanence of every life, all it can and cannot be, presented as in the instant of the incapacity of passage between life and death.

That said, a life is not simply a limit case of extreme circumstances, and again here Deleuze and Agamben are very close. Dying is a good example of a life, as in incapacity it produces *a* life when normally it remains invisible so to speak. Yet Deleuze stipulates, "A life is everywhere, in all the moments that a given living subject goes through and that are measured by given lived objects: an immanent life carrying with it the events or singularities that are merely actualized in subjects and objects. This indefinite life does not itself have moments, close as they may be one to another, but only between-times, between-moments".[5] In other words, as we saw in Agamben, *a* life is an indifferent life. Deleuze calls it here an indefinite life. It exists in the transition between moments, between actualisations, which Riderhood's near-death simply brings to clarity to the onlookers, including we readers. However, in a phrase that is not so clear in relation to Agamben, this life is everywhere. The ubiquity of a life will become an important bone of contention, for Agamben's method seems to suggest that indifference is a complex process achieved through a philosophical historiography, available only at certain moments, all in preparation for a philosophy to come. If you remember, his attack on Derridean concepts of law and justice is precisely to refute the ubiquity of indifference position. In contrast, for Deleuze immanence occurs between every actualisation, is bodily not historically based and is an end in itself inasmuch as there is nothing other than a life, and further a life is the basis of every potential counteractualisation. One might say of Deleuze that the philosophy to-come over which Agamben and Derrida's work dickers is always already here.

The remainder of the article reiterates points familiar to any reader of Deleuze: singularity is not individuality, the indefinite is not pure indetermination, the One is not a transcendent field to contain singularity but always multiple, transcendence is produced by immanence and the virtual is not opposed to the real but the actual. Deleuze ends, however, with a comment that pricks one's interest if one is considering, as we are here, the virtual in relation to the potential. Having said, consistent with his system laid out in *Difference and Repetition*, that singularities/events give

every actualised plane virtuality and the plane of immanence gives virtual events their reality (the crucial relation of quasi-causal cobelonging
further developed in *The Logic of Sense*),[6] he concludes, "The event considered as non-actualized (indefinite) is lacking in nothing. It suffices to
put it relation to its concomitants: a transcendental field, a plane of immanence, a life, singularities".[7]

In a sense this is just another way of saying that the virtual is as real as
the actual, only real in a different way. However, it also states that indefinite life is sufficient to itself. It is not in service of the actual, and the
actual is not its end. More than this, it speaks, I feel, of potentiality as well
as, in terms of its incapacity, impotentiality. As Agamben is at pains to
point out, potentiality is not actuality waiting to happen. It is a pure and
subsistent field protected, if you will, by impotentiality, which, when
needed, will sacrifice itself in actualisation so that potentiality can be
retained. This is the same point as Deleuze's in relation to the virtual. The
virtual is availability for actualisation and is defined by its determinability. Yet determination is not its goal or end point, and no amount of
actualisation in Deleuze will ever diminish the virtual. Finally, there will
never be a total determination. All actualisation is an apperceptive as-if
goal of wholeness, large or small, but counteractualisation will always
occur, interrupting actual wholeness with singular completions. The
question remains, for Agamben, is the same true for his system, and, if
not, is Agambenian messianic stasis to be preferred to Deleuzian redemption on this earth here and now, all the time?

VITALISM AS IMPOTENTIALITY

No consideration of the term life in Deleuze in relation to Agamben can
neglect the issue of Deleuze's much-touted vitalism, which, I have already stated, is at odds in the final analysis with Agamben's philosophical archaeology. Indeed, Agamben is clearly unhappy with Deleuze's two
examples of a life or bare life as they are presented in the article. Although Deleuze contends that *a* life is to be found between every moment
of every life, or impersonal virtuality is to be found between every actualisation, he falls back on two classic limit cases to express this, death and
birth. Here Agamben finally begins to be critical when he says of Deleuze, "One could say that the difficult attempt to clarify the vertigo of
immanence by means of 'a life' leads us instead into an area that is even
more uncertain, in which the child and the dying man present us with the
enigmatic cipher of bare biological life as such".[8] What Agamben seems
to be presenting us with here is a rather Derridean reading of Deleuze. It
cannot have escaped his attention that dying and birth are only extreme
examples for the sake of clarification; for Deleuze, after all, subjects are
constantly being born in that the virtual-actual is always genetic, and

dying in that counteractualisation is always destructive. Yet Agamben seems to feel that, all the same, it is no coincidence that *a* life is presented here in terms of the two special cases of human life to be found in the history of philosophy: birth and death, genesis and finitude. Agamben does not then develop on the suggestion that a life and bare life are different, perhaps at odds, and that bare life presents the limit of Deleuzian immanent vitalism, which would have been immeasurably illustrative, but rather moves backwards to Aristotle and his definition of life. Here he warns of associating life with the tradition of seeing a difference between human life and bare nutritive life which he assigns to Aristotelian scholarship and its influence on nineteenth-century science. Can, he wonders, Deleuzian vitalism survive the signature of all life in the West, the contentious yet remarkable persistent *zōe-bios* distinction it is assumed we inherited from the Greeks?

Agamben then 'saves' Deleuze from this error by indicating that central to the nutritive life model is its attribution of life to a subject, while what determines a life is that which can never be attributed to a subject "being instead the matrix of infinite desubjectification. *In Deleuze, the principle of immanence thus functions antithetically to Aristotle's principle of the ground*".[9] Here Agamben refers to the previous section, where he reveals Aristotelian life as always the classic two-part system of division-categorisation and then grounding. As we know, this is at the root of Agambenian indifference, and the same is true of Deleuze. Aristotle defines life as the ultimate exercise in genus and species, while Deleuzian immanence is a self-expressed exercise in the negation of this tradition in keeping with the wider context of his main beneficiaries, Agamben and Badiou. More than this, not only does immanence deny the grounding of all species on a single genus, but it also, by necessity, disallows the categorisation of hierarchy and separation typical of Aristotelian ontology up to Heidegger. Instead, "The plane of immanence thus functions as a principle of virtual indetermination, in which the vegetative and the animal, the inside and the outside . . . in passing through one another, cannot be told apart".[10] Agamben then cites the key section of the article "A Life Is Everywhere . . .", finally happy that Deleuze is not presenting a vitalism of difference such as he traces back to Aristotle.

That said, the nature of Deleuzian vitalism remains a source of concern for Agamben until, that is, he traces it to the concluding comments of *What Is Philosophy?* on the nature of vitalism. Deleuze, with Guattari, presents two alternatives for vitalism, an idea that acts but is not (does not come into objectal existence), which he rejects, and a force that exists but does not act, which he favours calling it "contemplation without knowledge". Agamben terms this a "force that preserves without acting",[11] the wording of which makes it clear how close this concept of vitalism is to Agamben's own conception of potentiality-impotentiality. He likens this to the Greek *theoria* but the more accurate name for this is

Deleuze's plane of immanence which constitutes the complex conception of the virtual that we traced in the previous chapter. We might then also call this the virtual-vital, a "living contemplation".[12] That this virtual-vital preserves without acting means that it has precisely the same characteristics of preservation and passivity that constitute potentiality in terms of its impotentiality. Impotentiality also preserves potentiality in actuality through its own passive, inactive mediality.[13]

BEATITUDE OF SELF-PREDICATION

Having drawn the parallel between potentiality and vitalism in terms of passivity and preservation, Agamben completes his analysis with a consideration of the other quality of living contemplation, what Deleuze terms its "potentiality, complete beatitude".[14] We have already traced this theme across the five essays that conclude the collection, but here specifically Agamben tries to develop a conception of complete beatitude again in terms of his own work, specifically his use of Russell's paradox of self-predication. The same conceptualisation is also present in Derridean grammatology, where there is no term for language that does not succumb to writing, and in Deleuze's linguistic pragmatism in *The Logic of Sense*. This problem can be found in Aristotle, is important to Kant and comes to be one of the central problems of modern set theory, which in turn informs Badiou's 'solution' to the problem.[15]

In terms of the varying different registers that this problem can be addressed under, in many senses *the* problem of modern and contemporary philosophy, Agamben traces, in a philological gesture typical of him, the relation of Spinoza to his native language of Ladino, still spoken in the northernmost reaches of Italy. In Ladino there are verbs that "present an action in which agent and patient enter a threshold of absolute indistinction: a walk as walking-oneself".[16] This verb, *pasearse*, presents to Spinoza, Agamben and, by implication, Deleuze a model of self-reflexivity that suspends the presuppositions of language. We found a similar operation in the essay "*Se*" and its consideration of self-reflexive verbs in romance languages. In such verbs the divisions of language, "active and passive, subject and object, transitive and intransitive lose their meaning. *Pasearse* is, furthermore, an action in which means and end, potentiality and actuality, faculty and use enter a zone of absolute indistinction".[17]

We are now more than familiar with this logic, but this passage does allow us to draw some additional conclusions. The first of these is that the signifier-signified division of the early work on language is always translatable across the totality of Agamben's work. Here it operates still in the linguistic field but in relation to verbs rather than nouns. This is important because, as mentioned, Deleuzian linguistics is a radical cri-

tique of structural linguistics based on a pragmatic context-verb formation. For Deleuze the issue is never one of naming the thing and all the
paradoxes therein but of the problematic causality of agent and action
within an already complete context of which naming is only a small
portion.[18] Beyond this Agamben also allows us to see that his critique of
the sign, intrinsic to his controversial reading of Derrida, is part of a
wider reconsideration of language in relation to action and existence, an
area he rightly indicates as not fully developed by grammatology. Finally, this construction clarifies the linguistic problem of self-reference,
through the expansion into verb and context, as a paradigm of the potential-actual dichotomy which then allows Agamben to present what he
believes to be Deleuzian beatitude: "*The immanence of desire to itself*". Deleuzian desire, as Agamben makes clear, is not determined by alterity or
lack. Rather, it should be defined as the capability of acting in an experi-
mental fashion. This capability exists in the plane of immanence in two
moments. The first of these is the capacity to actualise virtual forces in
any living being. The second is the capability to break sedimented and
territorialized situations through counteractualisation. Desire may then
be described as the simultaneous capacity to connect (bodies) and discon-
nect (states of affairs).[19]

Agamben stays with Spinoza here in explaining Deleuze by referring
to Spinoza's own concern over how a desire can stay within itself and still
be desire, for, after all, a desire is a potential for change into actualisation
(desire is another name for potential). He reads the Spinoza term *conatus*
in these terms as the Being of a thing through the desire: "to desire to
preserve one's own Being is to desire one's own desire, to constitute
oneself as desiring. *In* conatus, *desire and Being thus coincide without resi-
due.* . . . Spinoza defines life as *conatus*".[20] *Conatus* answers for Agamben a
fundamental question that is begged by his system of indifferent suspension: how can the negation of difference not result simply in the One? For
Agamben the Deleuzian plane of immanence satisfies precisely this question. On this plane, the plane of the virtual-vital as I am calling it, every
Being exists as movement, the desire to actualise, and as stasis, the reten-
tion of virtuality in actualisation by virtue of what Agamben calls the
impotential or incapacity of every potential-actual dynamic. This, for
Agamben at least, is Deleuzian vitalism.

We might express it more extensively in the following manner. The
plane of immanence is always already present in its meta-stability. All
potential actualisations are present there in the form of obscure, for now
inactive, potentialities. All of the life of to-green is contained in this plane.
In this sense the plane, which is composed entirely of desires (desire to
actualise and desire to counteractualise), is complete to itself.[21] Nothing
can be 'added' to this plane; rather, this plane can only be added to other
planes of territorialized construction. Agamben concludes, via Spinoza
and his construction of self-reflexive Latin terms to express the Ladino

idea of action and agent as indistinct, that Deleuzian beatitude is the resting of oneself through the desire of desire. By this he does not mean the want of desire due to its lack, rather simply that desire produces itself through experimentation. We will return to this final point in the final section of this chapter when we try to reconcile Deleuzian indifference at the level of the plane of immanence and Agambenian indifference. For now we need concern ourselves only with how this debate maps back onto Agamben's wider purpose.

AGAMBEN'S PHILOSOPHY OF LIFE TO COME

The essay finishes with a three-part program for future thought:

1. Life is the theme of any philosophy to come, contained in a mutual critique to be found between Foucauldian negative biopower and Deleuzian serene "A life . . . ": "we will have to see the element that marks subjection to biopower in the very paradigm of possible beatitude". Neither is correct; thus, it is wrong to either see Agamben as a thinker of biopower or concede that his concept of potential is simply a version of Deleuzian virtuality.

2. "To assume this legacy as a philosophical task it will be necessary to reconstruct a genealogy that will clearly distinguish in modern philosophy—which is, in a new sense, a philosophy of life—between a line of immanence and a line of transcendence", in other words, to take sides after Heidegger with the immanent thinkers of life, Foucault and Deleuze, rather than the 'transcendent' work of Levinas and Derrida.

3. One must match this with a genealogical enquiry into the term/ signature Life. In this way life will be presented not as a medical and scientific notion but as a "philosophical, political, and theological concept" which must "therefore be thought accordingly". This modality of thinking life, therefore, consists of moving far beyond division within the term "life" between, say, organic and animal, biological and contemplative, bare life and the life of the mind.[22]

There has, up to this point, and even later until the publication of *The Signature of All Things*, never been such a clear definition of Agamben's much-contested, because consistently misunderstood, messianism. A philosophy to come will take life as its central theme. That said, life is not a thing as such but a term constructed over time. He does not yet have access to the term "signature", but he means of course "signature". To understand life, you need genealogical critique. Yet such a critique must concede that at every turn, for example, late 19th- and early 20th-century scientific attempts to designate life such as are analysed in *The Open*, life is always a philosophical construct and cannot be understood otherwise.

These traditions are metaphysical, which means they are defined by a contingent and constructed philosophy of difference. Accordingly, one must suspend these differences and reveal them to be nonnecessary by retracing the history of their genealogical construction through philosophy, theology and politics. Locally this means taking sides with immanence, although globally this difference is itself imposed, and only rare thinkers are able, according to Agamben, to suspend this most pernicious of differences (Heidegger is the only one of the modern age). Even though Agamben sides with Foucault and Deleuze, therefore, he does so critically, seeing their immanence as the result, we presume, of choosing a difference. Foucault's biopower is necessarily critical; Agamben stresses after Derrida that critical philosophy of the genealogy of term construction is the essential business of philosophy, while Deleuzian beatitude is productive and positive, the two definitions of Deleuzian desire, in a manner which takes us away from philosophy as genealogical critique and towards a philosophy of forms of life to come.

Agamben's final words return to the question of vitalism or contemplation without knowledge:

> Life as contemplation without knowledge will have a precise correlate in thought that has freed itself of all cognition and intentionality. *Theoria* and the contemplative life, which the philosophical tradition has identified as its highest goal for centuries, will have to be dislocated onto a new plane of immanence. It is not certain that, in the process, political philosophy and epistemology will be able to maintain their present physiognomy and difference with respect to ontology. Today, blessed life lies on the same terrain as the biological body of the West.[23]

This is an almost impossibly compact set of statements which offer as much obfuscation in closing as the whole section proffers clarity in all other areas. He seems to be suggesting the following propositions:

- Deleuze is wrong in preferring potentiality without action over act without essence. The future of thought must be the correlation of both, reading correlation here as corelation or relational nonrelation.
- Yet at the same time, act without essence, pure abstract thought, must itself be dislocated onto the plane of vitalism. Each position must be suspended in relation to their other.
- When this happens the philosophy of Being and the philosophy of existence will lose the clear distinctions currently imposed upon them. Both transcendence and immanence are at fault, and their differentiation is to be suspended, perhaps resulting in what Nancy terms "trans-immanence".
- Yet all of this is to-come so that at the moment blessed life, or Deleuzian beatitude, is as unrealised as what one might call cursed life or the state of bare-life in Foucauldian biopolitics.

- Thus, we conclude that the philosophy to come must consider the theme life from the perspective of a doubly critical immanence: that of Deleuze and Foucault. Neither is correct, but both are usefully wrong in two specific ways. First, they present systems of immanence, whereas a philosophy to come suspends the transcendence-immanence division. Second, they are methodologically one-sided. Foucault presents genealogically consistent critical philosophy and Deleuze projective and productive messianic thinking. One needs both, and the indifferential system Agamben proposes seems to provide both.

As a clear statement of intent for the next two decades, the final lines of this essay make it another essential addition to the canon of Agamben's truly important contributions to the future development of philosophy out of his critique of the dominance of philosophy of difference.

CREATION FROM THE ABYSS

As previously mentioned, in 1993 Agamben published his essay "Bartleby, or On Contingency" alongside Deleuze's essay "Bartleby; or, The Formula." Although not a reading of Deleuze, in the centre of Agamben's essay is a sustained response to Deleuze's earlier work. The essay is divided into three parts on creation, the formula and decreation, respectively, and is now widely considered as one of Agamben's finest and most suggestive. The first section, "The Scribe, or On Creation", tackles several issues that are also covered in other essays as well as an original consideration of the role of the scribe (Bartleby is of course a scrivener). Specifically, Agamben traces the genealogy of the various paradigms of writing, copying, ink, tablets and so on in relation to thinking across the Western tradition. Specifically, Agamben is interested in the figure of the writing tablet, and here it returns in relation to Aristotle's model for thinking thought, specifically the tablet on which nothing is written. It is not so difficult for us now to see how this tablet serves Agamben's project of potentiality well. As he says, glossing on Aristotle's use of the figure of the *rasura tabulae*, the wax film covering the tablet which is his true model for potentiality, "The mind is therefore not a thing but a pure being of potentiality, and the image of the writing tablet on which nothing is written functions precisely to represent the mode in which pure potentiality exists".[24] Specifically, the wax tablet represents the impotentiality at the heart of potentiality so that "Just as the layer of sensitive wax is suddenly grazed by the scribe's stylus, so the potentiality of thought, which in itself is nothing, allows for the act of intelligence to take place".[25] The wax layer represents impotentiality. It is supported by a tablet which operates as the ground of potentiality, so that now in Deleuzian terms it is the plane of immanence. When you write on the tablet, you do not negate this pure potential support or ground because the wax takes the impression of actualisation leaving the tablet untouched and also, because of the nature of the wax, never negates its own potential to repeat this process of impotential sacrifice.

Having detailed how the tablet operates in relation to potentiality, he turns to one of his most important and confusing engagements with classical thought, Aristotle's model of thought that thinks itself or, as Agamben calls it in the earlier pages of *Potentialities*, the thing of thought itself, which he also likens to language. Again we have more than covered this in our various comments on self-reflexivity and self-predication in the sections above. Aristotle arrives at a problematic logical impasse in relation to thinking and potential. If thought thinks something, it becomes subordinate to this actualisation and, according to Aristotle, would never be actualised because it would be determined by something other than its essence, which means it remains in potential when actualised. Yet if thought thinks nothing and so remains pure potential, it is of course useless and profoundly inoperative. To escape this paradox Aristotle proposes the "famous idea of thought thinking itself, which is a kind of mean between thinking nothing and thinking something, between potentiality and actuality. . . . It thinks a pure potentiality (to think and not to think); and what thinks its own potentiality is what is most divine and blessed".[26] Such a formulation further strengthens the link between self-referentiality and beatitude. Agamben remains unsatisfied with this solution, as it raises several questions as to how one can actually think a pure potentiality, and how can a blank writing tablet impress itself? Thus, he turns to a scholastic work by Albert the Great, commenting on *De Anima*, who defines the blank self-impressing tablet of pure thought as "pure knowability and receptability", as if, "the letters, on their own, wrote themselves on the writing tablet".[27]

Agamben sees these comments as part of a wider genealogy whose signature is to be found across the three great monotheistic religions, namely the idea of creation *ex nihilo*. It is a problem whose signature is also to be found at the heart of modern philosophy in Kant's numerous refutations of the problem of infinite regress (how a condition can be first and thus by definition unconditioned) and of course informs contemporary onto-theological theories of the origin of the universe in the so-called big bang. In all its different manifestations up to Kant, what concerns these thinkers and theologians is that nothing can precede God in the act of creation, "such as matter (that is potential being)".[28] Yet at the same time the more these traditions looked into this nothing from which all things are created and which must be immaterial and not potential, the more they found that nothing resembled a something. This is in accord with Neoplatonic thought, which had already considered long and hard the problem of nothing, contending that it was the highest principle from which everything proceeds. To facilitate this, they bifurcated nothing into two orders: "Just as the Neoplatonists had distinguished two Nothings, one that, so to speak, transcends beings from above and one that exceeds then from below, so they distinguished two matters, one corporeal and the other incorporeal, the dark and eternal background of intelligible beings".[29]

However arcane this appears, it is worth keeping in mind the context of this essay. Students of Deleuze will be more than aware that these comments on Neoplatonic thought, whose master is Plotinus, pertain to the significance of darkness for the Deleuzian virtual that I have already referred to. As you will recall, Agamben's comments on the colour of darkness inform his appropriation of Aristotelian potentiality. We traced these same figures in relation to Deleuze's reliance on the obscurity-clarity formula that defines the essence of the virtual. The two figures then allowed us to map potentiality onto virtuality with some success but also resulted in several significant problems. We are now forced to contend with Deleuze's second use of darkness in the same text and how it relates directly to his use of indifference in *Difference and Repetition*, establishing the specificity of the terms "difference" and "repetition" in his work and also difference as always preceding identity. In so doing, Deleuze identifies two types of indifference: dark indifference and white or light indifference. Dark indifference is the easiest to understand, as it refers to the abyss of pure indetermination. In this zone each object is as yet undetermined, and so one object is as the same as another. They are not the same in terms of identity; it is just that they operate as indifferently different from each other and so appear as one and the same thing. It is advisable to keep in mind here Hegel's aporia of the One. The opposite of the dark realm of pure indetermination, which we will see is part of the deep, obscure, corporeal realm of virtuality, is the bright-light realm of absolute determination. Here each object is so totally determined that it finds no connection with any other object. These self-sufficient monads then are totally unique and fixed, a cold constellation of determination where singular identities are so strong that, ironically, the differences between them again become indifferent differences. Each monad, in being so determined from all the others, becomes indifferently identified as unique, pure singularity (Hegel's Alsos). Thus, Deleuze argues, the levels of both difference and repetition bear within them the threat of an unproductive indifference: the indifference of pure indetermination or absolute difference without repetition and the indifference of total determination of absolute repetition without difference.[30]

The necessity of thinking about Agamben's comments in light of these considerations of nonproductive indifference, specifically here the dark indifference of indetermination, is confirmed on the very next page when Agamben, ostensibly, is speaking of his beloved Cabalists but is actually referring to the work of Deleuze. Here he speaks of the mystical view of the "obscure matter that creation presupposes is nothing other than divine potentiality. The act of creation is God's descent into an abyss that is simply his own potentiality and impotentiality . . . and this undifferentiated abyss is the Nothing from which the world proceeds and on which it eternally rests. In this context, 'abyss' is not a metaphor".[31] Here the concentration is on the undifferentiated abyss of Nothing as that which precedes any act of creation. In other words, the abyss is the 'first' moment of the virtual, that is, the determinability of every series of singularities in the corporeal realm of the first desire of desire: the production of an actuality from a virtuality.[32]

That Deleuze calls this an abyss of indifference is due primarily to a misconception in philosophy as to the nature of this abyss. As Agamben's consideration of this signature shows, the abyss is a recurrent paradigm of Western thought in relation to the plate of creation: how can one create from nothing? For Deleuze the misconstrual of the abyss is of the same order as that of the misconstrual of the productive nature of philosophical obscurity. For him the abyss is never disassociated from creation, nor does it in any real sense precede it. Certainly, the desire of desire creates from nothing, but, like the Neoplatonists, for Deleuze nothing is decidedly *some thing*. Specifically, the realm of the abyss is not pure indetermination for the following reasons. The singularities in the abyss are always already reticulated. In this way there is never pure difference without repetition, as singularities by definition repeat their differences in terms of their common singularity and their common reticulation which, in linking two neutrally similar singularities, by definition distances them as specifically different by proposing a linked proximity.[33] Finally, this linked proximity is always available for actualisation and in fact is produced only as an aftereffect, essentially, of actualisation. All singularities are thus divisible series defined by their determinability, and this is why the darkness of the realm of the apparently indeterminate virtual is never the true darkness of pure indifferent indetermination.

Staying with the Neoplatonists, their double sense of nothing is also, surely, a reference to Deleuze's most important and troubling concept: quasi causality. Deleuze presents this in *The Logic of Sense* in terms of the Stoic's double consideration of indifference and their innovation of dividing causality into two. For them, and for Deleuze, as he wholeheartedly accepts this position, there are two realms. There is the realm of indifferent bodies and the realm of indifferent states of affairs. Bodies do not cause states, as they exist in entirely heterogeneous realms, but they cobelong. There can be no bodies unless they are manifested at some point in states of affairs, and no state of affairs can come about except from the preexistence of bodies.[34] Deleuze specifically uses the terms "corporeal" and "incorporeal" in reference to this theory, as does Agamben.[35] More than this, he identifies the corporeal realm with the virtual, now-renamed sense and the incorporeal with the actual, here considered in terms of language or abstract, incorporeal propositionality. In a typical fashion

that could be as much infuriating as it is exhilarating, Agamben appropriates Deleuze's conceptions of the abyss and indifferentiation whilst at the
same time inscribing them in a wider set of historically traceable, paradigmatic signatures. The stage is set, finally, for Agamben's last significant engagement with the modern thinker to whom he is most indebted,
specifically in relation to indifference, and from whom he must eventually find separation.

THE FORMULA: I PREFER NOT TO

The close relation between Deleuze and Agamben is never more apparent than in the opening comments of Deleuze in relation to what he calls
Bartleby's "great indeterminate formula, I PREFER NOT TO".[36] This is
not merely because Agamben too will concentrate on the precise wording
of the scrivener's refusal. He does not refuse to copy; he prefers not to
copy and in so doing consistently disarms those around him, uncertain
how to react to this statement of willed incapacity. Bartleby has not lost
the capacity to copy, but he has lost the will to copy or the preference for
actualisation; he permanently occupies his own incapacity *as* his capacity.
His preference not to actualise his potential becomes the actualisation of
his impotentiality, dramatizing a rare instance of impotentiality as such
revealing itself without sacrifice. Agamben unearths another startling example of this rare event in the piano playing of Glenn Gould wherein in
the latter stages of his mercurial career he plays with his capacity not to
play; in other words, he presents incapacity as actuality. Both men seem
to have sacrificed their actual lives in order to actualise their incapacity in
its full truth: namely, productive and positive creative noncreation. Other
examples might be Rimbaud's silence, Duchamp's descent into chess as
opposed to art and De Chirico's closing out his career with wilful bad
painting (perhaps even Damien Hirst's disastrous foray in still-life painting). Although Agamben does dwell on the scrivener's phrasing, it is the
language Deleuze uses to try to capture what he calls the formula that is
so startling to any scholar of Agamben. Deleuze says,

> The formula is devastating because it eliminates the preferable just as
> mercilessly as any nonpreferred. It not only abolishes the term it refers
> to, and that it rejects, but also abolishes the other term it seemed to
> preserve, and that becomes impossible. In fact, it renders then indis-
> tinct: it hollows out an ever expanding zone of indiscernibility or inde-
> termination between some nonpreferred activities and a preferable ac-
> tivity.[37]

Here Deleuze and Agamben speak in exactly the same terms, the zone of
indiscernibility and indetermination of Bartleby's decision to display incapacity as actualisation. Further, Deleuze then goes on immediately to
liken this to one of the key sources of Agamben's indifference when he

speaks of "Pure patient passivity, as Blanchot would say, Being as being, and nothing more".[38]

This is the first quite astonishing consonance between Deleuze and Agamben, and the reader would do well not to pass over it with any rapidity if his or her aim is a full understanding of Agamben's philosophy in relation to the wider context of thinkers of difference. It is of course implied on every page of this study that in relation to Agamben there can really be no other aim. The second consonance pertains to Deleuze's comments on language. Deleuze's theory of a minority language within the language of the majority is on display here when he speaks of the formula of negative preference as appearing almost like a bad translation of another language: "Perhaps it is the formula that carves out a kind of foreign language within language".[39] This foreign language within English, he argues, carries language "off", makes it "OUTLANDISH or Deterritorialized . . . and the effect, which is to sweep up language in its entirety, sending it into flight, pushing it to its very limit in order to discover its Outside, silence or music".[40] The formula, therefore, as is always the case in Agamben, ties the logic of impotentiality to that of the lack of word for the word or here a language of language (propositional self-predication).

Yet at the same time we could say that Deleuze's comments are in direct contravention of Agamben's views on this matter. For Deleuze the formula presents language as pure other, a total exteriority that can be conveyed in one of two ways, silence or semiotics. Agamben would certainly see this as another entry into the signature of language as ineffable, yet, as Deleuze develops his point, we come to see that part of Deleuze's project here is the negative staging of language as such or the foregrounding of language as pure, communicable incapacity. It in this vein that he says of the formula that "it hollows out a zone of indetermination that renders words indistinguishable, that creates a vacuum within language",[41] replacing the logic of presupposition (you are a copyist; therefore, you will copy) with that of preference (I prefer not to). This at least is in accord with Agamben's own methodology of staging the negations of the tradition. Language is revealed here as a field of pure, indeterminate indifference in a manner quite provocative in relation to our previous comments on dark and light indifference. For Deleuze, Bartleby makes the difference of his preference absolute difference or total indetermination. Indifference then is presented as entirely passive and static. This is not the indifference of determinability but rather the pure indifference of the indistinguishable.

In a sense one could say this is Bartleby's extreme response to the indifference of light which determines his previous existence and which his capacity names: copying. To copy, surely, as much represents repetition without difference or the indifference of pure determination, as 'preferring not to' represents the difference without repetition: the rendering of words indistinguishable. This is backed up by other elements of Bartleby's life of disconnection, such as his view on the wall or his reputed job immolating missives in the dead-letters section of the postal service. The postal service, after all, is the most Deleuzian of all institutions, and the differing response to dead letters helps better differentiate his approach to that of Derrida's. For Derrida, intrinsic is the possibility that any letter sent will fail to arrive, arrive at someone else's desk, arrive too late or arrive but not be received correctly. This is a beautiful model in his work for the logic of deferral as spacing. In contrast, for Deleuze, one could argue, dead letters are not dead at all and certainly should never be burnt. For him all the letters of the plane of virtual immanence could, in any case, never all be sent at once and certainly could not be received all at once. Dead letters are therefore obscure, dark virtual letters. I am extrapolating here; as far as I am aware Deleuze presents no postal philosophy of any note. That Bartleby is employed to destroy these dead letters explains quite neatly his actualised incapacity. If the virtual, potential letters of life are to be burnt while his job is to repeat without difference the already territorialised letters of business, then one of the greatest threats to Deleuze's system is realised: the fascistic state of total, static entropic territorialisation. Faced with this totalitarian threat, interestingly for Agamben's political works to be found at the heart of judicial, democratic due process, Bartleby's only mode of escape is negative indifferentiation of the order Agamben frowns upon but which, as in the case of bare life, he accepts as a moment of revelatory negative now-time that we all must pass through.

AGAMBEN ON DELEUZE ON BARTLEBY

Agamben commences the second section of his great essay, directly referring to Deleuze's formula, by confirming for us the status of Bartleby in relation to potentiality: "The scrivener has become the writing tablet; he is now nothing other than this white sheet",[42] or, as I have been suggesting and taking our lead also from Deleuze, he becomes his own incapacity and thus occupies the position of indifference. Bartleby is both the darkness and the light in a mode of radical suspended indistinction. This position is produced, Agamben says, by the peculiar relation of Bartleby's formula "I would prefer not to" and will. It is not that he doesn't want to but that he would prefer not to which "destroys all possibility of constructing a relation between being able and willing".[43] Bartleby is able and yet he does not, he is not unwilling and yet still he does not. Agamben calls this the indistinction between *potential absoluta* (God's absolute potential) and *potentia ordinata* (God's inability to act except according to his will). As we have been told quite often, God can do anything, even evil, but he cannot contravene his will, which is, of course, not to do evil.

It is not hard to see this as another example of Deleuze's system developed as a set of signed paradigms across a wider tradition of thought, a project Deleuze surely would have been happy to accept based on his own ideas on concept creation in *What Is Philosophy?*[44] Absolute potential is the equivalent of the relation between the virtual plane of immanence and its actualisations: anything can be connected to anything. Ordered potential is what you want to connect. Thus, capacity is the virtual plane and will the actualised one.

Having set up this resonance, Agamben then repeatedly reinscribes Deleuze's reading of the "zone of indistinction between yes and no" as indicative of both Agamben's own reading of this in terms of potential to be and not to be and a wider history of this logic of indifference. First, he relates it to the classical formula *ou mallon*, or "no more than", which Diogenes ascribes to the Sceptics, a "technical term with which the Skeptics denoted their most characteristic experience: *epokhe*, suspension".[45] This formula can be used constructively, one mythical creature exists no more than another, and negatively through a profound, sceptical self-referentiality. Following the same paradoxical logic as all statements are false, the phrase "no more than" is no more than it is not. In other words it names not a proper comparison but a suspension of doubt, A is no more likely than B, which itself infects the very statement so that its truth is no more than that it is not. Or, as Diogenes himself says, it is a truth held in an indifferent sense.

Agamben sees this as akin to Bartleby in one manner but notes that the sceptics also discover another inference from this self-reflexive statement of indifferent negation: one position is no more preferable than another. This other quality is also familiar to us. Diogenes says, "The Skeptic says the phenomenon and announces the affect without any opinion".[46] Agamben isolates the phrase *pathos apaggellien* and then relates the pathos element to the general meaning of the verbs *aggello* and *apagello*, which he says express the function of the messenger "who simply carries the message without adding anything, or who performatively announces the event".[47] He then reads this as yet another example of his concept of language as pure communicability as such so that in the "*epokhe* of the 'no more than', language is transformed into the angel of the phenomenon, the pure announcement of its passion" or an "announcement, which predicates nothing of nothing", which he calls "the intimation of Being without predication," a reference of course to Deleuze's reference to Blanchot.

Agamben develops the idea of suspension in sceptical thought by showing that for them, this also related to potentiality so that, according to Sextus, they saw suspension "not simply as indifference but as an experience of possibility or potentiality". From this he concludes that the suspension between being and non-being, sensible and intelligible and so on is not "the colorless abyss of the Nothing but the luminous spiral of the possible. To be able is *neither to posit nor to negate"*.[48] At this point Agamben recalls a key source text for the Deleuzian transcendental deduction, namely, the infinite comprehensibility of all things, which Deleuze modifies from the famous Leibniz contention of sufficient reason: there is a reason for which something does rather than does not exist. Returning to the sceptical 'no more than', on this formula he suggests that it calls into question this principle by occupying the 'rather' of the phrase 'does rather than does not exist' and placing there the 'no more than' so that the formula is not one of sufficient reason but one of indifferent reason: there is no more reason why something exists rather than does not.[49] Here the suspension between existence and inexistence is not the abyss of nothingness, that is, after all inexistence, but the suspensive indifference of incapacity.

It is into this world that Agamben now plunges Bartleby, presenting him in terms of a "'rather' fully freed of all *ratio*, and preference and a potentiality that no longer function to assure the supremacy of Being over Nothing but exist, without reason, in the indifference between Being and Nothing. The indifference of Being and Nothing is not, however, an equivalence between two opposing principles: rather, it is the mode of Being of potentiality that is purified of all reason".[50] This position allows Bartleby to modify Leibniz's formula, which, Agamben says, becomes "the fact there is no reason for something to exist rather than not to exist is the existence of something no more than nothing".[51] For Agamben, in a key comment on the dominance of binary ontology in our tradition, this contravenes Hamlet's choice and places a third option between to be or not to be, which is "a third term that transcends both: the 'rather' (or the 'no more than')".[52] Speaking of Bartleby's experimentation, referring to the Deleuzian idea of a formula, Agamben concludes that his is a great experiment where potential frees itself from the principle of reason, Leibniz's principle. Agamben's conclusion on the formula is "Emancipating itself from Being and non-Being alike, potentiality this creates its own ontology".[53]

This is an astonishing conclusion and speaks to our overall contention here that Agamben's is the first positive and productive philosophy of indifference, including here the ontology of potentiality, which is the ontology of indifference. Yet any reader would be legitimate in asking what Agamben is saying in relation to Deleuze's text which makes no use of these sources and ends on a very different conclusion pertaining to the relation of American fiction to American pragmatic philosophy. Earlier, I graciously suggested that one thing Agamben is attempting in this essay is to extend the signatories of Deleuze's observations, but as the section comes to a close, Agamben instead seems to be mounting a critique even more subtle and indirect than that posed against Derrida in *"Pardes"*. From what I can ascertain, he is attacking Deleuze on several fronts. First, in choosing Sceptical texts, he is emphasising an alternative history of indifference to that chosen by Deleuze. In *The Logic of Sense* the indifferential dynamic of the quasi cause is constructed from readings of the Stoics' division of causality as we saw. In contrast, Agamben is suggesting that indifference originates from Sceptical sources. Inasmuch as these two schools are traditionally placed in antinomy,[54] it would seem that Agamben is taking an opposing view of the genealogy of indifference or at the very least contesting the Deleuzian mode of finding origins for his own ideas in philosophical history in favour of a disseminating method of tracing signatures across the totality of the tradition.

Second, staying with *The Logic of Sense*, Deleuze clearly presents there a view of language as abstract propositionality occupying the position of stoical, incorporeal states of affairs, whereas Agamben seeks to liberate language from propositionality entirely and instead make it the division of the quasi cause between the corporeal and the incorporeal. Language is indifference for Agamben, whereas for Deleuze language is an actualisation of a virtuality located very much on one side of the equation although, through paradoxes and the like, able to give access to the nature of this quasi-causal cobelonging. For Deleuze any human territorialisation is first actualised in language, while the realm of pure sense, or the virtual, is as much prelinguistic as it is prephilosophical. In addition, as *The Logic of Sense* proceeds to the final section and in many ways deteriorates, Deleuze's choice of language as the actualisation of sense is precisely because, as in theories of the sign, it is bifurcated between the body (via speech and the mouth) and the incorporeal realm of propositionality,[55] none of which Agamben would accept. Finally, there is the critical reading of Leibniz's theory of sufficient reason which Deleuze modifies to form one part of his double system, along with the body-surface dialectic we have just rejected. The totality of Deleuze's philosophy is reducible to the transcendental deduction of infinite comprehensibility and the dialectic between body and surface with its relationship of quasi-causal cobelonging. The first of these is a modification of sufficient reason, removing God and denying the possibility of the convergence of all series in God. Yet Agamben directly criticises Leibniz's rational position, as we saw, contending that indifference negates the principle of sufficient reason by occupying the incapacity to be defined as something existing no more than not existing.

CONTINGENCY

We now enter into the most complex element of the relation between Agamben and Deleuze which is also a major fault line, I would argue, along which contemporary philosophy must be organised, completed, negated and renewed. This problem is so vexed that we have to break it into two components. Here we will address the specific differences be-

tween Deleuze and Agamben, considered under the heading of contingency. Then we must present schematically how these two systems come
to points of consonance and conflict in terms of their alternate, complex
presentations of a philosophy of indifference. Agamben, picking up a
central concern in *The Coming Community*, proposes absolute contingency
as the true value of indifference with contingency being defined as something that could have been otherwise. As he says in relation to first philosophy, "a being that can both be and not be is said to be contingent".
Agamben then remains in a position of radical appropriation of the Deleuzian source material by considering contingency in relation to Leibniz's four figures of modality: possible, impossible, necessary and contingent. Thus, a contingent is something that cannot do or be true, com-
pared, say, to the impossible, which is something that cannot do, or the
possible, which is something that can. Finally, then, we have the necessary, which is something that cannot not, necessity being opposed to
contingency, which is deemed the modality of freedom.[56]

Contingency, of all the modalities, has provided the greatest number
of contradictions; for example, if Being always preserves its potential not
to be (contingency), the very past itself could be called into question, and,
"moreover, no possibility would ever pass into actuality or remain in
actuality".[57] These two paradoxes present, in passing, the truly radical
nature of the Agambenian methodology, as the essay will go on to show,
namely, the possibility of 'changing' the past and of deactivating actualisation as a permanent realisation, so to speak, of the potential. Philosophy at large has wrestled with these two problems by proposing the
complementary laws of the irrevocability of the past or the "unrealizabil-
ity of the potential of the past"[58] and that of conditioned necessity which
effectively states that it is impossible for something to be and not be at the
same time, so that although contingency names the possibility of something being or not being, it is limited by the impossibility of it both being
and not being at the same time. The second law is the weaker of the two,
as Aristotle's principles of potentiality contravene it in that, in terms of
rational potential, it is possible to have the potential to walk and not walk
at the same time.

Inasmuch as this debate depends on the modalities of Leibniz and the
conditions of potentiality, it is always addressed to Deleuze, specifically
when Agamben speaks of Duns Scotus's theory of will in relation to
contingency, which names no decision (earlier Agamben analyses Bartleby in relation to choice) but refers "to the experience of the constitutive
and irreducible co-belonging of capacity to and capacity not to".[59] Directly utilising the Deleuzian relationality of cobelonging, Agamben does not
apply it to the relation between the virtual and the actual, as in Deleuze,
but rather describes it as being between capacity not to and capacity to.
This is named 'will' because, according to Duns Scotus, only the will is
indifferent to contrarieties in that it can both will to do and will not to do.

A third problem for contingency is that of future contingents wherein a necessary occurrence or nonoccurrence in the future "retroactively influences the moments of its predication, cancelling its contingency".[60] The example given is if you say that 'tomorrow there will be a battle'. If a battle then takes place the following day, then this was already true the day before it took place, meaning it could not not take place. In this case contingency is then replaced, retrospectively, with necessity, or, in the case of negative statements, impossibility.

All of these sophistries which exercised the great minds of our tradition are rendered inoperative by impotentiality, which is of course Agamben's point.[61] Because impotentiality is intrinsic to potentiality and negated in actuality in place of potentiality, contingency is never realised in any of these formulations. In this formulation the past is not irrevocable because in actualisation potentiality is never realised and negated so that the past remains always in potential. The second issue of conditioned necessity is negated because, as we have repeatedly seen, the logic of indifference suspends the being–not being dichotomy so that both can be in place at the same time by being rendered inoperative through suspension. Finally, the logic of retroactive temporality is actually embraced; it forms, for example, Agamben's thesis on temporal indifference and *kairos* in *The Time That Remains* inspired by Benjaminian now-time. The actualisation of an event never negates potentiality; rather, it negates impotentiality.

Agamben then tells a story from Leibniz's *Theodicy*, although it is again a direct reference to the work of Deleuze. This is the famous Palace of Destinies, a pyramid the top of which is the best of all possible worlds and then descending from this all the other possible worlds that could be, regressing downwards into an abyss. These alternatives are compossibilities; all exist alongside each other in their singularity and in their unrealised but real potentiality. As in each case when one alternative is realised, meaning the other or others are not, the pyramid ascends according to the famous principles of noncontradiction and identity of indiscernibles. Furthermore, the crowning moment of the pyramid and each choice that leads up to it is confirmed by the principles of the optimism and sufficient reason which result in the confirmation of the principle of plenitude. You will recall that Deleuze also adopts a similar system. As every singularity is a series, every singularity is subdivisible, thus retreating always down the pyramid's depths to finer and finer distinctions.

The debt to Leibniz's differential calculus and monadology is clear here. Similarly, as the Deleuzian ontology defines what is as what you are, every choice or actualisation is by definition the right one. What Deleuze removes from this model, however, is hierarchy and infinity. At the lowest level there is no infinite regress because all singularities already exist within the plane of immanence. Rather, the rule pertains to what happens when you divide. In Deleuze's system there is a permanent equilibrium of sorts between divisions and connections. There is an infinite yet limited number of singularities, and if one disconnects them, one increases their intensity, just as if one connects them, one increases their extensity. But pure intensity is never possible because each singularity must be a series, so that divisibility for him is always provided with the concomitant of a new reticulation. Similarly, pure extensity is impossible, as all such sedimented territorialisations connect only by virtue of their quasi-causal dependency on the singularities of the virtual. So again, every connection has built into it a future disconnection, meaning that when Agamben says, negatively, of the best of all possible worlds that it "projects an infinite shadow downward, which sinks lower and lower to the extreme universe . . . in which nothing is compossible with anything else and nothing can take place",[62] although the charge sticks when it comes to Leibniz, in terms of Deleuze it does not, and Agamben is more than aware of this.

This seems confirmed in the next section and its discourse on remembrance. Memory is a central feature of the Deleuzian system in that it relates to repetitions becoming actualised and also becoming static through force of habit.[63] Clarity-obscurity also works, in Deleuze's philosophy, in terms of memory and forgetting or, based on our previous comments, connection and division.[64] Agamben frames this in terms of Benjamin's theory of redemption, and at this precise moment our first comments on Agamben's method and this earlier work come into the clearest of focus. For Benjamin, the process of genealogical remembrance through material historical traces, which is also in part Agamben's method, is a means of redeeming the past, restoring possibility to it, making what did not happen happen and vice versa. Agamben says, "Remembrance is neither what happened nor what did not happen but, rather, their potentialization, their becoming possible again",[65] so that Bartleby's formula calls the past into question not by reliving it, redeeming it to live again, but by making it once again potential. This is especially poignant, as his job is copying, which is the most forced form of conditioned contingency, the only escape from which is the preference not to copy. Deleuze's version of this relates to his famous reading of Proust's presentation of Combray as always a new Combray in each act of remembrance, conveyed effectively by the verb "to-Combray".[66]

MESSIANIC DECREATION

We will pass over Agamben's reading of Nietzsche, although again it occupies precisely the same territory of Deleuze's comments on repetition in relation to eternal recurrence and will to power running throughout *Difference and Repetition*. Rather, we will conclude by looking at the final two pages of this revealing but also almost impossibly recondite and indirect essay. Agamben finishes with a flourish, picking up Deleuze's comment that Bartleby is the new Christ and deciding what order of messiah he can be. He is not a redeemer of what was but the saviour, via the logic of impotentiality, of what was not. Bartleby descends to the lowest level of the palace of destinies where compossibility is impossible. Finally, he does not bring a new table of law but rather fulfils the law by destroying it. This would usher in a second creation

> in which God summons all his potential not to be, creating on the basis of a point of indifference between potentiality and impotentiality. The creation that is now fulfilled is neither a re-creation nor an eternal repetition; it is, rather, a decreation in which what happened and what did not happen are returned to their originary unity in the mind of God, while what could not have been but was becomes indistinguishable from what could have been but was not. [67]

"Decreation" is not a term that repeats in Agamben's work after this point, but weak, small-case messianism often does and is often seized on by hostile critics as a kind of teleology. [68] In this instance messianism does not refer to the ideal final state, so that Agamben is not advocating Bartleby as a model for future practice. Rather, as is the case with bare life and with language under negation, and indeed negative aesthetics in his earliest work, decreation is, if you will, the real Heideggerian *Destruktion*. It represents Agamben's alternative to the Derridean deconstruction of metaphysics, an alternative which still makes extensive use of deconstruction; he says that his whole method is based on a deconstruction of genealogy but arrives at a negative position as the basis for a philosophy to come. This is the role of impotentiality, as we saw. It is sacrificed, in the same way that language is, to save potentiality from the implications of actualisation and to save actualisation from the deprecations of potentiality.

If we read potentiality now in this double register of history and also creation out of nothing, then we can argue the following. Historical potentiality is strictly monitored by philosophy so that the past cannot retain potentiality and the future cannot come back and modify an actuality. Yet, Agamben argues, the logic of potentiality depends on impotentiality. This being the case, the potentiality of the past, all the "might have beens" in the palace of destinies, remain potential. The rooms are not piled on top of each other hierarchically, and this structure is imposed through the power of identity through difference; rather, they are para-archaic. This means of course that difference alone cannot disrupt this structure, including Derridean and Deleuzian difference. The reason for this is because when a being is actualised, what is negated is impotentiality, so that potentiality is preserved and kept in reserve. The logic of this proposition means that one can indeed retain the potentiality of the past. What does this mean in reality? We have already seen this process in practice in the method. The past in the Agamben-Benjaminian proposal is always a potential to be realised in critical now-time. It can be accessed only when the time is right and is always a construct of the temporality of now, so that the past as such remains untouched or, better, nonactualised in this process.

The second half of the logic suggests that future contingents are also possible and, more than that, inevitable. Repeating this logic one last time, because of impotentiality the actualisation of any potential is actually the actualisation of impotentiality, which means that it always retains potentiality in reserve. Actualisation then is always marked by the trace of potential confirming the fact that the future will be able to redetermine the present. It does this in two ways. First, the present is always already past and so becomes available to the power of past potentiality. The second is that whatever happens in the future, the potential of the present moment, battles at sea or not, is retained and indeed comes to be potential only through the actualisation of a future moment. Again this can be mapped onto the method. The moment of arising and the signature of all things, whilst located historically and presented as *archē*- and genealogy, are accessible only in the now-time. It is only when one particular paradigm rises up that the other paradigms of which it is exemplary are composed as compossible. Thus, the historical origins, destinal distributions and paradigmatic organisations are all retained in potential even after they have become actualised in an act of philosophical philology or historiography. This is a crucial point for all critics of Agamben's use of such material. When these moments from the past are redeemed, their potentiality is not exhausted by Agamben's research; rather, they are constructed as potential sources for actual situations only from the perspective of these actualities. They remain in history potential sources for other redemptions, even contradictory ones. Similarly, in terms of these modern actualisations, they are themselves present only so as to succumb to the decreative powers of the potentiality they keep in reserve because they actualise the impotentialities of history and leave its potentiality intact.

THE TWO BARTLEBIES PART WAYS

Now, in closing, we need to ask the most challenging question of all: What does Agamben's reading of Bartleby tell us of his specific relationship with Deleuze's system? Nothing directly, as we have painfully seen, so we must reconstruct from all that we have learnt thus far of Agamben's work and add that into his specific comments on Deleuze in the two essays we have been considering. Let's begin by assuming that, for the most part, Agamben's potentiality is applicable to Deleuzian virtuality. What stands for impotentiality in this system is the precise nature of the quasi-causal cobelonging of virtual and actual in Deleuze essential to *Logic of Sense*. In this manner the two systems are identical. Where do they differ? I believe on two related and rather simple points. Deleuze contends that the virtual is determined by corporealities, and his indeterminate life depends on this model. Agamben never says anything remotely of this order and in this way is very much with Derrida that all such values are historically contingent and do not depend on any pre-philosophical or nonphilosophical ground. This means that, second, for Deleuze, the process of actualisation-counteractualisation is endless. Agamben again does not seem to agree with this and in this sense places Derrida and Deleuze together. For both of his predecessors the critical system alone is sufficient: difference and virtual sense are destination enough. Agamben, however, seems to hold with the dictum that the process of philosophical archaeology, so very similar in many ways to Deleuze and Guattari's concept-creation theory in *What Is Philosophy?*, has a limit, and we are at that limit. The messiah will repeatedly come, there is no one messiah, but there will come a time when the totality of the past as presented via the metaphysics of identity-difference is redeemed. This may in part be because the past is limited in a manner that bodies are not or also because the mode of redemption is determined by a specific moment in time, our moment, after which things will change, including what we term the Past as signature.

This then raises the question as to where the radical element belongs in potentiality and virtuality. For Deleuze every event is a potential counteractualisation. This is Badiou's criticism of the system, that it levels out all events and makes the radical of a par with the conservative.[69] This is precisely in agreement with Derridean conservatism. The only thing that is 'radical' is the insight into the process which naturally upsets many presuppositions, both conservative and progressive. At this point then, Agamben is much closer to Badiou in that he sees events as historically determined moments. However, unlike Badiou, these events are located in a diversity of fields, not just the four generic fields, and their relation to history is much more complex. Finally, these events happen many times, and, radically, Agamben wishes to negate them by tracing them back to their moment of arising so that their signature of difference through time can be finally suspended. For Agamben the radical element is historical, contingent and thus possessive of finitude. Something comes after concepts such as we have them now, something that would not be a concept but the suspension of the sensible-supersensible dichotomy.

We can, consequently, say of Agamben, in relation to Deleuze, that he sees the virtual as historically contingent, not embodied; that this means it has finitude or at least has finitude before it has immediacy; and, finally, that the critical decreative work, what is decreation but counteractualisation, is a means to an end of sorts, not an end in itself. Across these three issues then, the incredible consonance between Agamben and Deleuze comes to an end, and their two Bartlebies go their separate ways. Deleuze's returns to the dead-letter office from whence he was actualised, ready to be determined again but in a completely new fashion. Agamben's fulfils the real role of any messiah and is sacrificed so that the messiah can become the precursor to his own return.

NOTES

1. Gilles Deleuze, *Pure Immanence: Essays on Life*, trans. Anne Boyman (London: Verso, 1998), 25.

2. Deleuze, *Pure Immanence*, 27.

3. Orthodox in the sense that no philosopher of the last century does not accept the hermeneutic circle with Deleuze being a member of a wider tendency for twentieth-century philosophy that is basically hermeneutic phenomenology.

4. Deleuze, *Pure Immanence*, 28–29.

5. Deleuze, *Pure Immanence*, 29.

6. Gilles Deleuze, *The Logic of Sense*, trans. Mark Lester (London: Continuum, 2004),9.

7. Deleuze, *Pure Immanence*, 31.

8. Giorgio Agamben, *Potentialities*, trans. Daniel Heller-Roazen (Stanford, CA: Stanford University Press, 1999), 230.

9. Agamben, *Potentialities*, 232–33.

10. Agamben, *Potentialities*, 233.

11. Agamben, *Potentialities*, 233.

12. Agamben, *Potentialities*, 234.

13. On relation of language as communicability to mediality, see Giorgio Agamben, *State of Exception*, trans. Kevin Attell (Chicago: University of Chicago Press, 2005), 61–62.

14. Agamben, *Potentialities*, 234.

15. See Alain Badiou, *Being and Event*, trans. Oliver Feltham (London: Continuum, 2005), 38–48. It is apparent from this text that one of Cantor's great innovations in the development of axiomatic set theory is the means by which the axiomatic as a model transcends the paradoxes of mathematics around self-predication formulated by Frege and Russell, opening up a new chapter in mathematical thought in the last century.

16. Agamben, *Potentialities*, 234.

17. Agamben, *Potentialities*, 235.

18. Gilles Deleuze and Félix Guattari, *A Thousand Plateaus : Capitalism and Schizophrenia*, trans. Brian Massumi (London: Athlone Press, 1992), 75–85.

19. Deleuze and Guattari, *Thousand Plateaus*, 399–400.

20. Agamben, *Potentialities*, 236.

21. Deleuze and Guattari, *Thousand Plateaus*, 215.

22. Agamben, *Potentialities*, 239.

23. Agamben, *Potentialities*, 239.

24. Agamben, *Potentialities*, 245.

25. Agamben, *Potentialities*, 245.

26. Agamben, *Potentialities*, 249–50.

27. Agamben, *Potentialities*, 251.

28. Agamben, *Potentialities*, 252.

29. Agamben, *Potentialities*, 252.

30. Gilles Deleuze, *Difference and Repetition*, trans. Paul Patton (London: Athlone Press, 1994), 28–29.

31. Agamben, *Potentialities*, 253.

32. Deleuze, *Difference and Repetition*, 67–69.

33. Deleuze, *Difference and Repetition*, 1–27.

34. Deleuze, *Logic of Sense*, 194–201.

35. Deleuze, *Logic of Sense*, 7–10.

36. Gilles Deleuze, *Essays Critical and Clinical*, trans. Daniel W. Smith (Minneapolis: University of Minnesota Press, 1997), 69.

37. Deleuze, *Essays*, 71.

38. Deleuze, *Essays*, 71.

39. Deleuze, *Essays*, 71. See also Gilles Deleuze and Félix Guattari, *Kakfa: Toward a Minor Literature*, trans. Dana Polan (Minneapolis: University of Minnesota Press, 1986), and *Thousand Plateaus*, 105.

40. Deleuze, *Essays*, 72.

41. Deleuze, *Essays*, 73.

42. Agamben, *Potentialities*, 254.

43. Agamben, *Potentialities*, 255. See also Colby Dickinson, *Agamben and Theology* (London: Continuum, 2011), 41–50.

44. Gilles Deleuze and Félix Guattari, *What Is Philosophy?*, trans. Graham Burchell and Hugh Tomlinson (London: Verso, 1994), 15–34.

45. Agamben, *Potentialities*, 256.

46. Cited in Agamben, *Potentialities*, 256.

47. Agamben, *Potentialities*, 257.

48. Agamben, *Potentialities*, 257.

49. Here the necessity of contingency in Meillassoux's thesis and our own comments on indifference come together from what seems like opposite ends of the universe, Meillassoux's speculative realism and our own indifferent communicability.

50. Agamben, *Potentialities*, 259.

51. Agamben, *Potentialities*, 259.

52. Agamben, *Potentialities*, 259.

53. Agamben, *Potentialities*, 259.

54. Although for us they are both intrinsic parts of the first order of philosophical indifferentism up to Kant.

55. Deleuze, *Logic of Sense*, 214–24.

56. If Meillassoux is using Badiou's indifferent ontology as a launchpad for his conception of a material and hence real absolute contingency, our own project more modestly takes Agamben's indifferent archaeology to propose a conception of indifferent communicability as a form of absolute discursive contingency for the founding concepts of all philosophy: identity and difference. Both systems, however, share in common a rejection of what Meillassoux calls correlationism or what we term the metaphysics of identity-difference.

57. Agamben, *Potentialities*, 261.

58. Agamben, *Potentialities*, 262.

59. Agamben, *Potentialities*, 262.

60. Agamben, *Potentialities*, 263.

61. Meillassoux's various proofs as regards the aporias of causality in his work would buckle under the pressure of Agamben's logic of indifferent impotentiality.

62. Agamben, *Potentialities*, 266.

63. Deleuze, *Difference and Repetition*, 70–82.

64. Deleuze, *Difference and Repetition*, 79–85.

65. Agamben, *Potentialities*, 267.

66. Deleuze, *Difference and Repetition*, 84–85. Indeed, Agamben's first recorded use of the term "indifference" is in Agamben's introduction to Proust's rediscovered work "*L'indifférence*" in Giorgio Agamben, "*La passione dell'indifferenza* e il saggio di Philip Kolb, *Una novella perduta e ritrovata*," in Marcel Proust, *L'indifferente*, trans. Mariolina Bongiovanni Bertini (Torino: Einaudi, 1978).

67. Agamben, *Potentialities*, 270.

68. It is widely held that the origin of the term is to be found in the work of Simone Weil.

69. Alain Badiou, *Deleuze: The Clamour of Being*, trans. Louise Burchill (Minneapolis: University of Minnesota Press, 2000), 9–17.

Part III

The Indifference of Indifference: Politics, Language, Life

NINE

Homo Sacer and the Politics of Indifference

HOMO SACER REDUX

There is no need to rehearse the argument of *Homo Sacer*, for just as it is true that it has been misconstrued by some, it has also been the source of the most important and insightful work on Agamben in the past two decades. Rather, I want to look with fresh eyes at the key elements of the work through the neutralising filter of indifference. That said, my contention is that the essential component of this work and those which have resulted from it is indifference, and without a detailed engagement with this element, full understanding of *Homo Sacer* is lacking, which is not to say that critics have ignored indifference or at least the innumerable times it makes its presence felt through the text, most notably in the Deleuzian phrase "zone of indistinction", which Agamben makes regular use of. Yet, as we have seen, the complexity of what this actually means is profound and wide reaching. It does not simply indicate moments when there is a lack of distinction between concepts or discursive zones, although seeing it as such is not incorrect, just severely limited. If we take Agamben seriously in his ambition, then *Homo Sacer* as a political project can succeed only if indifference is understood in full as the logic that drives the whole work.

We have already seen that one cannot differentiate indifference at large from the indifferential method of paradigms, signatures and archaeology. Each element pertains to indifference. Paradigms present the logic of indifferential suspensive mediation between common and proper. Signatures operate in the same fashion between signifier and signified, permitting the intelligibility and transmission of signatures across discursive practices. Archaeology is a messianic project of the suspension of oppositions between contingent divisions presented as necessary by Western metaphysics. In each instance indifference, like impotential, has a negative operation for a positive result to come. Philosophy after indifference is the best description of this future project, described in *Homo Sacer* as the total suspension of oppositions or perhaps a return to the true meaning of oppositional terms. The negative suspension to open up a future avenue or, more ethically, the means by which negative zones of indistinction broach such an avenue is never more felt than in the nightmarish presentation of Western politics in *Homo Sacer*.

With a full comprehension of the method firmly in place, it is now relatively easy to recast *Homo Sacer* as exemplary of the indifferential philosophical archaeological method, a method not fully worked through, it must be said, at the time of the text's publication. So first of all, we note how the different elements of that text—homo sacer, sovereign, Muselmann, camps, Karen Quinlan, the führer, maverick doctors and so on—map onto the indifferential method as named paradigms to be found in the text of the wider signatures of Power and Life. We can also identify the key suspension in the text, named in the subtitle of the work in fact, sovereign power and bare life, and how sovereignty operates as the condition or common and bare life as the conditioned or proper. If we now turn attention to the more obscure issue of the signature, two elements can be noted: first, that Life is the primary signatory term in play in the text, as it was in the debate with Deleuze, moving from one discursive formation to the next without changing its form or its meaning, and, second, that one must now also consider the homo sacer project as a whole extending out from this astonishing source text and how the signatory term Power is transmitted across these often diverse works and indeed dispersed amongst other signatory elements. The second point will come to the fore when we consider the role of *oikos* in *Homo Sacer* and its extension into *oikonomia* in *The Kingdom and the Glory*. Finally, we can name the *zoē-bios* opposition and the homo sacer judicial exception as moments of arising that reveal our own political formation through an archaeology of its source in ancient political practice.

Although this analysis is schematic, I believe it to be accurate, and it is important that *Homo Sacer* can be presented in such an attenuated manner for future scholarship and a wider understanding. That said, it is insufficient in certain key areas. Therefore, in what follows, first I want to put some flesh on the bones of my contention by identifying the moments in the text where my model is supported. This is our first indifferential reading of the text inasmuch as the method is indifferential. After this I will retread the same ground looking at the specific instances of indifference therein, for, remember, this text was published nearly fifteen years before the method and, I assume, composed over many years before publication. To some degree it is only Agamben's second major work that is intimately engaged with indifference, *The Coming Community* being the first, and while the method has been in play since *Infancy and History* and is certainly fully formed in the pages of *Homo Sacer*, there is a clear development in terms of clarity and importance in the use of indifference between *Homo Sacer* and the recent works. Thus, I want to establish once and for all that at every key moment in the text, indifference is the essential logic, method and destination of Agamben's thoughts.

THE SIGNATURE OF LIFE

The introduction to *Homo Sacer* is an important moment in modern thought, yet it is also dense and at times unclear, specifically in its use of the term "bare life" to indicate *zoē*, which, as the text develops, we must say is not exactly the case.[1] The introduction is not, I will admit, always entirely consistent with the method, a method not fully realised for over a decade after. As such it stands in relation to *The Signature of All Things* the way *The Order of Things* stands in relation to *The Archaeology of Knowledge*; that is, I believe, the perfection of the method is not yet realised. For example, one gets the controversy over the use of terms such as 'secret' and 'hidden' here, whereas, in the more clearly Foucauldian sense of the method published subsequently, secret and hidden meanings are recast, as we saw in terms of Melandri's regression, as being the very opposite of repressed meaning. And we know that time and again Foucault attacks the trace of hidden meanings approach in his definition of the signature as what has been said of things. This has sound metaphysical reasons and also clearly differentiates the statement from the Derridean trace and his later work on secrecy, the spectre and so on.

Another troubling term here in the very early pages is reference to the key moment in the work. The book traces, after Foucault, the entry of life or *zoē* into the political sphere, or *bios*, during the modern era, resulting in what Foucault calls biopolitics. In miniature Agamben's thesis is that this is correct but that this happened at the moment of arising of the political in the West, Greek democracy and Roman law, not just during modernity. Speaking of "the politicization of bare life as such", he accepts, after Foucault, that it is "the decisive event of modernity" in that it "signals a radical transformation of the political-philosophical categories of modern thought".[2] What he is actually describing is the transmission of the signature Life through time and across discursive formations, here classical to modern thought. To call this a transformation is misleading, as theoretically the signature suffers no transformation in terms of form ("life" is still the material term used) or meaning (it still indicates the raw fact of existence before the political). Rather, what we see is a radical transmission of the signature Life, which allows both new things to be said of things and new statements to be formed by giving the double intelligibility of sanctioned usage (it can be said) and contextual support (said in such a way as groups of people can understand it). This not a radical transformation as such because the signature is transmitted from one tradition to the next and because nothing has changed except the potential or capacity to operate in a different way discursively. Here the usage of the term "bare life" is confusing because it suggests that bare life, *zoē*, is the same as bare life, say, in a concentration camp. What we are actually seeing is that Life, as a signature, has the same meaning in all contexts but allows for very different things to occur politically. In one sense then, life is always bare life, but in another Life is never the same statement even though it is the same signature. In that a statement is not determined by its meaning but by what it allows to happen, the operativity of Life in modernity is radically different than that in classical thought.

At precisely this point we have our first clear statement of the overall methodological underpinning of the text. Agamben says,

> The "enigmas" that our century has proposed to historical reason and that remain with us . . . will be solved only on the terrain—biopolitics— on which they were formed. Only within a biopolitical horizon will it be possible to decide whether the categories whose opposition founded modern politics . . . and which have been steadily dissolving, to the point of entering today into a real zone of indistinction—will have to be abandoned or will, instead, eventually regain the meaning lost in that very horizon.[3]

To this he adds, after Foucault and Benjamin, who, after all, compose the base of the method, only the questioning of the link between bare life and politics, "a link that secretly governs the modern ideologies seemingly most distant from one another, will be able to bring the political out of its concealment and, at the same time, return thought to its practical calling".[4] If we take Nazism as an example, Nazism as a discursive formation can be resolved only as an enigma: how can Nazism as a discursive practice occur from the same conditions as democracy during the same period in the same geographical location, from within the same discursive formation? This formation is not, as Habermas has it, for example, the enlightenment or democracy but biopolitics. Biopolitics as a formation reveals the archaeology of power, which is division into two opposing categories of condition (common) and conditioned (proper) distributed across time and different discourses through the signature of Life, which operates at various points as common, proper and now, in our age, the commonality of the proper or the individual's universal right to life. The movement of the signature Life has naturally called into question the division and the opposition of the terms through its capacity to operate on both sides and between the two. We are now then at the point, after the development of biopolitics and its localization of bare life within the camp, where the division, the distinction and the opposition of the founding terms of politics are indistinct: we cannot rely on their separation, their difference or their dialectical copresence.

The next proposition is more troubling. Agamben suggests that at the moment of indistinction we have two options which I have already mentioned. Difference as such will have to be abandoned, or terms will regain the meaning they lost when they entered into biopolitics. At this juncture we also have the problematic secret link between democracy and fascism. Here we can at least say that the secrecy in play is not that of a hidden trace or of repression but our lack of understanding of the operation of statements in these two discursive formations, the transmission of the signature Life across them so that life, for democracy, means operative sanctity and for fascism operative genocide, and the wider historical tradition they share in common: biopolitics as the origin of the political. Here Agamben outstrips Foucault by suggesting that biopolitical modernity is really only another discursive formation by virtue of the signatory shift of Life, a transmission, not an epistemic break or event. The last statement confers on us the true ambition of the work, and we will return to this. *Homo Sacer* calls for neither the renovation of the political nor the radicalisation of the philosophical but a mutual coimplication. Change in the political is due to ontological change which is due to change in the political. The two discursive realms, in other words, enter into indifferential indistinction. We can certainly conclude on this opening set of positions that there is much that is remarkable here, but it would be misleading to say that there is not also much that is troubling in relation to the consistency of the overall method. This is a recurrent problem in the book, the source of many misunderstandings and perhaps also the origin of its captivating power.

The signatory transmission of Life, although Agamben does not call it such and does not use the term "signature" in any sustained way for another decade or more, recurs in the later discussion on the consonance between the manner in which the living being has language and in what way bare life dwells in the *polis*. This structural indistinction between language (logos, philosophy) and *polis* is conducted through a brief but telling historical time line mapping life's signatory transmissions. This argument is promoted by a consideration of the Aristotelian good life. Criticising Foucault for not tracing the biopolitical back beyond modernity, Agamben radicalises Foucault's project by arguing the "the inclusion of bare life in the political realm constitutes the original—if concealed—nucleus of sovereign power. *It can even be said that the production of a biopolitical body is the original activity of sovereign power*",[5] meaning of course that biopolitics is at least as old as sovereign exception. This being the case, the definition of the *polis* found in Aristotle—and on the back of recent criticism, 'found' here is the correct word, meaning the manner in which statements by subject position Aristotle have been taken, translated and distributed, not necessarily what he actually said and meant—as the opposition between life (*zen*) and good life (*eu zen*) needs reworking. This assumed opposition is in fact "an implication of the first in the second, of bare life in politically qualified life".[6] Here we have one of the many examples of the law of exclusion pertaining to the signature life. Life, *zoē*, is included in politics, *polis*, through the qualification of life as good, only to be excluded by the same gesture; life on its own is not good without the *polis*. Politics then is not life but what is good about living, which is not included in life in its bare state. Agamben traces the signature of this tradition from its apparent moment of arising, Aristotle's distinction, which may not be his but merely the moment of arising of later constructions through the use of Aristotelian statements, through its traditional transmission as good life being the telos of the political. He then refutes this question and says, "We must instead ask why Western politics first constitutes itself through an exclusion (which is simultaneously an inclusion) of bare life".[7]

Agamben now turns to Foucault's reading of Aristotle for whom man is a living animal with an "additional capacity" for the political and the odd stipulation in Aristotle of being born in life but existing in good life. Obviously being, here being born in life or *zoē*, always includes the exclusion of *zoē* in the *polis*: "Almost as if politics were the place in which life had to transform itself into good life and in which what had to be politicised were always already bare life".[8] There is clarity and complexity of succession here. First, let's be clear in terms of the temporality. We now know that we are not dealing with origins or necessarily the first time a statement was made. In addition, while the subject of enunciation is Aristotle and the statements are associated with him, there is perhaps no other thinker who is less himself than Aristotle. When we speak of Aristotle we mean the position occupied by translated and interpreted statements authorised by the enunciative position: founder of Western thought. Anyway, the first line of succession traces the signatory transmission of life from "pre-Aristotelian" *zoē*, that is, what we have assumed to exist for the Greeks before what we assume Aristotle said about this, into the *polis* in terms of the stipulation good life. Then, in the modern 'biopolitical' era, good life becomes the sanctity of life so that *zoē* becomes the domain of the *polis*. Yet this bare life as we encounter it within our politics, the sanctity of individual life, appears here as the final or most recent destination of the signature, pure life—good life—bare life, and also seems to have at its telos its origin, bare life—pure life—good life—bare life. Agamben first indicates that bare life is peculiar in founding the city of men, the *polis*, through being included as that which is excluded. Further, we can add that Life here is presented in terms of its signatory transmission, intelligibility and inevitability as an origin that is its own telos and a telos that founds its own origin. This is possible only due to the temporal particularity of the archaeology method as I have outlined it.

HOMO SACER AND THE PROBLEM OF THE FIRST PARADIGM

We now encounter the first of several statements about paradigms. Much of the work is a delineation of paradigms, and the final section is a consideration of the camp as the "Biopolitical Paradigm of the Modern";[9] that said, I won't spend time on these paradigms, as it is enough to delineate their logic, which to a large degree we have already achieved. However, as again there has been controversy over the discovery of the homo sacer, the sacred man who may be killed and yet not sacrificed or murdered, as well as the originary status of the study, we ought to dwell on this initial paradigm long enough to dispel the fog. Agamben says here that the homo sacer is the "first paradigm of the political realm of the West".[10] What does that mean? One obvious concomitant is that all the controversy over the *zoē-bios* opposition for the Greeks is a reflection of the manner in which the signature Life has been distributed but does not found politics. It is added in later as originary in a manner effective even if Agamben's sources are, as has been suggested, the misreadings of Arendt and Foucault or his own investigations into the Aristotelian corpus that some scholars now suggest is false. If this is held to be the case, it does not matter, the paradigm is not foundational and the debate is not about the meaning of Aristotle's statements but what they were permitted to say and what they have permitted to be said. The foundation of the political in the West is not *zoē-bios* oppositions but the logic of the included exclusion paradigmatically represented by the forgotten figure of the homo sacer of which *zoē-bios* is another paradigmatic example.[11] Further, it matters not if homo sacer is a legitimate discovery or even, in fact, if Agamben is proven to be wrong over assigning it as the first. Indeed, following the strict logic of paradigmatic plates, there is no first paradigm even if the homo sacer is historically the first. That Agamben is excited by his philological discovery is not to be doubted, but if I may be more strictly Agambenian here than he is, by 'first' we can only say, retrospectively stipulated moment of arising for the commencement of an indifferentiation of oppositions. There is no 'first paradigm', just as in Foucault there is no founding statement. One might here bring into play Deleuze's law of the series of singularities: they are always multiple and divisible.

What is presented here as a complication is that homo sacer is the first paradigmatic presence of the logic of included exclusion. This helps us, if nothing else, differentiate once more the paradigm from the statement. Homo sacer is not a statement but rather a person or persons taking the paradigmatic method beyond that of language. Indeed, we have seen the method is a mode of indistinction between language (logos) and politics through the indifference of Life as the suspension between being and existence. The only resolution I can offer here, aside from perhaps that the purity of the work is lacking in relation to the method, not necessarily a criticism, is that when we speak of Life as the signature of *Homo Sacer*, it is the signature of the opposition sovereign—homo sacer distributed according to the persistent logic of the political, included exclusion, moving towards a weak messianic moment: suspension of all categories as the final political act.

This is again radically different from Foucault in that Agamben signs up to the Derridean project of metaphysics as categorical oppositional difference, and Foucault simply does not. So every signature in Agamben must be the transmission of this in terms of presupposed predivisive unity, distribution of opposition or indifferent suspension of opposition. In terms of life all three are clearly in play: pure life—good life—bare life. As we shall see, the sovereign occupies the position of pure life in that, like God, their word is fact, the homo sacer that of bare life, and 'normal' citizens varying degrees of good life. It is the slow creep of indistinction across these terms that constitutes our political history. As Agamben says of Foucault's reading, what matters is not that life becomes "a principle object of the projections and calculations of state power" but "the process by which . . . the realm of bare life—which is originally situated at the margins of the political order—gradually begins to coincide with the political realm, and exclusion and inclusion, outside and inside, *bios* and *zoē*, right and fact, enter into a zone of irreducible indistinction".[12] The inclusion-exclusion pairing, while seeming to name the logic of the whole process of the political, actually represents just another example of the common and proper in its operational mode of condition and conditioned.

A NEW POLITICS OF INDIFFERENCE

The final pages of the introduction establish a project that it is possible to support but impossible to endorse without a detailed understanding of the methodology of indifference. When Agamben says that the "idea of an inner solidarity between democracy and totalitarianism (which here we must, with every caution, advance) is obviously not . . . a historiographical claim which would authorize the liquidation and levelling of the enormous differences that characterize their history and their rivalry. Yet this idea must nevertheless be strongly maintained on a historico-philosophical level",[13] he means in terms of the method. This being the case, the nature of the solidarity between democracy and totalitarianism is to be found in the statement "Today politics knows no value (and, consequently, no nonvalue) other than life".[14] We now know that life here is not an actual biological or philosophical reference. Rather, it is the signatory manner that the sign Life is distributed across discursive formations to allow for certain things to be said and for certain acts to be sanctioned and performed. These things do not contain an ontological definition of life, for Life is not a referential sign here but a marker of a set of processual capacities or the pure divisibility of life as a caesura as he describes it in *The Open*.[15] This being the case, the messianic mode of the text, which is powerful but somewhat vague, is not the collapsing of two signs into one meaning. Life does not explain democracy or totalitarianism; it is the signature they have in common that allows them to operate intelligibly (in terms of being and transmissible meanings). In fact, Agamben's system is never aimed at levelling differences but at suspending them through and within indifference. This can be done only by retaining a degree of constructive indiscernability between politics and philosophy or here, methodologically speaking, 'history' and philosophy. Here then we are speaking of philosophical archaeology as a motivated method or a method whose aim is not revelation or illumination but change.

Agamben presents an example of the historical philosophical method when he gives us a judgemental history of politics, after Aristotle's distinction beautiful life versus political life, in terms of the metaphysics that it engenders and yet also accepts as its condition:

> In carrying out the metaphysical task that has led it more and more to assume the form of biopolitics, Western politics has not succeeding in constructing the link between *zoē* and *bios*, between voice and language, that would have healed the fracture. Bare life remains included in politics in the form of the exception. . . . How it is possible to "politicize" the "natural sweetness" of *zoē*? And first of all, does *zoē* really need to be politicized, or is politics not already contained in *zoē* as its most precious center?[16]

We have here a three-point philosophical history of politics in the West:

- Biopolitics as the moment of arising of the scission between life and politics revealed by its failure to heal this scission which, in fact, it engenders historically.
- Life as the signature in the form of a mode of operation rather than a set of meanings: the logic of exception which allows things to be said in political theories.
- Double paradoxical precondition for indifference: can one politicize life, or is politics not in the first instance part of life? Can one condition the unconditioned, or is the conditioned the condition of the condition?

The third issue here is indifference, of course, that life conditions politics that is the conditioned condition of the intelligibility of life. That Agamben then declares that until we have a completely new politics "no longer founded on the *exceptio* of bare life . . . every theory and every praxis will remain imprisoned and immobile"[17] gives us clear insight into the political status of indifference. Indifference is not the solution but the final revelation of the true problem. An archaeology of the signature of Life traced through its innumerable paradigms will reveal only what is wrong, while the suspensive state of indifference, itself a profound immobility, is where we have arrived but is not where we are going. So what is the new politics?

A new politics comes about by, first of all, suspending the signatory transmissibility of Life. This signature is not a set of meanings but a mode of organisation and sanction. Its logic of included exclusion is what is transmitted, and that is all Life is. Every political theory thus far has depended on the transmission of this mode to make intelligible its claims, by which we mean makes its claims possible through sanction, and operative through the context of their intelligibility. The only politics that can claim to be new is one that, directly facing up to the signature of all politics, refuses the sanction and operativity offered by Life as signatory included exclusion.

HOMO SACER AS PHILOSOPHICAL ARCHAEOLOGY

Having finished with the methodological elements of the introduction which indeed constitute those of the whole work, we can say the majority of the rest of book is an investigation of Life in its true modality, the signatory transmissible communicability of the structure of included exclusion. We will return to this to answer the fundamental question of the work, a question that I believe no one has yet raised, which is the direct relationship between exclusion and indifference. Now, however, I want to turn to the last "threshold" of the book, which functions as a conclusion and is as condensed and provocative as the opening salvos. Here I want to take as read the argument of exclusion, which I believe is very well articulated in the work of many critics, and look instead at how the conclusion of the book is sustained by the methodology I have applied. The 'conclusion' begins with a three-part designation of the conclusions of the inquiry:

1. The original political relation is the ban or the zone of indistinction of inclusion and exclusion to be found in the signature life.
2. Power produces life (as ban) as "originary political element" and "articulation between nature and culture".[18] Thus, power does nothing other than produce life as the double mode of unconditioned Being and of conditioned beings. The meaning of the term "production" here must be returned to.
3. We have a paradigm shift from the city to the camp. This last point interests our study the least except to say that it is the camp's role as the localization of the nonlocalizable or the clear inclusion of the excluded that determines its paradigmatic power. It is the latest structure of life as exception.

Agamben draws his own interim conclusions from these findings, which are interesting but less ambitious and far less significant than what is to follow.

Having dealt with the archaeology of Life, he then proceeds to the ontological aspect of his study. We have already seen that one of the most challenging indifferentiations in the work is that assumed between ontology (Being as condition) and politics (the conditions of beings). This is further ratified in the third chapter of the first section, "Potentiality and Law", where, representing the logic of potentiality and indifference which we found in greater detail in *Potentialities*, he explains that to think potentiality in terms of the impotential, one needs to think it in terms of an entirely new concept of relationality. This is a potential with no relation to "Being in the form of actuality" or indeed any concept of the gift of being and of letting be. "This," he says, "implies nothing less than thinking ontology and politics beyond every figure of relation, beyond even the limit relation that is the sovereign ban".[19]

He returns to this theme in the final pages by drawing parallels between the ontological concept of pure Being, *haplos*, and the definition of 'bare' in bare life. He notes that the isolation of pure Being operates as a signature in philosophy; he does not use this term, so we are extrapolating from the later work, in the same manner as bare life does in politics. This suggests of course a greater signature than Life or Being in that there is a signature which not only makes intelligible all of philosophy and another that makes communicable all of Western politics but that there is a further, meta-signature that distributes Being and Life as epi-signatures of a more common signature, the true signature of all things. Preparing us for this overwhelming and, to some degree, logically insupportable observation, Agamben relates how Being and life work in tandem so that "What constitutes man as a thinking animal has its exact counterpart in what constitutes him as a political animal".[20] What I would call the final indifference or the indifferentiation of indifference as such, a project I must admit Agamben does not achieve or openly sign up to. Thus, he says, just as the project ontologically is to isolate Being from the many senses of the term, so politically it is to separate bare life from the many forms of concrete life.

These two projects draw ontology and politics together in a common failure: "What is the link between the two constitutive processes by which metaphysics and politics seem, in isolating their proper element, simultaneously to run up against an unthinkable limit?"[21] What links Being and Life is in fact their nature as "empty and indeterminate concepts", their signatory operations, and thus their potential indistinction so that, as he argues here, thought passes over into politics and politics passes over to theory. This is perhaps the greatest enigma of the work. Why is Agamben not able to say at this point that it is the indistinction of the two great producers of indifference, philosophy and politics, that is the final project of thought, and that the signature of all things is the signatory law itself which promulgates the very project of isolation and separation through its apparent sanctioning of reticulation and combination, that is, that the method itself is nothing other than the arriving at the method as problem through the method as solution? Indifference itself must be indifferentiated before any new politics or any future for philosophy can be conceived. I am not sure of the answer to this question, but, by my own contention, there is no hierarchy of signatures, and so the signature of all things, the suspension of every signatory suspension, can be only the suspension of suspension as such or the indifference of indifference.

The final section of the conclusion then confirms, at least, that zones of indistinction, of which he has just revealed several as paradigms from the main body of the work, are the territory around which a new politics can be thought. Adding any new political space must now accept the moment of arising presented by the work: "That we no longer know anything of the classical distinction between *zoē* and *bios*, between private life and political existence, between man as a simple being living at home in the house and man's political existence in the city".[22] He then proposes the clearest determination so far as to what we should do next after *Homo Sacer*. This is formulated around a new signatory presence of life, the form of life. "This biopolitical body that is bare life must instead be transformed into the site for the constitution and installation of a form of life that is wholly exhausted in bare life and a *bios* that is only its own *zoē*".[23] In other words, we need a form of life that is constituted by the double indifference of bare life as where we are today, so that the division that is central to the signature of life is rendered inoperative. How do we do this? "How can a *bios* be only its own *zoē*, how can a form of life seize hold of the very *haplōs* that constitutes both the task and the enigma of Western metaphysics?"[24]

Agamben says that if we give the name form-of-life "to this being that is only its own bare existence and to this life that, being its own form, remains inseparable from it",[25] we will enter an entirely new field. And indeed he does take up this challenge in the essay "Form of Life", which is included in the collection *Means without Ends*, but it remains, after this, undeveloped as a project until the most very recent publications which complete the whole *Homo Sacer* project.[26] What is not undeveloped and abandoned at this point, however, is the method, and it is the method that the book ends on:

> First, however, it will be necessary to examine how it was possible for something like a bare life to be conceived within these disciplines, and how the historical development of these very disciplines has brought them to a limit beyond which they cannot venture without risking an unprecedented biopolitical catastrophe.[27]

The only way to do this, methodologically, we have come to realise, is via a fully worked out philosophical archaeology, and, judging from recent works, most notably *The Kingdom and the Glory*, it is this project which Agamben has committed his energies to.

NOTE ON SUSPENSION OF SUSPENSION

In my reading of Derrida, I denied the possibility that deconstruction could be indifferent precisely because the logic of the double suspension by definition means that dialectical movement qua oscillation can never be suspended. The logical conclusion that the suspension of suspension results in nonsuspensive movement is justified within the Derridean 'set' of terms and conditions. Why, one may ask, does not the suspension of suspension result in a similar movement in Agamben? Is not the indifference of indifference just another name for *différance*? Several things should be said at this juncture with the proviso that the full development of the indifference of indifference or the suspension of suspension is yet if ever to be expressed in Agamben's work. More than this, the formula, as I have already said, is in part a deduction on my part out of Agamben's work. This being the case, a full investigation of the indifference of indifference must be deferred for later studies, not least because within the method in play here, indifferentiated indifference is noncommunicable until indifference as such as become properly signatory.

Returning back to our qualifications, however, we can say that a suspension of suspension differs in Agamben and Derrida primarily because of the differing natures of their systems. In addition, suspension is only an element of the totality of what is meant by indifference, so that in a wider sense the indifference of indifference, whilst necessitating suspensions of suspensive states, is not reducible to just this gesture. Indeed, within the system the suspension of a suspensive state is able to exceed the classical logic of a double negative here, precisely because its aim is to make inoperative such binaristic, common-proper logical formations. Inasmuch as Derrida's nonmethod disallows the total suspension of metaphysical oscillation, then for him the suspension of suspension can mean only a return to movement. Inasmuch as Agamben's system is designed precisely to render said metaphysics permanently inoperative, it is available to him that the suspension of the dialectic, rendered at a standstill, can ever be only an interim state which must and will be overcome precisely by not falling back into the *oikonomia* of metaphysical articulation.

INDISTINCTION-INDIFFERENCE

As promised this analysis is in two parts, first the detail of how *Homo Sacer* accords with the method of philosophical archaeology, which I think we have achieved, and second how the text depends on indifference at every key moment. It is this second contention that I now want to proceed to justify. The instances of the use of indifference in *Homo Sacer* are too numerous to mention. First, we can argue, as we have done, that the methodological side of the text, still only just coming into clear view at this point, is dominated by the logic of indifference. More than this, again and again Agamben makes it clear here that the suspension of clear difference between terms such as *zoē-bios*, fact-law, homo sacer–sovereign, sacred-profane, home-city, animal-man, and *nomos-physis*, is the primary concern of the project. This is most commonly expressed by the term indistinction (*indistinzione*), specifically Deleuze's zone of indistinction, so that one hidden project of the text is the synthesis of Deleuzian metaphysics with Foucault's materialism such as we have already proposed. Finally, the controversial end point of the political analysis of the text depends on two key indistinctions, that between democracy and totalitarianism and the camp as zone of indistinction which replaces that of the city in classical politics. The main task here then is not to prove that indistinction is the basis of the text, the sheer weight of evidence performs that task, but to make it clear that indifference and indistinction are synonyms.

This can be proven by the many instances that Agamben uses various other synonyms for the same modality of thought, such as "indiscernibility," "indivisibility," "suspension" and "indifference". Second, it is almost impossible to find any clear definitional difference between "indistinction" and "indifference" and none at all between "difference" and "distinction". It is true that "distinction" has, in English, a more visual emphasis and that it can also mean "someone of importance", but "a person of indistinction" is not common usage, and the *Oxford English Dictionary* really leaves no doubt that of the two terms, it is "indifference" which is the richer, as it harbours one of the great emotional drivers of Western thought: lack of emotional commitment to either party or not caring. Thus, it is clear that first "indifference" and "indistinction" are synonyms in Agamben's work and that, more than this, the choice of "indifference" as the dominant term is justified because of this essential, extra meaning.

Of all these examples in the text, the most important use of indifference-indistinction pertains to the foundational political structure in the work, the signature of Life as the distributed logic of included exclusion leading to the indifference of the two terms in bare life and the concentration camp. The logic of this is as follows. There is a moment when life is divided into two elements in the Western philosophical and political traditions. These two elements, *zoē* and *bios*, define a certain political moment, the difference between the life of the home, the *oikos*, which is seen as nonpolitical life, or *zoē*, and the life of the city, which is *bios*, or political life. These two zones map onto the founding Greek distinctions of *physis* and *nomos* and the more contentious *zoē* and *bios*. Politics is founded on this difference, the private realm which belongs to us all, the common and unconditioned nature of day-to-day existence, and the public realm to which we all must belong in part, the proper and conditioned nature of public life. Yet, as we saw, as soon as the political element is developed in the Aristotelian tradition, something of pure life, specifically its goodness and sweetness, is included in the realm of political life. This begins the blurring of distinction by virtue of the shift of locales so that by the time of Roman law, the true origin of modern political life, the operativity of power depends on its indistinction. Both the sovereign and the homo sacer figure are included in the operative structure of law through their exclusion. The sovereign is the exception that founds the norm, and the homo sacer is the inclusion of one's own private life as central to the law's power in terms of it being something external to the law.[28] The law, normally, does not determine life as such; we leave aside here the issue of justified punishment, and to prove this to be the case, in Roman public life, there exist figures whose privacy is made public property. Here indistinction starts to develop, not only the inclusion of the excluded but also what life is; remember that Life is defined by Agamben as pure divisibility as such not a thing in itself, as well as the clear distinction between common and proper.

As these structures come to the fore in modern biopolitics, we see that in the case of fact and law, the commonality and unconditioned nature of human life, *zoē* or privacy, becomes instead the fact that the law passes judgement on. Thus, the law, the common law of all, is founded on the fact of existence. The fact of existence is of course common, common to all and the undifferentiated condition of our conditioned existence, yet in terms of law its facticity becomes the proper, and the propriety of the law becomes our commonality. This indistinction in terms of power is brought about by its reliance on the sovereign–homo sacer double structural indistinction, that they are both included as excluded and thus that they themselves fall into mutual indistinction in this regard. Modern law, because of this process, is itself a clear zone of indistinction between common and proper caused by its signatory reliance on life. Significantly, this is due to a second signature, that of *oikonomia*. In *Homo Sacer*, the *oikos*, or home in Greek thought, is assimilated into the definition of *zoē*, or life, as such. This is odd especially as *oikos* is the origin of the term *oikonomia*, or economy. Today it is impossible to think of economy as indistinct from life or as private and common. In *The Kingdom and the Glory*, as we shall see, the signatory shifts of Life occur against the background of a second signature, *oikonomia*, which traces the movement of governance from the home, through the kingdom of God, down to his theological economy on earth and on into political economy through a second signature called Secularisation.[29] As life becomes indistinct from law, so too does the home become indistinct from the city, resulting in the most horrific biopolitical paradigm of all, the camp as zone of double indistinction: the place where your private life becomes the property of law and where your home is entirely public.

Finally then, we find ourselves able to see this whole 'history' in terms of the following signatory shift. The division of Life into two elements is the moment when life as such becomes subject to the processes of discursive formation. There is no politics for us in the West without this. This initially does not take the form of one term split into two entities but two different senses of existence. These two terms then are forced together under one sign as two elements of the same phenomena: Life. This is then enshrined in the foundation of law and sovereign state power by the Romans. They use Life as a modality of establishing sovereign power by the double inclusion of exclusion, that of norm for the sovereign and fact for the homo sacer. Here already a switch occurs so that pure life, previously the common, now becomes facticity, the proper, allowing the sovereign to appropriate the 'natural' life of the common as their propriety to rule by natural law. Finally, in modern biopolitics, the difference between law and life becomes indifferentiated in states of exception. At these moments that which is excluded from law, your right to live privately, becomes the main domain of law. Law and Life then enter into a new zone of indistinction. When this occurs, the totality of the history of the signature of all things, Life, is finally, if horrifically, available to view. Now we must act.

SPECULATION ON THE FORMATION OF SIGNATURES

This is a complicated structure best considered now in the abstract in terms of repetition and difference. According to Agamben, at any moment in time within a defined discursive communicability, there are three elements in play. There are paradigmatic set consistencies which we call, after Foucault, discursive formations. As we have seen, the paradigms of these sets are determined in a specific way pertaining to the para-logic which defines the consistent and yet open nature of the sets. Then there are, overseeing the composition of the paradigm sets, certain statements that have become signatures. Signatures are paradigms that move, as we saw, outside the confines of a specific discursive formation or set. This movement determines at least three elements in relation to a set. First, it means a set can persist in and over time. Second, the set operativity can change using the same statements that, however, allow new things to be said. Third, it can influence other set formations, producing changes gifted with temporal persistence.

One question can and must be raised at this point as regards how signatures come about. Signatures, you will recall, are composed of statements which are then composed into paradigmatic sets. The order is, I believe, statement-signature-paradigm. However, this is a hermeneutic structure so that, for example, signatures must already exist to make statements communicable and paradigm sets must preexist signatures, for without them, signatures make operative nothing specific. The need for indifferent singularities to be inclined was, you may recall, the main stipulation of *The Coming Community*: that quodlibetality never be purely indifferent. In addition, we must remember that, due to the logic of now-time, the origin of a signature or indeed the presignatory realm is accessible only retroactively as an element of a contemporary moment of communicability. However, taking these provisos into consideration we can still present a kind of narrative of development of the different elements from the moment 'before' a signature takes hold. If we take the example of Life, there was before Life a prephilosophical conceptualisation of self-reflexive existence, one can presume. Over time, existence became not the sum total of lived experience per se but a set. Within the set there were paradigms, already indicating how the scattering of existence is being formalised into a genus defined by a set of species. Again, over time, within the set two paradigms were placed in a nonrelational relationality, home and city, which allowed for something to occur, at which point they become signatory potentials. That said, for Agamben, a signature is not two terms in relation but the relation of two nonrelational paradigms under one sign. Thus, home and city become articulated into one term: Life. This is why the Greeks had no term for life; they had no need for it, by which we mean for them life did not allow certain things to happen and so was noncommunicable. We are now in the realm of pure supposition, trying to keep attendant to the logic of the system if nothing else to test its consistency. First we must ask, Why do home and city become Life? Because they allow for something to happen, namely, sovereign power. Why does Life then get distributed over time? Because it continues to allow power to happen. Does power then precede home and city articulated into the signature life? No, rather Power itself is nothing other than a signature. What then does allow for this articulation? The same force that oversees every articulated signatory sanction of a specific set of communicability, the identity-difference logic of metaphysics.

In conclusion, of this speculation it is important to add that this process has a limited lifetime. The nature of signatory distribution is as follows:

> infinite indifferents → limited paradigms under signatory auspice → potential relationality of two paradigms → distinction of two paradigms as oppositional elements of one term → distribution of the term through time as signature → increasing indistinction as regards initial differentiation → point of indistinction in the moment of arising → suspension of difference

(There is much of Deleuze and Foucault here of course, or rather Deleuze's system is defined in terms of historical destiny, while Foucault's system of statements is given a Deleuzian way out.) In the heart of this system is the role of the inclusion of exclusion which, in *Homo Sacer* and then again more powerfully in *The Signature of All Things*, is presented as the very opposite of the paradigmatic example, which is exclusion of the inclusion. What we may be able to trace is a simple logic wherein the paradigm, an inclusion that is excluded, becomes the signature, the inclusion of the excluded, through the switch between the two logics, with indifference here operating as that which facilitates, polices and finally brings to an end this relationality resultant of the lack of distinction due to the repetition of the switch.

THE LOGIC OF EXCEPTION: INCLUDED EXCLUSION

The first chapter of *Homo Sacer* is concerned primarily with detailing the logic of exclusion beginning with the paradox of sovereign as being "at the same time, outside and inside the juridical order",[30] glossing on Schmitt, primarily, in relation to the exception to the determination of the rule of law via the establishment of a sovereign position. Here we then get the first major definition of the logic of exception:

> The exception itself is a kind of exclusion. What is excluded from the general rule is an individual case. But the most proper characteristic of the exception is that what is excluded in it is not, on account of being excluded, absolutely without relation to the rule. On the contrary, what is excluded in the exception maintains itself in relation to the rule in the form of the rule's suspension. *The rule applies to the exception in no longer applying, in withdrawing from it.* The state of exception is thus not the chaos that precedes order but rather the situation that results from its suspension. In this sense the exception is truly, according to its etymological root, *taken outside (ex-capere)*, and not simply excluded.[31]

This same logic applies to bare life, which is not pure life but denuded life or life made bare through politicisation.[32] In the same way the exception is taken outside. A state of exception or of law's suspension does not take one back to a primary lawlessness or state of nature in the Hobbesian sense; rather, it constructs lawlessness (anomie) through the law. Exclusion is the result of inclusion, or an element's being included in the set as that element which cannot be said to belong, what Badiou terms an excrescence. The rule then is founded on its exception: "The exception does not subtract itself from the rule; rather, the rule, suspending itself, gives rise to the exception and, maintaining itself in relation to the exception, first constitutes itself as a rule".[33] Agamben names this process the relation of exception or "the extreme form of relation by which something is included solely through its exclusion".[34] From this one can provisionally conclude that exteriority is a property of inclusion, a point made by Foucault in terms of statements which are the total inclusion of the purely exterior. There is, in this system, no otherness, therefore, no alterior and never-to-be-known other realm; rather, otherness is a product of system wherein every statement has no interior, no hidden meaning. On this reading exteriority, otherness, depth and so on are generated out of inclusion in a system by means of exclusion. If nothing else, this is a strong riposte to those traditions dependant on alterity, most specifically as we know for Agamben, Levinas and Derrida. For Agamben the trace is not that of the minimal otherness within identity that places otherness at the foundation and destination of thought, as in Derrida. Rather, the other is a construct of metaphysics, its most foundational construct, and there is no solution to the problem of metaphysics through otherness, only its continuing perpetuation through the logic of included exclusions.

This is further confirmed when Agamben speaks directly of the situation of exception as being neither that of fact nor that of right "but instead institutes a paradoxical threshold of indistinction between the two".[35] The excluded party, let us call it bare life, is not a fact because it is created out of law. As I have been arguing, it is a fact whose facticity is suspended or, better, constructed for it. Bare life then is lawful construction of life as fact. He adds that sovereign exception is not the "control or neutralization of an excess", which is the mainstream view of a politics of difference attributable with varying degrees of accuracy to Derrida, Deleuze and Foucault, but rather "the creation and definition of the very space in which the juridico-political order can have validity. In this sense sovereign exception is a fundamental localization (*Ortung*), which does not limit itself to distinguishing what is inside from what is outside but instead traces a threshold (the state of exception) between the two, on the basis of which outside and inside . . . enter into those complex topological relations that make validity of the juridical order possible".[36]

At this point the zone of indistinction then operates in a negative capacity in terms of the overall project of the book in that the zone of indifference that defines sovereignty is the precise locale where democratic sovereignty can cross over to totalitarianism and back again and where the biopolitical determination of bare life is composed as well. That said, at least we get a better sense of sovereignty here. It is a structure which allows power to happen, a signature, therefore, by which the determinant spaces of political thought, inside and outside, friend and enemy, right and fact, are constructed through the modality of their indifference. Indifference then determines the politics of the West rather than the assumed duality of friend (identity) and enemy (difference). And any future political theory must be a theory of indifference. Of course, because the structural operativity of sovereignty—the construction of a zone where inside and outside become indistinct because the presupposition of an outside against which we must construct a state is in fact a construct of a state to justify its foundation—is the indistinction of location, then the state of exception as such has no specific location. It is not a thing or a space in actuality but a process and a generation. Thus, the relation between localization (*Ortung*) and ordering (*Ordnung*) in Schmitt, which he determines as constitutive of our *nomos*, is in fact "an unlocalizable zone of indistinction or exception that, in the last analysis, necessarily acts against it as a principle of its infinite dislocation".[37]

We are in the last analysis precisely now in our contemporary situation, Agamben argues, wherein the localization of the political is so dependent on the unlocalizable distinction between inside and outside that we have arrived at a point of constructive crisis. We effectively live in a state of permanent exception, and more than that, in the camp, we have been able to grant "the unlocalizable a permanent and visible localization".[38] This is the positive outcome of indifference. That power operates via the modality of indifference means that it will always arrive at a moment where the zone of indistinction becomes the very zone of the political, not simply that which allows it to operate via the construction of sovereignty. At this point the political is at its most dangerous but also its most exposed. When this occurs, the moment of arising of power in the West is available for view in such a fashion that the indifferential suspension of inside and outside can itself be suspended. Indifference can be rendered indifferent, and a new politics be created.

At this point Agamben establishes a complex of relations between the nonlocalizable, language and potentiality. The rule is like the word. For the word to operate it must denote reality or an external fact, by suspending its own denotative power through its operativity as mere lexical usage with no actual relation to the thing denoted. This is the same with the rule, which pertains to the fact only by being in force due to sovereign exception. Here he likens sovereignty to the *langue*. Law then is a pure potentiality in "suspension of every actual reference".[39] "Language is the sovereign who, in a permanent state of exception, declares that there is nothing outside language and that language is always beyond itself".[40] In addition, just as language presupposes the nonlinguistic, that to which it refers and with which it must maintain a "virtual relation" so that it may denote it in actual usage, so too the law presupposes the nonjuridical (violence or chaos) "as that with which it maintains itself in a potential relation in the state of exception".[41] Thus, we can say that as is the object to the sign in language, so is violence to the law in power. We can add to this potentiality, of which there is a whole chapter devoted in this first section. At this stage, however, we can see that the nonlocalizability of power is the same as the impotentiality of potential. What is negated in the locale of power, city, state, camp and life is not the outside becoming inside (potential becoming actual) but the nonlocalizability of the locale becoming localized. Power, Language and Potentiality then all operate according to the same modality but across different discursive formations which match, I believe, the three zones in Foucault's work of statements, signs and propositions. This means, as I have been suggesting, that there is a meta-signatory level to the signature which is indifference as such, which is in force to allow indifference to operate across all discursive formations, and again must be termed here the signatory indifference of indifference.

EXAMPLE: AGAMBEN AND BADIOU

We have already seen how the example and the exception operate in opposite fashion. This is not, however, simply an interesting observation or a means of using the example to explain the exception. Rather, what is apparent from the short comment on this in *Homo Sacer* is the profound interrelation of these two modalities of relationality. As Agamben says, "Exception and example constitute the two modes by which a set tries to found and maintain its own coherence":[42] the exception by inclusive exclusion and the example by exclusive inclusion. With the benefit of hindsight and of course our own developments of the role of indifference, we can now say that exception and example provide two sides of the indifference process. The example designates the logic of indifference in the paradigmatic method as a positive means of suspending oppositions between common and proper. Exclusion rather indicates the mode by which the signature operates to arrive at a negative indistinction between common and proper. Perhaps we could propose the conjecture that, in one sense, the example comes before the signature in that a signature is an example on the move. Yet in another, we might say that the signature is the precondition for the operation of paradigms; thus, it prepares for the operativity of examples within a set. The truth is that in a hermeneutical and phenomenological sense, they cofound each other. From the perspective of the later work, the example is presented always as a positive opportunity to escape propositional and formal logic with a disruptive and productive analogic, while in *Homo Sacer* states of indifferential suspension are always at best examples of blindness, at worst the augurs of mass slaughter. However, as is indicated here, both example and exclusion are attempts to maintain set coherence that are bound to fail.

Agamben's concern here is with set composition, terms which do not feature as strongly in the later work, and we should always keep this in mind. Agamben is as aware as any of us the importance of Badiou's work and that it is Badiou's development of Deleuzian concepts that is the future direction of continental thought. In Badiou's controversial work on Deleuze, he claims that the central problem of philosophy and the circumscription of what it is possible to demand of philosophy is an "immanent conceptualization of the multiple",[43] going on to argue that what separates his own work from Deleuze is their conception of how this problem is to be addressed. We can easily add to this that Agamben is in agreement. His work is also an immanent conceptualization of the multiple, as is Foucault's, providing us with a clear trajectory as to where twenty-first-century philosophy must go. All four thinkers, Foucault, Deleuze, Badiou and Agamben, are set thinkers, looking not merely for a final answer as to what constitutes coherence and consistency but also for a convincing model for a workable philosophy of inconsistency. Where these thinkers differ from their forbears is that the answer to the question of set coherence is a prelude to a theory of how to break from the set in a consistent fashion.

Agamben mentions Badiou's work more than once, and, unlike his comments on Derrida, his relation to Badiou remains one of qualified agreement, no more so than in these closing pages of the first chapter of *Homo Sacer*. Agamben sets up the debate by concluding on the parallel relation of the example to the exclusion as follows:

> While the example is excluded from the set insofar as it belongs to it, the exception is included in the normal case precisely because it does not belong to it. And just as belonging to a class can be shown only by an example—that is, outside of the class itself—so non-belonging can be shown only at the center of the class, by an exception . . . exception and example are correlative concepts that are ultimately indistinguishable and that come into play every time the very sense of the belonging and commonality of individuals is to be defined. [44]

Before we move on to the relation of this idea to that of Badiou's event, two comments must be made. The first pertains to that last phrase suggesting that the parallel example-exclusion comes into play every time the issue of the commonality of individuals is to be defined. As the issue of the commonality of individuals is *the* political question, this is quite a precondition for any would-be twenty-first-century political theorists. Second, it also pertains to any ontology of our age, of which Badiou is the great exemplar. Finally, it refers to the very basis of epistemology and especially epistemological systems such as we find in the human sciences, which are nothing but the sciences of the commonality of individuals. This being the case, the sentence which precedes this assertion is fundamentally important to our own work, for we see there that example-exclusion, the two operativities of indifference, paradigm and signature, become indistinguishable 'ultimately', which I take to mean again the closing self-defeating element of the philosophy of indifference: the final indifferentiation of indifference itself.

Agamben's mapping of his own concerns onto Badiou's is rather rapid and rather neat. Set theory distinguishes between membership of a set, belonging, and inclusion. Membership is when all of a term's elements are included in the set. Inclusion is when a term is included in a set without being one of its members. We can speak of this in different terms by saying membership is akin to the condition and inclusion the conditioned. This is clarified when Badiou speaks of this politically and in relation to the terms "presentation" and "representation". Presentation is the quality of set membership wherein a political subject is a member of the situation they are a part of. A representation is included in a situation if it is represented in a meta-structure or the initial count is then re-counted. This allows Badiou to propose three political situations. Situations are normal when they both presented and represented, excrescent when they are represented but not presented and singular when they are presented and not represented. Mostly states are normal. Often they are produce excrescences. Rarely, they are singular (events).[45]

Agamben is well aware that a state of exception would seem to accord with the excrescent state, and I have already said as much, but his ambitions are well in excess of Badiou's schema. In a comment of real importance for modern thought because it debates the territory of its two most innovative thinkers, Agamben denies the representation of exclusion in Badiou's work, insisting that it is a presentation of a new category, the presentation of presentation as such: "What defines the character of the sovereign claim is precisely that it applies to the exception in no longer applying to it, that it includes what is outside itself. The sovereign exception is thus the figure in which singularity is represented as such, which is to say, insofar as it is unrepresentable. What cannot be included in any way is included in the form of the exception".[46] In other words, what is presented is the impossibility of the recuperation of the singular by the state, as the very basis of any state or set. Every set must include within itself the fact that there is something which is always presentable but never recuperable. Agamben then seems to extrapolate on Badiou's behalf a fourth term, "a threshold of indistinction between excrescence (representation without presentation) and singularity (presentation without representation), something like a paradoxical inclusion of membership itself. *The exception is what cannot be included in the whole of which it is a member and cannot be a member of the whole in which it is always already included.* What emerges in this limit figure is the radical crisis of every possibility of clearly distinguishing between memberships and inclusion, between what is outside and what is inside, between exception and rule".[47]

This allows Agamben to fully recuperate Badiou as a thinker of exception and the Badiou event as the structure of the exception: "An element of a situation such that its membership in the situation is undecidable from the perspective of the situation".[48] For the state, such a situation appears as an excrescence, while politically it is a revolution in that the exception-event shows to a system that it is impossible to make inclusion and membership coincide: "its reducing all its parts to a unity".[49] This not only is a subtle and prescient reading of Badiou but also recuperates Badiou, for our purposes, into the philosophy of indifference, an avenue we must now leave to grass over for a while before we return to claim our meagre crop. Finally, it uses Badiou to explain something that is missing in Foucault and too omnipresent in Deleuze: how does change come to a system? For Agamben the exception becomes exemplary of the state's perspective of excrescence, the exclusion of bare life, as a positive opportunity for the total suspension of the state. In politics, the attenuated and debased role of singularity, the presentation of unrepresentability, is also its most promising future, the suspension of the logic of exclusion-inclusion through the signature of life.

THE BAN: NONRELATIONAL RELATIONALITY

The chapter ends in the appropriation of another of Agamben's peers, Jean-Luc Nancy, and indeed it is notable that Agamben's most significant work up to this point, not *Language and Death* but *The Coming Community*, is a sustained engagement with Badiou and Nancy. Specifically, Agamben is speaking of the revision of the nature of sovereignty that the book presents, defining it, against the tradition, as "the originary structure in which law refers to life and includes it in itself by suspending it".[50] There is no more clear support for my reading of *Homo Sacer* than this. He then proposes to use the term *ban* to capture this process, taking inspiration from Nancy's concept of *abandoned being*. The term *ban* is excavated from the old Germanic, meant both banishment and the insignia of power. For Agamben, this presents perfectly the potentiality of law, meant in the powerfully Agambenian sense of potentiality and impotentiality. This is the ability of law to "maintain itself in its own privation, to apply in no longer applying"[51] or to "be in force without significance" as he goes on to define it in his famous reading of Kafka. His description of the ban or the person abandoned by law, the homo sacer, is of one about whom it is impossible to say if they are inside or outside the juridical order. Law's original relation to law then is one not of application, he argues, but of abandonment.

While the relation with Nancy is interesting, the engagement is of a different order here, and what interests us more is how this consideration of the ban allows Agamben to make two, for us, closing statements on the true intention of this confounding work. First, he says, "The matchless potential of the *nomos, its originary 'force of law,'* is that it holds life in its ban by abandoning it. This is the structure of the ban that we shall try to understand here, so that we can eventually call it into question".[52] Obviously, this is a description of bare life, the final zone of indistinction for politics in the West. Thus, we are able to see that the archaeology of bare life is designed to question and eventually suspend Life as the political signature of all things. The second point pertains to ban and relation, or its odd nature as relation. "[W]hat kind of relation is at issue here, when the ban has no positive content and the terms of the relation seem to exclude (and at the same time, to include) each other?".[53] Our answer is the kind of relation is that of indifference. Everything we have said so far supports this, as does what Agamben goes on to say: "The ban is the pure form of reference to something in general, which is to say, the simple positing of relation with the nonrelational. In this sense, the ban is identical with the limit form of relation".[54] The ban then is indifferent nonrelational relationality.

Agamben ends the chapter with a second programmatic call, this time a critique of the ban, which is what the book composes in the pages which follow, that will have to "put the very form of the relation into question".[55] If one is able to do this, and this is in miniature the entire project of Agamben's philosophy that I have attempted to present in terms of the philosophy of indifference, then one is finally entitled to "ask if the political fact is not perhaps thinkable beyond relation and, thus, no longer in the form of a connection".[56] If this is possible, and so far Agamben has not being able to think beyond the relation, only think the limits of relationality as such, I contend it is only viable to think this through indifference. All of this leads to a simple conclusion to this most complex work: the politics to come is the politics of indifference.

To arrive at this situation we can present the following programmatic archaeological representation. Accept that the signature of Power in the West is actually Life. Trace this philologically 'back' to two key moments of arising. The first is the articulation of life as divided, *zoē-bios*. The second is the signatory sanction of Power due to sovereign and sacred exclusions. Show how the biopolitical sphere, an operation of power based on the indistinction between life and state, extends back to the very origins of the signatures Life and Power. Describe the detail of the indistinction of Life within our age through various paradigms. Then offer this to a wider readership not just in terms of an insightful critique of contemporary politics, it is that, nor a genealogy of the origins of our situation, it is that too, but as a means of doing something about said situation. Then, at this moment, occupy a logical impossibility of the system: how can Life be a meta-signature for all other signatures when signatures are all distributed nonhierarchically? Such an occupation can be attained through, I contend, a simple logical deduction. The signature of all things, if it is to be the signature Life, must also be the method, hence the choice of the name for the work on method. Therefore, the only way one can act, politically, is through indifference as the suspension of the very signatory model of oppositional suspensions. Life, true life, the life to come by virtue of the form of life not as office nor occupation but as *theoria* or contemplation, is the indifferent suspension of the method of indifference. This is the only way that Life can be the meta-signature.

Any credible and operative politics of the future must be such a politics of indifference taken to be the indifferentiation of the oppositional

terms of political power, the identification of the centrality of the signature of Life as making these terms operative and then finally the indifference of the indifferential method as such. One implication to be drawn
from this is that if Life can be placed in the position of the last signature,
the final suspension, then this means that the presentation of power in
Homo Sacer is incomplete. For Life to suspend power, power must be
articulated fully, not just in terms of power as commonality, sovereignty,
but also in terms of particularity, propriety and facticity. The final articulation of power is not achieved by the end of *Homo Sacer*, is not achieved
for more than a decade after but, remarkably, it is achieved in the consideration of Power as articulation as such that is the basis of *The Kingdom
and the Glory*.

NOTES

1. See also Giorgio Agamben, *The Open: Man and Animal*, trans. Kevin Attell (Stanford, CA: Stanford University Press, 2004), 15–16, 38.
2. Giorgio Agamben, *Homo Sacer : Sovereign Power and Bare Life*, trans. Daniel
Heller-Roazen (Stanford, CA: Stanford University Press, 1998), 4.
3. Agamben, *Homo Sacer*, 4.
4. Agamben, *Homo Sacer*, 4–5.
5. Agamben, *Homo Sacer*, 6.
6. Agamben, *Homo Sacer*, 6.
7. Agamben, *Homo Sacer*, 7.
8. Agamben, *Homo Sacer*, 7.
9. Agamben, *Homo Sacer*, 117.
10. Agamben, *Homo Sacer*, 9.
11. See Giorgio Agamben, *Means without Ends*, trans. Vincenzo Binetti and Cesare
Casarino (Minneapolis: University of Minnesota Press, 2000), preface.
12. Agamben, *Homo Sacer*, 9.
13. Agamben, *Homo Sacer*, 10.
14. Agamben, *Homo Sacer*, 10.
15. See Agamben, *Open*, 33–38, 79–80.
16. Agamben, *Homo Sacer*, 11. See also Agamben, *Means*, 5–6.
17. Agamben, *Homo Sacer*, 11.
18. Agamben, *Homo Sacer*, 181.
19. Agamben, *Homo Sacer*, 47.
20. Agamben, *Homo Sacer*, 182.
21. Agamben, *Homo Sacer*, 182.
22. Agamben, *Homo Sacer*, 187.
23. Agamben, *Homo Sacer*, 188.
24. Agamben, *Homo Sacer*, 188.
25. Agamben, *Homo Sacer*, 188.
26. See Agamben, *Means*, 3–12. The most recent and as yet untranslated works by
Agamben, *Altissima Povertá*, *Opus Dei* and the unpublished *L'uso dei corpi*, form a final
set of statements on this issue whose significance is beyond the reach of this study.
27. Agamben, *Homo Sacer*, 188.
28. See also Giorgio Agamben, *State of Exception*, trans. Kevin Attell (Chicago: University of Chicago Press, 2005), 23, 33–40.
29. See Giorgio Agamben, *What Is an Apparatus? And Other Essays*, trans. David
Kishik and Stefan Pedatella (Stanford, CA: Stanford University Press, 2009), 12, 22.
30. Agamben, *Homo Sacer*, 15.

31. Agamben, *Homo Sacer*, 17–18.

32. See the essay "Nudity" in Giorgio Agamben, *Nudities*, trans. David Kishik and Stefan Pedatella (Stanford, CA: Stanford University Press, 2011), 55–90, for a final, definitive statement on this issue. See also Agamben, *Means*, 21.

33. Agamben, *Homo Sacer*, 18.

34. Agamben, *Homo Sacer*, 18.

35. Agamben, *Homo Sacer*, 18.

36. Agamben, *Homo Sacer*, 19.

37. Agamben, *Homo Sacer*, 19–20.

38. Agamben, *Homo Sacer*, 20.

39. Agamben, *Homo Sacer*, 20.

40. Agamben, *Homo Sacer*, 21.

41. Agamben, *Homo Sacer*, 21.

42. Agamben, *Homo Sacer*, 21.

43. Alain Badiou, *Deleuze: The Clamour of Being*, trans. Louise Burchill (Minneapolis: University of Minnesota Press, 2000), 4.

44. Agamben, *Homo Sacer*, 22. See also *Means*, 87–89, 109.

45. Badiou comments specifically on this issue in Alain Badiou, "Intervention dans le cadre du Collège international de philosophie sur le livre de Giorgio Agamben: *La Communauté qui vient, théorie de la singularité quelconque*", http://www.entretemps.asso.fr/Badiou/Agamben.htm, unpaginated.

46. Agamben, *Homo Sacer*, 24.

47. Agamben, *Homo Sacer*, 24–25.

48. Agamben, *Homo Sacer*, 25.

49. Agamben, *Homo Sacer*, 25.

50. Agamben, *Homo Sacer*, 28.

51. Agamben, *Homo Sacer*, 28.

52. Agamben, *Homo Sacer*, 29.

53. Agamben, *Homo Sacer*, 29.

54. Agamben, *Homo Sacer*, 29.

55. Agamben, *Homo Sacer*, 29.

56. Agamben, *Homo Sacer*, 29.

TEN

The Kingdom and the Glory: The Articulated Inoperativity of Power

AUCTORITAS AND POTESTAS: THE COMPLETE ARTICULATION OF POWER

To say *The Kingdom and the Glory* is an advance on *Homo Sacer* suggests something about the earlier text lags behind the later work, which is not the case; rather, what I mean is that *Homo Sacer* was never designed to be read in isolation but a part of sequence of texts. At this point, more than a decade later, due to the full availability of the method by the time it was composed, it can be asserted without controversy that *The Kingdom and the Glory* (*Homo Sacer* II, 2) is therefore a significant and perhaps predictable corrective development of *Homo Sacer* I, 1, in at least three senses. The first is that it presents an articulation of Power missing from the earlier study of sovereign power,[1] an articulation that not only suggests that Power is twofold but that Power is not merely to be presented as articulated into two contesting elements, kingdom and government, but that said articulation defines the operativity of Power as a signature. The second is that the use of paradigms in *Homo Sacer*, often its most controversial moments, is superseded to some degree by the development of the theory of signatures in this later work. In that the method is made up of an interpenetration of paradigmatic logic, signatory distribution and archaeological messianic reconstruction, the lack of any mention of the signature in *Homo Sacer* is certainly a limitation. This is particularly the case in relation to the later work where the signatures pertaining to Power in the form of *oikonomia*, Secularization, Glory, Order and so on present a much more complex and radical formation than those to be found in the

paradigms of the earlier piece. The third and final difference is the development of the Agambenian method of indifference. Indistinction, one of
the key synonyms for indifference in Agamben's work, is prominent in
Homo Sacer of course, but by the time of the publication of *The Kingdom
and the Glory*, the centrality of indifference to the method is fully developed. Through this method of indifference, while the complete articulation of power becomes available to view through our current access to the
history of its operations and the recent period of indiscernibility between
its two key elements, kingdom and government already impossible to
discern from *Homo Sacer*, the real purpose of the text is the role of inoperativity as such, specifically through the signature of Glory. In that *The
Kingdom and the Glory* takes us, in its final pages, towards a possible
suspension of inoperativity, it marks a significant advance in Agamben's
use of indifference, constituting in effect the inoperativity or indifferentiation of indifference as such.

Whatever one's opinions as to the particular relation of the two works,
what is clear is that they are articulated, primarily, by *State of Exception*
(2003). In the preface to *The Kingdom and the Glory*, Agamben contends
that the project of *Homo Sacer* was always a genealogy of power, and in
this sense he never intended it to be read in isolation as his theory of
politics. To better illustrate this point as to the development of a project
over time involving numerous volumes, he then concedes that *State of
Exception* (2003) is particularly significant in this regard in that its consideration of the correlation between *auctoritas* and *potestas* for the first time
clearly presents the division of power, which he names "the double structure of the governmental machine". If the theme of power is actually its
articulation through an economy, then *State of Exception* operates as the
economy of the two extremes of power presented in *Homo Sacer* and *The
Kingdom and the Glory*. It is this double structure or articulation that first
concerns us and that in *The Kingdom and the Glory* "takes the form of the
articulation between Kingdom and Government".[2] The necessity of the
articulation of power arises in response to the simple question "Why is
power split?";[3] it is not perhaps even clear in *Homo Sacer* that it is, and
Agamben's answer is that "the world is governed through the coordination of two principles, the *auctoritas* (that is, a power without actual execution) and the *potestas* (that is, a power that can be exercised); the Kingdom and the Government".[4] Aside from the articulation of power as
original thesis for *The Kingdom and the Glory*, it is also a significant development in relation to *Homo Sacer* which, although it presents the relation
of power to the double articulation of inside and outside as regards the
imposed division of *zoē* and *bios*, does not openly concede that power is
divided into two elements. If it appears in *Homo Sacer* that the double
articulation of inside and outside produces power which then grounds
the political, *The Kingdom and the Glory* radically modifies this claim by
showing how government effectively produces the power which grounds

it, making the kingdom (sovereign power) operative through the inoperativity of the power of glory. If this is proven to be the case, then *Homo Sacer* is a long way from Agamben's final word on power and politics, and just as power is articulated, then so too is Agamben's genealogy of power.

This discrepancy in *Homo Sacer* makes *State of Exception* all the more pertinent. Ostensibly, the text presents a genealogy of the state of exception structure from Roman law on, but it is the concluding chapter of the study that particularly concerns us dealing, as it does, with two designations of power in Roman law, *potestas*, power granted by the will of the people, and *auctoritas*, which we might call the power of authorisation. Agamben traces the roots of the term *auctoritas* to two seemingly contending definitions. On the one hand, *auctoritas* means someone who augments an act through the granting of authority: ratification. On the other, it means to create rather than augment what already exists. Agamben then notes that for the Greco-Roman world, the definition of creation was never *ex nihilo*, a concept we moderns have added to the signature, but always involved putting a stamp on an already existent but formless matter or substance. This means that every creation is a cocreation, and he cites historical sources which confirm that authorisation is never sufficient unto itself but must authorise something.[5] Here then *auctoritas* takes on a double existence which is not a contradiction but entirely within its remit as a signature. In the ideal act of law there are two subjects, one endowed with *auctoritas* and the other the acting agent. An agent cannot act without authority, but authority alone cannot act. This combination is the perfect moment of coincidence between authority and act. However, if there is no such perfect coincidence, in other words, where the authority of the act is not self-evident and self-authoring (which indeed it only is in the acts of gods and dictators), then *auctoritas* will be applied from the outside to ratify the act. This being the case, Agamben wonders where the authority of the *auctor* comes from, a question which sows the seeds of the study into kingdom and glory to come.

Tracing the genealogy of *auctoritas*, Agamben concludes, "The juridical system of the West appears as a double structure, formed by two heterogeneous yet coordinated elements: one that is normative and juridical in the strict sense (which we can for convenience inscribe under the rubric *potestas*) and one that is anomic and metajuridical (which we call by the name *auctoritas*)".[6] The normative element needs *auctoritas* to be applied, yet *auctoritas* can assert itself only by suspending the *potestas*. The state of exception is a device for articulating and holding together "the two aspects of the juridico-political machine by instituting a threshold of undecidability . . . between life and law, between *auctoritas* and *potestas*".[7] Agamben calls this dialectics a founding fiction. More interestingly for us, it shows that the operativity of sovereignty is the real definition of its power and that this operativity is based on a functional indif-

ference between two structures of power, that of governmental and juridical power. Indeed, we can concede that such an articulated power is by
the far the norm in our lives and that the founding authority for every
norm does not in fact precede the norm but is created as a founding
fiction from governance as such. Government, it can be said, articulates
its own foundation in sovereignty, which it disguises in the bizarre garb
and obscure insignia of glory.

At this point then, we can conclude on power as follows. Power is
divided, first of all, into two opposing elements, one common the other
proper. Second, conditioning power founds government and yet cannot
found anything alone: there is no authority without act, no law without
fact. Third, authority operates both as the assumed perfect coincidence of
act and law and as the pure externality of authority to law. It is thus, in
keeping with the logic of *Homo Sacer*, intrinsically extrinsic or better included because it can be excluded. Finally, fourth, the exclusion of power
is what founds the legitimacy of act by assuming authority as foundation
to, creative of, act. Yet no authority exists prior to act. Act is the granting
of power to authority, or the ratification of the agency of its own self-
ratification. This complex structure of division, distribution and comutual, ratifying foundation is the real essence of power in the West, government, whose main signature, *The Kingdom and the Glory* will go on to
argue, has been that of *oikonomia*, or economy. *Homo Sacer* concerns one
articulation of indifferentiation, sovereignty and bare life, as a first archaeology of power, but it is incomplete as it reveals the operation of only
one signature of power, *auctoritas*, whereas the real seat of power is that
which produces authority as its founding fiction: government. No understanding of Agamben's politics is complete without a full understanding
of power as, first, articulated of two opposing elements, kingdom and
government, and, second, that of power as such being, essentially, the
process of this articulation. If then Life suspends this oppositional articulation, by definition it suspends power.

Before we leave *State of Exception*, the final paragraphs give us some
further useful insights into the development of the methodology and its
relation to indifference in a wider sense. The penultimate section of the
book concerns our current political climate. Naturally, the eye is drawn to
declarations of our own permanent state of exception and its origins in
Roman law and the *arcanum imperii*, or secret of power, which Agamben
names as an empty space "in which a human action with no relation to
law stands before a norm with no relation to life".[8] Yet Agamben's aim is
not to reinstate a legitimate articulation between life (violence) and norm
(law) that has been suspended in the state of exception. Rather, what is
revealed is that there is no necessary relation between violence and law,
and this is what makes it possible to reveal its central fiction of foundation and operativity. He says of the assumed opposition between violence and law, "Alongside the movement that seeks to keep them in

relation at all costs, there is a countermovement that, working in an inverse direction in law and in life, always seeks to loosen what has been artificially and violently linked. That is to say, in the field of tension of our culture, two opposite forces act, one that institutes and makes, and one that deactivates and deposes".[9] From this he concludes what we must determine as the classic structure of the conversion of negative indifference to productive indifference, that the state of exception is the maximum point of tension between violence and law (condition and conditioned) and that which "threatens today to render them indiscernible".[10] Naturally, we might fear an age where the difference between violence and law is rendered indiscernible, but we ought not because the very terms "violence" and "law" are signatures, not signs carrying meaning. Violence and law are signatures that allow for power to be intelligible and operative, and the suspension of their difference does not result in a lawless state of violence; quite the obverse is true: the fiction of their difference is what founds law on violence for the West, resulting in the state as such as the lawful state of violence.

A second methodological point becomes clear here, and you can see in this text, almost ten years after *Homo Sacer*, the consistency of the method finally coming together. In the last section Agamben tackles the thesis that the articulation between life and law is "effective but fictional" by warning that "one can still not conclude from this that somewhere either beyond or before juridical apparatuses there is an immediate access to something whose fracture and impossible unification are represented by these apparatuses".[11] There is not, he says, first life as a "natural biological given" and then law; rather, the very possibility of distinguishing life and law "coincides with their articulation in the biopolitical machine. Bare life is a product of the machine and not something that preexists it".[12] Agamben is now able to present to us his project in the following manner:

> Life and law, anomie and *nomos*, *auctoritas* and *potestas*, result from the fracture of something to which we have no other access than through the fiction of their articulation and the patient work that, by unmasking the fiction, separates what it had claimed to unite. But disenchantment does not restore the enchanted thing to its original state: According to the principle that purity never lies at the origin, disenchantment gives it only the possibility of reaching a new condition.[13]

We are able to deduce from this the following thesis. Indifference is the philosophy of disenchantment whose first priority is, against the philosophy of difference, especially that found in Derrida and Deleuze, to reveal that difference does not precede identity but founds the fiction of identity. Any philosophy that wishes to destabilise the structures of metaphysical presence must concede difference as a production of metaphysics. Something then precedes difference. This something is not unity or identity, for unity and identity are products of difference. Nor is this something we can see or go back to, as our only access to it is the perfectly reasonable syllogism, If difference precedes identity, and identity produces differences, then what precedes difference is not identity but something that is neither difference nor identity. This also means that what is to come, which is both indifference and then the indifferentiation of indifference, results from access to the operativity of what is inaccessibly located before political scission through a positive disenchantment as a new condition of radical, indifferentiated political inoperativity. It is this state, named as glory, that *The Kingdom and the Glory* patiently unearths.

FROM THE PARADIGM TO THE SIGNATURE

We can summarise the main argument of *The Kingdom and the Glory* as follows. First, political power is always divided into sovereign and governmental power. In addition, through the signature of *oikonomia*, we find a "laboratory"[14] for observing the governmental machine. And finally, the true distribution of power in the West is to be found in the articulation between *oikonomia* and glory, "between power as government . . . and power as ceremonial and liturgical reality".[15] It is, in fact, the final point that is the main aspect of the total study and reflective of this is the final, dense chapter on the "Archaeology of Glory", which finds, in the paradox of the glory owed to God and the acts of glorification on earth, the key to the overall aim of this genealogy and Agamben's politics: the rendering inoperative of a political system based on founding sovereign violence and distributive and regulative acts of governance. It is to this final consideration of the inoperativity of power's articulation that our study will move, but to arrive there we will pass through the main moments of the book in a systematic fashion to consider the role of the signature, the machine-like process of economy and finally the inoperativity of glory.

Commencing with the role of the signature, we see that the first chapter of the book reveals a key structural difference between *Homo Sacer* and this later work. Entitled "The Two Paradigms", it considers the operativity of power in Western politics through the divisive articulation of two paradigms, "antinomical but functionally related". These paradigms derive from Christian theology. The first we are already very familiar with; coming from political theology, it is the theory of sovereign power which founds "the transcendence of sovereign power on the single God", in other words, the landscape of *Homo Sacer*. The other is the real subject of the book, an economic theology "which replaces this transcendence with the idea of an *oikonomia*, conceived as an immanent ordering".[16] The first paradigm makes intelligible political philosophy and modern theories of sovereign power, the second makes intelligible modern biopolitics and the "triumph of economy and government over every other aspect of social life".[17] Place these two paradigms together, and the true operativity of power as articulation of the two is finally available to view.

As wilful miscomprehension has been, in the past, rather typical of rapid responses to Agamben's work, let us make clear from the outset that the argument of the book is not that political economy derives from theological economy through a process of secularization. This would be to reproduce the usual 'worldview' arguments in this field and further obfuscate the truth as to what makes power operative, meaning we would never access the possibility of its inoperativity (the overall aim of Agamben's messianic political theory). Rather, as Agamben makes clear early on, secularization is not a historical process wherein theological concepts become profaned but is a signature that allows theological principles and profane ones to enter into a relationship of co-founding intelligibility: "The thesis according to which the economy could be a secularized theological paradigm acts retroactively on theology itself, since it implies that from the beginning theology conceives divine life and the history of humanity as an *oikonomia*".[18] This being the case, theology was always already economic and did not become economic later through the inevitability of the history of secularization. He adds that secularization does not reveal "*an identity of substance between theology and modernity*" but rather "*concerns a particular strategic relation that marks political concepts and refers them back to their theological origin. In other words, secularization is not a concept but a signature*".[19] This I think is a central stipulation for any future theological work on Agamben.

Signatory distribution presents a radically different theory of historical progression and influence than normal historiography, a logic which Agamben usefully explains as follows: "*The theological signature operates here as a sort of trompe l'oeil in which the very secularization of the world becomes the mark that identifies it as belonging to a divine oikonomia*".[20] This not only presents a clear demarcation of the method in its full realisation, clearly missing from *Homo Sacer*, but also makes a strong correction of the earlier text in emphasising that the issue of power is not sovereignty but *oikonomia*, allowing Agamben to conclude that the real issue of Western politics is "not sovereignty, but government" and that the real failure of political theory has been the designation of government "as mere execution of a general will and law". This miscomprehension of government has resulted in a history of political thought entirely unable to see and thus think governance, a history which is "nothing but the progressive coming to light of a substantial untruth of the primacy of legislative power and the consequent irreducibility of government to mere execution".[21]

Thanks to this rather explosive observation, we can now present the major development of the work: the division and distribution of sovereign power through the process of government as the very basis of the

Western conception of power in the paradox of a theological economy or the operation of God's power on the earth. We can also indicate the central consonance between the archaeological method and power as articulation. The signature of Secularization does not simply show how a conception of economy moves and mutates through time. Rather, our present moment of economy is made accessible through its origins in theological economy by virtue of the Greek concept of *oikonomia*, only inasmuch as these origins themselves are made accessible for the first time by our present situation. So we can say that Secularization makes possible its origins in divine economy by a retrospective gesture of founding precedence wherein theological economy is possible only as the origin of profane economy because profane economy allows this to be an operative structure of meaning. Again this disallows any straightforward theological recuperation of Agamben's terms, however tempting on the surface that might be. Even the logic of philosophical archaeology must submit to the law of the signature, revealing the final point here that a signature marks a process of knowledge formation and distribution both forward and backwards through time. Government is not the end point of sovereign power revealed by the continuing signatures of *oikonomia* and secularization; rather, government as much founds sovereign power by designating itself as the end point of said power, as it is founded by sovereign power. The two paradigms cofound, coimplicate, codistribute and cosuspend each other; and a signature such as Secularization merely reveals the details of this process.

OIKONOMIA: THE SIGNATORY PRAXIS OF ARTICULATING COMUTUAL COINTELLIGIBILITY

Zartaloudis presents such an excellent consideration of the term *oikonomia* that we do not need to dwell on the detail of the genealogy of this term too much, especially as, although this is the named interest of the book, for our purposes *oikonomia* is merely a signatory process or machine to arrive at Glory, the signature of the inoperativity of all things powerful.[22] We need only say that *oikonomia*, origin of the modern term "economy", means to the Greeks administration of the house, as opposed to that of the city. Good economy is taken by the Greeks to mean good household administration. That said, the *oikos*, or home, was a complex zone for the Greeks involving not just the family but an overlay of complex relations which Aristotle, being Aristotle, subdivides into relations between master and slave, father and children and husband and wife. Looked at from a Foucauldian perspective we can already see that, in the home, masculine power is in a constant process of becoming, or of constant shifts of enunciative positioning (master, father, husband). These differing relations are linked by an administrative paradigm that is not epistemic: "In other words, it is a matter of activity that is not bound to a system of rules. . . . This activity rather implies decisions and orders that cope with problems that are each time specific and concern the functional order (*taxis*) of the different parts of the *oikos*".[23] Agamben then closes on this definition by admitting that it is essentially a pragmatic model for the signature of operativity: "*Oikonomia* designates a practice and a non-epistemic knowledge that should be assessed only in the context of the aims that they pursue".[24]

Agamben proceeds to trace how the term is transposed into Christianity particularly through the relation of *oikonomia* to good rhetoric, a classic example of the signatory process where the sign retains the same meanings of order and division but in an entirely different sanctioning of discursive context. The Greek theory of home economics allows a group of subjects to say something about Christian ideas on rhetoric. Here the sense of *oikonomia* as mere divisive order is made more sophisticated, as it designates order in terms of choice and analysis of topics. This then means that as the signature *oikonomia* migrates from Greek to Christian culture, it is able to take on a new intelligibility as the divine plan of salvation, a 'meaning' that was not available before, as it could not be sanctioned or understood in the previous context.[25] At this point Agamben develops the signatory process by explaining that with *oikonomia* in its various different manifestations in different discursive formations, there is not a transformation of the sense of the word "*but rather a gradual analogical extension of its denotation*"[26] and further that it is the relative stability of the sense of the word that allows for its extension into new areas of denotation. That the term has a consistency of meaning means it can develop an almost unlimited universe of references and be said in any number of different senses whilst remaining intelligible and without affecting the meaning of the sign. Even when the signature reaches a point of radical indistinction, this is not a problem of the meaning of the term but rather a structural mode pertaining to a crisis in the field of denotative conflicts which become, over time, unsustainable. In this fashion the relation of the signature to the mode of the operation of the plane of consistency is clear. For Deleuze univocity guarantees inconsistency in every consistency, and by extension the signature does the same if we take indifferent suspension to be a moment of inconsistency. At the same time for precisely the same reasons, the difference between the two great men are as stark as they have ever been.

We now enter into one of the major historical observations of the work. Agamben considers a significant problem for theology as regards Gnosticism and the relation between God the Father and God the Son. The assumption of a Trinitarian model was initially to resolve the inherent threat of the Gnostic model, specifically how God can be complete in himself and also exist in material and limited form on earth. This alone is the basic structure of power and governance that we are concerned with.

To solve this problem the holy trinity was rendered operative as a paradigm from the signatory sanction of divine economy, engendering new
problems notably: how could the unity of God and son be reconciled
with the new Trinitarian model? It is Athenagoras who takes up the basic
meaning of *oikonomia* as activity and confers on it the additional status of
praxis for a purpose but also he who considers the *diaresis* between unity
and trinity in terms of *oikonomia*. This establishes a very particular structural dynamic for *oikonomia*, which is also the more general logic of the
signatory method as such. Through a wide variety of theological texts,
the signature of economy becomes that of the "harmonic composition of
the threefold divine activity in a single 'symphony'",[27] meaning that
economy as ordered arrangement is that which "articulates the divine
being into a trinity and, at the same time, preserves and 'harmonizes' it
into a unity".[28]

A citation from Hippolytus is revealing here presenting the following
logic. The Father is one, but he is two persons, Father and Son, and then
there is a third, the Holy Spirit. The third mediates between Father and
Son, first in that the Father gives orders which are performed by the logos
revealed in the Son. Then the Son, through belief, is accorded to the
Father as the one who performs the Father's will. In other words, economy, the Holy Spirit, is a doubly mediating articulation that does not
actually reconcile Trinitarian and Gnostic theology but does solve the
age-old theological problem of how God's will is actuated on the earth
without undermining all the elements of God's power, such as omniscience, atemporality, the will of good resulting in the existence of evil and
so on. We can translocate the theology here by reconsidering the problem
in terms of its signatory presence in the philosophical paradigms of conditioned and unconditioned which actually precede and in this sense
found Christianity by making *oikonomia* communicable as a dynamic. The
question for philosophy is, as ever, this: how can the unconditioned operate as the condition of the conditioned by remaining unconditioned but
in such a way that it can have a relationality with the conditioned? I
would articulate this model as the 1-3-2-3-1 model, which is the fictional
presentation of power (1)-administration (3)-governance (2)-administra-
tion (3)-power (1). In fact, the model is better presented as 2-3-1-3-2 in
that, as we increasingly see, governance founds its founding power
through the signatory action of economy.

The 1-3-2 or 2-3-1 model is repeated several times in the theological
texts that compose the large majority of this work, indicating their profound dependence on pagan deductive sources rather than Christian revelatory ones. Thus, later in relation to Aquinas, we have his logic that
"Things are ordered insofar as they have a specific relation among themselves, but this relation is nothing other than the expression of their relation to the divine end. And, vice versa, things are ordered insofar as they
have a certain relation to God, but this relation expresses itself only by

means of the reciprocal relation of things. The only content of the transcendent order is the immanent order, but the meaning of the immanent order is nothing other than the relation to the transcendent end".[29] This conception of order as relation occurs repeatedly in this chapter, specifically through a reading of the Aristotelian concept of taxis, which Agamben opposes, to what is separated and what is for itself, which, he says "decidedly inscribes the concept of order in the sphere of the category of relation".[30] Adding Heidegger into the mix, Agamben is then able to abstract the maxim that "Order is the theoretical apparatus that allows us to think the relation between the two objects"[31] before realising that the "reciprocal coordination" of transcendence and immanence, which is after all the real topic of the book, not Christianity per se, matches precisely the task of splitting metaphysics in two, followed by the attempt to then keep the two parts together in a dialectic, relational construct (the fundamental critique of metaphysics to be found on every page of every major work by Agamben). "Yet the aporia lies in the fact that order (that is, a figure of relation) becomes the way in which the separate substance is present and acts in the world".[32]

It is these observation that lead Agamben to the conclusion that order as such is an *"empty concept . . . a* signature" that *"produces a displacement of the privileged place of ontology from the category of substance to the categories of relation and praxis; this displacement is perhaps medieval thought's most important contribution to ontology".*[33] Additionally, we can also say more expansively that Order is the very signature of metaphysics and the mode that differentiates Agamben's philosophy from that of the philosophers of difference who directly precede him, namely, Derrida and Deleuze. Order is what articulates the metaphysics of division in both senses of the term, seems to join together a division and also makes speak the truth of the philosophy of division which is that neither the split nor the presupposed unity are anything other than historical contingencies. Using the terminology in play in the following chapter on being, acting and in this instance will as *oikonomia*, order is the anarchic foundation of transcendence from within the governance of immanence,[34] so that while Agamben has in the past allied himself with a certain immanentist strain of philosophy, as we saw, his overall project is the suspension of such contingent divisions.

We have then a specific division of division, presenting two orders of division, substantial separation, Father and Son, and economic articulation, Father (Spirit) Son. This is expressed in Tertullian, as while there is no substantial difference between Father and Son, there is an articulation of difference in terms of their "economic disposition". Agamben further contextualises this, explaining that substance is a single reality articulated into innumerable individualities and that in this light economy always forms a single field of heterogeneity which is substantially one and therefore whose heterogeneity "does not concern being and ontology, but rather action and praxis".[35] The trinity is nothing other than the praxis of divine being or how God's will, which is eternal, complete and atempo- ral, orders his earthly kingdom, which is limited, incomplete and deter- mined by a genesis and a destiny. Over time this comes to be called the economy of the mystery of God's will, but the mystery is of a specific nature. What is patently not obscure is what God wants or wills; rather, it is the economy of his will on earth that is mysterious, "the very praxis by means of which God arranges the divine life . . . and the world of crea- tures".[36] Or, to put it in other terms, God's mystery consists in the rela- tion between sovereign power and governance with which we com- menced by considering in relation to *auctoritas* and *potestas*. There is noth- ing specifically theological about this mystery; it is merely the signatory distribution of *oikonomia* from Greek thought to Christian and beyond.

The signatory role of *oikonomia* then "makes possible a reconciliation in which a transcendent God, who is both one and triune at the same time, can—while remaining transcendent—take charge of the world and found an immanent praxis of government whose supermundane mystery coincides with the history of humanity",[37] specifically in terms of fate, providence and redemption. This vision has led to the assumption that *oikonomia* has two contradictory meanings for Christian theology, as we have seen in fact a clear indicator of the presence of a signature. First, economy is the organisation of God's unity in relation to the trinity and a second meaning relating to "the historical dispensation of salvation".[38] Rather than a contradiction, what we are confronted with is one of the most significant examples of the signatory logic of indifference in the history of Western thought. The signature *oikonomia* does not have two meanings, two senses, but rather represents "the attempt to articulate in a single semantic sphere . . . a series of levels whose reconciliation ap- peared problematic: noninvolvement in the world and government of the world; unity in being and plurality of actions; ontology and history".[39] Instead of this being a contradiction indicative of the modality of tradi- tional logic, the two elements in play operate according to the paradig- matic ana-logic of Melandri, so that Agamben says the two levels "do not contradict themselves, but they are correlated and become fully intelli- gible only in their functional relation. That is to say, they constitute the two sides of a single divine *oikonomia*, in which ontology and pragmat- ics . . . refer back to each other for the solution of their aporias".[40] This final statement allows us then to step back from the theological detail and focus on what is truly significant in this text for our study: the full devel- opment of the logic of a praxis of articulating comutual cointelligibility. This is the true mystery of power, and until we can see it for what it is, we will never be able to suspend these oppositions, which in fact are not necessarily oppositional at all, and move into a new, for which read 'first actual', political and philosophical situation.

THE PROVIDENTIAL MACHINE

There is, perhaps, encased in two opposing definitions of providence in English, the core of the philosophical and political argument we are pursuing through theological means or paradigms. Providence is both "The foreknowing and protective care and government of a spiritual power" which becomes in a secular sphere "prudent management" based on "anticipation of and preparation for the future". On a regular basis all over the world, innumerable individuals make just such providential plans often termed risk assessment or risk management. In the secular age or in the intelligibility provided for providence through the signature of secularization, providence has become the presupposition that something that one cannot predict will go wrong, whereas in terms of theology of course it represents the perfect primary will of God in the creation of this world. This opens up a second contesting meaning, "divine intervention", which in English took the qualifier "special providence." This second sense of the term refers to the central paradox of providence: if God in his foreknowledge has provided for the world, where is our will, why did he send down his only son, why is there anarchy that requires governance in the form of theological *oikonomia*, why must he intervene in special cases, and how does primary providence relate to secondary providence or the redemption of humanity? More succinctly put, in terms of providence, how do primary and secondary providence relate?

Zartaloudis expresses this problem in the following formulation around the issue of the reconciliation of the freedom of man and God's providential will:

> The true root of the problem of such reconciliation is not so much the freedom of man, but the possibility of the divine government of the world. If kingdom and government in God are not seen as separate, then a divine government of the world does not seem possible: on the one part, one locates an impotent sovereignty and, on the other, a series of infinite and chaotic multiplicities of action on the basis of particular providences. Government is only possible if kingdom and government are correlated in a bipolar machine formed between general and particular or special providences. [41]

Aside from this being an excellent summation of the issues to hand in the text, Zartaloudis's choice to name the relationality of the whole text as examples of the "providential machine" is the first truly developed moment in Agamben criticism where the indifferential nature of the whole project is given something close to its due. Later, summarising Agamben, Zartaloudis expresses this as "a duplex *modus* of the activity of the government of the world which at times is presented as transcendent, at times immanent. . . . Thus, providence presents itself as a machine that rearticulates at the same time the two planes of the fracture evident in *gubernatio dei* (the divine governance of the world)".[42] Although one can understand why Zartaloudis uses the intermittent and oscillating "at times" structure, the second comment here is the more accurate. It is not the case of a kind of Derridean oscillation between, say, space and time, two of the categories Zartaloudis applies here, but rather that of the rearticulation of two planes whose fracture is the apparent precondition of the machine; there can be no rearticulation without articulation, although in actual fact the machine is what produces the fracture through articulation, the presupposition of the primary cause in its secondary causality. And, finally, the inevitability of the machine's shuttling back and forth results in first blurring, where one cannot tell primary from secondary, and eventually malfunction, with the shuttle jamming and the machinic *oikonomia* suspended.

Zartaloudis's third comment then is perhaps the most telling at least for our study:

> The two planes remain correlated in the alleged mode in which the first founds, legitimates and makes possible the second (as its condition of possibility); and in turn the second realizes concretely the causes and effects of the general (sovereign) decisions of the divine will. The government of the world *is* this mythologeme of functional correlation. As a result, the key paradigm of governmental *praxis*, in its pure form (as a functional *relation* or apparatus) lies in its *collateral effects*.[43]

As he goes on to explain, government is a collateral or concomitant effect of the zone of undecidability between law and general economy that it regulates or corelates. It is not directed at any aim, any ideological telos or strategy, but appears as merely tactical, as we said firefighting. Government is the product of the providential machine or *oikonomia* between first and second cause or divine providential will and earthly providential fate and human free will.[44]

I cite Zartaloudis at length here for a few reasons, the first of which is loneliness. His is the first work, I believe, that makes the structure of undecidability the centre of an argument. The second is to give another voice to the ideas present in the work, mine being concerned primarily with philosophical modalities, his being much more attuned to real issues of law and governance. A third is to take the opportunity to clarify, from our perspective, that government is a collateral effect of the undecidability between law and economy but that at the same time the oppositions which generate governance are themselves generated by the machine of governance. Another way of saying this is that the collateral effect works both ways; the machine is produced from that which it produces and thus when the basic term of the machine is rendered inoperative, namely, there is no founding power, so too the other element of the machine is rendered inoperative, nor are there such things as facts or effects. At this moment the machine itself, what Zartaloudis calls providential but what we term more widely indifference, will itself cease to have efficacy. When this transpires we are faced with the indifference of indifferentiation, its inoperativity, as the key moment in Western thought, a conclusion necessarily out of the remit of Zartaloudis's study, which contents itself with 'merely' the suspensive inoperativity of Western political power.

A fourth benefit is of course that, as Zartaloudis consistently does such a good job with his reading of the main thrust of the text, we can move more rapidly through these elements concentrating on our main concern and also moving towards the most significant part of the text for us, the final chapter. Chapter 5, "The Providential Machine", begins with a point made first, I believe, in *Homo Sacer* as to Foucault's failed project to reconcile structures of power in relation to subjective interpellation. Naturally, this interests Agamben inordinately because, in certain ways, Agamben's politics is a completion and critical modification of Foucault, although Foucault is merely giving alternative voice to the wider traditions of phenomenology, hermeneutics and pragmatism. Here the concern is less the contention that biopolitics is 'older' than modernity and more that governmentality is produced from the economy of relation between founding law and subjective fact, an eventuality Foucault never completely arrived at in his too brief lifetime. Agamben then traces this back to, once again, the Stoic philosophy of primary and secondary causes in relation to fate. Here then the combination of Stoic thought and Foucault is the justification for the claim that "government is possible only if the Kingdom and the Government are correlated in a bipolar machine: the government is precisely what results from the coordination and articulation of special and general providence".[45] For this thesis the rest of the chapter is clearly divisible into two parts, first the sustained reading of Alexander of Aphrodisias's consideration of providence, then a seven-part summary of what Agamben calls vicarious ontology, which provide the archaeological basis for the radical and conclusion that government is a collateral effect.

If we summarise the argument of Alexander, we find him struggling with not two but three types of providence in his second-century treatise. We have divine providence for itself, then worldly or accidental providence, but Alexander looks also for "an intermediate model, which neutralizes these oppositions",[46] a model which is involuntary and yet accidental. Alexander develops here the idea of a collateral effect, the accidental providence of human fate and free will, which in some way was calculated by divine providential will. He does not wish to simply found the government of the world on divine will, but the correlation of the general and particular as regards will means that government "results, in a contingent but knowing way, from the universal providence. The god that reigns, yet does not govern, thus makes possible the government".[47] It is from Alexander then that we get the Christian canon of *gubernatio* of the world, but at the same time he passes on the more complex signatory and indifferential logic of power in the West through his presentation of world governance as neither divine providence nor accidental providence but "through the knowing anticipation of the collateral effects that arise from the very nature of things and remain absolutely contingent in their singularity".[48] A proposition of the knowing calculation of collateral effects, from the second century, is shocking in its prescience of a world of management of risk and of course modern warfare, for it proposes absolute power as the calculated anticipation of the unknown or the care for the uncared for.

The logical nadir of collateral effects is surely the now-famous adage of Rumsfeld made in the apotheosis of modern collateral governmentality, the press conference. Rumsfeld's known unknowns and unknown unknowns has received a degree of serious consideration, and we do not wish to belabour the point here except to say that, perhaps unwittingly, Rumsfeld lets slip the key concept of government according to Agamben, the providential foreknowledge of the accident. Having said this, Rumsfeld is part of an administration that, if anything, was rolling back history to before the second century in its brief and ill-fated attempt to make America a world sovereign with a clear providential plan. In fact then, in Rumsfeld's comments we have the conflict of government with kingdom represented by the press conference wherein God has to explain his actions to a group of human beings who, unlike God, cannot see where this is going to end. The final irony is that we could all see where it was going to end, and it did indeed end there, in committees, in hearings, and finally in the replacement of God, Bush, with an Angel, Obama, an Angel in Agambenian terms, namely, one of God's bureaucrats.[49]

From this ancient and startlingly modern text, Agamben is able to make the local point about collateral effects in modern warfare,[50] but he is also able to present the greater point, which is that while Alexander had no interest in developing a governmental paradigm, in his presentation of this third element of providence, that of calculated collateral effects, he develops a providence-fate machine "functioning as a bipolar system that ends up producing a kind of zone of indifference between what is primary and what is secondary, the general and the particular, the final cause and its effects".[51] This Agamben calls an effectual ontology in which government is not aimed at either general or particular, providence or fate, "but their functional correlation", or as we would put it, their indifferentiation.[52] This then allows us to abstract from Agamben's general comment that the government of the world is not the application of a general law "but from the correlation between the general law and the contingent level of second causes" that government is nothing other than the application of the logic of indifference in the field of the political economy, a comment that gathers more power and credence when Agamben defines modern government as the management of absolute contingencies in that, as we saw in *The Coming Community*, it is the pure contingent that defines the truly indifferent: everything that is could also be otherwise.

Agamben chooses the term "vicarious" here to designate the operation of government in relation to the kingdom. Specifically, as he says, "The Government certainly acts vicariously with regard to the Kingdom" but only in terms of a logic in which "the two powers depend on each other".[53] Such an ontology of dependency via an asymmetrical logic of substitution replaces, for Agamben, classical ontology, the relation of beings to Being, with an economic paradigm. Economic ontology presents a topology wherein no single being can be in the position of the *arche*, while at the same time what is original is "the very Trinitarian relation, whereby each figure *gerit vices*, deputizes for the other".[54] This being the case, Agamben makes the almost offhand conclusion that there is no substance to power, only an economy. The political implications are explosive of course, not least in the genealogy of theology and politics but also in the complete reconsideration of the nature of modern governance and its dependency on a founding power that it itself founded by becoming the functional origin of a to-be-confirmed founding sovereignty.

To return to a moment to Rumsfeld's other most famous comment, in response to questions about collateral damage in the invasion of Iraq, the modern power of governance is based on the providential intimation that "shit happens." Providential foreknowledge of random happenings then needs to be transformed into a system of power which justifies action, how we manage the crisis, and founds legitimacy; we are in power because we will be able to manage the next crisis best of all. In actual fact, government is neither good management nor the authority of good managers but the process of articulation between the unconditioned condition of *auctoritas* and the conditioned sanction of *potestas*, represented first in theology by the trinity and then by glory.

It is to glory that we must now turn to end our consideration of this remarkable text, the ramifications of which we can only at this point guess at. Yet before we get there, we cannot neglect to mention to seven-part characteristics of this new ontology of the acts of government as they are laid out in the conclusion to this chapter:

1. Providence or government is the coming to terms of the split that constitutes classical ontology and, indeed, according to Agamben's other earlier works, metaphysics as such. This split, we have consistently argued, is ostensibly between paradigms of the common and the proper. Providence is a machine that joins together the two elements in the model of a divine government of the world, but we might add that it is also, through its indifferential logic of archaeological moments of arising, the very institution of the split.

2. Providence as a signature is the result of the historical battle between a Gnostic view of God as foreign to a world he governs and

the Trinitarian solution to this which, in order to function, must accept a double extraneousness of power. God is alien to the world, which is corrupted and which he must redeem. The son is in this world tasked with redeeming it for a Kingdom to arrive that is not, however, of this world. Thus, sovereign power and governmental power operate as immanent to a world which remains always extraneous, the external nature of this world in relation to God's Kingdom and the alien nature of this kingdom to come in relation to the world it would redeem.

3. The providential machine matches perfectly the logic of indifference. It is unity that articulates itself, because of its unitary status, into two different planes of transcendence and immanence. As he says, in a comment so central that it must be quoted in its entirety,

4. The two levels are strictly entwined, so that the first founds, legitimates, and makes possible the second, while the second concretely puts into practice in the chain of causes and effects the general decisions of the divine mind. The government of the world is what results from this functional correlation.[55]

5. Thus, the "paradigm of the act of government is, consequently, the collateral effect . . . an area of undecidability between what is general and what is particular, between what is calculated and what is not-wanted".[56] Again to reassert this, government is indifference in its effect here of operativity, it makes intelligible power, and later, as we shall see in glory, in its inoperativity, it makes intelligible power's vacuity.

6. The division of the levels is consubstantial with the machine. The levels do not compose the machine; the machine and the levels are cocollateral, as we saw in our analysis of the Trinitarian model.

7. The ontology of power is insubstantial because it is entirely vicarious; one element is always deputising for another. Again we must then stress our contention that the secondary effects found the primary effects just as must as the primary is presented as the founding of the secondary. What is actually founded is the economy of the split and positionality of oppositional parts.

The good news of all of this is that power is never in actual fact despotic, and, contrary to the prevailing opinion, an act of violence is not needed to found power. Power does not do violence to its creatures but "presupposes the freedom of those that are governed" in terms of their being anarchic, chaotic, accidental happenings that must be provided for. Once all the knives are in the drawer, the parent is happy to allow its toddlers to roam the kitchen, accepting that there may be an unknown unknown which could still injure them.

From this ontology Agamben presents two powerful political arguments. The first is that democratic power is the result of the providential-

economic paradigm, just as despotic power is the result of the theological-political. This is a word of warning, for, as we saw, power is always
divided and not just between condition and conditioned but between the
two orders of power, power as ordering and power qua order or dictat.
The second is that government is a collateral effect of Being and beings,
order and chaos. Of this Agamben says three powerful things. First,
governmental aims are arrived at collaterally only from the overlap of
general and particular; they cannot be willed except as the willed provi-
sion of the known unknowns of the Rumsfeldian "shit happens". Second,
governing must allow for general economy to arise, founding power of
some order, yet this is totally ineffective on its own. Power as *auctoritas*
alone is power that has no effects. And, third, a very significant comment
on modern ontology to rival that of Badiou and presenting a major modification of our Heideggerian inheritance, effects do not depend on being,
government on kingdom, "but rather that being consists of its effects:
such is the vicarious and effectual ontology that defines the acts of
government".[57] In one way this is an actual completion of the phenomenological and hermeneutic logic of early Heidegger, yet it also represents
in another form Agamben's radical ontology of indifferent existentialism
or a being that consists only of the indifference of its singular effects.

GLORY: ARTICULATED INOPERATIVITY

The first original contribution of the text in question is this consideration
of *oikonomia* as an economy of power between kingdom and government.
Yet the second and, in the end, more original contribution does not come
into play until the final chapters and concerns the prevalence of glory
within political systems. In some sense the logic is the same as you would
expect from a thinker of such systematic consistency. There are, theologi-
cally, two elements of glory. There is the glory of God, which is unconditioned and not of the world, and then there is the glory we owe to god,
which we might call glorification.[58] This glorification is not needed for
God's *auctoritas*, and so why, Agamben wonders, is it so central to the
church, especially in the manner in which it determines ceremonial and
doxological elements? Agamben commences the argument around the
activity of angels whose primary role is God's glorification. He notes a
central aporia in the theory of redemption which is the role of angels
when God's kingdom is resumed, considering that they previously operated as God's emissaries in leading men to salvation.[59] Agamben is then
able to clarify the radical structure of the theory of redemption as an
unlimited period of God's kingdom, the briefest of interregnum during
which time the issue of economy and government comes about in the fix
between Gnostic duality and Christian Trinitarianism, followed by another eternal period of kingdom: "Government is nothing but the brief

interval running between two eternal and glorious figures of King-dom".[60]

The theological problem of the end of economy is raised here. As Angels are God's bureaucrats, in answer to the question as to what is left for them to do when they become inoperative after redemption, Agamben explains that they survive "as a hymnological hierarchy, as contemplation and praise of the glory of the divine" (KG 162). In other words, Angels, left without act or praxis as God's will has been completed so that he is, yet again, pure Being without any further act, represent, through their songs of praise, God's inoperativity (he no longer needs to act on earth). This opens up the meaning of the term "glory" for Agamben in a truly original fashion so that he is able to observe, *"Hence glory is what must cover with its splendour the unaccountable figure of divine inoperativity"*.[61] This figure of the inoperative Angel forms a pair with the rendering inoperative of the law in the Pauline Messianic canon so that both are deactivated in being reconciled with God. Redemption means then the end of act in terms of Being as regards either the divine economy represented by Angels or law. "The ultimate and glorious telos of the law and of the angelic powers, as well as of the profane powers, is to be deactivated and made inoperative".[62] It is then the relation between glory and inoperativity that the final part of the text is based around.

In the following chapter Agamben pursues these two elements of glory. Angelic glory has a juridical element in that it constitutes the liturgy. There is then also a parallel phenomenon as regards the tradition of acclamation, which is effectively a public glorification of people power. Thus, glory is the public exclamation of *auctoritas* and acclamation that of *potestas*. He then relates this to a regular theme of his, language as performative, especially the oath.[63] In making an acclamation, the people commit a linguistic act that is also an existential fact: they acclaim themselves and make themselves a people by the speech act of acclamation. In fact, both glory and acclamation have this gestic element;[64] they use language to remove the assumed division between word and thing in that use of language is a thing: God is glory as we glorify him, or we are a people as we declare that we are a people here and now. Agamben then traces with relish the whole history of ceremonial power as gestic, glorifying acclamation before arriving at a key double definition. First, he confirms, secular modes of glorification and acclamation have a religious origin only if we refuse to place the magical-religious as prior to the political as has traditionally been the case. Second, acclamation and glory have a relation that exists before their clear differentiation, but this relation is not one of precedence and influence but rather, as ever, consists of a threshold of indistinction "where the juridical and the religious become truly indistinguishable".[65]

The first threshold of this type pertains to the sacred and was investigated at length in *Homo Sacer*. This being the case, Agamben is able to

reveal again why *The Kingdom and the Glory* is such an essential development from that earlier text: "If we now call 'glory' the uncertain zone in
which acclamations, ceremonies, liturgies, and insignia operate, we will
see a field of research open before us that is equally relevant and, at least
in part, as yet unexplored".[66] The implication of this is that the study of
power in the West is of two orders, the famous two swords indeed. The
first is the indifferential relation between sovereignty and the sacred, the
second between government and glory. Power is bifurcated in a zone of
indifference between kingdom and government, and each element is further bifurcated in an indistinction named as sacred and glorious, respectively. Finally, it is the signature of economy that articulates this double
articulation, rendering the process operative only on the basis of the operativity of this indistinction which is destined, as the world and God are,
for inoperativity, and at which point all articulations are suspended in a
relational nonrelation.

Obviously, a key issue here is the relation of the theological and the
political as it determines Western power. It is now more than apparent
that the relationship between divine and political economy is not just a
simple case of influence but rather a more complex determination of
moments of arising composing statements into sets through paradigms
and distributing paradigm-sets across discourses and time in the form of
signatures. These signatures, through the careful archaeology of the text,
present us in our contemporary moment with a moment of arising which,
when placed together, allow for a moment of indistinction between kingdom and government due to glory that, paradoxically, makes the problem of power distinct as primarily the modality of indifferential indistinction. For Agamben glory is important because it is "precisely the place at
which this bi-lateral (or bi-univocal) character of the relation between
theology and politics clearly emerges into the light. . . . The theology of
glory constitutes, in this sense, the secret point of contact through which
theology and politics continuously communicate and exchange parts
with one another. . . . Like many of the concepts we have encountered in
our investigation, this garment of glory is a signature".[67] Thus, glory
constitutes the final and, in fact, most significant signature of Western
power, for it renders articulate and indifferent the two key modalities of
power, not just the sacred power of the sovereign but also the glorious
power of government. Glory is the name of the economy of power, the
signature of political signatures par excellence.

The final, huge chapter of the work now reveals its true colours. For
students of politics, law, and theology the book is perhaps rich enough
up to this point. However, Agamben's project is more ambitious than the
revealing of new historical resonances, and thus the archaeology of glory,
not its history, is what the book ends on. The chapter starts with a summary of the ostensible argument of the book. Theology differentiates two
trinities, the economic trinity of revelation and the immanent trinity of

substance (God as he is in himself). These match the division between praxis and ontology that make up economic theology or God's operativity in the world. Immanent trinity reveals ontology and theology and economic trinity praxis and *oikonomia*. Together these have formed the basis of what he terms the machine of the divine government of the world around the poles of transcendent and immanent order. In relation to this structure, "Glory is the place where theology attempts to think the difficult conciliation between immanent trinity and economic trinity. . . . In glory, economic trinity and immanent trinity, God's praxis of salvation and his being are conjoined and move through each other".[68] Inasmuch as it can be said that the Father glorifies the Son just as the Son glorifies the Father, then economy glorifies being and being glorifies economy. In this "mirror of glory . . . being and economy, Kingdom and Government appear to coincide for an instant".[69] The result is a symmetry of indifferential reciprocity that is ruined by redemption, a profoundly asymmetrical concept. On the day of judgement, after all, only the economic trinity is completed. This asymmetry will have deep ramifications, for, at the moment of the revelation of economic inoperativity, what is revealed is that God is composed of glory, and in rendering inoperative glorification we reveal that the essential Being of God is itself void.

When glory returns to God in its purely immanent element at the end of time, what we see is that God, in rendering his economy inoperative, reveals himself to be, fundamentally, nothing other than inoperativity as such. Agamben suggests, "Perhaps the distinction between internal glory and external glory serves precisely to cover over this intimate link between glorification and the substance of the divinity. What appears in God when the distinction breaks down is something that theology absolutely does not want to see, a nudity that must be covered by a garment of light at any cost".[70] Parallels with the homo sacer and bare life can be felt here. Just as bare life is the denuding of the concept of life which reveals the essence of biopolitical power, so too here the denuding of God's Being as fundamentally inoperative reveals the essence of sovereign power.

Now Agamben turns his attention to the final inoperativity at the end of time which defines redemption. It is, he notes, a recurrent theme that redemption is akin to inoperativity: "Glory occupies the place of postjudicial inoperativity; it is the eternal *amen* in which all works and all divine and human words are resolved".[71] This he then traces through the Judaic tradition via the figure of inoperativity as the name most fitting for God, or God as Sabbath. In the Pauline canon this takes on the name sabbatism or the inoperativity that awaits the people of God, an element Agamben considers in the Messianic 'as not' in *The Time That Remains*.[72] Citing source after source Agamben reveals this special signature of God's Being, a divine inoperativity, and his kingdom, that of the eternal Saturday. This reaches an apotheosis or crisis point in the work of Augustine, who struggles to conceive of an eternal Saturday in which there will be no *acedia* (listlessness or sloth) or need. Agamben explains, "He finds no other adequate expression for the blessed inoperativity, which is neither a doing nor a not-doing, than 'becoming Sabbath'. . . . Here, in a stuttering attempt to think the unthinkable, Augustine defines the final condition as a sabbatism to the nth degree, a making the Sabbath take rest in the Sabbath, a resolving of inoperativity into inoperativity".[73]

Inasmuch as one definition of *acedia* is "indifference", we can see in a perpetual Sabbath that indifference is itself articulated and that indifference has, as its final destination, what can be called only the indifference of indifference. Why is this necessary? For the simple reason that any resolution of difference that itself can remain operative for us must not be a resolution of difference into identity or the reinstatement of the origin within the specific temporal category of the Agamben *archē*. In that a suspension or indistinction retains the opposing elements even if it renders them indiscernible, it is not a state that one can find redemption in, for indiscernibility is a feature of the political, the theological and the philosophical. Indifference is the logical end point of the process, and so one cannot accede to a dwelling in this indifference. *Homo Sacer* makes this apparent with its paradigms of indifference: bare life, concentration camps, coma patients and so on. These cannot be utopian political states for the future, not least because they belong to the intelligibility of our political system.

The concomitant conclusion is that indifference as a future potential cannot remain as it is within the providential machine; it cannot return to an unconditioned origin because its inoperativity extends precisely to the kingdom, rendering it a fictive void of foundation. This being the case, the only option available is to somehow indifferentiate indifference:

> At the beginning and the end of the highest power there stands . . . a figure not of action and government but of inoperativity. . . . Glory . . . is precisely what takes the place of that unthinkable emptiness that amounts to the inoperativity of power. And yet, precisely this unsayable vacuity is what nourishes and feeds power (or, rather, what the machine of power transforms into nourishment). That means that the center of the governmental apparatus, the threshold at which Kingdom and Government ceaselessly communicate and ceaselessly distinguish themselves from one another is, in reality, empty.[74]

This vacuity is symbolised most powerfully in the famous figure of the empty throne, an image of which adorns the front cover of the English translation. The throne, Agamben states, captures not the readiness of power, as is usually assumed, but its inoperativity.

INOPERATIVITY: THE INDIFFERENTIATION OF INDIFFERENCE

Glory presents a double inoperativity through the logic of redemption. On the one hand, we have power's essential vacuity, that of Being without act, or God's pure and perfect self-presence. This inoperativity bookends a secondary inoperativity to be found in the cessation of action on this earth with the second coming of God's kingdom. These form two sides of the intelligibility of Western political power, that of *auctoritas*, or power through authoritative founding violence, and *potestas*, the power of the people through the judicial process.[75] Yet inasmuch as power is composed of two signatures, that of the sacred and the glorious, real power resides in neither camp. Power as such 'resides' in economy. It is through *oikonomia* that the intelligibility of power through two paradigms distributed across two signatures becomes visible to us now. But it is also through the activity of the economy that runs between the two paradigms and also composes the two paradigms internally that power is distributed. Economy is the signature of all political signatures in that signatures mark the movement of content through time and place, and glory comes to stand for this signature in a particularly revealing way. It is wrong to look at power as founding government. It is also wrong to look at government as subsequently composing the empty fiction of power. And it is wrong to look at economy as merely the machine that shuttles between the two forms of power, creating the totality of power through imposed division, assumed originary unity and destinal indifferentiation. Economy is no more the machine that fuels power, Agamben speaks of nourishment, than government is the activity that makes inoperative founding power fictively operative. Rather, power is both the fuel of its economy and also that which is fuelled by its economy.

Where this becomes particularly significant is the moment that glory and the sacred combine, for example, in the form of doxology, ceremonies and the festival. These events capture the inoperativity essential to human life in a separate sphere. This is a complex process of *a-lethia*, showing a particular debt to Heidegger: "The *oikonomia* of power places firmly at its heart, in the form of festival and glory, what appears to its eyes as the inoperativity of man and God, which cannot be looked at. Human life is inoperative and without purpose, but precisely this *argia* and this absence of aim make the incomparable operativity [*operosità*] of the human species possible".[76] These comments relate directly to the sometimes misunderstood bareness of bare life in *Homo Sacer*. Bare life and glory both present or generate an emptiness. Glory makes visible our essential inoperativity by placing it in a separate sphere. This separation then generates what one might call the motion of inoperativity, primarily between the inoperativity of eternal kingdom and the inoperativity of human destiny. The endless movement between these two inoperativities is profoundly operative in the mode of its making intelligible inoperativity, and, in showing us emptiness, in the same way that biopolitics shows us bare life, power is rendered intelligible. And so it is that when we see an empty throne, we see an image full of 'emptiness' rendered functional, ironically, due to the actual emptiness of the power structures it sets into motion.

If this were not complicated enough, bareness and emptiness themselves constitute the actual machine of true signatory inoperativity. For example, Agamben argues, man is dedicated to labor to hide his fundamental ontological inoperativity, thus bringing the arguments of human life and eternal life into a perfect, machinic motion: "And just as the machine of the theological *oikonomia* can function only if it writes within its core a doxological threshold in which economic trinity and immanent trinity are ceaselessly and liturgically (that is politically) in motion, each passing into the other, so the governmental apparatus functions because it has captured in its empty centre the inoperativity of the human essence".[77] As Zartaloudis explains,[78] at the heart of sovereign power is a double void: both Being and beings are inoperative. A pure founding power is as fictive as a pure essence of human being, and, in fact, it is the double inoperativity of Being and beings that constitutes the real ontico-ontological difference, a difference we might now term the ontico-ontological *indifference*. There is no pure state of nature to which man can retreat from the dirty politics of the city, for bare life is the construct of the polis. By the same gesture there is no pure glory of the unconditioned to which man aims at the end of his life of strife, for the unconditioned is a construct of the contingent conditions of life.

Agamben expresses this with great beauty when he speaks of the utopian gesture of politics or a world of perpetual Saturdays, which he sees very much as a signature of theological-political power. These visions, he says,

> are the enigmatic relics that the economical-theological machine abandons on the water's edge of civilization and that each time men question anew, nostalgically and in vain. Nostalgically because they appear to contain something that belongs to the human essence, but in vain because really they are nothing but the waste products of the immaterial and glorious fuel burnt by the motor of the machine as it turns, and that cannot be stopped.[79]

In a more prosaic register this can be summarised by the statement that there is no human origin and no posthuman destination. Endings and beginnings are just the paradoxical fictive necessities of the philosophy of pure immanence as an endless, processing, eternal becoming. But if this machine cannot be stopped, then indifference as such is meaningless, functioning as a mere precursor, the second coming of a John the Baptist that must submit to a radical decollation if the true Christ is ever to arrive. Indifference must finally render itself indifferent.

Aristotle, it would seem, toyed with the idea that man is naturally functionless, establishing the theme of a possible inoperativity of the human species. If the human is that which has capacity and incapacity, then what is the function of capacity in general, returning to Agamben's question in *Potentialities* as to what it means to have a capacity, or to be capable of capacity?[80] Aristotle rapidly moves against this idea by making logos the purpose of life, but the possible operation of the idea of the essential inoperativity of the human was sanctioned. It finds, of course, its greatest exponent in the concept of eternal life captured in the Greek term *aion*. Eternal life, Agamben argues, results from the world, from its corruptibility, even though the world exists only for its own redemption back into eternity. As such, then the structure emulates that of the founding myth of kingdom only in reverse. Whereas, thus far, kingdom was the foundation for the government which actually founds it through economy, now kingdom is the purpose or aim of government, which moves towards a completion it composes from its own radical contingency. So it is that Agamben notes that eternal life has never been a mere temporal category "but designates a special quality of life and, more precisely, the transformation that human life undergoes in the world to come" a transformation into an incorruptible and carefree life.[81] This explains, Agamben thinks, the rabbinical tradition of seeing future life as in opposition to the present life and "at the same time, in a singular contiguity with it; that is, as a deactivation of biological functions and bad instincts".[82]

Agamben then directly compares the eternal life of salvation to that of the messianic calling such as he describes in *The Time That Remains*. In the messianic *klesis*, the subject is required to give up their capacity and live the life of the *hōs me*, or 'as not'. For Paul this means that eternal life is not a reward to come but a quality of life within messianic time. Living life under the interdiction of the 'as not' means living life under the suspension of law, subjectivity and time. It is, then, the ultimate zone of indistinction within the Western tradition. As Agamben says,

> Under the 'as not,' life cannot coincide with itself and is divided into a life that we live (*vitam quam vivimus*, the set of facts and events that define our biography) and a life for which and in which we live (*vita qua vivimus*, what renders life livable and gives it a meaning and a form). To live in the Messiah means precisely to revoke and render inoperative at each instant every aspect of the life that we live, and to make the life for which we live, which Paul calls the 'life of Jesus' (*zōē tou Iesou* — *zōē* not *bios*!) appear within it.[83]

This is divisible, if you wish, into the essential facticity of beings or *Dasein* and the ethical value of Being as such. What it expresses is that for our capacity or potential to live to operate, the central intelligibility of that life is its inoperativity, or its *hōs me*. For Agamben specifically, it means "The messianic life is the impossibility that life might coincide with a predetermined form".[84] For Paul, the messianic inoperativity is anything but passive, while in contrast he sees, as others do, the future *aion* as the glorious inoperativity of God. This has the recognisable effect of ruining the inoperativity of messianic life by effectively making it an inoperativity *for* something. "Life, which rendered all forms inoperative, itself becomes a form in glory. Impassivity, agility, subtlety, and clarity thereby become the characters that define the life of the glorious body".[85] What is at stake here is perhaps best expressed in the language of potential. If, in potential, the specific capacity to be able to do something is made possible only by the presence of an incapacity or essential inoperativity and if this inoperativity ceases to be indifferentiation but becomes the capacity for indifference, then indifference ceases to be the potential for a form of life and instead becomes indifference as the form of life. At precisely the moment of the appropriation of indifference, indifference ceases to operate, as it does in the activity of messianic life, and instead becomes total rest. Indifference at rest is, at this moment, meaningless inasmuch as its primary essence is its mobility, even if it is also always defined in terms of its suspensive nature.

Agamben finds another tradition of inoperativity as rest in the Western conception of thought as contemplation. Referring to the verb form invented by Spinoza to convey being at rest with oneself, *acquiescentia* (echoing a similar analysis of the term *pasearse* or "to walk with oneself" in Spinoza[86]), Agamben considers the idea of self-contentment or self-resting of the self in terms of whether it represents sabbatical glory, literal inaction or another more complex form resulting from the act that contemplates its own power to act. "The life, which contemplates its (own) power to act, renders itself inoperative in all its operations, and lives only (its) livability. . . . 'Self,' subjectivity, is what opens itself as a central inoperativity in every operation, like the live-*ability* of every life. In this inoperativity, the life that we live is only the life through which we live; only our power of acting and living, our act-*ability* and our live-*ability*. Here the *bios* coincides with the *zōē* without remainder".[87] This defines, for Agamben, the basic model of the Western contemplative tradition, which is also that of Christian glorious sabbatism and the basis of the most recent addition to the Homo Sacer project, the monastic order. The structure is as follows: that which defines the human in terms of its praxis is the ability to contemplate its life as such only through the rendering of life as praxis as inoperative. This means, of course, that the praxis of the human is the rendering inoperative of praxis, so that praxis can appear as the operativity of the human. For Agamben, terms such as "contemplation" and "inoperativity" are "the metaphysical operators of anthropogenesis" in that they free man from biological and social destiny on this earth, fate, resulting in the dimension we tend to call politics but in actual fact, as it is a fundamental inoperativity as such, is better defined as glory.

It was, then, Aristotle's division of the contemplative and political life as two *bioi* that "deflected politics and philosophy from their trajectory and, at the same time, delineated the paradigm in which the economy-glory apparatus would model itself".[88] The Agamben method is very apparent in these phrases. As ever, there is a moment of arising wherein a contingently imposed division, here between contemplative and political beings for the human, both determines the future direction of signatures across time and place and also retroactively installs a predivisive, fictive perfection. As we saw in *Homo Sacer*, at issue there was the idea of a predivided human life (in fact Agamben comes to define the signature Life as division as such),[89] while here the issue is as much the projection forward of an eternal life as the installation after the event of a bare or predivided life. He goes on, in a key phrase, "The political is neither a *bios* nor a *zōē*, but the dimension that the inoperativity of contemplation, by deactivating linguistic and corporeal, material and immaterial praxes, ceaselessly opens and assigns to the living".[90] In other words, politics is indifference as a process, the endless movement between the two forms opened up by the division, based on a foundation of prescission perfection, and hurtling towards a final moment of cessation when such division is rendered once more inoperative. This being the case, he concludes, it is perfectly natural that theological *oikonomia*, the subject of the study, must incorporate inoperativity through the figure of eternal life. It is eternal life, that to which government is heading through the paradox of economy, which is the inoperative center of the human "that the machine of the economy and of glory ceaselessly attempts to capture within itself".[91]

What is left uncertain here is the role of inoperativity through indifference. Although indifference determines Agamben's method and is to be found at the heart of every element of his work from potentiality through included exclusion to, here, the role of economy, as these comments reveal indifference as such as an inoperativity is capable of being appropriated at precisely the moment it opens up the system's potential to be rendered inoperative. In other words, there are two inoperativities. The first is the appropriation of inoperativity as the fuel for an economic system of kingdom-government. This first inoperativity is life as that which is doubly inoperative. On the earth it is biological pure life as total indetermination. In the kingdom it is instead eternal life as final destination where biological life will fall away. In this manner one can see that bare life is, at any moment, the determined foundation of a governmental, earthly existence, while eternal life is the determined completion of this life and its falling away. Bare life is a myth of foundation that allows for eternal life as a myth of destiny. Operating as two inoperativities on either side of praxis, this concept of the political-inoperative fuels the economic systems of the West.

Then again there is another inoperativity defined as the rendering transparent of the system at precisely the moments of appropriated indifference, so that the system of indifference can itself be suspended. This is what I would call the indifference or inoperativity of indifference, and Agamben ends this complex section with a reference to the poem as a strong analogy for this function. In the same manner that the poem makes the communicative and denotative elements of language inoperative in favour of foregrounding the semiotic as such, so that the power of saying is potentially opened for a new use, so too must we conceive of a kind of political poetics. This includes not merely the opening up of the sayability of language, its intelligibility as we have been calling it, but also the process of desubjectivization regularly taken up by the poet in the act of writing and found in Foucault's work in the concept of subjective enunciations.[92] In other words, at the moment, in the poem, that language is made inoperative due to its being pure sayability, so too the subject is rendered inoperative in that her enunciative position is entirely dependent on the 'said' of a statement. Thinking of Foucault for a moment, if the intelligibility of a statement is determined by the enunciative position, then the poem makes intelligibility as such intelligible, rendering any specific enunciative position fundamentally indifferent. At this moment pure intelligibility denies the subject any of the myths of life that have been sustaining her determined enunciative position, providing an opportunity for a subjectivity that is not subject to a predetermined form of life: bare, political or eternal. "*What the poem accomplishes for the power of saying, politics and philosophy must accomplish for the power of acting. By rendering economic and biological operations inoperative, they demonstrate what the human body* can do; *they open it up to a new, possible use*".[93]

Inoperativity and indifference present a unique opportunity. In the first instance indifference is the negative driver of metaphysical systems, not issues of presence or difference as has previously been assumed. Second, it reveals the total structure of the system at key moments of revelatory indistinction. Third, at these moments what is provided is not only historical or analytical clarity but also a window of opportunity to bring about 'change' or something new, specifically here a new idea as to what the human can do, their actual operativity. What this operativity will be is to be determined by the final two parts of the Homo Sacer project and their consideration of *uso* (use, custom) and *ufficio* (office, duty, vocation), texts beyond the remit of this analysis. What we can say, however, is that until the signatures of power are themselves revealed in their inoperativity and, more than this, until the indifferential logic of their inoperativity is itself rendered indifferent or inoperative, the oft-promised key to the totality of the Homo Sacer project, namely, the full delineation of a form-of-life, a life that cannot be separated from its form,[94] remains unintelligible. It is for this reason that *The Kingdom and the Glory* may come to be seen not only as one of Agamben's most important statements but also as the fundamental work of political philosophy of our age.

THRESHOLD: THE AESTHETICS OF INDIFFERENCE (POETRY AS SIGNATURE)

Poetry is a signature in Agamben. It operates according to the logic of the common and proper by assigning prose to the realm of the common and the poetic or semiotic to that of the proper. Agamben repeatedly talks about the signature of poetry in terms of the semantic/semiotic split, the age-old antagonism between philosophy and poetry or indeed that between prose and poetry.[95] The semantic element of this signature is assumed to be writing that places the communication of meaning ahead of that of the medium of communication. Poetry, represented by the technique of enjambment, interrupts clarity and coherence of communication by favouring the semiotic over the semantic.[96] Thus, simply put, a sentence in a poem, if it is longer than the designated syllabic allocation stipulated by the metrics in play, let us say here ten syllables, will be interrupted by a line break, the sentence concluded therefore on the next line. The line break naturally imposes a pause; it traditionally gives extra emphasis to the word at the end of the line due to where it is, not what it says, an emphasis often enforced by the use of rhyme and by semantic-semiotic shifters, such as ending lines on words like "fall," "dead," "drop," "pause" and so on. Enjambment is not the only technique that foregrounds the semiotic in poetry, but it is the strongest paradigm amongst all the various semiotic techniques to hand, especially because of the relation between enjambment and caesura. The caesura interrupts the flow of the line, in the opposite manner to the way in which enjambment interrupts the coherence of the sentence. The model or signatory paradigm is to be found in a pronounced fashion both in Derrida's work on Literature/literature and in Deleuze's work on the relation between segment and flow in the theory of the assemblage. Put simply, the semiotic is made operative only by means of its rendering momentarily inoperative the semantic.

The complexity here that perhaps was beyond my previous study is that poetry is defined in Agamben as the tension between the semantic and the semiotic, not as, it has seemed so far, the material singularity of the semiotic. There are then two poetries in play here. Small p poetry is the foregrounding of the semiotic, while large P Poetry is the relation between semantic and semiotic. Thus, Poetry as signature is the *oikonomia* between the semantic and the semiotic in our tradition, whose moment of arising is Plato's *Republic* and the "expulsion of the poets" myth promulgated there and further confused by Agamben coming to call this the Idea of Prose. Prose is actually, after Agamben, Benjamin and Walser, indifferent Poetry. The distraction is the assumption that, after Heidegger, and more recently Derrida, Nancy, Lacoue-Labarthe and Badiou, it is the singularity of the poetic in terms of its asemantic materiality that defines its nature as a signature or, to paraphrase Badiou, poetry's *poiesis* as opposed to philosophical *dianioa*.[97] Rather, what now must be concluded is that Poetry is the impossible economy between philosophy as *dianoia* or as universal truth irrespective of its mode of communication and poetry as *poiesis* or material singularity that communicates nothing but communicability as such. Such a viewpoint is strongly supported by my own comments here as to the origins of communicability in Kant's third critique and its extension by Heidegger's work on art which eventually became attenuated to considerations of poetry alone. Thus, poetry's tension is the constant interchange between its meaning and its form, and its definition as this tension between the semantic and the semiotic is not its definition as object but rather its revelation as process in the modern sources cited by Agamben: Valéry, Milner, Heidegger and so on.[98]

This being the case, Poetry is the inoperativity of the ancient metaphysical division of thought and its expression. In this way it is a special signature which again makes its excavation rather tricky. For example, it suspends the signature through which we come to understand indifferent suspension: philosophy. In addition, it suspends the quality of singularity that *The Coming Community* defines as central to indifference. In that it is concerned with semantic and semiotic, it of course suspends language as a signature and its reliance on signified and signifier in metaphysics. In that the semiotic has been defined as the essence of poetry as the art of all arts since Hegel, reified almost by Heidegger's later work and the manner in which poetry as the material singularity of language per se catches hold of such thinkers as Derrida, Nancy, Lacoue-Labarthe and to some degree Badiou and as it often seems in the earlier work of Agamben, Poetry renders indifferent and thus inoperative the signature Art of which it should be epiphenomenal. Naturally, in Agamben's paradigm-signature model there is no epiphenomenal relation here, meaning that poetry must be a paradigm of the arts.[99] Finally, as the semiotic is presented by this tradition as the foregrounding of language *as such* as the communication of communication per se, before above or to the side of what is being communicated, in other words, communicability as such, if poetry is suspended, so too is communicability.

Poetry then is a special case. First, it is a signature and a paradigm in Agamben's work. Second, when it is a paradigm, it is a paradigm of art as such in terms of its semiotic materiality, although Agamben does not pursue this signature. Third, when it is a signature, it suspends another key signature, Philosophy. Fourth, in so doing, it also suspends a second signature, the most important of all, Language. Fifth, as it is defined as the foregrounding of language as such as semiotic, Poetry is another name for the communicability as such of language encountered in terms of its material support for all signatures, a materiality whose being, however, it also suspends in terms of its traditional counterdefinition as not-semantic, not-communication, not-philosophy, not-universal, not-true.

Two final points in this regard. If Poetry as signature suspends poetry as paradigm of singularity while at the same time rendering indifferent Philosophy as the common to poetry's singular propriety, then the post-Heideggerian tradition of thinkers around poetic singularity are in a state of suspension too, an issue most pertinent in relation to Badiou, who ends the suturing of philosophy to poetry after two hundred years in 1970 with the death of Celan. Badiou is clear that philosophy is sutured to poetry, not in a state of comutual cofounding, yet in his *Inaesthetics* he clearly defines *poiesis* contra to *dianioa* in a manner that demonstrates he still thinks of poetry in terms of the metaphysics of identity-difference.[100] The dispute over the precise relation of *poiesis* to philosophy then is likely to be one of the fault lines along which future studies start to connect and divide the two men in terms of the *oikonomia* of our contemporary philosophical moment.

Second, in the opposite register, if Poetry is a signature which means it is not an epiphenomenon of Art or of Literature, both taken here as signatures, then any future aesthetics of indifference, what I have called logopoiesis,[101] and any future literary theory of indifference, the poetics of indifference perhaps, must take into account the signatory specificity of Poetry, Literature, Art and Prose and perhaps finally accept that these four do not form a set on a plate or plateau but are just four separate signatures with nothing in common discursively beyond the mode of their communicability. This being the case, meaning that we are concerned with what these signatures sanction to occur, not what they express as commonality of meaning and qualities, these signatures sanction radically singular operativities and participate in heterogeneous modes and temporalities of suspension. Suspend one, say Poetry, which is in our tradition the art of arts, and you do not suspend the others. Any future aesthetics and poetics of indifference must take this limited diversity into account resulting in neither aesthetics nor inaesthetics but The Aesthetics, in a limited plurality of nonmutual nonrelationality which we have corralled into a single set through the operative power of the term Aesthetics, finding its point of arising in Baumgarten-Kant.

If this is the case, then Aesthetics as a signature is defined in the first instance as indifferent suspension between reason and understanding and in the final analysis in Heidegger and those who came after as pure communicability as such. Any future study of aesthetics then must be a simultaneous study of indifference and communicability, this much is clear. What is less obvious but equally true is that any future study of indifference must also be a consideration of the aesthetic, marking a new kind of relationship between philosophy and poetry, and any future study of our ontology of epistemology, or what I am calling communicability, meaning I suppose the totality of the humanities and the majority of the social sciences, must also be a sustained engagement with the moment of arising of the aesthetic when it ceased to be the science of sensation and became the objective subjectivity of the common sense of the beautiful.

NOTES

1. Although Agamben is not entirely consistent, I try to capitalise the first letter of words like Power, Language, Glory and so on when they are considered as signatures.

2. Giorgio Agamben, *The Kingdom and the Glory: For a Theological Genealogy of Economy and Government*, trans. Lorenzo Chiesa with Matteo Mandarini (Stanford, CA: Stanford University Press, 2011), xi.

3. Agamben, *Kingdom*, 100.

4. Agamben, *Kingdom*, 103.

5. See also Giorgio Agamben, *State of Exception*, trans. Kevin Attell (Chicago: University of Chicago Press, 2005), 76.

6. Agamben, *State of Exception*, 85–86.

7. Agamben, *State of Exception*, 86.

8. Agamben, *State of Exception*, 86.

9. Agamben, *State of Exception*, 87.

10. Agamben, *State of Exception*, 87.

11. Agamben, *State of Exception*, 87.

12. Agamben, *State of Exception*, 87–88.

13. Agamben, *State of Exception*, 88.

14. Agamben, *Kingdom*, xi.

15. Agamben, *Kingdom*, xii.

16. Agamben, *Kingdom*, 1.

17. Agamben, *Kingdom*, 1.

18. Agamben, *Kingdom*, 3.

19. Agamben, *Kingdom*, 4.

20. Agamben, *Kingdom*, 4.

21. Agamben, *Kingdom*, 276.

22. Thanos Zartaloudis, *Giorgio Agamben: Power, Law and the Uses of Criticism* (London: Routledge, 2010), 56–65.

23. Agamben, *Kingdom*, 17–18.

24. Agamben, *Kingdom*, 19.

25. See the essay "Creation and Salvation" for an extension of these topics into other areas, particularly aesthetics (Giorgio Agamben, *Nudities*, trans. David Kishik and Stefan Pedatella [Stanford, CA: Stanford University Press, 2011], 1–9).

26. Agamben, *Kingdom*, 20.

27. Agamben, *Kingdom*, 39.

28. Agamben, *Kingdom*, 39.

29. Agamben, *Kingdom*, 87.

30. Agamben, *Kingdom*, 82.

31. Agamben, *Kingdom*, 83.

32. Agamben, *Kingdom*, 83.

33. Agamben, *Kingdom*, 87–88.

34. Agamben, *Kingdom*, 64–65.

35. Agamben, *Kingdom*, 41.

36. Agamben, *Kingdom*, 50.

37. Agamben, *Kingdom*, 50–51.
38. Agamben, *Kingdom*, 51.
39. Agamben, *Kingdom*, 51.
40. Agamben, *Kingdom*, 51.
41. Zartaloudis, *Giorgio Agamben*, 75.
42. Zartaloudis, *Giorgio Agamben*, 80–81.
43. Zartaloudis, *Giorgio Agamben*, 81–82.
44. Naturally, a large part of this theory of government in Agamben is taken from Foucault's idea of governmentality.
45. Agamben, *Kingdom*, 114.
46. Agamben, *Kingdom*, 116.
47. Agamben, *Kingdom*, 118.
48. Agamben, *Kingdom*, 118–19.
49. For a consideration of U.S. domestic policy in relation to Agamben, see Slavoj Žižek, *Violence: Six Sideways Reflections* (London: Profile Books, 2008), 79.
50. Agamben, *Kingdom*, 119–20.
51. Agamben, *Kingdom*, 122.
52. Agamben, *Kingdom*, 122.
53. Agamben, *Kingdom*, 139.
54. Agamben, *Kingdom*, 139.
55. Agamben, *Kingdom*, 141.
56. Agamben, *Kingdom*, 141.
57. Agamben, *Kingdom*, 142.
58. For an excellent explanation of glory see Agamben, *Nudities*, 101–2.
59. On Angels and temporality see Agamben, *Nudities*, 4.
60. Agamben, *Kingdom*, 162.
61. Agamben, *Kingdom*, 163.
62. Agamben, *Kingdom*, 163.
63. See also Giorgio Agamben, *The Time That Remains*, trans. Patricia Dailey (Stanford, CA: Stanford University Press, 2005), 132–33.
64. Agamben, *Kingdom*, 180.
65. Agamben, *Kingdom*, 188.
66. Agamben, *Kingdom*, 188.
67. Agamben, *Kingdom*, 193–94.
68. Agamben, *Kingdom*, 208–9.
69. Agamben, *Kingdom*, 209.
70. Agamben, *Kingdom*, 221.
71. Agamben, *Kingdom*, 239.
72. Agamben, *Time That Remains*, 19–43; William Watkin, *The Literary Agamben: Adventures in Logopoiesis* (London: Continuum, 2010), 88–91.
73. Agamben, *Kingdom*, 241.
74. Agamben, *Kingdom*, 242.
75. See Slavoj Žižek, *Iraq: The Borrowed Kettle* (London: Verso, 2004), 158–60.
76. Agamben, *Kingdom*, 245–46.
77. Agamben, *Kingdom*, 246.
78. Zartaloudis, *Giorgio Agamben*, 89–93.
79. Agamben, *Kingdom*, 246.
80. Giorgio Agamben, *Potentialities*, trans. Daniel Heller-Roazen (Stanford, CA: Stanford University Press, 1999), 179.
81. Agamben, *Kingdom*, 247.
82. Agamben, *Kingdom*, 247.
83. Agamben, *Kingdom*, 248.
84. Agamben, *Kingdom*, 248.
85. Agamben, *Kingdom*, 249.
86. Agamben, *Potentialities*, 234–35.
87. Agamben, *Kingdom*, 251.

88. Agamben, *Kingdom*, 251.

89. Giorgio Agamben, *The Open: Man and Animal*, trans. Kevin Attell (Stanford, CA: Stanford University Press, 2004), 13–16.

90. Agamben, *Kingdom*, 251.

91. Agamben, *Kingdom*, 251.

92. See Michel Foucault, *The Archaeology of Knowledge*, trans. A. M. Sheridan Smith (London: Routledge, 1972), 50–55, 88–107. See also Giorgio Agamben, *Infancy and History: On the Destruction of Experience*, trans. Liz Heron (London: Verso, 1993), 50–60; Agamben, *Potentialities*, 112–32; and Watkin, *Literary Agamben*, 23–31, 107–16.

93. Agamben, *Kingdom*, 252.

94. See Giorgio Agamben, *Means without Ends*, trans. Vincenzo Binetti and Cesare Casarino (Minneapolis: University of Minnesota Press, 2000), 3–4, and Giorgio Agamben, *Altissima povert à* (Vicenza: Neri Pozza, 2011), 9–10.

95. I have written extensively on this in *Literary Agamben* and said that Agamben makes a recent comment on the relation that I have not previously considered. See Agamben, *Nudities*, 5–6. In fact, Agamben's concern with this imposed scission begins in his earlier work. See Giorgio Agamben, *Man without Content*, trans. Georgia Albert (Stanford, CA: Stanford University Press, 1999), 52–53. While his first comments on messianism are also tied into this issue (Giorgio Agamben, *Stanzas: Word and Phantasm in Western Culture*, trans. Ronald L. Martinez [Minneapolis: University of Minnesota Press, 1993], 131), here he also makes clear that philosophy is based on the presupposed division that constitutes the sign (*Stanzas*, 136).

96. Giorgio Agamben, *End of Poem*, trans. Daniel Heller-Roazen (Stanford, CA: Stanford University Press, 1999), 109–15.

97. See Alain Badiou, *The Handbook of Inaesthetics*, trans. Alberto Tosacano (Stanford, CA: Stanford University Press, 2005), 16–27.

98. See Agamben, *Time That Remains*, 131.

99. See my reading of Nancy's reading of Hegel here as regards the relation between poetry and art in "Poetry's Promiscuous Plurality: On a Part of Jean-Luc Nancy's The Muses" in *Jean-Luc Nancy and Plural Thinking*, ed. Peter Gratton and Marie-Eve Morin (Albany: State University of New York Press, 2012), 191–212.

100. The relation between Badiou's inaesthetics and Agamben's comments on Aristotle's "perception of imperception or a pure *anaisthesis*", as I called it, is a frontier beyond which any analysis of the two men's works must at some point travel.

101. See Watkin, *Literary Agamben*.

ELEVEN

The Sacrament of Language: **Language as Communicability**

One of the earliest pieces of important Agamben criticism, Düttman's introduction to *Idea of Prose*, attempts to delineate the key element of language for Agamben's thought: communicability.[1] Düttman concentrates on the Benjamin source for the term, specifically the idea that communicability communicates nothing other than language's capacity to communicate. It does this only through its praxis or act, its contingency, context, operativity and intelligibility. Yet at no point can language communicate its communicability; it can only demonstrate it through its being a communicable medium or process. This relates to Agamben's interest in the Russell-Frege paradox of statement self-predication, although, as we shall see, an important element of communicability is that it concerns compound linguistic series, not individual words. Perhaps at this stage we should progress through an admission of failure. In my own extended comments on communicability in my earlier work, while I approached this quality and delineated some of its key aspects, I did not arrive at a state of clarity in terms of its definition. I am certainly to blame for this lack of perspicuity and so many other dark obfuscations. Having said that, with the publication of *The Sacrament of Language*, *The Kingdom and the Glory* and *The Signature of All Things*, it is now increasingly impossible not to be lucid over what Agamben takes to be language's primary characteristic: *its communicability defined in terms of its intelligibility or its operativity*. It has been a long road for many of us to this refuge point, itself only the gate to a whole new territory for which we remain woefully ill equipped and with little to guide us beyond sketches on the backs of matchbooks, outlandish stories from the mouths of the mad, that sort of thing.

Already back in 1978, Agamben is laying out the linguistic theories, specifically those of Benveniste, that will underpin his first major philosophical work, *Language and Death*, and come to define the first significant inroad of his philosophy into his messianic project of suspending oppositional metaphysical structures located within paradigms and distributed through signatures. Yet not until the works of the last few years is it really clear why the thing of thought itself is language, his thesis in the at times obscure essay "The Thing Itself",[2] and also why language is to be defined in terms of communicability. So, a sad story of failure with a happy ending, for as we have seen, communicability is now rather simple to define and its true ramifications finally traceable: not what a statement means but that it can mean, not what it says but that it can be said due to sovereign sanction and subjective complicity. Communicability is not the meaning of a statement but the meaning of the fact that such and such a statement can be said by such and such a subject position at such and such a time in such a way as it is taken to be meaningful at large.

WITTGENSTEIN'S PUBLIC LANGUAGE THEORY

One problem with the obscurity surrounding the understanding of communicability is that in the earlier work the source of the term seemed to be found in just a few provocative statements in the work of Benjamin, specifically the dense essay "On Language as Such and on the Language of Man", and some unpublished fragments that Agamben makes available in his studies of his great precursor. To his great credit Zartaloudis identifies an element of Agamben's method which helps us to understand his manner of putting together concepts which is always in accordance with his method. Thus, communicability was never simply an interpretation on Agamben's part of something Benjamin touched upon. Rather, all of Agamben's concepts are themselves signatory in the manner in which they allow certain things to be said, to be intelligible, through the presentation of a number of paradigms from the history of Western thought or, better, Western discourse formations. And so it is with communicability, which, if we step back from Agamben a moment, is one of the central topics of modern philosophy albeit in an unspoken manner. Agamben's communicability, therefore, sourced in Benjamin, was really only a moment of arising for his work within a full understanding of this signature that dominates a key element of philosophy and also oversees philosophy's disastrous internal differentiation at the beginning of the twentieth century into the so-called analytic and continental traditions. As we saw, communicability was first developed for modern thought in Kant's third critique concerning the aesthetic and then revitalised in the early part of last century in Heidegger's essays on art. It relates directly to Russell's self-predication paradox and is another name for Wittgenstein's public language theory made communicable by forms of life.

Wittgenstein's theory of private language and the Russell-Frege self-predicative paradox combine together in Agamben's work to further develop his conceptualisation of language as communicability. That Agamben is able to combine these works with those of a thinker like Benjamin and find equal value in each is testament to the remarkably generous and inclusive thinker he can be but also the archaeological nature of his analysis.

As is well documented in *Philosophical Investigations*, Wittgenstein works to disprove the idea that there is such a thing as a private language. While it has been contested that no one was promulgating such a theory at this time in any case so that Wittgenstein disproves an issue no one was promoting, in fact Wittgenstein is giving voice to a deeply felt problem within the traditions of philosophy. The question is, of course, Does a subject possess an actual consciousness, or is consciousness always shared through the communicability of its mediation, at all points, in language? The idea that there can be private sensations, experiences and thoughts that somehow belong to the subject alone is a fundamental one to our culture, as powerful as the counterbalance that there is out there an objective world which all subjects are subject to in the same way. Wittgenstein gives the examples of pain and diaries.

Pain is a sensation so immediate that, he suggests, it is a strong contender for the privacy of sensation argument: no one else can feel my pain or go through it for me. Yet he also asks, How can we know that it is pain to such a degree that we can say that this pain of mine is private to me? In other words, the conceptualisation of pain must already be public for us to determine that it possesses also a privacy, or what I would prefer to call subjective singularity. The other example relates to this. Every time one feels a specific sensation, he suggests as a thought experiment, one inscribes it in a diary using a random signifier: S. But again here the problem of succession of consistent experience is raised. How does one know it is the same sensation, and how does one also realise that the first time it is a singular experience as such? This results of course in an argument of infinite regress: there can be no determined singular sensation without a previous sensation which determines it as singular, and there can be no confirmation that each time I write S, I am correct in identifying the same sensation, as this is verifiable only publicly. As Wittgenstein points out, in a truly private language the concept of right does not pertain.

Of specific interest to the work of Agamben in this regard is the consideration of the diary entry in section 258, where Wittgenstein says that after deciding on the sign designation S for this particular private sensation, "I will remark first of all that a definition of the sign cannot be formulated. — But still I can give myself a kind of ostensive definition. —

How? Can I point to the sensation? Not in the ordinary sense. But I speak, or write the sign down, and at the same time I concentrate my attention on the sensation—and so, as it were, point to it inwardly.—But what is this ceremony for? for that is all it seems to be!"[3] Three terms here stand out. The first is the concentration on ostension, for, as we shall see, Agamben's most convincing presentation of language pertains to the ostensive functioning of the oath. The second is the problem of pointing in that Agamben's earliest comments on language pertain to the role of deixis. Finally, third, the negation of this mode of pointing to a private sensation is brought about by the negative designation of the activity as mere 'ceremony', but, as the previous chapter showed, empty ceremony is, in fact, essential to the public communicability of language. I think that at this stage it is adequate to say that Wittgenstein's great demonstration, that language is always public and that thus there is no means of making the concept of a private sensation communicable, is accepted by the tradition that Agamben belongs to, namely, the Foucauldian and Deleuzian view of language as immanent intelligibility. Agamben agrees with Wittgenstein that the definition of language is its public nature, yet he radically disagrees with him that this is an intrinsic quality of language; rather, he argues that the public nature of language, its operativity, is historically contingent, and he strongly argues for the possibility of a future for language where the private-ostensive and the public-referential come together in perfect suspension.

On the basis of this discussion we can now go further and say that communicability, preexistent public existence of singular private experience, is also the basis of Derrida's implied refutation of Wittgenstein's public language theory through Derrida's insistence that every statement, due to *différance*, has an element which is other, by definition 'private' (although we know to be careful with such auto-affective designations). To summarise one of Derrida's greatest arguments within this Wittgenstein framework, it is the repeatability of signs that means they are always communicable (common or public) even when what they are communicating is something singular, yet it is this iterability that means they are never communicable in full so that some element remains in the public realm yet, ostensibly, private. It is difficult within this context to say if communicability is a significant term because it reveals the nature of the signature Language or if Language is significant because it makes communicable the structure of communicability for the first time as subject to indifference. Either way it is fitting that we end with language and communicability because Agamben's work began with language and negativity, and his overall method comes to a point of suspension through the act of making communicability transparent, communicable and ultimately inoperative and thus noncommunicable.

THE SUSTAINED QUESTION OF WHAT IT MEANS FOR HUMAN BEINGS TO HAVE LANGUAGE

Murray's recent introduction to Agamben's work begins by asserting, perfectly rationally, that Agamben's philosophy is reducible to a conceptualisation of language.[4] The literature supports this. There is no period of Agamben's work that is not intimately concerned with the mapping out of his ideas on language, and, of course, he is on the record as saying the thing of thought is language.[5] Yet in *The Sacrament of Language* (2009), to date his most important statement on the topic, he says in the very final section, "It is perhaps time to call into question the prestige that language has enjoyed and continues to enjoy in our culture, as a tool of incomparable potency, efficacy, and beauty. And yet, considered in itself, it is no more beautiful than birdsong, no more efficacious than the signals insects exchange, no more powerful than the roar with which the lion asserts his dominion".[6] Murray did not have this text in front of him when he wrote his introductory remarks, nor do they necessarily make his summation less accurate than those, say, of Mills in another excellent introduction when she defines Agamben's work as primarily what it means to have something.[7] Here Mills is reducing Agamben's work to the logic of potential, capacity, in the same way that Murray reduces it to language. Indeed, the two are also interrelated and not necessarily mutually exclusive in that, from an early point, Agamben has concentrated not on language as such but on what it means for human beings to *have* language, to come to possess it through a period he defines as infancy (linguistic capacity).[8]

Our study comes at the issue differently by asserting Agamben's work is reducible to the logic of indifference, but all three statements must take warning from Agamben's turn against language here. In fact language, capacity and indifference itself are all historical contingencies that at some point must be rendered inoperative because they emanate from a metaphysical tradition that is now finally exhausted. To return to Murray's contention, Agamben's philosophy of language is operative only if, built into it, there is the certainty of its inoperativity, and it is to this end that Agamben's qualification of his reneging on language moves:

> The decisive element that confers on human language its peculiar virtue is not in the tool itself but in the place it leaves to the speaker, in the fact that it prepares within itself a hollowed-out form that the speaker must always assume in order to speak—that is to say, in the ethical relation that is established between the speaker and his language. *The human being is that living being that, in order to speak, must say "I," must "take the word," assume it and make it his own.*[9]

This is a statement which could have been made thirty years earlier, and it remains a constant in Agamben's work, although nowhere is it as clearly expressed as in the 2009 study. It is a statement that owes much to Foucault, as Agamben concedes here, but in terms of its relation to communicability can be located in a much wider philosophical context. It also vindicates Murray as much as Mills, as we see that it is the operativity of the signature language that is being contested here, its assumed qualities of power (politics), efficacy (philosophy) and beauty (aesthetics), not language as such, and that central to any conceptualisation of language is the problem of the unique human capacity for language. Agamben is not repeating the ancient argument that we are *zoon logon echon* but rather expressing a peculiarity of the communicability of language which is the human element of language.[10]

Human beings possess a capacity for language; everything else simply has language (irrational potential). Thus, it is the impotential element of linguistic capacity here and the praxis of coming to have that capacity (making it rational potential) that define the human element of language, certainly, but also the human as that which takes possession of its life at the moments it takes possession of its enunciation. If *The Signature of All Things* is a sustained study of the statement element of Foucault's masterwork, *The Sacrament of Language* completes this study by taking on the enunciative element in the same way that, for example, Deleuze and Guattari address the role of the persona in their late, great consideration of communicability: *What Is Philosophy?* As we progress then, we have before us three modes of series. The first is the consistency in Agamben from *Infancy and History* to *The Sacrament of Language* in terms of the question of what it means for human beings to have language. The second is the development of this question from the earlier considerations of signs, deixis, desubjectivization, infancy, voice, the semiotic and communicability to the much clearer recent work with its focus on communicability as intelligibility and operativity. And finally, third, how this recent work makes the overall project for language in Agamben's study, its radical presentation of a truly ostensive language that does not succumb to the Wittgensteinian arguments of privacy or the Derridean objection of *différance*, that is, a language that is truly communicable through the suspension of the traditional oppositions of spatial difference, inside and out, and temporal, immediate and mediated (repeated), available through linguistic inoperative indifference. It is to this third point that we will push towards in the pages which follow.

ACCLAMATION AND THE OATH

The oath is defined early on *The Sacrament of Language* as follows: "The oath does not concern the statement as such but the guarantees of its efficacy: what is in question is not the semiotic or cognitive function of language as such but the assurance of its truthfulness and its actualization".[11] Immediately, we are struck by how the oath conveys precisely the qualities of intelligibility of discourses through the presence of signatures. Like a signature, the semiotic and semantic element is not of concern; rather, the oath participates in the process of operativity. Irrespective of the content of the oath, what Agamben will calls its dictum 'I swear that . . .', the fundamental nature of the oath is simply a guarantee that said statement is communicable. Its communicability here is guaranteed by the oath's swearing as to the two ontological bases of communicability: that the statement can be made in this manner (actualization) and that it can be taken within this context to convey truthfulness. Both are elements of public language: this statement has been made in the presence of others, and they are able to find intelligible its veracity. It is to this element of language that Agamben returns towards the end of the book when he explains, through Foucault, that human beings are unique because they put their lives at stake, or their subjective position, when they use language, not because of the shortfall or disjuncture between what they say and what they would like to mean but because each speech act is a statement of one's trustworthiness which you guarantee with your 'life', sometimes literally.

With this in mind Agamben attempts a gesture that he first put into place in the final pages of *Stanzas*, which is to wrest contemporary debates about language away from signification and move them instead into issues of guarantee, authentication and promise. Criticising Levi-Strauss here, but we must assume that an implied critique of Derrida as well as the early work in *Stanzas* is concerned primarily with his near contemporary and great rival, he says that the moment of arising of language in the human did not create the problem of "the cognitive aspect of the inadequation of signifier and signified that constitutes the limit of human knowledge".[12] Rather, what was more decisive for the human who "found himself speaking", in other words, was possessed with a self-reflexivity as to its capacity for speech that, say, the animals it was hunting did not show, "is the problem of the efficacy and truthfulness of his word, that is, of what can guarantee the original connection between names and things, and between the subject who has become a speaker— and, thus capable of asserting and promising—and his actions".[13]

What this amounts to saying is the manner in which human beings have language is not related to assumed referential agreement models, such as we find being founded and developed in Wittgenstein for the analytic and ordinary language thinkers to follow, and the problematisation of this model in work such as Levi-Strauss and Derrida of course. The issue of reference in its specificity is irrelevant in fact, faced with the indifference of the guarantee. What human language communicates is not the correctness or limits of specific acts of linguistic reference, 'this is an elk let's hunt it' or 'here is a root let's unearth it', but the indifferent or general guarantee that what it points to is what the subject says it is. This guarantee is then based not on a public act of agreement, several people gathering around said root and saying 'yes, this is indeed an edible root', but on a statement of subjective placement: I take up this position and guarantee its efficacy through my promise of its truthfulness.

This then is the true nature of communicability, not the truth of a reference through communal agreement but the constant guarantees of the operativity of communicability through oaths of actualisation and truthfulness. The specificity of the reference is either irrelevant or at the very least comes later. Prior to this is the indifferentiation of the oath as such. Here then language as oath is defined as fundamentally performative but performative without context. What I say is an act: I guarantee it. If this can be proven to be the case, then Agamben has performed the trick of retaining Wittgenstein's public language through the very quality he wished to negate: ostension. At the same time he will have been able to prove that Derrida's radical contention as to the *différance* of each speech act is correct, for example, like Derrida, the specific context of a speech act cannot be vouchsafed to determine referential agreement, but is to a degree irrelevant. It is not a matter of reference identity or referential *différance*, language, but that of operativity. Language does not communicate amongst subjects but makes subjectivity as such a communicable position.

A good analogue to this position is developed in terms of acclamation in *The Kingdom and the Glory*. Acclamation is opposed, there, to glory as two means of making power operative through ceremony. In terms of the two orders of power conveyed in that text, the *auctoritas* of God and the *potestas* of the people, acclamation is defined, via Schmitt, as "the pure and immediate expression of the people as constituent democratic power",[14] to which Agamben adds from Schmitt's nemesis Peterson, "What is an acclamation? It is an exclamation of praise, of triumph . . . of laudation or of disapproval . . . yelled by a crowd in determinate circumstances".[15] These acclamations are irrelevant in content and specific context and in the case of Amen can in fact become automated, empty ceremonies. However, their vacuity is irrelevant, for their purpose is not to convey meaning but to affirm the basis of communicability: we are the people, we are the congregation. It is Schmitt who notes, in a troubling observation, the loss of acclamation in the secret ballot, and there is some truth in that. In a ballot we choose, and in so doing we occlude language; language's assumed secrecy is a key element of Agamben's critique of language and voice as we know. In acclamation we assert nonchoice in the act of being one voice. Thus, we can see here a complex linguistics of power through choice. Oppositional choices are linguistic acts that accept division and must then occur in silence. Mass affirmations of power are linguistic acts that state operativity and explode in acts of public noise-making.

PERFORMATIVITY

Agamben then develops this idea of acclamation in relation to an earlier idea of the gestural which again up to this point remained a rather confusing possibility rather than a clearly stated thesis (as my own limited attempts to contend with gesture in the earlier study show).[16] In this instance what is made clear is the manner in which gestures do not support speech but themselves speak as pure act: "The gestures become words, the words become facts".[17] The gestural then is that element of language which is defined as performative, "the insoluble interweaving of words and facts".[18] What interests Agamben about Austin's performative theory, and again there is an implied critique of Derrida's "Signature Event Context" here, is the manner in which a linguistic utterance immediately can be taken as fact "insofar as its meaning coincides with a reality that it produces".[19] This theme is actually of great significance for the final section of the magisterial Homo Sacer project. For example, the study of poverty and use through a consideration of the rules of monastic orders, *Altissima povertà*, is concerned primarily with a similar instance where the monastic vow is not a commitment to follow a specific set of rules or precepts which, if broken specifically would lead to punitive measures, the juridical norm for lawmaking, but a total commitment to live your life in every aspect according to your vow. There the form-of-life of monastic orders sees no division between every moment that you live and the vow you have made to live according to rules. If you break a specific rule, you have broken your vow in the totality of its efficacy; in effect, you have transgressed your very own life.[20] As Agamben tells us that the form-of-life is set to answer the question as to what to do after the indifference of all the signatures of all things Western, his project after all, we can see here that the special consonance between an oath, a gesture, a performative utterance and a vow is of particular significance. It is worth noting also that the phrase form-of-life originates in Wittgenstein to indicate a general sense of the totality of base communicability of the life we all live in common and take as a given. Form-of-life then is the dream of a truly publicised being, one that is not dependent on Wittgenstein's profoundly metaphysical reliance on public (common) private (proper) differential articulation.

Agamben now raises an issue in terms of the sign that we have already touched upon. If the linguistic position is that there is an abyss between word and thing, or, more accurately, signifier and signified (a basic maxim of Saussurian structural linguistics retained by Agamben's favoured, ontologically orientated linguist Benveniste), then what are we to make of performatives which work in the opposite manner? They do not, in fact, heal this rift; rather, they take it for granted that there is no such rift. In performatives your word is your act, so that the presupposition of the sign as bifurcated is in suspension: "The performative is al-

ways constituted through a suspension of the normal, denotative character of the sign".[21] Agamben illustrates this with reference to the afore-
mentioned dictum. If one assumes that the oath consists of the act and its
dictum, I swear and I swear that, then a performative suspends the dictum. Your promise is your act; it is not the subject of a factical dictum.

Philosophically speaking, this observation is rather incendiary. As has
been the project of a number of thinkers, the oath suspends the subject-
predicate law of Aristotelian thought. It negates the need for an ontico-
ontological difference. It questions the presupposition of the common
and proper dialectic at the heart of Western thought structures. It removes the referential from philosophy, as at issue here is certainly not an
agreement between a sign and what it indicates as a meaning. And in the
end it suspends difference and, in so doing, negates identity. This last
point is the most telling in that it encourages a realisation, contrary to
Derrida and Deleuze, for example, that to suspend the predominance of
the metaphysics of presence/identity, one does not turn to difference;
rather, one actually in some way negates or suspends difference. In a
phrase that may shock most thinkers from this tradition, there is something other than identity and difference, a modality that suspends difference and yet does not then return to identity.

Agamben then proposes that the mode in which a performative suspends a dictum, resulting in a fact that is not proper and a norm that is
not common, means that a performative utterance is not a sign but a
signature: "One that marks the *dictum* in order to suspend its value and
displace it into a new nondenotative sphere that takes the place of the
former".[22] In other words, performatives are not signs that carry meaning
through the semiotic mode of referentiality wherein the truth of something is determined by agreement: yes this sign refers to that thing. Rather, they make operative the dictum as a mode of mobile or communicative intelligibility by virtue of a meaning-neutral communicability of a set
of public-sanctioned meanings. This again marks a radical attack on Wittgenstein or, better, a significant development from his work. The very
aspect of a sign that Wittgenstein denies is its inability to be truly ostensive. On the contrary, Agamben argues, it is the ostensive nature of the
sign that makes communicability possible through a sign becoming a
modality of ostension he calls the signature.

Agamben goes even further in this text by showing that empty ceremonies, acts of glory and of spontaneous acclamation, are actually essential for the vouchsafing of communicability. God's glory, for example, is
self-sufficient, by which I mean his very being is his glorification. In
contrast acclamation makes a people through the communal act of self-
declaration: we are the people! The ceremony then is all important to
access these two peculiar ontological states and of course as ontology is
primarily a pseudoproblem for Wittgenstein; the intelligibility of this
idea is rendered inoperative for him through his adherence to the para-

digms of the analytical tradition, which are themselves two sides of an ontology of indifferent inoperativity. In terms of God's Being, his existence is his utterance. In the case of the being of the people, their utterance actuates their existence. The suspension of subjectivity then occurs due to the double inoperativity of Being and beings through the empty ceremony of all performative utterances. In *A Thousand Plateaus*, Deleuze and Guattari declare that all language is a command and thus that language as such is a performative,[23] while Foucault contends that all subjectivity is determined by one's placement in discursive formations.[24] These two ideas then come to the fore in Agamben's consideration of performative forms such as oaths and explain his thesis as a whole: that all language is an oath because it is through oaths that the subject puts its life into question. It is towards these two conceptions of language that we are moving through a close consideration of the signature of oaths that Agamben constructs.

AN ARCHAEOLOGY OF THE OATH

The specifics of the arguments of the archaeology of the oath are not of direct concern to us here. Suffice it to say that debates over the religious or juridical origins of the oath are recast in line with the archaeological method, whose moment of arising is not to be found in either area but rather allows us to question the idea of the origins of both in a coimplicating fashion. The same structure is developed in *The Kingdom and the Glory* in relation to the signature of secularization. Thus, there are speculations that there existed an archaic prelaw age that preceded law and religion. In relation to this Agamben says that it would be better to call this prelaw period *x*; we could also call it the moment of arising, "practicing a sort of archaeological *epoché* that suspends, at least provisionally, the attribution of predicates with which we are used to defining religion and law".[25] The moment of arising leads to an investigation of a "threshold of indistinction" between the two terms, also as we saw between word and thing in linguistics, that is not a somehow prehistoric age for which we lack documentation "but an internal limit, the comprehension of which, by way of calling into question the accepted distinction, can lead to a new definition of the phenomenon".[26] This is the strong methodological basis of the whole study that has wider implications for the most recent work on vows as law in *Altissima povertà*.

So there are the terms of the study of historical interest from which we will glean time and again statements of great clarity pertained to the overall consideration of language as communicable intelligibility. For example, when summarising in the early pages Philo's thesis of the oath, we find, using the language of religion, an ancient presentation of the signatory power of the performative utterance. Philo notes that oaths are the verification of words in facts. As regards God's words, all are facts, and thus all his words are oaths. It is for this reason that only God can swear truly, as it is impossible for him to do otherwise: what he says is logos, a saying-doing. God, then, is the being whose *logoi* are *horkoi*, whose words are acts, and, as we can never know God, the only definition we have is one "whose word testifies with absolute certainty for itself".[27] Philo concludes in terms of God that he spoke and that it was done with no interval between the two. God's being is his language as pure, immediate act: the ideal of communicability. To this end he shares a great deal in common, according to *Homo Sacer*, with the Führer, whereas for we humans our oaths are our attempt to conform as much as possible to this model. The logic of the oath leads to a problem of indistinction or productive logical suspension: "On the one hand, in the oath human language communicates with that of God; on the other, if God is the being whose words are oaths, it is completely impossible to decide if he is reliable because of the oath or if the oath is reliable because of God".[28] At this point of indistinction the structure of the indifferential suspension of power is repeated. Just as kingdom is demonstrable through government in a manner where one cannot say if power founds governance or governance produces power, so here we have the same issue. The oath has at its centre a central inoperativity: it is guaranteed by a force, here God, that itself cannot be guaranteed except through its acting as guarantee.

The indifferential inoperativity of the oath then is its foundational moment and is soon to be revealed in the formation of "the co-originality of blessing and curse, which are constitutively copresent in the oath".[29] The copresence of blessing and curse is specifically related to the conceptions of perjury and blasphemy. In relation to blasphemy, Agamben defines it as *"an oath, in which the name of a god is extracted from the assertorial or promissory context and is uttered in itself, in vain, independently of a semantic content"*.[30] Thus, he argues that the apotropaic nature of the oath, blessing and curse, produces the oath from the co-originality of benediction and male-diction. We have presented these in terms of the ceremonial. The blessing is glory, while blasphemy is acclamation. A true oath operates through the operativity between the two.

Agamben is able to widen the scope of the study even more dramatically when he notes that the blessing and the curse "are born as specific institutions from the division of the experience of speech that was in question in the oath".[31] Although Agamben does not say this here, we can easily surmise that this means that speech and oath are also cooriginary and that the divisions attendant on the oath are traceable to the power of speech as divided into signifier and signified, a power vouchsafed by the specific instance of the oath. In terms of language then, speech operates as the common, the powerful, the blessing that founds the proper example of the oath or the performative. This being the case then, the structure of the indifferentiation of language is finally before us. Speech as divided, what Agamben calls in *Language and Death* Voice, founds the possibility of the facts of speech presented to us by linguistics, here the performative. However, the performativity of the fact, guaranteed by the norm, co-originates the norm. The aim then is to suspend speech by way of the oath so that language as indifference can be perceived as the final moment of oppositional Western thinking structuration before we plunge into the real of language as pure communicability as such or the God-like state of nonintervalic speech, what is said is what one does, brought down to earth so that in this form-of-life, the problem is not whether we mean what we say but a world in which means have no ends so that what we need to ask is whether we act as we speak.

The final part of this archaeological study that concerns us before we move to consider the totality of Agamben's statements on language pertains to the pagan use of naming. Agamben considers the disciplinary consideration of naming gods through Usener's study *Götternamen*. Usener notes that pagan gods were named after the acts and events they influenced on earth, the specific example being the times of the year one must plough. These special names, *Söndergotter*, Agamben notes, divinise "the very event of the name; nomination itself. . . . The *nomen* is immediately *numen* and the *numen* immediately *nomen*".[32] The indistinction of word and act in pagan *Götternamen* explains a point made in terms of punishment for breaking one's vow in *Altissima povertà* that the oath, like the vow, is not guaranteed by God's punishing you if you break the vow. This is not how one swears by God. Rather, God "represents, he *is* the very event of language in which words and things are indissolubly linked. Every naming, every act of speech is, in this sense, an oath".[33]

This logic then becomes transposed into the field of monotheism, where, as there is only one God and consequently only one name for God, the performative element of language as a series of particular oaths becomes instead the exact coincidence of the name of God and that of language. God's word is his oath both in terms of this faithfulness and in terms of his immediate performative linguistic praxis; his words are deeds which is the double sense of the logos, faithfulness to one's word and one's word as act, that becomes the Western conception of language which Agamben is renaming here an oath.

Agamben goes on to use a constellation of familiar sources, Scholem, Benjamin and Mainonides, to consider the nature of God's name in terms of its negation of predication in the act of nomination. The proper name of God is not an attribute added to his being, naming his Being as an object. Rather, the proper name is the operativity of Being or as Agamben says, "To pronounce the name of God means to understand it as that experience of language in which it is impossible to separate name and being, words and things. . . . It is a matter that is to say, above all, of an experience of language. . . . The name of God expresses the status of the *logos* in the dimension of the *fides* oath, in which nomination immediately actualizes the existence of what it names". [34]

Taking these three statements and transferring them into a wider, secular environment through the signature of communicability-intelligibility has been the lifelong project of Agamben thus far. This is indicated immediately here by the shift in emphasis to that mainstay of the history of Western thought and the analytical traditions that seem always under the surface here, predication. Agamben argues that through the oath of God's word, the archetype for language as logos in the West, every name used is transformed into a pronoun: "That is, it ceases to indicate, like every name, a substance plus an attribute and, being emptied of its content, now designates, like pronouns or proper names, pure existence . . . the pure act of speech as such". [35] Significant here is not only the move from the theological to the analytical with these comments on pure ostensive speech acts devoid of reference or predicate but also the care with which Agamben weaves into this study the terms of his earlier concerns pertaining to the pure experience of language, deictic pronouns, and the voice. Every phrase is an echo of those earlier, sometimes confusing studies, reproduced here with incredible confidence born of experience, philosophical maturity, methodological brilliance and historical distribution.

The final comments tackle that other key element of Agamben's thoughts on language, Russell's self-predicative nominal paradox. Here Agamben 'solves' this paradox by what we might term a paradigm shift made operative through the tradition of exegesis that one presumes Russell would have found dubious. Reading Aquinas on the phrase *qui est* as it refers to God, Aquinas notes that this cannot signify what God is but "a sea of existence that is infinite and as if indeterminate". [36] We need not remind the reader at this stage the similarities here between Aquinas and Deleuze's central conception of indifference in the form of the plane of immanence. This sea of indeterminate existence then leads Agamben to conclude that the name of God can carry no semantic content but can only each time affirm "a pure experience of speech a pure and bare experience", an indifferent experience. [37] If this is the case, then yes, the oath is the experience of language that "treats all language as a proper name" or empty act of pronominal deixis to be exact. "Pure existence—the existence of the name—is not the result of a recognition, nor of a logical deduction: it is something that cannot be signified but only sworn, that is affirmed as a name". [38]

That this section ends with a consideration of Wittgenstein is apt, for a mainstay of modern positivism is at stake here in terms of reference. If we break down the above phrase into its component parts, we can say first that the existence of anything is determined by its name. All existence then is linguistic or, better, discursive. Existence on this reading is not an ontological game of Being but the praxis of communicability. Here

Agamben seems to support the view that there can be no private language of pure ostension. Yet, he goes on, the truth of naming is not truth as agreement typified by public language theories. A name is not operative due to the recognition of the relation between the arbitrary sign and the publicly sanctioned process of accepting that sign for that thing. Nor can the relation of the name to the thing be produced through the semi-private or restricted access language of pure logic. Thus, we are left with one option: the oath.

Agamben now reads Wittgenstein's own comments on the need to take the name on trust in *On Certainty*. Wittgenstein is forced to admit that he cannot be certain that his name refers to his existence in the same way that he can be certain of other empirical facts, like having been on the moon (a little-reported achievement in the bulging portfolio of this belated and reluctant Renaissance man), but rather is the referential link between his name and who he is the "'rule' of the game that language is".[39] Here Agamben is clearly co-opting Wittgenstein into a more pragmatic register which would better ally a certain strand of analytical thought with the tradition Agamben is operating in here of immanent thinkers such as Foucault and Deleuze. More troublingly, he then reduces the analytical tradition to a theological signature when he reveals that this same logic, of having to take the name on trust as something made operative and communicable within the rules of certain discursive practices, pertains to the problem of the name of God:

> The name of God names the name that is always and only true, that is, the experience of language that it is not possible to doubt. For man this experience is the oath. In this sense every name is an oath, and in every name a "faith" is in question, because the certainty of the name is not of an empirico-constative or logico-epistemic type but rather puts in play the commitment and praxis of men. To speak is, above all, to swear, to believe in the name.[40]

This is a significant moment in Agamben's work. Certainly, it reveals that presuppositions from that other tradition represented by Frege, Russell and Wittgenstein are problematic and that naming has to do with neither reference or deduction. Yet this is not our main task here. Rather, what is important is the manner in which the linguistic ideas of the early work come into clear agreement with the methodological clarity of the later work. The communicability of language, arguably Agamben's first major idea compound, is represented here as the intelligibility of signatures. This means first that we finally grasp a conception of language that retains the public yet accepts difference, the ideal combination of two traditions: analytical and phenomenological. By this I mean that the oath of language depends in each instance on public sanction, "the commitment and praxis of men". Yet in each oath there is retained an element of difference which is, we might say, Derrida's lasting contribution to the cause.

There is, in every oath, a private and a privative moment; for example, the proof of faith can never be published. While I can test specific speech acts, failure to keep promises has never been an effective way of negating the signifying power of language. In the end, the oath of language as such can never be tested, and the basis of our faith is always private because it is absolutely and totally public. It is an issue that I think Agamben is retaining from his engagement with Deleuze. In Deleuze, when the deep rises to the surface, it becomes absolutely mappable onto the surface in every aspect, but the two remain permanently heterogeneous. This is in fact a comment on the oath; remember that Deleuze is led to the same conclusion that all language is a form of an order, a particular view of the nature of the oath. If for Deleuze the performative element of language is You must do, Agamben's view is more profoundly interpolative, as it conforms to the promissory, I promise I will. There is, in other words, no need for coercion. That we have adopted a linguistic structure of the oath means that language is the ultimate ISA reminding us that hegemony is a distinctly Italian conceptual invention.

To return to the more complex point, language remains unknown, private and privative, in that it is the facilitation of communication. Each name, each word, is an oath; thus, each public act is vouchsafed by a private act of trustworthiness in the public arena of trust. Second, as we said, while we can test certain promises, if every word is a promise, how can we test language? Third, because language is nothing other than pure communicability, it is literally everywhere but can never be seen, as it is a process, or isolated, as it is the infinite sea of indetermination. Language then, in a simple but fundamental disagreement with Heidegger and his disputative beneficiaries, shows that while there is a clear difference between Being and beings, Being as such is never in withdrawal; rather, it is always and everywhere totally open and present, absolutely consonant with beings. Consequently, we have Agamben's innovation: the synthesis of the public language theories of early analytical philosophy, with the dependence on difference of the phenomenological-hermeneutic tradition of the so-called continental school.

A comment then reveals the final private element of the system: it is historically contingent. Here Agamben parts company with Wittgenstein and Derrida or, better, rids himself of one by the application of the other. Derridean *différance* necessitates the temporal-logical contingency of any theory of self-presence, even that of the self-presence of the public as regards their sanctioned meanings. Wittgensteinian public language, however, negates the possibility that something like a fundamental otherness or difference of language can exist. If the logic of reference and deduction is historical and the logic of difference itself an identity, then the only possible conclusion is that public-private is, itself, a definition not of language as such but of language as our modality of communicability. If this is proven to be the case, then the opposition in language between public and private, much more significant than that between thing and word because it makes operative the same debates around common and proper, can and must be suspended. It is then this impending indifference of language that promotes Agamben to, rather wearily, suggest we give up the prestige of language in the philosophical works to come.

INFANCY AND HISTORY: THE HUMAN CAPACITY FOR LANGUAGE

Of all the signatures we have thus far considered, power, glory, kingdom, government, order, life, potentiality, poetry, secularisation, the oath, *oikonomia*, sovereignty and so on, language still holds something of a privileged place if only because it concerns Agamben for the longest period of time, his whole career thus far. Language's special status in Agamben explains my focus in my earlier study, along with others emerging at the same time, each giving great prominence to the many texts on language in Agamben's oeuvre. That one cannot come to a clear actualisation of this concept of language until the publication of *The Sacrament of Language* is now apparent to me and obvious from my past failings, and so naturally I want to restrict the detail of my comments to this text. Yet, having said that, now is the time to delineate all the elements previous to this text which, I believe, find their completion only therein. As I have already written extensively on this matter and as several other excellent studies of the topic also exist, I will then restrict myself to a summary of the issues and refer to those other texts for the detail.

Agamben's first major work on language is his second book, *Infancy and History*. Here he testifies as to the future work which would consist of a study of the human voice, a study never completed in actuality but under the surface of much that was to follow. Here he explains that his main topic is the meaning of "there is language" and the meaning of "I speak".[41] What is quite remarkable is how we can see that the method, especially in its debts to Foucault, reproduces precisely these two components of language as intelligibility. The first concerns the means by which there can be intelligibility, the second the impact this has on subjective enunciation. We could then say that communicability as such is composed, as I have already proposed, of the fact of language as intelligible and the event of the subject as placement of enunciation. This, we also saw, is the final destination of *The Sacrament of Language*. Remarkable it is then that the 'juvenile' Agamben is in total agreement with the mature works.

The earlier study investigates specifically the ancient, Aristotelian presentation of the Greek adage that the definition of the human is "*zoon logon echon*", or the living being that has language, a commentary that justifies the reductions of both Mills and Murray. Specifically, what concerns Agamben is the self-conscious possession of language that human beings participate in: that they take up a place as a Being by means of their awareness of their capacity for language which, as we saw, is the only basis in our lives for the sustained prestige of language. As he says in *Infancy and History*, again in *Language and Death* and again in *The End of a Poem*, central to the human experience of speech is the simple lack of a term for the human voice akin to that of crickets which chirp, pigs that oink and so on. We are unable to find a term for our voice wherein there is no separation between speech and being, a term which as regards animals is not needed, as their being is enacted in their voice, whose role is entirely to make something happen. In the later work then, Agamben is finally able to express this in a manner that, for me at least, is impossible to question. We will never have a name for the human voice; rather, the act of naming is precisely the eradication of a difference between speaking and acting in that all acts of language are speech acts and all speech acts are oaths.

These ideas feed into the idea of infancy which I, at least, found troubling in this earlier work. The proposition of a developmental stage wherein infants come to learn language and thus separation from it, a stage animals do not experience, seemed doomed to failure in terms of developments in the science of speech acquisition. Agamben states that animals do not enter language but are always already inside of it, while man has an infancy which precedes speech and thus splits the single language: "In order to speak, has to constitute himself as the subject of language".[42] It is perhaps my failing combined with the choice of language and a lack of clarity of the method that makes this early study on infancy questionable. When, for example, Agamben goes on to suggest that if language is man's true nature, then this nature is split at the source meaning that "the historicity of the human being has its basis in this difference and discontinuity",[43] the sense is that this is actually the case, whereas from the contemporary perspective we can say that language is not man's true nature but rather is a historically presented signature of man's true nature. More than this, we can also conclude that language must be split at the source, as, for Agamben, all signatures are split at the moment of arising, for that *is* the moment of arising. Finally, the historicity of the human being then is actually an archaeological, not an ontological, statement. The history of the human in the West is dependent on the prestige of language as defining being that needs a sense of infancy or of language capacity. We could restate this and say that human being needs to have its capacity to be based on the fundamental incapacity at the heart of its most treasured capacity: language. Infancy then is a term rare in

Agamben and indicative of an early relationship to a nascent method. In general, Agamben never invents terms or concepts but traces signatures, and as infancy is not a recognised signature across the various discourses pertaining to language, it is perhaps not surprising that he jettisons this term as his work progresses, preferring instead to use speech, sign and voice.

DEIXIS

The other major innovation of *Infancy and History* pertains to the consideration of deixis and deictic shifters as regards what he calls, in these earlier works and then again in *Remnant of Auschwitz*, desubjectivization.[44] This is, of course, a related point to that of infancy that marks the place of subjective enunciation. Enunciation then is a signature that Agamben traces across the work of Benveniste here, with reference to De Saussure and Jacobson, finds present in the reliance on deixis in the statements of Hegel and Heidegger on linguistic ineffability and is still in place as we saw in the most recent work. To summarise, Being, for Agamben, is nothing other than enunciation. A subject comes to being when they occupy a place within a discourse wherein a certain set of statements become intelligible to them either as participant in a discourse, a leading voice in the making operative of that discourse or a mere observer. Deixis is the activity of pointing which, in linguistics through the use of words such as "this", "that", "here", "there", "it", "he", "she" and so on, seems to refer to a specific external reality but which, in terms of its linguistic operativity, does nothing of the kind. Rather, it reveals first the total lack of exteriority of Being and specifically language.

In accordance with Wittgenstein, deixis shows that there is no private sphere but that all meaning is publicly expressed through discourse. Second, it shows, in discord with Wittgenstein, that meaning is never determined by reference for, as deixis proves, you are able to point to something as purely neutral: this thing. If you recall Wittgenstein's objection was that in private language it was impossible to indicate a singularity using a modality of generality, this singular thing. What Agamben argues is that in fact this is all you are able to do. Each speech act is an act of indifferent deixis: it points to the indifferent precondition of general communicability. These positions are usually represented linguistically by the presumed division of the sign into signifier and signified. A general term is agreed upon to refer to the singularity of an experience, singular because it is only repeatable as we saw through referential signs. No sign can be singular, while every experience must be so if it is an experience that requires secondary support through indicative acts. If it were not singular but general, then in fact we would not need a general form to indicate it. Taken to its logical extreme in a true system of communicability, language as signification would not be needed, a state Agamben presumes animals occupy and which he calls Idea of Prose in one study, using a term from an obscure work by Benjamin.[45]

We can now appreciate the second significance for deixis. Not only does it make operative subjective enunciation, by which we mean the appropriation of a human subjectivity by the agreement to act within language as something we have gained a capacity for or Being as gained intelligibility, but it also reveals the central inoperativity at the heart of Western conceptions of language, an inoperativity made apparent in what Benveniste and Jacobson note as deictic shifters. A fundamental law of signification enshrined for the modern age in the work of De Saussure is the lack of communicability between signifier and signified. The semiotic and the semantic are fundamentally divided so that the sign can have a double compound structure. Agamben, like Derrida and others, sees this division as an imposition of metaphysics, not a linguistic fact (indeed contemporary linguistics has little use for this stipulation). Specifically, Agamben notes that the function of deixis is to indicate, which means it is fundamentally semantic-referential. Yet the content of the sign is empty, this thing, which means that the only significant component of it is its physical presence so that it is fundamentally semiotic. The ability of deixis to shift across the barrier assumed by Western thought between reference and referent is not a special case but in fact the indication that the inoperativity of the barrier in this instance is indeed the inoperativity of language as a whole.

Looking over the previous comments on the oath, this is confirmed. As all language is an oath in that all names operate as pronouns, then all words operate as deixis in at least three ways. First, each word does not refer to a meaning or thing but points to the fact of intelligibility. Second, the act of language is that of deictic enunciation that says this language is intelligible to me because I have chosen to occupy this available subjective position wherein such an intelligibility is operative. Third, deixis renders inoperative the assumed division between signifier and signified, which is, as we saw, the primary effect of an oath: the removal of an interval or spacing of difference between saying and doing.

THE SIGN AND THE STANZA: THE BAR AND THE BOX[46]

We have already addressed in detail Agamben's theory of the sign, so we can simply reiterate it here. For Agamben the Western tradition of the sign as the basis of language is not necessary but contingent or not the result of sustained empirical observation as much as the result of the signatory structures of Western metaphysics. It is not a coincidence that this theory of language splits language, that it bars the two elements from any kind of relationship other than heterogeneous and conflictual and that the two elements, signifier and signified, occupy the tradition common and proper positions. Yet the sign is an early example of the archaeological method in that the supposed bar between signifier and signified is, as we saw, eminently crossable by specific yet fairly common instances of deixis. Deixis carries no semantic content and is thus semiotic, yet it is the basis of all semantic content, namely, indicative reference.

What the later works add to this is that any theory of language in terms of reference or deduction submits to this same logic and, further, that all human utterances are performative-indicative speech acts. Inasmuch as all oaths are examples of deixis and all speech acts are oaths, then all speech acts are deictic at root. The porous line between signifier and signified is a very early example of the indifferential method. Although Agamben is still bound up with a certain logic of revelatory negation in these early works such as we find in *The Man Without Content* as regards modern art, in *Language and Death* as regards the metaphysics of linguistic occlusions and here in *Stanzas* as regards the sign, the model is clearly present in Agamben's mind. The line between signifier and signified, the barrier as he calls it, allows one to see the true intelligibility and inoperativity of the historical signature of language through the act of negation. The same argument becomes in the later work the moment of indifferential suspension wherein the oppositional system is momentarily revealed in its inoperativity, giving one an opportunity to render it permanently so.

What we have not touched on although I have covered it at length in my early work is the image of the stanza that Agamben uses. Through a series of philological moves pertaining to twelfth-century poetics, Agamben reveals that the stanza, for troubadour poets, meant the very nucleus of their poetry, defined as "capacious dwelling, receptacle".[47] Over time, due to the qualities associated with it, the stanza came also to be seen as a womb and also to represent the hidden aim of all such poetry, the love object. These reflections allow Agamben to present to us just how far reaching the logic of language as split has been absorbed into our tradition. The stanza operates in the poem in the same manner as deixis. Stanzas are, after all, semantic organising elements, yet they themselves are just empty boxes or rooms for the poetry. As such, they work as perfect signatures for the operativity of language, secured by the values of capacity, dwelling and receptivity, of the ontogenetic suggestion of the womb and the fated future direction towards a never-to-be-attained love object.

The stanza is the key means by which poetry reveals the secret it possesses in our culture in that, being a semantic unit that places the semiotic before the semantic, in terms of word use for sound only, enjambment, caesura, stanzaic structure and overall reiterative structure, it occupies the position of the line in the sign. That said, significant here is that this line is in fact dimensional. It is not a line but, as we have already seen in relation to the subject, an empty space which the poet/subject comes to occupy so that certain concepts become intelligible. The stanza is the opening up of the line to a box-like structure wherein the indifference of language can be made communicable, yet the very space itself remains always, like the love object, out of reach. This logic of the necessary occlusion of language so as to render it visible will then come to occupy the pages of Agamben's next major comment in the areas covered by *Language and Death*. Before we leave *Stanzas* it is worth noting that at this very early stage the sign is being replaced by the logic of the signature even if the term itself is not yet in use. Such a logic can be proposed, in fact, as Agamben's major contribution to philosophical understanding of language: a critique of the predominance of the sign through its recasting as a signature represented here by the expansion of the line into a box-like structure or stanza.

LANGUAGE AS SIGNATURE: A CONCLUSION

Communicability is pursued through several texts such as *Language and Death*, *Idea of Prose* and most specifically the essays bundled into the first part of *Potentialities*. Each of these is provocative, but, we might argue, the reader would have been better placed if an archaeology of language through communicability had been presented. That this did not happen seems in part due to Agamben's slow accumulation of evidential support for his ideas, culminating in the full-length study of communicability as intelligibility in *The Signature of All Things*, a text that reveals that several of my own assumptions about language we off-key, for example, my belief that the singularity of language is based on its semiotic materiality, a quasi-Heideggerian reading which itself is not a very illustrious reading of Heidegger or Agamben. We can now see, for example, that the semiotic is actually a precondition for materiality because communicability is a philosophy of what is, not of otherness or the ineffable. A statement must be made, Foucault argues, in a material and transferrable form for it to become public. And when we say that language never has the floor because it is the floor, Agamben's argument pertaining to the tablet of language, this is not a material presence of support except in the basic ontico-empirical sense of we must be dealing with some thing. In fact, what is meant is that language is communicability as such or, simply put, that language is not representation, expression or communication even but the specific conditions of the communicability of certain concepts by way of signatures. Even the role of poetry is now clarified in that, as he says in *The Kingdom and the Glory*, what poetry does for saying, philosophy and politics must do for acting. Or the poem does nothing other than reveal most clearly the inoperativity of a conceptualisation of language as bifurcated between semiotic and semantic. Poetry's own in-decisiveness on this point suspends this opposition long enough for us to conceive of a fundamental inoperativity of language as such as communi-cability. Now philosophy and politics must do the same with acting, for, as we saw, the prize is the final indifferentiation of the West, the suspen-sive inoperativity of the fundamental communicability of all our signa-tures, the opposition between saying and doing. It is this massive task that the final pages of *The Sacrament of Language* taken on.

Agamben notes, drawing a distinction between his own ideas and those of Derrida's without openly stating it, that performatives have been treated by linguists over the last century as a kind of magical stage of language. A form of utterance that does not describe a state of affairs but is a state of affairs in that it "immediately produces a fact"[48] is indeed a rarity in our conceptualisation of language although, for Agamben, not a rarity at all in actual fact in how we operate in language but something ubiquitous. Agamben's study of the prehistorical signature of the oath is at this stage then mapped onto performatives, but, and this is crucial, not to be in agreement with critics of the oath and the performative, these modes are somehow vestigial remnants of a predivisive age of language use where one's word was one's act. Agamben concedes that oaths do represent a remnant of a period when the connection between words was not "semantic-denotative but performative", yet he then stipulates how we are to take this idea of remnant: "This is not, as we have seen, a magico-religious stage but a structure antecedent to (or contemporane-ous with) the distinction between sense and denotation, which is perhaps not, as we have been accustomed to believe, an original and eternal char-acteristic of human language but a historical product (which, as such, has not always existed and could one day cease to exist)",[49] a statement of no small significance as regards the history of the oath, which actually does not concern this study overmuch, but more than that for language as such, which does.

Imagine if you will, he asks the reader, that the assumed division that constitutes our sense of language, between sense and denotation, sig-nified and signifier as we can also write this, was nothing other than a deeply felt and long-standing historical contingency. If so, then language is nothing other than a signature, and its essence is made up of only the operativity of its historical existence. All of this means that one day we can live without the signature language because that is all it is, just as we might assume that we once lived without it. And if this is true of lan-guage, then, and here is the simple, radical conclusion of the totality of Agamben's work, it is true of all other concepts which are themselves signatures subject to radical historical contingency whose sole existence is to make communicable certain statements and acts. Further, the es-sence of these signature-concepts, namely, difference, must always con-tain that element we call indifference, which allows difference to be operative but which also leaves a space in difference for its inoperativity. What is true for language is true for politics, power, being, life, poetry, philosophy and so on. One could end our study of Agamben right here if it were not for the richness of the analysis of language which follows and also the complexity of the task to hand: the indifference of saying and acting that becomes the concept of the form-of-life in the most recent studies.

NOTES

1. Alexander Garcia Düttman, "Integral Actuality", in Giorgio Agamben, *Idea of Prose*, trans. Michael Sullivan and Sam Whitsitt (Albany: State University of New York Press, 1995), 3–28.
2. Giorgio Agamben, *Potentialities*, trans. Daniel Heller-Roazen (Stanford, CA: Stanford University Press, 1999), 27–38.
3. Ludwig Wittgenstein, *Philosophical Investigations* (Oxford: Blackwell, 1953), 92.
4. See Alex Murray, *Giorgio Agamben* (London: Routledge, 2010), 11.
5. See Agamben, *Potentialities*, 27–38.
6. Giorgio Agamben, *The Sacrament of Language: An Archaeology of the Oath*, trans. Adam Kotsko (Stanford, CA: Stanford University Press, 2010), 71.
7. Catherine Mills, *The Philosophy of Agamben* (Stocksfield: Acumen, 2008), 21, backed up by Agamben in *Potentialities*, trans. Daniel Heller-Roazen (Stanford, CA: Stanford University Press, 1999), 178.
8. See Giorgio Agamben, *Infancy and History: On the Destruction of Experience*, trans. (Liz Heron (London: Verso, 1993), 13–72.
9. Agamben, *Sacrament of Language*, 71.
10. Giorgio Agamben, *Remnants of Auschwitz: The Witness and the Archive*, trans. Daniel Heller-Roazen (New York: Zone Books, 2002), 128–29.
11. Agamben, *Sacrament of Language*, 4.
12. Agamben, *Sacrament of Language*, 68.
13. Agamben, *Sacrament of Language*, 68.
14. Giorgio Agamben, *The Kingdom and the Glory: For a Theological Genealogy of Economy and Government*, trans. Lorenzo Chiesa with Matteo Mandarini (Stanford, CA: Stanford University Press, 2011), 170.
15. Agamben, *Kingdom*, 169.
16. See William Watkin, *The Literary Agamben : Adventures in Logopoiesis* (London: Continuum, 2010), 58–60. See also Mills, *Agamben*, 47–49, and Murray, *Agamben*, 86–90.
17. Agamben, *Kingdom*, 181.
18. Agamben, *Kingdom*, 181.
19. Agamben, *Kingdom*, 181.
20. See Giorgio Agamben, *Altissima povertà* (Vicenza: Neri Pozza, 2011),71–78.
21. Agamben, *Kingdom*, 181.
22. Agamben, *Kingdom*, 181.
23. See Gilles Deleuze and Félix Guattari, *A Thousand Plateaus: Capitalism and Schizophrenia*, trans. Brian Massumi (London: Athlone Press, 1992), 77–79. On Agamben, God, creation and the command see Giorgio Agamben, *Nudities*, trans. David Kishik and Stefan Pedatella (Stanford, CA: Stanford University Press, 2011), 2–3.
24. See Michel Foucault, *The Archaeology of Knowledge*, trans. A. M. Sheridan Smith (London: Routledge, 1972), 50–55.
25. Agamben, *Sacrament of Language*, 17.
26. Agamben, *Sacrament of Language*, 17.
27. Agamben, *Sacrament of Language*, 21.
28. Agamben, *Sacrament of Language*, 22.

29. Agamben, *Sacrament of Language*, 36.
30. Agamben, *Sacrament of Language*, 40.
31. Agamben, *Sacrament of Language*, 44.
32. Agamben, *Sacrament of Language*, 46.
33. Agamben, *Sacrament of Language*, 46.
34. Agamben, *Sacrament of Language*, 52–53.
35. Agamben, *Sacrament of Language*, 53.
36. Cited in Agamben, *Sacrament of Language*, 53.
37. Agamben, *Sacrament of Language*, 53.
38. Agamben, *Sacrament of Language*, 53.
39. Agamben, *Sacrament of Language*, 54.
40. Agamben, *Sacrament of Language*, 54.
41. Agamben, *Infancy and History*, 6.
42. Agamben, *Infancy and History*, 7.
43. Agamben, *Infancy and History*, 7.
44. See Agamben, *Infancy and History*, 53–70, for the full debate. See also Giorgio Agamben, *Language and Death: The Place of Negativity*, trans. Karen E. Pinkus with Michael Hardt (Minneapolis: University of Minnesota Press, 1991), 19–26, 73–77, and Agamben, *Potentialities*, 62, and *Remnants*, 115–17.
45. See Giorgio Agamben, *Idea of Prose*, 39, and *State of Exception*, trans. Kevin Attell (Chicago: University of Chicago Press, 2005), 88.
46. See Giorgio Agamben, *Stanzas: Word and Phantasm in Western Culture*, trans. Ronald L. Martinez (Minneapolis: University of Minnesota Press, 1993), 124–57, for the full debate.
47. Agamben, *Stanzas*, xv.
48. Agamben, *Sacrament of Language*, 54.
49. Agamben, *Sacrament of Language*, 55.

Conclusion: The End of Lying, the Birth of Living

THE OPERATIVITY OF THE PERFORMATIVE IN THE OATH

Agamben takes it on himself, at the end of *The Sacrament of Language*, to work through the nature of the operativity of the performative, a wise decision considering everything depends on this. The question is, How can a statement be immediately and entirely a fact, negating our ancient assumption of the 'abyss' between words and things? Using Benveniste's study, Agamben focuses on the self-referentiality of the performative, which is not limited to the statement taking itself as its referent, although this is true, but more than this "that the self-referentiality of the performative is constituted always by means of a suspension of the normal denotative character of language".[1] By this is meant specifically that every performative is a verb followed by a *dictum*, I swear that, but that in fact the performative suspends the denotative element of the *dictum*. "That is to say, the performative substitutes for the denotative relationship between speech and fact a self-referential relation that, putting the former out of play, puts itself forward as the decisive fact. The model of truth here is not that of the adequation between words and things but the performative one in which speech unfailingly actualizes its meaning".[2] Showing a clear debt here to Deleuze as well as Foucault, the truth as agreement model of public language theory is replaced by the truth as operative model of the postpragmatic, hermeneutical-phenomenological other tradition. Language is not now the adequation or not between what is said and what is meant but simply the fact that you can say such and such and be intelligible (communicability).

At this moment is raised an issue that first comes to the fore in *Homo Sacer* as regards the close consonance between the suspension of language and that of law. There Agamben states, "The question 'In what way does the living being have language?' corresponds exactly to the question 'In what way does bare life dwell in the *polis*?' The living being has *logos* by taking away and conserving its own voice in it, even as it dwells in the *polis* by letting its own bare life be excluded, as an exception, within it".[3] Two decades later the same point is reiterated: "Just as, in the state of exception, the law suspends its own application only to found, in this way, its being in force, so in the performative, language

271

suspends its denotation precisely and solely to found its existential connection with things".[4] The performative nature of the oath does not tell us what language really is; rather, as is the case with bare life, it presents us with the truth of how language operates through inoperativity, and thus, due to the radical contingency of this revelation plus the nature of inoperativity, it suggests to us what language outside of this historical existence could be. Yet inasmuch as the method in question is dependent on this linguistic communicability, we are faced here with a radical proposal akin to my own contention that indifference is a self-negating operation. The totality of Agamben's system of communicability which gives us access to the intelligibility of our entire culture through the operative communicability of its signatures must be rendered inoperative. Indifference must be indifferentiated before we can proceed to anything approximating a legitimate form of life.

In a rather dense couple of pages, Agamben then moves on to the relation of language as performative to ontotheological metaphysics in general. He commences this consideration with a paraphrase of Wittgenstein: "The existence of language is the performative expression of the existence of the world".[5] Wittgenstein's hinted at thesis of the form of life which is really just a quasi-transcendental version of Foucault's discursive formations without the law of dispersal, namely, the matrix of circumstances that allow us to make statements that can generate public meaning through agreement even across language differences. It is a conception that has found powerful expression in Habermas's theory of communicative action but can also be found in Heidegger's conception of how art makes a world in "The Origin of the Work of Art". All thinkers here are in agreement over the centrality of communicability, which is that while what one says can be proven true or false, one's language as a whole cannot. Where they differ of course is what is at root of all of this, a basic set of unchanging ways of existing (Wittgenstein), enlightenment traditions (Habermas), the operations of power (Foucault), the destinal epochality of a people (Heidegger) or metaphysical historical contingency (Agamben). This being the case, ontotheology is entirely dependent on the oath structure or the performance of language, and its power or decline depends on the power or decline of oath structures. "In this sense metaphysics, the science of pure being, is itself historical and coincides with the experience of the event of language to which man devotes himself in the oath. If the oath is declining, if the name of God is withdrawing from language . . . then metaphysics also reaches its completion".[6] Said metaphysics depends on the "co-originality of the performative structure and the denotative structure", which themselves determine all the oppositions of the *logos* which are given both at the same time "co-originally, but in such a way that they cannot perfectly coincide".[7]

We have here then the clearest statement Agamben has ever made about his version of the end of metaphysics. The decline of the authority of God results in the weakening of the power of the oath to the end that the suspension of language, swearing without a *dictum*, is itself suspended. Said suspension is our opportunity to think something new, but are we in a position to take it? If we do so, we cannot depend on an ontotheological thinking of the one or on a differential thinking of the many. Nor can we then say rather that we will now think from or by virtue of indifference. All we can say is that indifference has suspended metaphysics but that it itself must be suspended before anything like a philosophy of the future can become operative.

ASSERTORIC AND VERIDICTIVE

The sections which follow move us away from general concerns pertaining to the nature of language as oath to specific observations pertaining to the archaeology of the oath. Agamben explains that the oath is split into assertoric and promissory elements over time, shielding our eyes from the true nature of the oath, which he calls veridiction, taking yet another term from Foucault. Veridiction names the processes we have been unearthing here, that the subject puts itself into play through the act of the oath, puts its life on the line so to speak, and that veridiction recognises no division between speech and act for this reason. The enunciative function, so central to Foucault's schema, is effectively historicised and valorised in these considerations of the specificity of the oath. More than this, Agamben argues that the signature of performative is nothing other than a relic of the nature of the oath so that not only can Foucault's system be made radically contingent, but even the assertoric, deductive logic of modern linguistics and analytic common language philosophy has its moment of arising revealed in the oath. Logic, he notes, comes after the oath, and indeed it is the moment that the oath becomes split into assertoric, I swear that, and veridictive, I swear as such, that problems such as perjury and blasphemy occur. Religion and law, he tells us, are also younger than the oath and arise precisely because of the act of formulating a veridiction as an assertion. It is undoubtedly a question of ontology and metaphysics also, from the position of I have Being because I speak, we developed the model: I am a human Being because I speak in this way. The split between Being and beings is the result of the degradation of the oath as veridiction. In a conclusion which forms a pair with the comments on secularization from this same period and which presents a clear sense of his uneasy relation to theology, he says, "Religion and law do not pre-exist the performative experience of language that is in question in the oath, but rather they were invented to guarantee the truth and trustworthiness of the *logos*".[8]

Agamben goes further in this vein when he asserts that the division of religion and law is matched in terms of a wider division of faculties or disciplines so that the split between disciplines-faculties depends also on the oath's division. Assertoric statements are watched over by new disciplines such as logic and science, while veridictive disciplines spring up also such as law, religion, poetry and literature, presenting a much clearer sense of the age-old antagonism between literature and philosophy, with philosophy taken here to be assertoric.[9] Yet, he argues, the real division is not between poetry and philosophy for, on the side of veridiction there are other disciplines aside from poetry, and further the real capacity for philosophy is neither logical nor scientific. "In the middle is philosophy, which, abiding in both truth and error, seeks to safeguard the performative experience of speech without renouncing the possibility of lying and, in every assertorial discourse, experiences the veridiction that takes place in it".[10] We are then presented with a clear sense of what Agamben takes to be the capacities of philosophical thought. First, that philosophy abides in truth and falsehood, that it oversees the overall process where a truth could be said to be intelligible through comparison with a falsehood. Second, that philosophy concerns the conditions for assertion by virtue of its analysis of the nature of its veridiction, or, to use another set of terms from Foucault, it concerns the study of an enunciative field in relation to an associated domain.[11]

These comments then lead to the three-part statement of the book's thesis. First, that the magico-religious sphere does not precede the oath as scholars have assumed but vice versa. The oath explains religion, not the other way around. Second, the attempt to reconcile acts of faith "as the performative experience of a veridiction" with dogmatic beliefs "of an assertive type" represents the central contradiction of the Christian Church, a statement which needs to be mapped onto the reading of power in *The Kingdom and the Glory*, although we do not have time for that here. This means that philosophy has the role of operating as the "true religion", as "it does not seek to fix veridiction into a codified system of truth but, in every event of language, puts into words and exposes the veridiction which founds it".[12] Again then, we have a clear task for our third-millennial philosophy: *to expose the verification which founds every statement's communicable intelligibility*. Now we can finally draw a clear line between Foucault's concept of intelligibility of statements through the enunciative function of which he says time and again that it is entirely hermeneutic, knowing no foundation and no destiny, and Agamben's system which calls into question the system of the intelligibility of statements, his own system, remember, through the enunciative function's dependence on a fundamental veridiction. Agamben's philosophy then is not content to present an archaeology of statements; his is effectively an archaeology of the archaeology itself, which is the significance of indifference in his work.

Indifference is key because it suspends the very system itself, and so philosophy is not concerned with mapping the systemisation of veridictions, what Deleuze would term territorialization, nor is Agamben's interest in deterritorialization limited to freeing veridictions from systems of truth. Rather, again like Deleuze, his main concern is the veridiction which facilitates every systemisation and indeed every statement in a language. Whether we can call this veridiction a plane of immanence is a question again perhaps exterior to the confines of this study, but what one can say is that veridiction is not the same as communicability. Veridiction is not, phenomenologically speaking, the fund of every statement that could be made in the plane of determinable singularities. Rather, it is the perfect coincidence of the plane of immanence with that of its actualisation with no remainder. The best way I can think of expressing this is to accept that Being and beings are of the same numerical order and that in fact there is therefore no quantitative difference between them. The illimited realm of Being and the infinite singularity of beings is negated in favour of a philosophical system which shows, here through a consideration of language and the oath, that just as one can both speak and act with no interval, so of course one can be and exist in the same fashion.

APOTROPAICISM: THE END OF LYING AND THE BIRTH OF LIVING

The third and final point draws our attention to the relation between the oath and the sacred; it is, after all, a sacrament of language that we are considering. Here Agamben extends the logic of the oath onto the wider political project we have detailed by showing that there is a foundational political bifurcation of the oath. Just as we saw that the oath becomes split into the apotropaic system of blessing and curse, so too in the figure of the homo sacer the sacralisation of life produces an untenable but deep-seated relation, in law, between a sacrament and a curse: "Only a politics that has broken this original connection with the curse will be able one day to make possible another use of speech and of the law".[13] Or, in the movement from the oath as singular, I put my life into action through my act of speaking, to that of bifurcated, I swear on another authority that what I am saying is the truth, we have the same degradation of a life from a form-of life, where form and life know no distinction, as we saw in terms of bare life. In bare life as in the oath, the act of veridiction is split by the inclusion of the assertoric: I swear that, or I live as. So as in language the only way to solve the problem of falsehood is to move to a language in which one cannot lie because what one says is what one does, so in politics we need to move to a system of jurisprudence where one cannot be cursed by the law.

Perjury in speech is the equivalent of being cursed in act; both are the result of historical contingencies as regards their intelligibility and thus can be removed. An age where we do not lie and commit no crimes is possible, not by changing our essential 'human nature' but by modifying

the communicability of such discursive formations as Human and Nature. As Deleuze shows in relation to philosophy, falsehood is only the
result of a certain mode of communicating what a problem is, that is, as
that which wants a solution rather than as something which opens up a
pursuit. We need, in this sense, a Deleuze of the act, and I think Agamben
fulfils this enunciative persona well, although his work far exceeds this
role. If it is the case that we only lie within a communicable discursive
function wherein lying can be an enunciative position, then, more than
that, surely it is possible that we can have a jurisprudence freed from the
curse of crime, by which I do not mean simply describing crimes otherwise and letting the murders persist—it cannot, although in international
relations this remains a commonplace—but rather beginning again as
regards the actual object of law. If the real object of philosophy is the
manifestation of the veridiction of every speech act, so the real object of
law and politics should be the obverse, the making manifest of the veridiction of every act-statement. Philosophy must suspend the difference
between word and thing from the position of the word, politics from the
position of the thing, leading us to one final indifference: that between
philosophy and politics, speech and act, which Agamben calls form-of-
life.

Agamben ends his study with a radical overhaul of the Western metaphysical system of language as the profound heterogeneity between
word and thing, locating language instead within trustworthiness. It is
not the difference between word and thing that is the definition of language as communication but rather the guarantee of a speaking subject of
the connection between words and things and, at the same time, "between the subject who has become a speaker—and, thus capable of asserting and promising—and his actions".[14] All linguistic acts are primarily an ethos; as he goes on to explain, when man speaks "*he has . . . put his
very nature at stake in language*".[15] On this reading language is not one
capacity amongst others that the human has; rather, it is the capacity of
all capacities, by which we mean the human capacity to life as a human
being. Here the statement that the human is the animal whose politics
puts its life in question, so key to Foucault, is matched by the Agamben
statement that language performs the same function, primarily because
the political and the linguistic are fundamentally linked. As he says of
politics and language, "These two statements are, in fact, inseparable and
constitutively dependant on each other".[16]

The phrasing here gives us cause for pause. Clearly at any stage of
such a comutual interdependency of a common and a proper, language
and the political (speech and act), the point of the archaeological study is
to reveal the moment of arising of this division and suspend it indifferen-
tially. These comments then frame the following statement on the oath:
"The oath is situated at their intersection, understood as the anthropogenic operator by means of which the living being, who has discovered

itself speaking, has decided to be responsible for his words",[17] so that she commits herself to the logos and becomes *zoon logon echon*. The oath then is the signature that allows us to trace a very ancient moment of arising for, he tells us, the possibility of an oath (I swear) presupposes a division between word and deed. We can recast this in terms of glory and glorification if you wish. God's glory is self-sufficient and needs no expression; he exists as his glory. The same is true of his words. Our glorification of God reveals the moment of arising of the division of power which is actually the beginning of the development of the founding fiction of power in governance: a being whose existence is its glory. Exactly the same occurs with the oath. The oath retroactively instates a God-life figure whose word is its deed, as the necessary founding for the process of the oath as guarantee of trustworthiness. God then sanctions the invention of lying, what else?

Language occurs "in the moment in which the living being, who found itself co-originally exposed to the possibility of both truth and lie, committed itself to respond with its life for its words, to testify in the first person for them".[18] From the fact, this is true, comes the act, and I say this is so. So every oath asks the human animal to put its life at stake in speech by agreeing to occupy the enunciative positioning required for the guarantee of truthfulness. This means simply that language is the act of enunciation represented by the indifferent deictic indicator "I", plus the performative "swear" that suspends the difference between word and deed that "I" originated, plus the datum of the performance "that" which consecrates this division in the deep historical contingency of the assumed division between the common, truth as a whole, and the specific, the truth of this statement. This is also that of the common, Being as such, and the proper, 'I' am this being taking up this enunciative position as regards the truthfulness of this statement within the formation of its communicability. At this juncture words, things and actions are bound together by language "in a political and ethical connection".[19]

The oath bequeaths to us the fundamental apotropaic nature of Western discursive structures by means of signatures. Apotropaicism is the ancient Greek rhetorical term for a charm but came over time in a modality we can *not* see as inevitable if we but choose, as that which both repels evil and attracts luck. Apotropaicism names the totality of the dynamic experience of thought that can be called Western metaphysics and can be identified in the relation of reason to understanding via taste in Kant, the Hegelian dialectic, the Appolline-Dionysiac drive system of Nietzsche and the tense relation between Being and beings expressed in Heidegger's concepts of earth and world. Apotropaicism also explains the success of Freudianism, which expresses nothing other than the communicability of truth as such via apotropaicism (repression).

One can see here the integral nature of apotropaicism to indifference. A division is called up in such a manner that a difference of opposition occurs which yet is bound together in a structure of mutuality. I am in agreement with Agamben on this point. All modalities of thought within the West as founded on this structure and are also marred by it. It is impossible at present to think in the West except by insisting on the shackling together of two mutually antipathic examples of common and proper which, however, depend on their other for their mutual cofounding and comutual intelligibility. The logic here allows us to add that intelligibility or communicability as such, for us, thus far, is apotropaic, a blessing which is our curse and a curse which could lead to our benediction. Apotropaicism is Agamben's great revelation in terms of the nature of the sacred and here in terms of the blessing and the curse of the oath. Agamben says of the ethical nature of enunciation (language as we call it using one of the most ancient and troubling of signatures),

> It is in the wake of this decision, in faithfulness to this oath, that the human species, to its misfortune as much as to its good fortune, in a certain way still lives. Every naming is, in fact, double: it is a blessing or a curse. A blessing, if the word is full, if there is a correspondence between the signifier and the signifier . . . ; a curse if the word is empty, if there remains, between the semiotic and the semantic, a void and a gap. Oath and perjury, bene-diction and male-diction correspond to the double possibility inscribed in the *logos*.[20]

Our logocentric tradition then is one of apotropaicism.

Agamben follows this up with a comment on our current age, where the "anthropogenic experience of the word in the oath and the curse" has over time been located in institutions which have formalised this comutual opposition into truly separate spheres of existence. Subsequently, the oath element, the sacrament of language, becomes *auctoritas*, the force of law on a foundational power of language to self-guarantee. If this is so, then our current situation can be clearly explained in the following phrases: "On the one hand, there is the living being, more and more reduced to a purely biological reality and to bare life. On the other, there is the speaking being, artificially divided from the former, through a multiplicity of techno-mediatic apparatuses".[21] Yet this is not to suggest that we live in an age where the oath is at its weakest, and thus we are in the mess we are in. Agamben is not advocating a return to a mythical age where my word is my bond, far from it. In the last page of this rather miraculous little book, he explains that "Philosophy is . . . constitutively a critique of the oath: that is, it puts into question the sacramental bond that links the human being to language, without for that reason, simply speaking haphazardly". Thus, he adds, in an age when politics "can only assume the form of an *oikonomia*, that is, of a governance of empty speech over bare life, it is once more from philosophy that there can come, in the sober awareness of the extreme situation at which the living human being that has language has arrived in its history, the indication of a line of resistance and of change".[22]

Agamben says of language that it has taken us two millennia to isolate the enunciative function. The definition of deictic shifters is the fundamental discovery of this science. In these moments the subject assumes language through a concrete act. Yet linguistics was not in a position to explain the profound ethos of this act that "determines the extraordinary implication of the subject in his word".[23] Only politics and the social sciences were capable of that, specifically in the work of Foucault and Agamben's completion-development of his project. Yet neither linguistics nor politics is able to reveal the fundamental apotropaic structure at the heart of this revelation, namely, the movement of the shifter across the barrier that separates word and thing. It is philosophy that must be called in to reveal for us the true historically determined nature of language as that which enunciates the human subject through the neutral indifference of deixis to the division of word and thing assumed in the sign. What the indifference of the shifter shows is both the nature of the difference, the moment that difference arose revealing the contingency of difference, and, at certain moments, the inoperativity of this difference.

It is not necessarily a period that one relishes living in, an age of internment camps on one side and Twitter on the other, yet if it is true that we live in a great and terrible Age of Indifference where the current human ethos is a politics of exposed flesh and gossip, bare life and vain speech, the indifference of the shifter, those little words, should give us cause for hope. If one can remain truly, philosophically, technically indifferent to our own indifferent age, then our contemporary *acedia* can be transformed into a future of productive inoperativity. If our Western mode of discourse which determines not just how we live but also the means by which we can be said to live is marked by an unbearable tension between living as if blessed and as if cursed and if this mode of life is deep and ancient yet historically contingent, then we could choose to live otherwise or better opt to be alive otherwise.

threshold of suspension

> To render inoperative the machine that governs our conception of man will therefore mean no longer to seek new—more effective or authentic—articulations, but rather to show that the central emptiness, the haitus that—within man—separates man and animal, and to risk ourselves in this emptiness: the suspension of suspension.[24]

We are left then with an impossible maxim which, due to the law of communicability, is now less impossible than it was, I hope, as we commenced our brief sojourn together. *Communicability makes communicability communicable, and, if this is so, it opens up the potential for making itself permanently noncommunicable.* The only theory of political, philosophical and anthropological change of any worth must be a theory wherein the very signature Change alters beyond recognition. This is what Agamben's work seems to offer us. Indifference is not, after Badiou or Deleuze an event; it does not 'happen' in any real sense of that word, but even if it were, it is what 'happens' after indifference which is the central concern here. If it is clear that any theory of difference as change, intermittent (Badiou), constant (Deleuze) or oscillating (Derrida), produces no change to the system which facilitates it, merely an advance, reorganisation or incremental undermining of metaphysics, then the only communicable option left to us is a form of change that is *not* different, although nor can it be the same. It might seem incredible to insist on a revolution in the term "revolution" itself, a change to the conception of change as difference, perhaps even logically insupportable: what can change mean without things being different? This being the case, this is what we must demand, and indifference is, as far as I can ascertain, the only register from which the failure of change to actually change anything does not lead to a defeatist, fatalistic form of life pragmatism—things are the way they are because that is the way they are—or a valorisation of events as exceptionally rare moments of absolute interruption after which the world cannot help but be different.

Indifference suspends once and for all the first communication of philosophy; there is stability and there is flux, which is the first and lasting economy of the West.[25] Surely after more than two millennia, we are ready to think otherwise. Even a simple statement like "there is stability, there is flux and there is something else", opens up new vistas of thinking, mostly neglected by our tradition. Make that statement: there is stability-flux and its indifference", and the position is improved immeasurably. Conclude with "there is stability-flux, its indifference *and* the indifferentiation of this indifference that does not revert back to stability-flux", and one is proposing a new 'first' philosophy. Agamben's genius has been not to delineate what this new first philosophy would consist of (note here that our phrasing 'new first' is still within the modalities of the moment of arising) but rather, with characteristic diffidence and indirection, to make the possibility of thinking, speaking and acting otherwise (not different but otherwise in whatever fashion) communicable amongst us for the first time. If, I as contend, modern philosophy began with a flight from indifferentism (Kant) coupled to the valorisation of pure difference (Hegel), it ends with embracing indifference as the means by which one is able to think beyond difference in a consistent fashion that is, however, not identity, the One, repetition or foundation.

We are left in a state of suspension in communicability, made communicable by a series of statements made under the signatory sanction of the title of this book: Agamben and Indifference. However, Agamben's advice for all of us is clear and consistent. Suspending the machine is not enough indeed, as the machine tends to suspend its own economy, it is perhaps not even very much. Look around you reader, I exhort you, the machine lies about us in disarray. It is the suspension of the suspension that is, naturally, the ticklish portion. How to make indifference itself, a logic of course entirely communicable under the signature of our metaphysics, indifferentiated without recourse to the common, the proper or any of the permutations of their articulation available to us or indeed any new form of articulation? All I can say in closing is that the machine is broken, and, under Agamben's permissive sanction, I am not working to fix it. Even if, at some future date, it gets its bullying pistons pumping under its own steam, wheezing and overbearing, violent and immense, absolutely omnipresent in its false confidence at its total omniscience, I will not be subject to its economy. Whether it judders or whether it jolts is a matter of indifference to me. Once you have seen its mechanisms laid bare, they remain permanently reductive, self-serving, tedious, unconvincing, illogical, evanescent, tyrannical, ultimately risible. I have no more need of philosophical difference, and in making this position communicable I have sown a seed, proposed a sanction, which may or may not be taken up by others but which now at least has a potential, thanks to Agambenian indifference, to think in a novel and consistent manner permanently to the side of the identity-difference copula.

NOTES

1. Giorgio Agamben, *The Sacrament of Language: An Archaeology of the Oath*, trans. Adam Kotsko (Stanford, CA: Stanford University Press, 2010), 55.
2. Agamben, *Sacrament of Language*, 55–56.
3. Giorgio Agamben, *Homo Sacer: Sovereign Power and Bare Life*, trans. Daniel Heller-Roazen (Stanford, CA: Stanford University Press, 1998), 8.
4. Agamben, *Sacrament of Language*, 56.
5. Agamben, *Sacrament of Language*, 56.
6. Agamben, *Sacrament of Language*, 56.
7. Agamben, *Sacrament of Language*, 56.
8. Agamben, *Sacrament of Language*, 59.
9. As primarily a study of this theme, see William Watkin, *The Literary Agamben : Adventures in Logopoiesis* (London: Continuum, 2010). A recent, alternative statement in the field can also be found in Colby Dickinson, "The Poetic Atheology of Giorgio Agamben: Defining the Scission between Poetry and Philosophy", *Mosaic* 45, no. 1 (2012): 203–17.
10. Agamben, *Sacrament of Language*, 59.
11. See Michel Foucault, *The Archaeology of Knowledge*, trans. A. M. Sheridan Smith (London: Routledge, 1972), 96–100.
12. Agamben, *Sacrament of Language*, 66.
13. Agamben, *Sacrament of Language*, 66.
14. Agamben, *Sacrament of Language*, 68.
15. Agamben, *Sacrament of Language*, 68.
16. Agamben, *Sacrament of Language*, 69. There is a methodological issue here that I have not been able to solve, and it is too late in the study to tackle. My rationalisation of philosophical archaeology does not allow for signatory sets, so to speak, as is suggested here by language and politics. Space and time would be another such set. Nor can there be a hierarchy of signatures. The system needs a maximum limit to

avoid issues of a theological infinity solved by Cantor's actual infinity, according to Badiou. To make this system work, I have allowed a signature of all signatures. For me this is indifference, but only with the proviso that it permanently suspends the method at this point. I cannot say from Agamben's perspective how interested he is in a formalisation of his method to this degree, but speaking for my own part the twin problems of signature sets and signature hierarchies threaten the viability of the method unless there is indifference of indifference.

17. Agamben, *Sacrament of Language*, 69.
18. Agamben, *Sacrament of Language*, 69.
19. Agamben, *Sacrament of Language*, 69.
20. Agamben, *Sacrament of Language*, 69–70.
21. Agamben, *Sacrament of Language*, 70.
22. Agamben, *Sacrament of Language*, 72.
23. Agamben, *Sacrament of Language*, 71.
24. Giorgio Agamben, *The Open: Man and Animal*, trans. Kevin Attell (Stanford, CA: Stanford University Press, 2004), 92.
25. This is also the basis of Laruelle's proposal of a radical nonphilosophy after difference; see François Laruelle, *Philosophies of Difference: A Critical Introduction to Non-Philosophy*, trans. Rocco Gangle (London: Continuum, 2010), 6–9, 14–17.

Bibliography

Agamben, Giorgio. *Altissima povertà*. Vicenza: Neri Pozza, 2011.

———. *Homo Sacer: Sovereign Power and Bare Life*. Translated by Daniel Heller-Roazen. Stanford, CA: Stanford University Press, 1998.

———. *Idea of Prose*. Translated by Michael Sullivan and Sam Whitsitt. Albany: State University of New York Press, 1995.

———. *Infancy and History: On the Destruction of Experience*. Translated by Liz Heron. London: Verso, 1993.

———. 'K'. In *The Work of Giorgio Agamben: Law, Literature, Life*, edited by Justin Clemens, Nicholas Heron, and Alex Murray. Edinburgh: Edinburgh University Press, 2008, 13–27.

———. *La Potenza del pensiero: Saggi e conferenze*. Vicenza: Neri Pozza, 2005.

———. *Language and Death: The Place of Negativity*. Translated by Karen E. Pinkus with Michael Hardt. Minneapolis: University of Minnesota Press, 1991.

———. *L'uso dei corpi*. Forthcoming.

———. *Means without Ends*. Translated by Vincenzo Binetti and Cesare Casarino. Minneapolis: University of Minnesota Press, 2000.

———. *Ninfe*. Torino: Bollati Boringhieri, 2008.

———. *Nudities*. Translated by David Kishik and Stefan Pedatella. Stanford, CA: Stanford University Press, 2011.

———. *Nymphs*. Kolkata: Seagull Books, 2013.

———. *Potentialities*. Translated by Daniel Heller-Roazen. Stanford, CA: Stanford University Press, 1999.

———. *Opus Dei. Archeologia dell'ufficio*. Torino: Bollati Boringhieri, 2012.

———. *Profanations*. Translated by Jeff Fort. New York: Zone Books, 2007.

———. *Remnants of Auschwitz: The Witness and the Archive*. Translated by Daniel Heller-Roazen. New York: Zone Books, 2002.

———. *Signatura rerum: Sul metodo*. Torino: Bollati Boringhieri, 2008.

———. *Stanzas: Word and Phantasm in Western Culture*. Translated by Ronald L. Martinez. Minneapolis: University of Minnesota Press, 1993.

———. *State of Exception*. Translated by Kevin Attell. Chicago: University of Chicago Press, 2005.

———. *The Church and Its Reign*. Chicago: University of Chicago Press, 2013.

———. *The Coming Community*. Translated by Michael Hardt. Minneapolis: University of Minnesota Press, 1993.

———. *The End of the Poem*. Translated by Daniel Heller-Roazen. Stanford, CA: Stanford University Press, 1999.

———. *The Highest Poverty: Monastic Rules and Form-of-Life*. Translated by Adam Kotsko. Stanford, CA: Stanford University Press, 2013.

———. *The Kingdom and the Glory: For a Theological Genealogy of Economy and Government*. Translated by Lorenzo Chiesa with Matteo Mandarini. Stanford, CA: Stanford University Press, 2001.

———. *The Man without Content*. Translated by Georgia Albert. Stanford, CA: Stanford University Press, 1999.

———. *The Open: Man and Animal*. Translated by Kevin Attell. Stanford, CA: Stanford University Press, 2004.

———. *The Sacrament of Language: An Archaeology of the Oath*. Translated by Adam Kotsko. Stanford, CA: Stanford University Press, 2010.

———. *The Signature of All Things: On Method*. Translated by Luca D'Isanto and Kevin Attell. New York: Zone Books, 2009.

———. *The Time That Remains*. Translated by Patricia Dailey. Stanford, CA: Stanford University Press, 2005.

———. *The Unspeakable Girl*. Translated by Leland de la Durantaye. Chicago: University of Chicago Press, 2013.

———. *What Is an Apparatus? And Other Essays*. Translated by David Kishik and Stefan Pedatella. Stanford, CA: Stanford University Press, 2009.

Agamben, Giorgio, and Gilles Deleuze. *Bartleby: La Formula della creazione*. Macerata: Quodlibet, 1993.

Badiou, Alain. *Being and Event*. Translated by Oliver Feltham. London: Continuum, 2005.

———. *Deleuze: The Clamour of Being*. Translated by Louise Burchill. Minneapolis: University of Minnesota Press, 2000.

———. *Handbook of Inaesthetics*. Translated by Alberto Toscano. Stanford, CA: Stanford University Press, 2005.

———. 'Intervention dans le cadre du Collège international de philosophie sur le livre de Giorgio Agamben: *La Communauté qui vient, théorie de la singularité quelconque*'. http://www.entretemps.asso.fr/Badiou/Agamben.htm.

———. *Logics of Worlds*. Translated by Alberto Toscano. London: Continuum, 2009.

Benjamin, Walter. *The Arcades Project*. Translated by Howard Eiland and Kevin McLaughlin. Cambridge, MA: Harvard University Press, 1999.

Blanchot, Maurice. *The Work of Fire*. Translated by Charlotte Mandell. Stanford, CA: Stanford University Press, 1995.

Bowden, Sean. *The Priority of Events: Deleuze's Logic of Sense*. Edinburgh: Edinburgh University Press, 2011.

Calarco, Matthew, and Steven DeCaroli, eds. *Sovereignty and Life*. Stanford, CA: Stanford University Press, 2007.

Clemens, Justin, Nicholas Heron, and Alex Murray, eds. *The Work of Giorgio Agamben: Law, Literature, Life*. Edinburgh: Edinburgh University Press, 2008.

de la Durantaye, Leland. *Giorgio Agamben: A Critical Introduction*. Stanford, CA: Stanford University Press, 2009.

Deleuze, Gilles. *Difference and Repetition*. Translated by Paul Patton. London: Athlone Press, 1994.

———. *Essays Critical and Clinical*. Translated by Daniel W. Smith. Minneapolis: University of Minnesota Press, 1997.

———. *Pure Immanence: Essays on Life*. Translated by Anne Boyman. London: Verso, 1998.

———. *The Logic of Sense*. Translated by Mark Lester. London: Continuum, 2004.

Deleuze, Gilles, and Félix Guattari. *A Thousand Plateaus: Capitalism and Schizophrenia*. Translated by Brian Massumi. London: Athlone Press, 1992.

———. *Kakfa: Toward a Minor Literature*. Translated by Dana Polan. Minneapolis: University of Minnesota Press, 1986.

———. *What Is Philosophy?* Translated by Graham Burchell and Hugh Tomlinson. London: Verso, 1994.

Derrida, Jacques. *Acts of Literature*. Edited by Derek Attridge. London: Routledge, 1992.

———. *Margins of Philosophy*. Translated by Alan Bass. London: Harvester Wheatsheaf, 1982.

———. *Positions*. Translated by Alan Bass. Chicago: University of Chicago Press, 1981.

———. *Speech and Phenomena*. Translated by David B. Allison. Evanston, IL: Northwestern University Press, 1973.

Dickinson, Colby. *Agamben and Theology*. London: Continuum, 2011.

Dubreuil, Laurent. 'Leaving Politics: Bios Zoe, Life'. *Diacritics* 36, no. 2 (2006): 83–98.

Düttman, Alexander García. 'Integral Actuality'. In Giorgio Agamben, *Idea of Prose*. Translated by Michael Sullivan and Sam Whitsitt. Albany: State University of New York Press, 1995, 1–28.

Foucault, Michel. *The Archaeology of Knowledge*. Translated by A. M. Sheridan Smith. London: Routledge, 1972.

Gaston, Sean. *Derrida, Literature and War*. London: Continuum, 2009.

Gibson, Andrew. *Intermittency: The Concept of Historical Reason in Recent French Philosophy*. Edinburgh: Edinburgh University Press, 2012.

Godzich, Wlad, and Jeffrey Kittay. *The Emergence of Prose: An Essay in Prosaics*. Minneapolis: University of Minnesota Press, 1987.

Havercamp, Anselm. 'Notes on the "Dialectical Image" (How Deconstructive Is It?)'. *Diacritics* 22, no. 3–4 (1992): 69–80.

Hegel, G. W. F. *Science of Logic*. Translated by A. V. Miller. New York: Humanity Books, 1969.

———. *The Phenomenology of Spirit*. Translated by A. V. Miller. Oxford: Oxford University Press, 1977.

Heidegger, Martin. *Identity and Difference*. Translated by Joan Stambaugh. Chicago: University of Chicago Press, 1969.

Kant, Immanuel. *Critique of Pure Reason*. Translated by Marcus Wiegelt. London: Penguin, 2007.

———. *The Critique of Judgement*. Translated by James Creed Meredith. Oxford: Clarendon Press, 1952.

Kishik, David. *The Power of Life*. Stanford, CA: Stanford University Press, 2012.

Laruelle, François. *Philosophies of Difference: A Critical Introduction to Non-Philosophy*. Translated by Rocco Gangle. London: Continuum, 2010.

Meillassoux, Quentin. *After Finitude: An Essay on the Necessity of Contingency*. Translated by Ray Brassier. London: Continuum, 2008.

Mills, Catherine. *The Philosophy of Agamben*. Stocksfield: Acumen, 2008.

Murray, Alex. *Giorgio Agamben*. London: Routledge, 2010.

Murray, Alex, and Jessica Whyte, eds. *The Agamben Dictionary*. Edinburgh: Edinburgh University Press, 2011.

Norris, Andrew, ed. *Politics, Metaphysics and Death: Essays on Giorgio Agamben's Homo Sacer*. Durham, NC: Duke University Press, 2005.

Norris, Christopher. *Badiou's Being and Event*. London: Continuum, 2009.

Paragraph 25, no. 2 (2002). Agamben special issue.

Plato. *Republic*. Translated by Robin Waterfield. Oxford: Oxford World's Classics, 2008.

Ross, Alison, ed. *The Agamben Effect. The South Atlantic Quarterly* 106, no. 2 (2007). Special issue.

Royle, Nicholas. *Deconstruction: A User's Guide*. Basingstoke: Palgrave Macmillan, 2000.

Stern, Robert. *Hegel and the Phenomenology of Spirit*. London; Routledge, 2002.

Svirsky, Marcelo, and Simone Bignall, eds. *Agamben and Colonialism*. Edinburgh: Edinburgh University Press, 2012.

Thurschwell, Adam. 'Cutting the Branches for Akiba, Agamben's Critique of Derrida'. In *Politics, Metaphysics and Death: Essays on Giorgio Agamben's Homo Sacer*, edited by Andrew Norris. Durham, NC: Duke University Press, 2005, 173–97.

Vallega, Alejandro A., ed. *Giorgio Agamben: The Potency of Negativity in the Age of Sovereign Exception, Epoché* 16, no. 1 (2011). Special issue.

Wall, Thomas Carl. *Radical Passivity: Lévinas, Blanchot and Agamben*. New York: State University of New York Press, 1999.

Watkin, William. 'Poetry's Promiscuous Plurality: On a Part of Jean-Luc Nancy's The Muses'. In *Jean-Luc Nancy and Plural Thinking*, edited by Peter Gratton and Marie-Eve Morin. Albany: State University of New York Press, 2012, 191–212.

———. *The Literary Agamben: Adventures in Logopoiesis*. London: Continuum, 2010.

————. 'The Materialization of Prose: *Poiesis* versus *Dianoia* in the work of Godzich & Kittay, Shklovsky, Silliman and Agamben'' *Paragraph* 31, no. 3 (2008): 344–64.

Williams, James. *Gilles Deleuze's* Difference and Repetition. Edinburgh: Edinburgh University Press, 2003.

————. *Gilles Deleuze's* Logic of Sense. Edinburgh: Edinburgh University Press, 2008.

Wohlfarth, Irving. 'On the Messianic Structures of Walter Benjamin's Last Reflections'. In *Walter Benjamin: Critical Evaluations in Cultural Theory*, edited by Peter Osborne. London: Taylor and Francis, 2004, 169–231.

Zartaloudis, Thanos. *Giorgio Agamben: Power, Law and the Uses of Criticism*. London: Routledge, 2010.

Žižek, Slavoj. *Did Someone Say Totalitarianism? Four Interventions in the (Mis)Use of a Notion*. London: Verso, 2011.

————. 'Neighbours and Other Monsters: A Plea for Ethical Violence'. In Slavoj Žižek, Eric L. Santner, and Kenneth Reinhard, *The Neighbour: Three Enquiries in Political Theology*. Chicago: Chicago University Press, 2005.

————. *Iraq: The Borrowed Kettle*. London: Verso, 2004.

Index